Living the Enlightenment

Living the Enlightenment

Freemasonry and Politics in Eighteenth-Century Europe

MARGARET C. JACOB

New York Oxford
OXFORD UNIVERSITY PRESS
1991

Oxford University Press

Oxford New York Toronto
Delhi Bombay Calcutta Madras Karachi
Petaling Jaya Singapore Hong Kong Tokyo
Nairobi Dar es Salaam Cape Town
Melbourne Auckland

and associated companies in
Berlin Ibadan

Published by Oxford University Press, Inc.,
198 Madison Avenue, New York, New York 10016-4314

Library of Congress Cataloging-in-Publication Data
Jacob, Margaret C., 1943-
Living the enlightenment :
freemasonry and politics in eighteenth-century Europe /
Margaret C. Jacob.
p. cm. Includes index.
ISBN 0-19-506992-7 (cloth).
— ISBN 0-19-507051-8 (paper)
1. Freemasons—Europe—History—18th century.
2. Freemasonry—Political aspects—Europe—History—18th century.
3. Enlightenment—Europe. 4. Europe—Politics and government—1648-1789.
I. Title. HS416.J33 1991 366'.1'096609033—dc20 91-8354

Photographic reproductions of books in its collection were kindly supplied by the library of the Grand Lodge of The Netherlands and its librarian, E. Kwaadgras. These appear in plates 1–9.

9 8 7 6 5 4 3 2
Printed in the United States of America
on acid-free paper

To Christopher Hill and Lynn Hunt
guides in matters revolutionary

Acknowledgments

The historian who works in many countries incurs more than the usual number of debts. Although mine mounted by the day through the late 1980s, first and foremost remained the Guggenheim Foundation and the New School for Social Research, both of which provided the financial support for a year of leave time. Also at the New School my assistant, Ursula Levelt, provided superb linguistic skills, patience, and care.

Because I am writing here about a private society that is still very much alive, particularly in Continental Europe, I have been unusually dependent upon private archives and archivists. By far my greatest debt is to the members of La Bien Aimée, the lodge in Amsterdam with its extraordinary set of records. None of the chapters that depend on those archives would have been possible without the gracious assistance of Hilco Rodermond, who photocopied the entire eighteenth-century archive for me; and J. Kistemaker, who provided conversation and wisdom. Not least, I have been helped by the earlier historical studies of the Dutch historian Willem Kat. Of course the history of European freemasonry in the eighteenth century could barely be written without the splendid library of the Grand Lodge of the Netherlands and its librarian emeritus, B. C. van Uchelen. Readers wishing to consult that collection, which is strong in French and German freemasonry, as well as Dutch, should know that at this time (1990) efforts are being made to relocate it at the Royal Library in The Hague. Wherever it is housed, scholars can only be assisted by its enormous and rich collection and the willingness of the Grand Lodge to help and encourage them. In Belgium, L. Verlee provided gracious assistance in locating private archives, which, due to local circumstances, are not automatically available to the general public.

At the Bibliothèque Nationale in Paris the librarian of the masonic collection, Florence de Lussy, gave assistance far above the call of duty. At the Central Library, Dundee, Scotland, I was assisted with bibliographical material, and I also want to thank Iain Fleet, archivist, Archive and Record Centre, City Chambers, Dundee. Permission to use the primary source material at Dundee came from B. N. Bowman, clerk to the Three United Trades, Dundee; they hold the copyright on GD/GRW/M 1/1, Sederunt book 1736–1807; GD/GRW/M 2/1 Boxmaster's account book 1706–1760; and GD/GRW/M 3/1 Register of entries of masters and journeymen 1659–1779. The Lockit Book, still in use, is in the possession of the clerk.

Some publishers and libraries need to be thanked for permission to reprint or to cite manuscript material. E. J. Brill Inc. allowed me to reprint portions of chapter 2, which had appeared in an earlier version, originally a lecture at the Clark Library given in 1981 and then collected in a volume edited by Richard H. Popkin. Haworth Press, Inc., gave me permission to publish portions of chapter 5, which first appeared in an essay in *Women and the Enlightenment,* a collection published by Haworth, Binghamton, New York, in 1976 for The Institute for Research in History. Dr. Williams's Library, London, and its librarian, John Creasey, gave permission to quote from one letter in the Kenrick–Wodrow correspondence. The archivist at the municipal library in Namur, René Leboutte, also made every effort to assist.

Various American and European scholars shared their knowledge of archives or read portions of the text: Herbert Rowen, Ferenc Feher, Hugo de Schampheleire, Els Witte, N. Luitse, Gordon DesBrisay, and not least, Wijnand Mijnhardt, with whom I have had many important conversations. Martin Weiner read a portion of chapter 1 and said very helpful things. Larry Stewart located an important masonic manuscript at the Royal Society of London. J. Appleby read, queried, and inspired. The editors at Oxford University Press have been prompt and efficient. None of these generous and helpful people are responsible for any of the errors that may still exist.

Janja Lalich proved to be a supremely competent editor for the opening chapters. Carroll Joynes, Don Scott, and the members of the Pro-Seminar on Knowledge, Culture and Power at the New School were good and kind critics. Janet M. Burke has been willing to share her important work on women freemasons.

The book's dedication speaks from my own history, intellectual and personal.

Contents

Abbreviations

B.A.	the manuscripts of the Amsterdam lodge, La Bien Aimée, to be found at the library in the Grand Lodge of the Netherlands, 22 Fluwelenburgwal, The Hague
B.L.	British Library, London
B.N.	Bibliothèque Nationale, Paris
B.N.U.	Bibliothèque Nationale et Universitaire, Strasbourg
FM	Freemasonry collection, Bibliothèque Nationale, Paris
G.L.	the library in the Grand Lodge of the Netherlands, The Hague
Kloss MSS	always refers to the collection of that title in the library of the Grand Lodge of the Netherlands, The Hague

In general I have neither modernized the foreign languages nor sought to provide French accent marks not supplied by the original eighteenth-century authors. The original language is given in footnotes for the specialist reader; translations are intended to give the sense of the text with specialists expected to consult the original for the full text. It should be remembered that many Dutch writers of French were using a second language and, as a result, their French can be somewhat eccentric. Many scribes recorded masonic minutes, but not for twentieth-century readers. Every effort has been made to keep this author's errors of transcription to a minimum.

Living the Enlightenment

Introduction
The European Enlightenment: The Birth of Modern Civil Society

In the 1740s the Parisian police arrested, searched, and systematically interrogated freemasons. We know about these events because the reports of what was said made their way into the records housed in the Bastille.[1] Spies, and at least one local priest with a grudge to satisfy, helped the authorities gather their information. In some confusion the police described their new detainees as "frimassons" or "frey-maçons," but it was not the name that worried them. The detailed interrogation reports reveal their concern. Repeatedly they asked the prisoners: "Is it not true that this assembly was for the purpose of electing a master of the lodge who in turn would choose two surveillants; is it not true that the record of the Election would be handed over to the secretary of the order who is M. Perret, notary?"[2] Is it not true "that with various other freemasons you signed an act of Convocation in order to be assembled . . . and that this assembly was for the purpose of electing a master of the Lodge? Did you write that act?"[3]

Elections, signed acts of convocation permitting an assembly, a legal record prepared by a notary, an assembly held with the expressed purpose of conducting elections—these were the elements that alarmed the authorities, these were the words they used to describe the meetings. The answers they invariably got from the detained brothers and lodge officers, who displayed remarkable amnesia on many other details, was invariably "oui." With equal alarm the police wanted to know whether the lodge met "under the arms of M. the Count of Clermont," who in 1743 became the masonic Grand Master of France.

Clearly the authorities were confused. Was this a new corporate entity with pretensions at self-government, using forms of representative assembly possibly alien, possibly subversive? In other words, was this imported form of social behavior inherently political, and thus almost inevitably criminal? "All association (as one representative of the police put it) is always dangerous to the state, especially when it takes on the secret and appearance of religion."[4] Or was this another kind of potentially subversive assembly, one more familiar and alarmingly commonplace in

French history: a cabal organized under the arms of a prominent aristocrat? The nature of the gathering was doubly confusing because on another occasion the police arrived just at the moment when an elaborate feast was being prepared. The problem was that some of the men present were of the most ordinary status: a lapidary (or jeweler), a minor official of the poultry market, a gardener, a tapestry merchant, worse still, an actor in the Comédie Italienne, and perhaps most remarkable of all, "a Negro who serves as a trumpeter in the King's Guard."[5] There were also a wine merchant as master of the lodge, army officers, a secretary to a nobleman, three Benedictine priests, a valet at court, a "gentleman," a "bourgeois," a surgeon; and, on the raid conducted in June 1744, four women, unmarried, were also rounded up. Such a wide range of occupations and status conforms to other masonic records from the 1730s. In them we find accountants, a black musketeer, merchants, and an official of a provincial tax court who was also a prominent champagne merchant. All addressed one another as brother and openly discussed their new loyalty to freemasonry. At that early date they were also being persecuted and forced as a result to change regularly their place of meeting.[6]

The confusion of the police should not become ours. The private society whose meetings and police interrogations we are now considering was not a throwback to the aristocratic cabals of earlier days or even to the secrecy and practices of the traditional guilds. Nor did its secrecy imitate the practices of monasteries, religious orders, and persecuted sects of the ancien régime. Rather the lodges on the Continent were replicas of British lodges and brought with them forms of governance and social behavior developed within the distinctive political culture of that island. Men had voted at meetings for centuries and on either side of the Channel. Only in Britain did they do so within a constitutional structure and at a national legislative assembly where voting was by individual and not by estate or locality. With this distinctive form of political culture came a new form of civil society. Individuals with voting rights, then a distinct minority in Britain, identified with political parties and issues on both a local and national level. They read and debated, formed reading societies, clubs, and lodges, where they exercised their talents as orators and commentators, or as devotees of philosophy and literature. Only in the lodges men also became legislators and constitution makers. It was precisely that aspect of their behavior that the Parisian police picked up on, and it alarmed them.

It would seem that the constitutional and legislative environment was what attracted men on the Continent to the first lodges. Within their confines brothers adjudicated new forms of personal power and they could imagine themselves as involved in governance as well as in opposition. One of the earliest letters we have from a French freemason to a brother in the provinces makes the point nicely. Apparently a change has occurred in local masonic leadership in Paris. Our correspondent there, one M. Calviere, an avid orderer and (one presumes) drinker of champagne, writes to his brother, a wine merchant in Epernay in the heart of champagne country: "You will find our venerable order a little changed at your return; the legislative power has passed to other hands, more elevated in truth but less accustomed to the manner of the trowel [i.e., to masonic practices]." This change has alarmed M. Calviere. What fascinates us is the way he expresses his alarm: "It is even to be feared that some hint of despotism will creep in; but you know this better than I. It is the most dangerous poison for every kind of society, and an omen almost certainly for the fall of the best founded republics."[7] We are witness in this statement to a new form of sociability, which will eventually have implications for how societies and governments can be organized. Perhaps we have finally located the earliest moments in the formation of modern civil society. The lodge, the philosophical society, the scientific academy became the underpinning, as philosophers like J. Habermas and some historians have long believed, for the republican and democratic forms of government that evolved slowly and fitfully in Western Europe from the late eighteenth century on. We should return to the police reports, for they have much to tell us.

Frequently the arrests in Paris were made in private homes.[8] Yet the police records also indicate that sometimes the masons assembled in local cabarets.[9] Most of the men were young and involved in trade, yet significantly they came from different quarters of the city and their occupations would have put them in touch with a wide variety of people. Motley, as a description, does not quite do justice to the cast of characters upon which the police had stumbled. There seemed to them no obvious explanation, other than intrigue or debauchery (the suspicion of sodomy turns up in one report), to explain why men of such disparate circumstances, unrelated by any obvious common interest, neighborhood, inclination, or attribute, save perhaps commerce, would willingly assemble, sign legal documents, regard themselves as "constituted" by an act of convocation—which they might have written—then feast together, both with and without women, and finally, and not least, involve priests, in whom the police showed a particular interest.[10] At the one meeting where women were present there is no reason to assume they were anything other than full participants, despite the subsequent attempt to bar them entirely from French freemasonry, a step taken precisely in the late 1740s.

For the masonic officers arrested—ordinary brothers were let go with a warning that such assemblies were prohibited—it must have been a disturbing experience. In the different prisons to which they were deliberately sent to be separated during interrogation were housed an assortment of the socially undesirable, at least as the police saw it. Their reports list the freemasons along with such routine detainees as prostitutes, Jansenists, sellers of illegal books, a man who thought he was the true son of Louis XIV and his mistress, Madame de Maintenon,[11] and another who caused a public uproar at the opera. Despite the protests of the freemasons, who maintained they had done "nothing against Religion, against the State, nor contrary to good morals," the police wanted to know about their secret passwords, their initiation ceremonies, and why they were holding these meetings in the first place. One of the spies had used disturbing analogies and metaphors in his report on masonic ceremonies and clothing. He spoke about "the pontiff of the masons" with "his august and pontifical vestments" and "shining set of masonic instruments," reporting that "the grand masonic pontiff had become a grand priest."[12] Could these be religious heretics in new garb? Possibly they were another version of the hated Jansenists, religious reformers who always worried the authorities and upon whom they spied unrelentingly.

When asked why they had become freemasons and paid the not insubstantial entry fee of 24 livres, one detainee answered "because honorable men had introduced him to it and because he believed that the assembly had been authorized by the Count of Clermont." In short he shifted the responsibility onto his social superiors. Reasonably placated, the police released the freemasons, although a few were heavily fined, and all were warned that these assemblies had been forbidden.[13] Cardinal Fleury (d. 1743), the chief minister of state, had indeed banned them. He saw them as British and hence the import, inevitably subversive, of his great rival. His concern had undoubtedly been aggravated by the war that raged to the north, where in 1744 the French finally (and once again) invaded the Austrian Netherlands. Undaunted by official harassment, French freemasons continued to meet. By the 1750s, long after Fleury's death, the fraternity became increasingly respectable, and hence tolerable to the authorities. But this had been a gradual process, one that had begun as early as the 1720s.[14] In those earlier decades assemblies had been strictly prohibited because in them, as the police code put it, "enemies of order seek to weaken in people's spirits the principles of religion and of subordination to the Powers, established by God."[15] By the reasoning of the authorities private assemblies possessed an inherently public meaning.

Yet even before achieving respectability, the newly constituted assemblies did not scare easily. They answered their accusers in print, although from the safety of anonymity. In 1744 Parisian freemasons took to the presses to argue that "freemasonry is justly called the School of Virtue. . . . The fraternity that reigns among them represents . . . the first time that men really concerned themselves with the needs of one another. Paris and London are the two cities in the world where they are the most numerous."[16] But what about their persecutors and defamers? "Profanes are men who sacrifice their probity for interest and the honors that come along in this life."[17] In the masonic vocabulary the hostile nonmason is the "profane." Against their attacks the masons were particularly eager to refute the charge of licentiousness. And throughout the century they will be harassed by charges of libertinism and sodomy. Partly in response, freemasons would alternatively encourage women's participation and seek to exclude them. In the eyes of their frequently clerical opponents the reason for this exclusion was simple: Why would women wish to be involved in the practices of government?[18]

Juxtaposed to the supposed selfishness of the profane, the masonic creed proclaimed a universalist ethic: "All honest men are freemasons; their laws are common and general to all men." But what in the end will work to replace the "excesses caused by the passions" and establish order among human beings? The answer given in the anonymous masonic tract of 1744 was uncompromising: "The sacred Laws of the Masons; it is to you that this work is reserved; it is up to you to eliminate crime, to strike the criminal, to defend the innocent, to prop up the weak, to force men to become happy. Oh, the disgrace of nature! Oh, the confusion of humanity! which makes it that a man cannot be free without being a criminal. Must he be rendered a slave in order to be virtuous? Yes, my brothers, that is our condition; our passions require laws, our unjust and reckless desires must be restrained."[19]

There were some strong words in the masonic defense and justification: freedom versus slavery, innocence contrasted to vanity and self-interest. The implications of such language, had anyone wanted to draw them out, were subversive indeed. But the masonic approach toward state power being proposed here was to turn inward toward self-reform, toward virtue, and most important, toward reason. Public self-defense, even "under the pain of being punished," must also occur, but the real "work" of the freemason should mean that "in his presence, everything changes, all things in the universe are renewed and reformed, order is established, the rule and measure of things is understood, duty is followed, reason listened to, wisdom comprehended; and mortals, without changing their essence, appear as new men."[20] In short, these new men are self-disciplined, as well as charitable toward one another, and their new ethics come from their recently discovered idealism as embodied in their dedication to freemasonry.

The implications of finding one's morality in secular fraternizing and "the laws" proclaimed through sociability might not augur well for the religious institutions traditionally in charge of establishing the laws and rules of ethical and, not least, charitable conduct. But what about the implications for the state? Did the secular authorities, in fact, have anything to worry about? On this rather crucial point the freemasons sought in this early tract to reassure. They did so by explaining their understanding of civic virtue and their own role in "the republic." First, they explained that they had a role. Indeed they speculated about why it was that only men of certain occupations and professions, which, they claimed, are in fact of little use to "the republic," nevertheless receive most of the esteem and respect.[21] The real heroes and wise men, the freemasons explained, are of two kinds: those who brave all hazard, including death, to defend their fellow citizens, to avenge the injuries of the Nation, and thus to extend the boundaries of the Empire. "Les Sages" make the laws. Of course the two are completely compatible: "A great Legislator and a great warrior gives the Republic the equal advantage of laws and arms." And then comes the message: "True masons are "Héros et Sages." In addition, they believe in God and are faithful to the prince. The true prince, in turn, is the father of his people; he is good and just.

The only problem with this statement of the true mason's political role in the state is that it was being prescribed for men as diverse and humble as gardeners, Negro trumpeters, and small merchants. Within the political vocabularies of the eighteenth century the prescription was essentially, if vaguely, republican. The appeal, written in wartime, was also nationalist, possibly because among the few things such men had in common as they met in their new and exotic society was their Frenchness. In the words of the Grand Master of 1740, "the Order of Free-masons exists to form men, agreeable men, good citizens, good subjects . . . to form in the course of time a totally spiritual nation, where without denigrating from the various duties required by different states [or conditions], one [nevertheless] creates a new people."[22]

What must have surprised the authorities who knew at least some of the men and women behind the anonymous voice of 1744 was the claim upon the state that was being advanced. The identification was with power as well as with reforms. These were heady sentiments coming from people who would have been experiencing their first "election" after having signed their first "act of convocation." It could be argued that the authorities did in fact need reassuring.

In their alarm, the Parisian police left us a cultural record of precisely what was new, and hence inexplicable, as well as disturbing, about these assemblies. They asked, understandably enough, why join them, and what were they all about, and what was their meaning in relation to the familiar and the commonplace, to Catholicism, and not least, to the interests and procedures of the state? Although reasonably placated by what they discovered, and thus able to release their prisoners, the representatives of the absolutist state probably did not read the tracts just described very carefully, if at all, or ponder the meaning of their rather florid rhetoric. But we should.

The Paris police asked the same questions about freemasonry that other, less menacing, contemporaries asked; they are also the same questions that historians since the 1790s have raised. Like the Parisian police, historians have been less than convinced that men of wholly disparate backgrounds, without any easily identified common interests, joined lodges simply because their betters led the way. As these police reports show, some of the very earliest Continental freemasons were not only the most ordinary of men; they were also not rooted in their neighborhoods but rather in larger economic or cultural universes. They were also sometimes among the least socially acceptable. Actors were often despised; black trumpeters in their rarity can be seen as marginal men.[23] Merchants could be respectable enough, but if the nature of their trade took them far afield, they could be without a strong local or neighborhood identity.[24]

Although eighteenth-century European freemasonry could oftentimes be significantly aristocratic, there remains the statistical reality, documented by many scholars working in various countries, that membership in the lodges cut through the literate and modestly to greatly affluent classes.[25] This is not to suggest, as some historians have recently suggested (p. 13), that the lodges were inherently democratic in the modern sense. Although they spoke of all brothers as "equal," this did not obviate the role the lodges played as places that replicated social hierarchy and order, based not on birth per se but on an ideology of merit. From the earliest records Continental (as well as British) freemasons distinguished themselves from "the common people" to whom those truths fit only for "the man of merit" should not be communicated.[26] In the lodges throughout western Europe, on both sides of the Channel, national leadership in the so-called Grand Lodges fell almost invariably to the aristocracy. Embracing an ideology that was democratic in implication and reforming if not utopian, British, French, Belgian, and Dutch aristocrats offered their version of enlightened leadership. Those historians who have emphasized only the democratic elements in masonic government miss the obvious: The lodges mirrored the old order just as they were creating a form of civil society that would ultimately replace it.[27] The challenge for the historian lies in understanding the lodges as embedded in their time and place and yet as practicing and speaking in new ways. It is the same challenge that the eighteenth century as a whole presents to the cultural historian: How to understand the Enlightenment within the context of an often rigid and deeply hierarchical social and political order, within various manifestations of anciens régimes.

The diversity of social groupings present in many of the early Continental lodges is striking. Merchants, teachers, lawyers, minor officials were commonplace; later in the century so too were military men and aristocrats. The men and few women who joined did so primarily as individuals, not as members of an estate, a craft or profession, a guild, or a confraternity. In that membership, which could encompass a lifetime, corporate identity gave way to individual identity, which was augmented by the new and evolving masonic subculture. It in turn could vary from country to country, city to city, even lodge to lodge.

Yet the culture of freemasonry did possess certain ubiquitous characteristics. Universally masonic identity was unrelentingly secular; masonic discourse, in whatever western European language, although permitting the expression of local interests and circumstances, did so within the framework of a rhetoric that was British in origin as well as invariably civic, hence political, and most frequently progressive and reformist. Central to masonic identity was the belief that merit and not birth constitutes the foundation for social and political order. While possessing many sources, that belief was most central to and most easily identified with the English republican tradition that crystallized in the 1650s.[28] The masonic message that made its way to Continental Europe would never lose its originally British associations.

In examining the masonic phenomenon and its role in the Enlightenment we are reminded that then (as now) there was a European culture that could at moments transcend national borders and is best approached from an international perspective. Given the secular and distinctively "modern" social character of international freemasonry, perhaps we can understand why the earliest response of Continental historical commentators resembled that of the Parisian police. They saw conspiracy and intrigue in these inexplicable assemblies. In France as early as 1789 the opponents of the French Revolution blamed the fraternity.[29] At first the condemning voice argued that the lodges represented the resurgence of the mystical and theosophical, hence of what Europeans then called, with fear and derision, enthusiasm. The term always had a political connotation: Sects of religious enthusiasts threaten established authority.

This earliest condemnation of the lodges written within a revolutionary context, and it would seem after July 1789, makes an interesting observation in passing about the phenomenon of masonic sociability, indeed we might argue about potentially all forms of eighteenth-century sociability: The "work" of the lodge provides an occasion for association; association leads to assemblies; assemblies are completed by eloquent discourse; such discourse (and here the logic becomes hostile and obsessed) is really the same thing as religious fanaticism; such discourse excites the desire to know.[30] We can be much more benign about the purpose of such assemblies, ignore the nonsense about their being conspiratorial and fanatic, and still find in this contemporary critique an apt description of what was unique about the lodges.

Within the first year of the French Revolution, the accusations grew more fearful, claiming that the masonic circles had become centers for spying, in which is born "ce plan de conjuration, ce club de la propaganda."[31] They are even given a symbolic color, both on the colored title page of the accusatory tract and, according to it, in the daily life of these subversive enclaves. They are red lodges. According to another hostile account the freemasons began in England under Cromwell (see pp. 24–25); they embody the attributes of new and would-be "priests and magistrates"; and, not least, they are the "quintessence of all the heresies that divided Germany in the sixteenth century." In addition, their members are "atheists and deists" who seek to create a "new temple" and to form "a democratic government." The divisions within the republic "into classes and regions" permit the masonic lodges to flourish.[32]

By 1790 the lodges have ceased in the minds of their opponents to be centers of religious fanaticism; they are now the Enlightenment fanaticized. They retain the sectarian quality of the enthusiasts, we are told, only now they have adopted a secular political and religious agenda. They are in effect the old revolutionary Puritans of the seventeenth century transformed into new revolutionary philosophes. Ironically, had the seventeenth-century opponents of popular revolution in England turned up in Paris in 1790, they might have agreed: "Atheism and enthusiasm, though they seem so extremely opposite one another, yet in many things do very nearly agree." The statement was made in England in 1655 by a staunch supporter of Church and King.[33]

To the contemporaneous right-wing opponents of the French Revolution, the National Assembly imitates the masonic form of government and owes its origin to masonic practices, which are republican and democratic.[34] Masonic national government is in turn duplicated by the new revolutionary government, which, like the lodges, governs locally, and hence centralizes, through a system of departments, districts, and so on. Even the officers of the masonic order, given their rhetoric of civic virtue and discipline, resemble the new magistracy established by the Revolution. Ironically, some French freemasons of the 1780s may have themselves believed in the resemblance. A provincial lodge writing to the Paris Grand Lodge almost offhandedly remarked that "in the civil order the deputies of a province represent the general assemblies of the Nation; it is the same in the lodges."[35]

In the hands of the antimasons these were serious charges, framed around what must have seemed a remarkable parallelism. In a stroke, opponents of the Revolution laid claim to a thesis that would haunt the study of eighteenth-century European freemasonry evermore: The freemasons were responsible—more than any group—for causing the French Revolution. Everything about them, it has been subsequently claimed, stood in conflict with the ancien régime. Forever, and hence to this day in some quarters, freemasonry would be associated with conspiracy and subversion.[36] The most famous—and paranoid—historian of eighteenth-century freemasonry, the abbé Augustin de Barruel (1741–1820), elaborated upon this theme of conspiracy and subversion and made the thesis his own. In a once widely read book, available in many languages, he proclaimed that freemasonry was "one of the great causes of the French Revolution."[37]

It is worth pausing to deal with right-wing French historiography about eighteenth-century freemasonry. It is significant because of the insights, as well as the errors, it contains. Not least, it was the first historical commentary about freemasonry that enunciated a subsidiary, and still widely accepted, thesis: The Enlightenment had also, in some sense, caused the French Revolution. From any perspective this linkage, still contested and only partially understood, remains a central component in the narrative history of Western political and cultural development. How that causal relationship between Enlightenment and Revolution worked had seemed straightforward enough to the abbé Barruel: "All the famous Conspirators had been in most cases in the same lodge, the initiates of d'Holbach . . . [and] the atheistic, deistic and pantheistic Masons."[38]

Barruel, of course, was an old hand at attacking the Enlightenment. Among his earliest published work is a reasonably sophisticated assault on scientifically inspired materialism with particular attention to Buffon, Diderot, La Mettrie, and d'Holbach. But Barruel was no straightforward reactionary; in fact, he was a proponent of Newtonian science as well as a monarchist who supported the French intervention in the American colonies and their struggle for "liberty."[39] As a Jesuit Barruel had been among those expelled from France in 1764. He had traveled extensively, returning home as a secular priest only to be exiled once again in 1792.

His subsequent embrace of the conspiracy theory of history as applied to the freemasons appeared in 1797. If we treat Barruel as a primary source rather than a historian, and if we try to read through his "paranoia," we can find a starting place for our approach to European freemasonry. His writings also offer a point of departure for understanding the relationship between the Continental Enlightenment, as it was lived in the clubs, societies, and lodges of the eighteenth century, and the outbreak of the democratic revolutions in the late 1780s in Amsterdam, Brussels, and, most important, Paris. Ironically and disturbingly, the themes he first proclaimed—among them the persecution of the innocent by the forces of revolution rather than by monarchy, army, or police—recur to this day in the historiography of the French Revolution, although not in most historical writing about other European revolutions. Since Barruel, historical writing about the French Revolution has almost universally ignored the international context of the democratic revolutions throughout western Europe in the 1780s and 1790s; thus critics of the Revolution have seized upon the freemasons in France as causal and simply ignored the fact that the lodges were everywhere in western Europe and, despite local variations, remarkably similar in the civic life they sought to create.[40] Only in Britain did masonic civic life and system of governance closely resemble the political and constitutional order.

Reasonably, in what was otherwise a polemic, Barruel argued for a distinction between English and Continental freemasonry, and thus between English and French circumstances. Like most subsequent historians of the French Revolution, he never dealt with the circumstances and causes of the American and other Continental democratic revolutions, although the political unrest in the Holy Roman Empire, (i.e., Germany) did concern him. In contrasting the British and French cases he dwelt upon language and its use within a specific context: In both places freemasons use the words "liberty" and "equality," but in Britain, the lodge masters preach that this masonic equality should never interfere with "the marks of respect, the deference that social convention attached to [a man's] rank in the world, or to the different grades and political titles."[41]

Barruel's focus is on "language," on the intentionality in the use of words which endows them with new meaning or with an imagined universality. He further argues that words spoken in private can have a public meaning: "In the language of the Masons, all their lodges are only temples made to represent the universe itself."[42] To make his point about the universality of the masonic vision he quotes from published masonic discourses, and he lays great emphasis on "the first words of masonry, equality, liberty . . . an explication of these words . . . [which] lies in the trials, the oaths and in the grades."[43] He claims to have seen with his own eyes that English freemasons avoid "the Jacobin explication" of those words, but "the German lodges and the French ones," practicing "philosophical masonry," take up that explication, "the abuse of the same words."[44] What we can salvage from Barruel's approach is the realization that language spoken in organized groups, with rules and constitutions, rituals and oaths, can have a special force. Its sound is larger than the single voice speaking; the hearer transforms the sound and is transformed by it. In one sense the text becomes its context.

In his more subtle moments even Barruel—who had a penchant for wild and unsupportable interpretations—recognizes that the Channel voyage of this private society wrought changes in the meaning of its originally British, but increasingly universalist, vocabulary. He is also clear that on both sides of the Channel the masonic temple was intended as a public as well as a private space. He believes that the masonic language about equality, liberty, and fraternity bears relation to the radical and democratic phase of the French Revolution, that is, to Jacobin language. A similar point was made by the British historian Michael Roberts, writing in the 1970s.[45] In a highly rigorous and scholarly essay he noted that the slogan "liberty, equality, fraternity" bears closer relation to masonic sloganizing than it does to any other eighteenth-century antecedent. The American historian R. R. Palmer called to our attention the fact that those three words, in just that order and as a slogan, were first used in 1795 in the revolutionary Dutch Republic.[46] This fact might suggest common values and interests among revolutionaries in both places, to their possession of a common culture. But rather than starting with that insight which we owe to Palmer, many recent historians of the French Revolution continue to dwell upon the unique and, from their perspective, particularly reprehensible nature of French Jacobinism. With this in mind they are obsessed with, in effect, the masonic origins of the Terror.

We can easily concede the point about the filiation of masonic language, ritual, and symbol and certain aspects of Jacobin rhetoric. Crane Brinton made this point some years ago,[47] as did some freemasons of the 1790s. They said that freemasonry "was necessary only in a despotic society." Once abolished, masonry lost its raison d'être.[48] Prior to this abolition it could be seen as having been a school of civic sociability, an alternative to the traditional. Certainly the historical phenomenon of freemasonry has significance in the interesting similarity of its rhetoric with that of the first modern democratic and radical movements. But we shall approach it for what it can tell us about the eighteenth-century Enlightenment. We cannot let our discoveries be shaped by subsequent critics of the Terror. The nature of the political experience created in the lodges differed profoundly from the political experience of democrats anywhere in western Europe after the late 1780s. But this should not blind us to the civic and hence political nature of this particular form of secular fraternizing, to the creation of civil society within the culture of the European Enlightenment.

A balanced and empirically focused approach to the political nature of the masonic experience has eluded not just Barruel but also most subsequent French historians, however scholarly and nonconspiratorial their understanding has been. In the 1970s the most influential historian of his generation, François Furet, revived the writings of a Catholic historian and follower of Durkheim, Augustin Cochin (d.1916), and drew from them a new, and disturbing, interpretation of the philosophical society and, in particular, of freemasonry. In the hands of Cochin the "plot" of Barruel became rarefied into the "machine" of ideological purity and harmony. In the eighteenth-century lodges, Cochin asserted, and Furet elaborated upon, the interpretation that "the consensus was produced by a discussion among equals that did not concern real situations but was exclusively devoted to the relationship of individuals with a set of stated goals."[49] Lost, as it were, in the closed universe of its own rhetoric the lodge becomes for Furet a metaphor for the antidemocratic, a "political party that claimed to embody both society and the State, which were now identical." Albeit unwittingly, the masonic lodges of the eighteenth century became, as the police of the 1740s had begun to suspect might happen, the breeding ground for "militant minorities in whom the new legitimacy" might be vested.[50] We need to know much more than what the police, or Furet, imagine about the new sociability. We need to know about private and voluntary associations which were bound to aspects of the old order and yet capable of permitting impulses that challenged and undermined it.

The influence of Furet's approach pervades French scholarship, and its impact extends from the study of the lodges to our very understanding of the French Enlightenment. Picking up on the thought of Cochin and Furet, Ran Halévi has given us a portrait of the eighteenth-century lodges as enclaves of democratic practice. Attempting to quantify every aspect of masonic practice and even language, this sociological approach presents a picture frozen in time, with little nuancing from decade to decade and with the assumption unchallenged that the lodges engaged in direct democracy.[51] While recognizing their relationship to commerce and the growth of urbanization, Halévi's vision of the lodges shows little interest in the language spoken or the practices embraced.

The problem lies not with the quantitative research, which is superb, but rather with the limited value of the method employed. An essentially sociological approach leads to a homogenizing of all the forms of sociability. In Daniel Roche's version of the method, the dimensions of masonic sociability make it remarkably similar to the sociability found in the French academies: Men gathered, discussed, gave speeches, sought self-improvement, and so on.[52] He does, of course, note certain important differences in the membership of the lodges as distinct from the academies; for example, no bishops appear in the masonic temple (the Church had condemned the order in 1738), and on balance the plurality of French brothers, unlike the academicians, were bourgeois. But he asserts that the "social ethic" of the lodges was no different from that of the academies. Roche is the most important French practitioner of the sociological approach. For all of its strengths it misses the distinctively civic quality of masonic sociability—its building of the polity within sociability, the political content of its moral vision and its discourse; its imitation and initiation of forms of governance, not least its quasi-religious quality. Just as significantly, it misses the connection between the values of the lodges and British political culture.

Emphasizing the political dimension of the masonic experience does not lead to the conclusion that it was purely and simply the source of Jacobin language. Some French historians now routinely tell us that Jacobin discourse grew out of the "societies of thought," hence out of the Enlightenment.[53] Such blanket simplifications should arouse suspicion, especially when they are based upon little reference to the content of eighteenth-century discourse within the new enclaves of sociability. Not least, they attempt to treat an international phenomenon nationally and not comparatively.

The actual evidence from the lodges of western Europe, from Britain, The Netherlands, Belgium, and France, suggests that we need to discard the ideological interpretation of Cochin and Furet and all that it, perhaps through no fault of its own, has been used to support. And a great deal has evolved out of this reading of the political implications, rather than the political reality, of enlightened sociability. It is now fashionable in some quarters to equate the excesses of the Reign of Terror with the principles articulated in 1789 and, from that assumption, to find the horrors of the twentieth century embodied in the Jacobins and their ideals: "The myth of revolutionary equality . . . is the justification for a total aspiration to Vengeance. It announces the worse: Marat, Robespierre, Lenin, Pol Pot."[54] From such an imagined vantage point, some contemporary French historians seek—more in the spirit of Barruel than they would perhaps wish to admit—to devalue the secular ideals of the Enlightenment, to find disparate philosophes such as Voltaire or even Babeuf, united by their "having been masons" and as such having subscribed to an "egalitarian, communitarian and libertarian anarchy."[55] Such statements have a long lineage in twentieth-century Continental thought about freemasonry. They harken back to the attacks on the fraternity initiated in the 1930s. During the war the Nazis turned the Grand Lodges in The Hague, Brussels, and Paris into museums for the display of antimasonic propaganda. The Enlightenment, perhaps more than any other secular cultural movement of modern times, has managed to arouse hostile, even violent, reactions.

Thus some French historians have seen in the philosophical society the seeds, not simply of modern civil society, but of revolutionary and democratic activism with particularly terrifying implications. On the other hand, some German historians such as Reinhart Koselleck have seen it as all of that and more. In a book written in German in the 1950s but republished in English in the 1980s, Koselleck maintained that the "mystery" of freemasonry "signified an intellectual front cutting through the world of Absolutist States."[56] "Its social function" was "to unite the bourgeois world" and to do so under the mantle of secrecy.[57] From Koselleck's perspective the politically radical Illuminati, founded in Germany in 1776, are not simply imitative of masonic forms; they are the logical outgrowth, the inevitable shift from social to political activism.[58] Their "secret plan to abolish the State" derived its self-confidence from the certitudes of the masonic moral vision that extolled secular virtue, education, and fraternal charity as the prerequisites to unceasing progress.[59] Similar to Furet's masonically inspired radicals who equate the state with society and hence look toward the totalitarian enterprise lurking ominously in direct democracy, Koselleck's radicals seek the abolition of the state.[60] The end product of both radicalisms ironically remains the same. Having

abolished the absolutist state, Koselleck's fraternity of the enlightened righteous, armed with the slogan of the general will as provided them conveniently by Rousseau, also embark down the road toward dictatorship. "Quite in keeping with the lodges," the bourgeois elite seek now to control "not only actions, but above all ideas; [these] must be co-ordinated."[61] In Koselleck's analysis, the Enlightenment literally contains the seeds of its own destruction. Its power "which grew invisibly and secretly, became the victim of its own disguise."[62] At the heart of the disguise, according to Koselleck, lay a fatally flawed utopian vision, the "ultimate answer to Absolutism." A misguided utopianism fraught with totalitarian implications is the usher escorting in the modern age.[63]

By ignoring the actual roots of the European Enlightenment, which lay in the English revolutionary experience against Stuart absolutism as well as in the Continental opposition to French absolutism situated after 1685 until the death of Louis XIV (1715) largely in the Dutch Republic, Koselleck can naively condemn its idealism as hopelessly utopian. He fails to recognize the early Enlightenment's direct relationship to lived political experience. Having set up the model of a benighted, even duplicitous, Enlightenment, he then grafts onto it the Continental masonic experience, which he analyzes almost entirely from German literature of the 1770s. In this interpretation freemasonry stands in relation to the Enlightenment rather like Voltaire's God: if the lodges did not already exist one or another philosophe would had to have invented them. Both Koselleck and Furet condemn the Enlightenment to a sinister politics, the bastard legacy of Absolutism, and hence one bereft of modern liberal and socially democratic institutions or thought processes, meaningless as an anchor upon which to rest either modernity or postmodernity.

As we enter into the post-postwar era this seems an appropriate historiographical moment to reassess both freemasonry and the Enlightenment. The constitutional principles and legislative assemblies of 1789, it will be argued here, have more to do with the practices and the ideals of the masonic lodges, and hence with the Enlightenment, than has been previously understood. Modern civil society was invented during the Enlightenment in the new enclaves of sociability of which freemasonry was the most avowedly constitutional and aggressively civic. The nature of masonic sociability has not been understood because historians have seldom looked at actual masonic practice. Since almost all the masonic archives were opened at the end of World War II, the mirage of secrecy does not explain the webs of interpretation that contemporary historians have spun out about the lodges. And of course vast quantities of masonic tracts and discourses spoken at lodge meetings were routinely published at the time and have been available ever since.

By their own admission and by their meeting records, the European lodges emerge as societies organized around British constitutional principles, around elections, majority rule, and representative government. The earliest French description of the lodges speaks of "elections." "the consent of all brothers," the authority of the master and Grand master, "pluralities," "consent or opposition," "representatives," and "government."[64] In tandem with this structure came the assumption that reform of society and government, if only in this private public sphere, is possible through virtuous and self-disciplined leadership. The cultivation of individual virtue and reason was universally presumed by the lodges to have meaning for civil society and hence for the larger polity. That meaning could differ enormously. In chapter 2 we will find masonic discourse that could be court and Whig, or even Jacobite or country in Britain. In chapter 4 we will find that it could be nationalist and centralizing in the midcentury Dutch Republic. Later in the century we will find lodges that were fawningly Josephine in the Austrian Netherlands under Joseph II[65] or imperial and cultlike in their adoration of Frederick II in the 1740s in Prussia. And we must not forget the republican and egalitarian brothers we have just met among the youthful and marginal in Paris. They probably would have become followers of Rousseau had they kept writing into the 1760s. In chapter 6 we will find a Rousseauian tinge in masonic thought of the 1760s and beyond. By then, however, we can easily find French freemasons who are monarchist, yet reformist; such were men and women freemasons in late eighteenth-century Burgundy. Not least, in chapter 8 we will find that freemasonry could be mystical, with Catholic undertones, and aristocratic in Strasbourg and its environs. The point about the masonic impulse wherever we find it is that it strove to be political, without ever being overtly partisan, in places where the politics of the old order frequently saw little or no need for its forms of governance, for the constitutional, the legislative, or the centralizing and nationalist.

Not least in every European country the lodges sought to integrate the titles and status of their members within their new fraternal identity. The more baroque the symbols of rank and class, the more elaborate were the masonic degrees and ceremonies as they sought to redefine the meaning of rank and place while seeking at every turn to reinforce and extol it. In chapter 8 we can see this dedication to degress particularly within French freemasonry, but it is also present in every European lodge. In Amsterdam in 1795 the main lodge, La Bien Aimée, welcomed officers of the French army and openly embraced the principles of the French Revolution. It also self-consciously changed its ceremonies at that moment to reflect the new ideology of equality (see pp. 175–76). The lodges were as much of the old order as they were dissonant with its most fundamental assumptions.[66] Historians have found French lodges in 1789 that were aggressively supportive of the old order, of estates, of a social order at that moment deeply menaced by the forces of change and modernity.[67]

None of this activity—*pace* Furet—signals a machinelike search for ideological purity among an eccentric minority. Instead, Continental lodges were imitating forms of political organization exported from Britain, seeking within those forms a means of expressing the disparate interests of their members in society and government. Harmless enough, we might assume, were it not for the reality of society and governance at moments in any country in eighteenth-century Europe. The police in Paris sought to protect that reality; so too did the States of Holland when it outlawed the fraternity in 1735; so too did Joseph II when he closed down all but one lodge in every Belgian province in 1787. The beliefs and values subsumed under that all-too-abstract term "Enlightenment" were different from the beliefs and values that had benefited the old elites in most European societies for centuries, but not so different as to be everywhere and at every moment dangerous or radical. Thus the police had to arrest the freemasons; they also let them go.

It is the contention of this book that the masonic experience in every western European context, from Edinburgh to Berlin, from the 1730s to the 1780s, was resolutely civil and hence political. Masonic language from those decades does not merely provide vocabulary words for the "real" politics of the 1790s. It is too simplistic to assume that although the Jacobins had some similarity with the philosophical societies of the Enlightenment—with freemasonry as the most important of these antecedents—"their involvement *in politics* sets the earliest [Jacobin] societies apart from pre-revolutionary circles and lodges."[68] The political nature of enlightened discourse and sociability can be understood on its own terms provided we do not approach it stereotypically, either from the unproven and unprovable supposition that it was conspiratorial, or from the equally flawed perception found in the writings of François Furet, that "the philosophical societies . . . set up a model for pure, not representative, democracy, in which the collective will always lays down the law."[69] From such a perspective it is not hard to imagine that the roots of totalitarianism lie in the Enlightenment and not in its opposition.

Condemning 1789 also condemns the Enlightenment, not only its philosophical dreams but also its schools of political practice and discourse, which is what the lodges were, particularly on the Continent. But contrary to seeing these settings as seedbeds of a hegemonic egalitarianism, as breeding grounds for consensus based upon ideology rather than upon interest, hence for ideology that entraps rather than informs the political individual, this book argues from the sources for a very different and much more benign reading of the political meaning of enlightened sociability. In so doing it seeks to challenge an essentially right-of-center historiographical tradition that is entrenched in some places, ignored mindlessly in others. At the major conference to celebrate the French Revolution held in July 1989 and sponsored by French Marxists, not a single paper out of well over two hundred was devoted to French freemasonry.[70] It was as if the topic had ceased to be important or, worse still, was allowed to stand indicted of tendencies dark and forbidding, and hence best left to others.

It is quite simply wrong to state that the philosophical society known as freemasonry ever intended to practice, or actually practiced, direct democracy in the lodges of western Europe. Elected representatives, that is, lodge officers, were central to the social and constitutional life of the lodges, and in some lodges were almost authoritarian in their governance. In France this hierarchical character is evident right into the 1770s and 1780s when the Grand Orient in Paris consolidated its power and instituted a national General Assembly complete with committees to adjudicate the awarding of degrees as well as the distribution of charity to brothers fallen on hard times. Thus it is wrong to presume, as does Furet, that the dominant ideology in French freemasonry was Rousseauian. As we shall see, masonic discourse with its extraordinary porosity, its ability to absorb the theoretical and the political, could indeed at moments be Rousseauian (p. 155); first and foremost, it could also be, and was, right into the late 1760s Lockean, as well as republican. As the Paris freemasons demonstrate in their published self-defense, republican language could readily echo in the masonic voice. In the 1740s that language almost certainly derived from the rhetoric of the republic of letters where English ideas, as translated by the French Huguenots exiled in the Dutch Republic, figured so prominently. Vaguely republican language even turns up as early as the 1730s in the masonic speeches of the Catholic Jacobite Chevalier Ramsey and was repeated incessantly, eventually to merge with Rousseau, or with American, or Dutch republican discourse, even with d'Holbachian fantasies about enlightened monarchy. In the early nineteenth century aged and exiled French Jacobins could still naively lay claim to the myth that the English Revolution was the historical moment when speculative freemasonry with its progressive vision was born. As one exile put it, that birth in the 1640s distinguished the "free mason [maçon libre]" from the ordinary mason. The epoch of the English Revolution, it was believed, had been when freemasonry "took an entirely new direction . . . applicable to the moral conduct of wise men so designated because of their practice of social virtue."[71] As we shall see in chapter 1, such myths were widespread and capable of remarkable survival.

There is another reality about European freemasonry that present-day European historiography does not address, namely, its international character. Furet as well as his followers would designate the French philosophical societies as the place where it was possible "to substitute an egalitarian ideology and the principle of direct democracy for religion, the king and traditional hierarchies."[72] As such, "freemasonry transformed a social phenomenon into politics and opinion into action. In this sense, it embodied the origin of Jacobinism."[73] If the masonic lodges were the seedbeds of Jacobinism, then why did they not spawn it in Philadelphia in 1780 or in Brussels and Amsterdam in the 1790s? Throughout the century there was hardly ever a lodge meeting in any major European city when foreign visitors were not present. Even in less important cities, such as Bordeaux, visitors can be found at over half the meetings.[74] In addition, lodges were in regular communication with their foreign counterparts and, even in moments of dispute, capable of seeking affiliation with foreign Grand Lodges (p. 105). In all these comings and goings, visitations, and delegations, described in letters and signed visitors' books preserved in archives from Stockholm to Strasbourg, I know of no record suggesting that French freemasonry was perceived to be markedly different in its fundamental practices and ideals from Dutch, or British, or Belgian, or American masonry.

When the young Jean Paul Marat visited the Amsterdam lodge in 1774 he would have discovered discourses and ceremonies comfortably familiar.[75] True, French degree ceremonies were more frequent and elaborate; the hierarchical structure in France was undoubtedly greater and more complex with its more aristocratic lodges openly critical of the frequent elections and rotation of leadership that were common practices in Dutch, and also British, freemasonry. In short, on the scale of democratic practice the eighteenth-century French lodges were less, rather than more democratic, with the significant exception of women's participation, which was marked in French aristocratic circles by the 1770s. This is not to suggest that the masonic mentality which labeled the unenlightened as "the profane" does not present the historian with troubling antecendents to the politics of exclusion based upon class, or gender, or ideology. It is to suggest, however, and once again in alliance with a moderate and liberal reading of the French Revolution, that we must look to the tensions within the ancien régime, to the repressions and excesses, to the police who did the interrogations and extracted the fines, in order to give an adequate and balanced account of the radical direction that French sociability took in the Jacobin clubs of the 1790s. It seems a singularly presentist perspective to lay blame for the abuses of democracy primarily on the progenitors of modern social and political behavior, however philosophical and hence inevitably abstract their stance under the old order. Outside of countries where the Inquisition was strong, I know of no records of interrogations, detentions, and spying on masons, or others, comparable to what can be found in the eighteenth-century records of the Bastille. Modern civil society struggled to be born and the more powerful Continental absolutist states, particularly with a strong, unreformed clergy, did nothing to encourage its nativity.

In attempting to rediscover freemasonry we are seeking another, more constructive approach to the Enlightenment. For in addition to being freemasons, our cast of historical characters is made up primarily of men and women of the Enlightenment. This term, Enlightenment, ironically veils as much as it illuminates. It conjures up a vast historiography as liberal and self-assured as the phenomenon it seeks to describe. It presumes a taxonomy of eighteenth-century ideas, first dissected brilliantly by the German historian Ernst Cassirer in the 1930s, that rightly, but abstractly, places the science of Newton at the heart of enlightened discourse and adds to it contract theory, associated with the writings of John Locke, as well as rational religiosity, oftentimes described as deism and frequently combined with anticlericalism. To this taxonomy the traditional historian of ideas adds various natural philosophical impulses, such as materialism and pantheism, stemming in complex ways from Descartes and Spinoza.

The resulting map of enlightened ideas arrays these verities on a landscape perceived from a lofty and rather static distance. This book seeks to revise that traditional account, in effect to shorten the distance, to make us at the least pedestrians, or at the most invited guests, witnessing private meetings, reading, as it were, other people's letters and records, to find out what it may have been like to live out the ideals of the so-called age of Enlightenment. If in the process we "politicize" the Enlightenment by making it civic, then, I would argue, we have become closer to the intentions of many of its participants. My intention here remains focused by the text, in this instance by words spoken socially, in decorated rooms amid precise ceremonies, as well as in published defenses and explications. It is not my intention to count or measure, to quantify the texts or their listeners. It is the content of discourse to which we shall return repeatedly as we seek to unlock the meaning of the historical experience lived by actors speaking on a distant stage from which modernity evolved.

In our journey we may discard the map provided by Cassirer and others, at moments finding their taxonomy so idealized as to mislead. In so doing we will have seen the point of entering the realm of private discourse in order to illuminate general history. New ways will have been found to answer some old yet timeless historical questions: Did that eighteenth-century explosion of enlightened discourse, rooted in the new science, actually produce a new variety of Western religiosity, in short a new ethical posture available to only the most literate, not necessarily better or worse yet profoundly different from the doctrinal Christianity it rivaled? Are the gentlemen and women who identified with progressive thought and fraternized in the lodges significantly different from their pious counterparts? Are they given to forays or interventions into the established orders of society and government for the purpose of changing them? And if so, does their posture in the world tell us something about the actually revolutionary or, in Britain, simply reforming political movements that transformed European political institutions at the end of the eighteenth century? Did the Enlightenment, so called, have anything to do with the actual birth of modern and progressive social and political institutions, with the late eighteenth-century revolutions in western Europe? The answer presented here is qualified and nuanced, but it is for the most part affirmative.

Should a collection of characters chosen for their largely masonic affiliations be allowed to posture as sources for the unraveling of such important historical questions? This book treats freemasonry as but one—unique—form of the new private sociability. Certain characteristics of masonic association differ not at all from the many other private societies that sprang up throughout Europe in the course of the eighteenth century. Members, proposed and chosen by other members, paid dues, attended meetings, voted and discussed, gave loyalty, and sought conviviality, if not self-improvement, from their association. What is characteristic of the new private societies of the eighteenth century is also characteristic of freemasonry. Members were literate and affluent. Most important, they met out of mutual interest and not as a result of confessional affiliation, birth, or rank in society per se. And they always met separately from their families, although not necessarily from their spouses. In short, they met as individuals.

Yet the freemasons did more than simply convene and converse. In their private sociability, I shall be arguing, they reconstituted the polity and established a constitutional form of self-government, complete with constitutions and laws, elections and representatives. To this government they gave allegiance, and they bestowed sovereignty upon it. Yet this government could in turn be altered or removed by the consent of a majority of brothers. The lodges became microscopic civil polities, new public spaces, in effect schools for constitutional government. On the Continent, in every European country, even the Dutch Republic, the practice of this sort of governance was unique. It is also historically significant that this education in self-government excluded the majority of Europeans—almost all women, as well as the illiterate and the nonaffluent.

The German philosopher, Jürgen Habermas has argued that such an exclusion was almost inevitable. The public space being delineated was created by and for the European bourgeoisie. The "bourgeois public sphere" was intended to regulate civil society, and it was possible because of "the background experience of a private sphere that had become interiorized human closeness." Out of that more egalitarian intimacy the public sphere arose "as an expansion . . . and . . . completion."[76] Out of the bourgeois family, as well as out of the habits and practice of commerce, Habermas believes, arose the "public sphere." With extraordinary insight he argues for its appearance first in England in the 1690s, in the aftermath of the English Revolution. And he sees freemasonry as anticipating the European-wide adoption of this sphere as an alternative to absolutism.[77]

Although Habermas's analysis has merit, it still remains flawed. It cannot explain why the values of a more egalitarian intimacy produced a public sphere intended solely for men. It may be that rather than the private permitting a new public sphere, however idealized, the reverse is true. We need to consider the possibility that ideologies and behavior intended for the public realm shaped the family, providing it with an egalitarian ethos that never actually redefined the inequality of gender relations. A politically meaningful public sphere—as well as the first speculative lodge—did emerge in England during the 1690s, after the establishment of parliamentary government and constitutional monarchy. As the ideal of the public sphere spread throughout Europe under the mantle of the Enlightenment, women's place in it, as Joan Landes has shown, was ambiguous and fraught with contradiction.[78] Women participated in the new sociability but, as we shall see in chapter 5, in paradoxical ways. The masonic lodges provide a particularly clarifying insight into women's relationship to the Enlightenment.

In the lodges, small enclaves with habits that could be simultaneously formal and intensely personal, the private became the public in ways that were deeply ambiguous. In the human order the private implies the domestic. Predictably lodges at moments self-consciously imitated the domestic and sought to inculcate ethical values. They even used the language of domesticity: founding lodges became mothers, the good master was the good and benevolent father; members were brothers, other neighboring lodges were sisters. Lodges not recognized by legitimate lodges became "bastards." Yet in the lodges that admitted women as "equals" and sisters, ceremonies and discourses by women emphasized only the ethical, private virtues, never governance (see chapter 5). Their virtues, at least in theory, could be transformed into civic virtues and used in the governance of civil society, but that was the work of their brothers. They articulated how that transformation should occur. The dominance and importance of the public sphere over the private, of men over women, is never actually contested. Amid their equality in the lodges the dominance of men over women is ironically reinforced.

The virtues sought by the lodges were simply presumed to be applicable to governance, to social order and harmony, to the public sphere. This is what I mean by the ambiguity between the personal and the public, between the search for virtue and the inevitability of the political. It just may be that the egalitarian family was the creation of civil society, and not the reverse. Whatever the sequence of development, by the late eighteenth century on the Continent, the private sphere came to be seen as subservient to the work of public order and governance. There can be no revolutions without the predominance, if only for a time, of the public sphere, of politics and political discourse over all other forms of human behavior and discourse.

The Enlightenment provided the rudiments of a new Western identity. The secular men it created ceased to understand how to separate the language of power from ordered behavior and an ideology of improvement, moral and material, that is, from ethical discourse in tandem with self-interest. Only the literate and educated, it came to be believed, could be trusted to act ethically and to think disinterestedly in the interests of society, government, and improvement. The importance of the lodges lay in their ability to teach men identified by their supposed merit how to integrate enlightened values with the habits of governance. The lodges sought to civilize, to teach manners and decorum, to augment the order and harmony of civil society. They taught men to speak in public, to keep records, to pay "taxes," to be tolerant, to debate freely, to vote, to moderate their feasting, and to give lifelong devotion to the other citizens of their order. By the late eighteenth century such men might assume a variety of political postures. Rather than imagine their affiliations with monarchs or democrats, we are on far firmer ground in arguing that they would have had affiliations, that they possessed a civic consciousness, that in one place if only for hours in the month, they had become citizens.

What draws the historian to freemasonry is not simply its secrecy, although that may intrigue, not the lifelong dedication that it could elicit from its brothers (and, as we shall see, its sisters); more important, we are compelled by the content of the moral, ethical, and political prescriptions permeating masonic rituals and discourse. Once divorced from its guild origins, the new freemasonry, as it spread from London first to the towns and cities of western Europe and then beyond, came to embody a variety of ethical prescriptions for living in this world, a stance that was secular and philosophical as distinct from religious and doctrinal. Masonic idealism gives life to those various taxonomies drawn by Cassirer and others. More so than any of the other forms of private sociability, freemasonry wove enlightened ideas into a tapestry of rituals and oaths, rules of conduct intended to induce loyalty and civility, in short into a way of life for its most dedicated followers. There is an all-pervasive religiosity about masonic sociability. In it we may find that "heavenly city" offered by the new secular philosophies of the eighteenth century to their worldly and cosmopolitan followers.

1

The Public Becomes the Private: The English Revolution and the Origins of European Freemasonry

From early in its European history freemasonry was accused of possessing democratic and republican intentions, if not communistic ones. An anonymous French polemic, published in Brussels in 1744, claimed to expose the freemasons as seeking to establish "a universal and democratic republic which would also hold in common all that the earth and the talents of its inhabitants, are capable of producing."[1] In Amsterdam at the height of the Revolution of 1747, another exposé accused the freemasons of being followers of Oliver Cromwell,[2] of being the heirs to the English revolutionary and republican tradition. In yet another anonymous repetition of the charge, also published in Amsterdam, the freemasons became "this Cromwellist Society," enraptured by "enthusiasm" for the common people (*du menu peuple*), as well as being the enemies of religion, elite men (*de gens plus elits*) who threaten the security of the state.[3] In 1791 the Cromwell charge was repeated; this time by opponents of the French Revolution.[4]

Many of these attacks were of a clerical origin. In 1738 the Papacy condemned freemasonry, partly in response to the popularity of the lodge in Rome, and Catholic apologists who promulgated the Papal Bull explicated its logic in detail. At the top of their list of masonic offenses was republicanism. The ingenuity of the English nation, they explained, has revived the purity of freemasonry, and "this society . . . imitates an aspect of the government of Republics. Its leaders are chosen, or dismissed, at its will."[5] Just like the Paris police in the 1740s, Catholic opponents of the fraternity fixated on its custom of holding elections.

These paranoid fantasies, conjuring up beasts that were almost entirely republican or democratic, were, on one level, just that, fantasies. Their appearance relatively early in the century foreshadows the vast antimasonic, and largely monarchist literature produced during and after the French Revolution. Yet in one respect

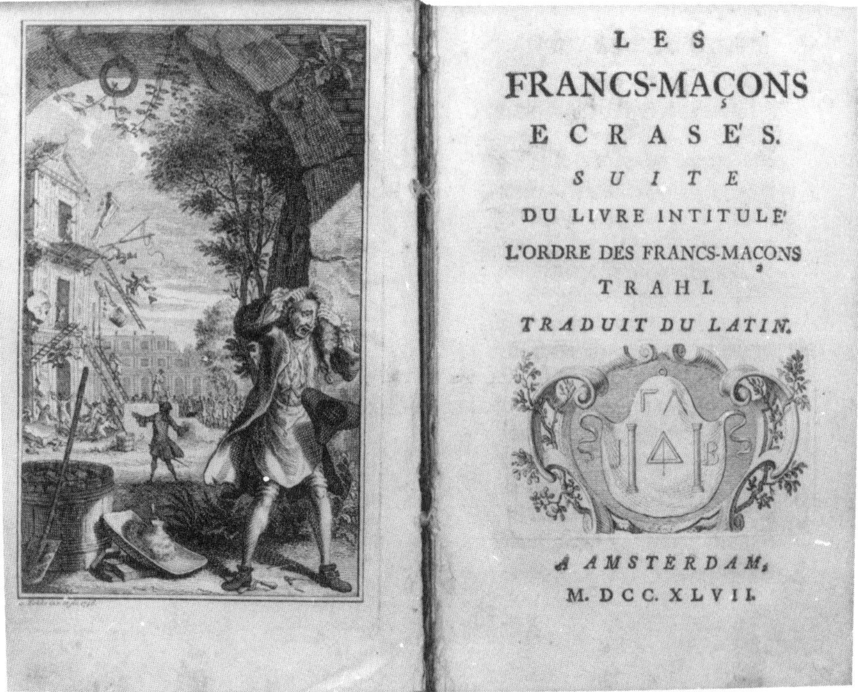

LES
FRANCS-MAÇONS
ECRASE'S.
SUITE
DU LIVRE INTITULE'
L'ORDRE DES FRANCS-MAÇONS
TRAHI.
TRADUIT DU LATIN.

A AMSTERDAM,
M. DCC. XLVII.

FIG. 1. Engraved frontispiece and title page from one of the earliest and most famous antimasonic works wherein the myth of Cromwell as the founder of freemasonry is used against the order. The place and date of publication, Amsterdam 1747, coincide with the Dutch Revolution of that year.

the European, and primarily Continental reaction, however fanciful, did contain a simple truth. This private society was a British, not a Continental invention. As such it brought with it forms of behavior and values first articulated in that foreign context. From an eighteenth-century European perspective the British context was nothing short of extraordinary. In contrast to the monarchical absolutism that had come to dominate much of Continental Europe in the course of the seventeenth century, the English, as a result of their revolutionary experience in both 1640 and 1688–89, had secured constitutional and parliamentary government. In the 1730s the myth was born that freemasonry was linked to that experience.

We need to know how this happened. We need to know how and why freemasonry acquired its mythical history because it is mythical only to us. We know that the seventeenth-century English and Scottish masons' guild and its craftsmen had absolutely nothing to do with causing, or probably even participating in the English Revolution, either of 1640 or 1688–89. There is not a shred of historical evidence from that period to confirm or even to suggest a direct linkage, yet a century later we find Continental freemasons, writing in French in the 1770s and 1780s, telling themselves that Cromwell was the founder of modern freemasonry.

In that period French freemasons were still attempting to reconstruct the history of the order. Throughout the eighteenth century the exercise in historical reconstruction had always occupied devout freemasons on both sides of the Channel. In their effort to ensure respectability, particularly in the face of rival and purely aristocratic orders of medieval origin, Continental freemasons sought a careful reconstruction of a history they believed extended back to Hiram, the builder of Solomon's Temple. They went on to tie the history of their fraternity to the Crusades, then to the Knights Templar, and finally they picked up the story again in seventeenth-century England. We have manuscript histories by French freemasons stating, almost in passing, that freemasonry was associated with Oliver Cromwell. "He had revived the order" and had also "made the revolution in England." These devout freemasons accepted Cromwell as their founder, and they wanted to believe that although they were descended from the events that transformed seventeenth-century England, they were not responsible for them. "Our order has been blamed for the rebellion!" stated one history indignantly. In 1776 a pious masonic historian asserted that the Jesuits were largely responsible for distorting masonic history and "rendering the order an object of hatred."[6] In the same year a lengthy masonic dialogue admitted that the mason sees himself as an "English legislator," indebted to Cromwell for his origins, and then argues that there is nothing subversive or revolutionary about this identification.[7] In the 1780s the orator in a lodge in Bordeaux gave a lecture on "a masonic work translated from English on the true origin of masonry," and the topic was discussed for some weeks to come.[8] Even the official history of French freemasonry located the beginning of speculative freemasonry in mid–seventeenth-century England, mentioning, in passing, Christopher Wren's involvement in the lodges.[9] The official history discreetly left out the Cromwell story.

Masonic reformers, often aristocratic and interested in making the society more conscious of "degrees" and harder to join, claimed they were reviving the freemasonry associated with "the celebrated and unfortunate Prince Charles I, King of England" and his descendants through the Pretender.[10] In general, aristocratic French freemasons of the latter part of the century preferred to imagine that the society had been founded by Crusading princes returning from the Holy Land. In one version of the story, which came from the Jacobite Chevalier Ramsay, masonry came to France via the medieval kings of Scotland, and the period of the English Revolution never figures in that mythical history.[11] Even in the early nineteenth century French freemasons believed that "the customs of the English, and the spirit of liberty they hold in their laws is the principal cause of the establishment and the favor that freemasonry has in England."[12] In this account the sociable and tolerant Druids, conjectured to be priests of the ancient Anglo-Saxons, developed a religion that was "uniquely universal and immutable, that is to say, freemasonry."

Perhaps only British freemasons realized just how potentially damaging and inflammatory the association with the English Revolution could prove. The official British masonic *Constitutions* (1723) never mentioned it. George Smith, an English mathematical lecturer who lived at midcentury in Amsterdam, lectured his brothers there on the origins of the order and skipped everything from "King Charles I who was a Master Mason . . . to King George the first was a good Master Mason . . . and his Royal Successor, George II, our present king is a Master Mason."[13] He simply pretended that the Revolution had never occurred. But by the

1780s, if not earlier, in Germany freemasonry was associated with the English Revolution, and with "our freedom" and the "tradition of the British Nation."[14] The myth that English societies and fraternities were directly associated with the English Revolution must have been widespread. In 1790 we can find supporters of the French Revolution establishing a "Society of the Revolution like those that had been established in London in 1688."[15] English historians might have trouble imagining what these French revolutionaries could have had in mind; the Whig party might be the closest we could imagine. Myths create history as much as they transmit versions of the past needed in the present.

On the Continent generally, only devoutly Catholic lodges with Jacobite tendencies avoided (or attacked) the Cromwell story. We can find the Jacobite version being constructed as early as 1740 when a loyalist of the exiled Stuarts, the Chevalier Ramsay, held great sway in some of the French lodges.[16] When a new degree was introduced in the lodges of the 1780s, the degree of Chevalier or knight, it was noted that in England during the last century the name had been associated with "a very great error. The Revolutions" had in turn brought no good to the order.[17] But for those freemasons who held to Cromwell, republican and king killer, as their perceived patron, they could hardly have expected better treatment at the hands of the ideological supporters of courts, princes, and established churches.

Most of what Continental freemasons, and their detractors, knew about the early history and practices of their society came from a series of anonymous tracts that began to appear in French in the late 1730s, and subsequently became known as "exposures." In these they learned everything from history to rituals, and in that literature was born the myth of Cromwell. We would dearly like to know who wrote the exposures, but those identities are probably lost forever. Whoever the anonymous authors were, they were often quite knowledgeable about the new fraternity they sought to describe.

Sometimes it is clear from the tone and voice of the anonymous writer where his, and occasionally it was claimed her, sympathies lay. Disaffected freemasons, imposters, but also apologists and devotees had a hand at "exposing" this new secret and foreign society to the curious. Despite all of the interest we need to explain this particular accusation, this association, however delusional, of freemasonry with republicanism. Certainly the specifically British origins of freemasonry rendered it suspect in almost all Continental countries where parliaments, revolutions, constitutions, bills of rights, and acts of toleration were seen as inherently subversive. In addition, by the 1730s, however oligarchic we may imagine Britain to have been, it was widely perceived as a country governed by Parliament and the constitution. By that decade both Whig and Tory newspapers commonly spoke of "our Constitution [which] hath thought fit that the Representatives of the People should not have Time to forget that they are such; that they are empowered to act for the People, not against them" and that "the Constitution of England is King, Lords and Commons making Laws."[18] In addition, in The Netherlands and in France close ties existed between the first official lodges and Whig politicians resident in those countries, thus the suspicion that lodge membership signaled a pro-British attitude on foreign policy. Many of the first most visible Continental freemasons of the 1730s were in the entourage of the claimant to the office of stadtholder of the Dutch republic. This was almost certainly the main reason the authorities in the province of Holland disbanded the lodge in 1735.[19] Such associations helped to establish the lodges as breeding grounds for British ideas and practices.

Freemasons were also regarded as subversive in Portugal in the early 1740s, where a freemason was arrested and tortured and the lodge accused of riotous behavior during the Lenten season.[20] In 1738 the French authorities raided British ambassador Lord Waldegrave's residence because a lodge meeting had occurred there.[21] French police reports, as we saw in the introduction, provide valuable information about the early development of French freemasonry. They seem to confirm the existence of a Paris lodge founded by Jacobite exiles in the mid-1720s, and then a separate group sponsored by Whigs, or at least anti-Jacobites, in the 1730s. By the 1740s, again as noted in the introduction, masonic lodges in Paris embraced men—and even some women—of rather humble occupations.

Being either Jacobite or Whig might strike us as a significant difference. Yet on the Continent both were first and foremost British and foreign. Not least, both shared in similar social practices and political values—aside from the monarch they revered—which were more, rather than less homogeneous, and again distinctively British.[22] Among the most important of these was the habit of political parties, ideologies, and movements that cut across lines of class and caste. Thus it is possible to speak of a popular and organized Jacobitism, just as there was Whiggery among small merchants and freeholders.

Whether Whig or Jacobite, freemasonry on the Continent implied subversion. Predictably some of the most violent antimasonic writing from the French ancien régime also contained the most explicit defenses of monarchical absolutism.[23] In most absolutist countries the ultimate form of subversion was republicanism. Thus this particular accusation was leveled against the freemasons. It is not the charge itself that concerns us here, but rather we shall focus upon the common thread running through the earliest opposition mounted against the freemasons. Whatever the interests or motives of the authorities, we are struck by their assumption that this voluntary private society with its ritual and secrecy, and its international connections, posed a threat to the state. Perhaps not every instance was considered a specifically republican threat, but nevertheless this unlicensed exercise in fraternal association and conviviality was regarded as more than harmless festivity. It was almost immediately perceived as an incursion into realms, whether religious or political, reserved for the legitimate civil authorities. A curious fusion of the private into the public had occurred in the minds of the authorities, and we need to understand the reasons why this connection was so readily made.

Masonic literature assisted the authorities in presuming that this British movement possessed political meaning. An early and anonymous masonic treatise of 1738 made the point explicitly and linked the origin of freemasonry precisely to the English Revolution. From this particular exposure arose the myth, as far as we can trace it, that Cromwell had sponsored the freemasons. The tract pretended to be simply a French translation of an earlier English exposé, the widely read (over twenty editions in English—a remarkable number) and commented upon *Masonry Dissected,* published in London in 1730 by a disaffected but genuine freemason, Samuel Prichard. But the French translation, which itself went through seventeen editions as well as translation into German and Dutch, in fact altered and elaborated upon Prichard, making new and bold claims for the English origins of freemasonry. Most important, it was written by someone who knew a great deal about English history, indeed by an amateur historian of seventeenth-century Europe. Into the narrative of the English Revolution this historian wove the origins of the fraternity. The history explained the derivation of the name "freemason" in this way:

> It is composed of two words with a double significance, by mason one seeks to denote this society founded on a solid foundation . . . by the word Franc which precedes it, one wants to say that in general this society works perpetually for the franchise or liberty of the nation. . . this franchise consists in the free election of the members of Parliament, and in the liberty to speak one's mind according to Magna Charta.[24]

Freemasonry, we are told, began at this "most famous of Revolutions," and quickly came to include

> princes, dukes . . . in short the leading lords of the country who now shared in working perpetually for the liberty of the Nation. The Freemason is a free worker. Taking these two words together in a political sense, they bear an entirely different explanation. The Society which had chosen the virtues, attached separately to each part of this composite, prides itself in a great freedom, in voting and in manners.[25]

The posture of liberty is then immediately related to

> the milieu of the seventeenth century, during the troubles which agitated Britain, the general malcontentment of the English and the Scottish against the government of Charles I, there were born different associations, for the purpose of resisting the will of the prince, who was suspected of seeking absolute power, and following the doctrine of resistance, one of these assemblies, envisioning a total liberty and franchise, took the name, Freemasons, and as they were persuaded that Cromwell had been of the same sentiment, this society was formed in his time.

At the time of Cromwell its membership was all from "the sect of the Enthusiasts." But as England evolved after 1660, so too did the freemasons. After the expulsion of James II in 1688, the latter-day followers of Cromwell revived and restored the freemasons. Prichard's exposé had claimed that the new lodges began only in 1691. The French-language account took liberties with the text and emphasized the link with the English republic, and it asserted the lodges' dedication to parliamentary government; the French text pushed the date back and reinforced the linkage with the midcentury English Revolution.

Whoever wrote this French exposé knew in depth the history of that revolution. He recounted in detail the events leading up to the civil wars, the beheading of Charles I—"a unique example in Christianity of a king decapitated by his subjects"—and then proceeded to the reign of Charles II, who ruled "without virtue" and became "a pensioner of Louis XIV."[26] William III was "the restorer of English liberty," the Tories, "for the most part Jacobites," are the supporters of the dethroned king, James II, and by far the greater part of the Whigs are "attached to the present government." Yet the freemasons accept Whigs and Tories "indifferently," and a considerable number of them are even Jacobites. "The Statutes of this order were drafted after the last revolution, and it is in the form of Colleges, regulating contact and imposing taxes and the compliance of the classes."[27] Note that in this account the differences between Whigs and Jacobites, which we might think were great, are skillfully minimized. In one manner or another they are all revolutionaries and they are certainly all men with political agendas. Not least the French tract works subtle but important linguistic changes: lodges become "Colleges," a cowan (outsider) becomes a stranger (*un étranger*) and later in the same text, "un prophane." Such changes signal the appearance of a cultural transformation.

This earliest Continental explication of masonic history, linking it to the political history of seventeenth-century England, is an extraordinary document. Its tone is anti-French and pro-Austrian, suggesting that it was written by a French speaker in the Low Countries, either in The Netherlands or in Belgium. The end of the tract claimed that it could be bought in the book shop of Jacques Jacob in Liège. There was such a publisher who had a shop in that independent principality in this period, and that fits well enough into the story of freemasonry in Catholic Europe. The fraternity had just been condemned by the papacy, a decree enforced in the bordering Austrian Netherlands by the pious Maria Theresa. Liège was directly across the border. Although the local bishop exercised control, he was indifferent to the decree and Liège was a safe enough place in 1738 to sell an anonymous pamphlet about the freemasons.[28] This pamphlet began a powerful myth that remained a part of masonic belief throughout the eighteenth century. The 1776 French manuscript history of the order that linked it to Cromwell even uses some of the same language.

The 1738 pamphlet was a part of the literature that advocated the Triple Alliance of Britain, the Dutch Republic, and the Austrian Empire, which was intended to contain the French colossus.[29] With documents such as these it is little wonder that the detractors and accusers of freemasonry from the 1730s on found political meaning in every move the fraternity made. From then on, masonic apologists tried to deny the accusation of republicanism and to deny that the order "had implicated itself, as it were, in all of the Revolutions which had on more than one occasion put the Kingdom of England on the brink of ruin, according to which of the Parties stood for or against the monarchy."[30] Apologists responded, Have the great princes themselves not belonged to the order? Yet the charge of fomenting revolution would not go away.

What the accusations against freemasonry suggest, at the very least, is the creation of a new and unacceptable means by which private men intruded themselves into the domain of public and governmental authority. At first glance this seems curious. Private associations, often with civic duties and responsibilities, were hardly new to the social landscape of any European urban society. Indeed the medieval guilds, from which freemasonry derived, still possessed in many European countries various civic functions; some guilds were nearly as old as the cities themselves. By the last quarter of the seventeenth century, salons and coffeehouse or café coteries were commonly found in towns and cities from Amsterdam to Paris.

By the 1730s reading societies flourished. It would seem though, that something made all these groups different from the freemasons.

By the freemason's own admission, even boast, and certainly by the accusations of their detractors, there was indeed something unique about this society—a difference that could easily enough arouse suspicion. Here we may legitimately ask, What was the difference? Or to put the matter another way: What made freemasonry similar yet so different from these other eighteenth-century clubs, societies, and associations that its appeal was never simply local, although each lodge always possessed a highly localized character? Why did freemasonry spread so rapidly once it had broken out of its guild origins? Why especially did it become international so quickly, moving by the 1720s, if not before, from Britain to The Netherlands and France, and then to the whole of urban Europe? Complementing this cosmopolitanism, as we shall see, was a remarkable consistency, from country to country, language to language, in what freemasons said about themselves at their meetings, and occasionally in the content of the accusations leveled by their detractors. Answering these questions will require in the chapters to follow that we travel throughout western Europe with the fraternity, witnessing its meetings and the discourses of its orators, first for the remainder of this chapter, at its place of origin, in Scotland and England, then in other parts of Continental Europe. In choosing to make such a journey we are presuming that much of what has been written about eighteenth-century sociability misses the distinctive character of the lodges. Of course they were like the philosophical societies and reading clubs, yet they were also different. Many historians, particularly writing about the societies and lodges in France, have chosen to treat them as of a piece. But it will become evident that such an essentially sociological approach obscures as much as it illuminates.

There is one other question that will recur repeatedly in the story we are about to tell: Why did masonic idealism inspire such loyalty and why did its form, in turn, lead, by the late eighteenth century, to countless imitations? Some of these were of a politically subversive character, the Illuminati in the German-speaking lands being probably the most famous.[31]

These questions go to the heart of the political meaning that could be extracted by devotees of the new secular culture that emerged in eighteenth-century Europe. In the first instance this culture was not specifically political. Rather it was centered around urban sociability, invariably found in the ambience of purposeful social gatherings, coteries located in coffeehouses, as well as in clubs, salons, scientific academies, literary and philosophical societies, and most markedly, or we might say extremely, in the masonic lodges. In all those places men—and only very rarely women—met as individuals, separate from family, church, confraternity, or other traditional corporate bodies that primarily reflected their status and rank in the larger society. The new gatherings were places where literate men could articulate an identity for themselves that was different from, or complementary to, their established place in a social system that was profoundly hierarchical, patriarchal, and traditional. Out of that new identity as a man of letters, or a man of science, or simply as an informed reader and discussant of the new journals and newspapers, a new political meaning—as well as a religious meaning—could also begin to emerge. In the older guilds men were joined because of commonly held attributes, what it was that they did for a living and the social place accorded to them on the basis of that status. In the lodges of the new freemasonry there was no single identifying mark or status shared by everyone present. Men met there because of who they were, not because of their occupations or status per se. According to the practices of the English and Scottish lodges of the early eighteenth century, brothers had only to be literate, of good character, and able to afford the dues, which were not insubstantial. To define a common social identity in this way, even within the confines of a private gathering, had implications for the whole of human experience, for the values, mores, and beliefs by which lodge brothers lived their daily lives. Lodges could meet as often as six times a month and some meetings, particularly on the Continent, could take up to five or six hours.[32]

It is not accidental that this form of socializing arose first in Britain. Its crafts and guilds had been weakened earlier than was the case on the Continent. The market economy was further advanced there than on the Continent. Even the Scottish merchant guilds had been denied their monopoly privileges by the Scottish parliament as early as 1672.[33] By the 1720s British society permitted more open and relaxed social interaction (although not necessarily marriage) between lords, gentry, and commoners. A young French visitor to London in the 1720s, Voltaire, wrote about and made that familiarity famous. With it came a degree of religious toleration unknown except in the Dutch Republic.

In early modern Europe, religion—whether confessional or heretical—possessed political implications. The reverse is also true. In every European country religious minorities were watched closely by the authorities, if not persecuted. In 1739, for example, the French ambassador to Great Britain wrote a confidential report to his king about the possibility of dissension and rebellion within the kingdom of this powerful rival. Remarkably, he pointed to the Methodists, and to the Unitarians, as possible factions out of which sectarian disorder might spread.[34] Particularly on the Continent, any organized body with religious beliefs different from the established church was regarded as potentially subversive. Masonic beliefs, in particular their emphasis on relative religious toleration, combined with the invention of ritual practices, played into this fear.

It was only in the masonic lodges, of all the new forms of sociability, that the deity of enlightened culture, the Grand Architect of the Universe, was ceremonially invoked. These pious invocations, first articulated within a British context, seemed to equate the Grand Architect with the deity of the new science, the guarantor of the order and harmony originally proclaimed by Descartes, but codified most especially by Newton. This was not necessarily the understanding of the deity invoked by pious Calvinists or Catholics. It need not, however, have been taken as different. Yet, as clerical critics were quick to point out, the masonic deity was at best suspect, or at worst the god of the deists.

Once invoked in masonic discourse, the Grand Architect was mentioned on the whole infrequently; what interested the masonic brothers was their fraternal sociability. Through rituals and orations their most cherished ideals were expressed in language that made them universal, intended for the lodges "spread over the surface of the earth," intended ultimately for all of humankind. Distinct from most other societies, academies, and salons, the lodges existed to promote the virtue of their members, and they were not shy about disciplining brothers by reprimands and fines, or even by expulsions. Freemasons claimed to be creating perfectly harmonious societies within the lodge. Their purpose was both social and moral. The self-knowledge and education sought by freemasons cannot be divorced from an idealism that connected enlightenment with virtue, in an ethical sense, as well as with personal and social improvement. The key to improvement lay in order and harmony. The masonic concern for both was unrelenting. Then, as now, order requires authority, and authority implies governance.

The thrust of masonic rhetoric was invariably civic. The polities created were intended to possess an internal government, as well as to be social and intellectual in character. They were never intended, in the first instance, to be political—as that term denotes state power, access to, or protection from. When we speak of freemasonry and politics we are saying that the civic consciousness developed in the lodges perforce addressed the nature and purpose of the polity. In that sense the lodges were deeply concerned about the political without ever wishing to engage in day-to-day politics. Nevertheless, hostile critics made the point—and then went on to imagine that their insight conformed to reality—that this separation of masonic idealism from actual political intervention was bogus. The separation, we now know, was never bogus. Masonic records are clear on the lack of specific political involvement on the part of almost any European lodge. The official masonic *Constitutions* published in London in 1723 prohibited "any quarrels about religion, or nations, or state policy . . . we . . . are resolved against all Politicks, as what never yet conduc'd to the Welfare of the Lodge."[35] But we need to know what London freemasons meant by politics.

The First British Lodges

By the 1720s politics in Britain meant something rather different from what it meant in the rest of Europe. In speaking of "politics" the masonic *Constitutions* meant party politics, the rage of party brought on by the creation of a new political nation as the result of the Revolution Settlement of 1688–89. Politics was the contest for power between Whig and Tory, between court and country, even between Jacobite and Hanoverian, within the context of a constitutionally protected system of parliamentary elections for which approximately one-fifth of the male population was enfranchised. To eschew politics in this context—or for that matter in any other—did not necessarily mean to deny the civic. Quite the reverse could be true. Indeed, the condemnation of factions and parties was a commonplace of the era, dominated as it was by just that. British masonic idealism proclaimed the civic as a realm for contemplation and idealization. As the *Constitutions* proclaimed, freemasonry was the "Royal Art," practiced by the "free born . . . from the beginning of the world, in the polite nations, especially in times of peace, and when the civil powers, abhorring tyranny and slavery, gave due scope to the bright and free genius of their happy subjects. . . then always masons, above all other artists, were the favorites of the eminent."[36] The conditions of the social harmony of working men and their betters depended upon peace and freedom as guaranteed by the civil authorities. The

FIG. 2. Engraved frontispiece from James Anderson, *The Constitutions of the Freemasons* (London 1723). Men of genteel dress and hence rank, possibly one of them Jean Desaguliers, an Anglican minister, are passing on the *Constitutions*.

public, and hence political meaning to be extracted from private lodge sociability, as distinct from other forms of eighteenth-century enlightened sociability, began only with the adulation accorded the post-1689 political order. Unlike most other clubs and societies, the lodges were governed not just by rules or contracts among their members. They possessed what the freemasons called their constitutions, which came to mean in the course of the early eighteenth-century normative laws governing these private societies in ways that made them capable of being transformed into microscopic, and contractually founded and constitutionally governed, civil societies. It seems hardly accidental that only literate men with some surplus income—a few shillings a month—could qualify for membership in a lodge. These same men would be the most likely to meet the property qualifications for voting in eighteenth-century British elections. They would almost certainly have been among that 20 percent of the male population who could actually do so.

The *Constitutions* were codified and published in 1723 by the London lodges which had organized themselves into the Grand Lodge of London. The preface to that work explicitly linked the development of freemasonry to the political history of England. Prince Edwin, the son of the tenth-century Saxon king Athelstan, assembled the first general meeting of all the masons. "That assembly did frame the Constitution and Charges of an English Lodge, made a Law to preserve and observe the same in all time coming." From that time on, and with the approval of the aristocracy, most of whom became masons, the Constitution was read to every new working mason. The first Stuart king, James I (d. 1625), favored the masons and imported the Augustan style of architecture from Renaissance Italy; but his son, Charles I, was "diverted by the Civil Wars" (he was beheaded in 1649). Cultivated by Charles II (d. 1685), scorned by his successor, the deposed James II, since the Revolution of 1688–89 and the reign of William III, the masons have flourished. Both the Scottish and English nations, "freeborn . . . and enjoying the fruits of peace and liberty," have cultivated "the Royal Art."[37] At moments we need to recall that not a shred of historical evidence existed, then or now, to prove this account. Indeed, late eighteenth-century American freemasons subtly altered the account, noting that at times parliament had persecuted the masons and that in 1775 the Boston Grand Master had been slain "contending for the liberties of his country."[38]

In their private assemblies eighteenth-century British freemasons, armed with this mythic history, could attempt to recreate the order, civility, and harmony they imagined embodied in the post-1689 Augustan style. The constitutions of the freemasons gradually became identified with the practices of ancient constitutional government enshrined in the Revolution Settlement of 1689. Once identified with originally British practices of government, the lodges, when exported, or even on native ground, could become, in effect, private exercises in self-government. If the mores and governing practices of the lodges then were taken to have meaning, to be exemplary for the larger civil polity, they also could have seriously divisive implications, even if not intentions, particularly in those European states governed by absolute monarchies.

The civil society of the lodges also differed from the salons and academies of the period—many of them no less socially exclusive—in articulating a hostility toward "the world." To hold it at a distance masonic rhetoric defined the nonmasonic as the "profane." The term "cowan" used in the British lodges to denote an outsider quickly evolved into "stranger," and then, on the Continent, into "les profanes."[39] With the new word came new meaning; the profane were not just different, but morally, and often intellectually, inferior. This masonic sense of uniqueness was further reinforced by rituals of initiation and advancement in the masonic mysteries that bonded all brothers, supposedly for life. Added to this ritual bond were significant dues and a commitment to charity for brothers, or their families, fallen on hard times. In the masonic experience of the eighteenth century we have more than simply another example of the new sociability of literate and urban elites. For its devotees, freemasonry became the cult of Enlightenment, presenting a set of distinctive values by which men and some women might now organize their lives.

What became cultic for some educated and idealistic men by the middle of the eighteenth century had roots, probably no less intensely felt, in the experience of working men. Eighteenth-century freemasonry evolved out of the Scottish and English guilds of seventeenth-century stonemasons. That evolution, to this day only partially understood, makes for a fascinating story, well worth telling, however briefly, and illustrating here with the example of one Scottish lodge. The lodge in Dundee, Scotland, experienced the transformation from a guild, or lodge, of workingmen—"operatives" as they are called in masonic literature—to a private society of "free and accepted" masons within a few decades, from roughly 1700 to 1730. These decades coincide with the consolidation of parliament's power to govern the nation (after 1707 both England and Scotland) and with the ascendancy of the Whig party as keeper of the revolutionary heritage created in 1688–89. They also coincide with the decline in the real economic power of the craft guilds. As we shall see, the political transformations worked their way into actual practices, as well as into the ideals found in the *Constitutions* of the new masonic lodges. That document in its turn glorified the practices of British constitutional government and also condemned the restrictive economic practices of the old guilds.

British Origins: The Constitution and Civil Society

The surviving manuscript records from the lodge in Dundee, Scotland, permit us to watch, almost year by year, the transformation from a workingman's guild to a society constitutionally governed by gentlemen. These records are rare for their completeness, although other Scottish lodges leave similar archives documenting this transformation. The very richness of these records has led the historian who has worked most extensively with them, David Stevenson, to argue that the freemasonry bequeathed to the eighteenth century was a Scottish invention.[40] By this he means that the transformation from a guild of stonemasons to a society dominated by gentlemen, if not completely devoid of handworkers, occurred first in Scotland, gradually spreading to England. The freemasonry of merchants and gentlemen, which was finally organized under the Grand Lodge of London in 1717, was therefore not English at its origin, despite the fact that most masonic historians, being English themselves, have insisted that it was.

Stevenson further argues that the mysteries and secrets associated with freemasonry, and in particular its mystical language about God as the Grand Architect, about Solomon's Temple as a masonic construction, and about the search for wisdom and enlightenment, owe much to the influence of intellectual traditions that predate the European Enlightenment by a century or more. Stevenson claims that the masonic devotion to the mystical and to the search for perfection grew out of intellectual traditions established in the early seventeenth century by Scottish masonic reformers. In particular one William Schaw, master of the king's works, was imbued with the reforming and mystical Hermeticism of the late Renaissance. He brought this to the lodges of the 1590s. Within a few decades freemasons also developed an affinity toward Rosicrucianism, an originally German form of mystical idealism that called for universal education and reform in terms that evoked the late Renaissance devotion to the Hermetic quest for human perfection. Many channels brought Hermeticism to Scotland; not least, a discipline of the Renaissance Hermeticist Giordano Bruno brought it to the Stuart court in the late 1590s. Schaw was an intimate of those circles.[41]

This account of the links between freemasonry and Renaissance Hermeticism is actually not a new argument. In the 1960s the great historian of Hermeticism and biographer of Bruno, Frances Yates, had hypothesized the existence of just such a link. Now we have some evidence for it.[42] We are told by Stevenson that Schaw may have gone around the lodges of early seventeenth-century Scotland relating their craft traditions, their use of secret passwords, their knowledge of mathematics and the principles of architecture to the search for mystical knowledge about nature, to the art of memory as the key to unlocking the secrets of the universe (the ultimate goal of one version of the Hermetic quest). This link would have been plausible enough to craftsmen who, through oral traditions, had been initiated into myths that, quite fancifully, made Euclid into an ancient Egyptian mason. If this was what Schaw did, then he and his followers gave the stonemasons in these lodges an even more elevated sense of their own history, while also turning their lodges into objects of curiosity.

Hermetic philosophical currents turn up in seventeenth-century Scottish texts that relate the Mason's Word, the secret password of lodge members, to the practices of the Brothers of the Rosy Cross, or Rosicrucians. Some masonic writings also make reference to the sun in language that is Hermetic and mystical. Not least, early eighteenth-century opponents of the order, among them the Papacy, linked it to the "Rosy-Crucians and Adepts, Brothers of the same Fraternity, or Order, who derived themselves from Hermes Trismegistus."[43] One version of the masonic *Constitutions* published in 1726 laid claim to Hermes as a great masonic teacher: "If ye will give me your children to govern, I will teach them one of the seven sciences, whereby they may live honestly, as gentlemen should, under condition that ye will grant them, and that I may have power to rule them, after the manner that science ought to be ruled. And then this worthy clerk Hermes . . . taught them the science of geometry in practick, for to work in stone."[44] Certainly by 1710 in London freemasons were known to possess "the Word, Mark, or Token of a certain Company . . . which is well known to every Member of that Sage Society, but kept a mightly Secret from all the World."[45] These mystical philosophical traditions, grafted onto a craft of medieval origin, only made it more interesting, undoubtedly providing one explanation of why some gentlemen with philosophical interests sought to join it.

The resulting philosophical freemasonry became known as speculative. It may indeed have been invented in Scotland and then exported south; but what returned to Scotland in the early eighteenth century, in a reverse migration from England, was quite different. The freemasonry that we find throughout Europe in the period beginning the 1730s appears to owe more to England than it does to Scotland, and that includes the freemasonry found by that time in Scottish lodges like Dundee. We can be very specific about the nature of the debt: the emphasis on constitutions, laws, and governance originated in London, the city of party politics and parliamentary debate. We normally use the term British only to describe the inhabitants of England and Scotland after the Act of Union in 1707. But in the case of freemasonry, as it evolved on the island during the late seventeenth century, we appear to have a phenomenon that was truly British, *avant la lettre*. In addition, Scottish burghs possessed rich traditions of societies, fellowships, and fraternities that met locally and could be seen by Scottish commentators to fulfill the ideal of communal citizenship preached by Bodin, or by two great Roman lawgivers and philosophers of the commonwealth, Cicero and Lycurgus.[46]

There is nothing mysterious or unusual about the evolution of freemasonry by the late seventeenth century if we bear in mind that of all the early modern guild members, master masons could be of higher social standing that certain other tradesmen such as bakers and dyers. Once established and accepted by their craft, masters were small, often prosperous businessmen, literate and often mathematical, who performed a function that by the early nineteenth century would be done by architects.[47] In effect, seventeenth-century master masons practiced a craft that sometimes bordered on engineering, and predictably in midcentury Scotland there were engineers who were admitted to the lodges.[48] In addition, of all the craft guilds the masons possessed one of the most elaborate mythologies. These myths adorned their history as the builders of palaces and churches. By the mid-seventeenth century English masons wrote manuscript histories that extolled the liberal arts and sciences, emphasized their knowledge of geometry, and even laid claim to Solomon's Temple as one of the many masonic achievements.[49] These myths and stories undoubtedly circulated among local craftsmen, in both Scotland and England, and they gave pride and edification. They could also be found attractive by men of some education or by seekers of ancient wisdom.

We know that the Oxford antiquarian and student of alchemy Elias Ashmole was admitted to a guild in the 1640s.[50] His membership may also have been connected to his mathematical skills and his service as an artillery officer. In this period the skill of a master mason often included knowledge of ballistics; indeed, it was not uncommon for the king's local master of works to be appointed master gunner. In effect the same man was put in charge of the castle and its cannon.[51] A similar commonality of interests may help to explain why in 1641 members of the masonic lodge of Edinburgh, who were serving in the army of the covenanters which had occupied northern England, met in Newcastle and admitted two parliamentary rebel officers as "fellow crafts and masters." Both Alexander Hamilton and Robert Moray were skilled in artillery and possessed some scientific knowledge about the principles of local motion as well as technical expertise. In effect they were themselves already practicing aspects of the mason's craft. Their admission to the guild at this time had more to do, however, with political alliances between covenanters and parliamentarians than it did with anything "secretive."

The admissions are important on two counts. They are among the earliest examples we have of a process that would eventually turn the Scottish and English masons' guilds into societies of gentlemen. In addition, Moray was a figure of some intellectual importance in the early Royal Society of London. Its interest in the practice and history of the trades, as part of applied science, led Moray to attempt a history of masonry for the Society. By the 1720s Fellows of the Royal Society were noticeably present in the earliest London lodges. The masonic myths fascinated Moray for much of his life, as did the more mystical and scientific writers of the late Renaissance.[52] This fascination with ancient and "secret" wisdom, so commonplace among educated gentlemen in the period, could nurture an attraction to any originally medieval institution that claimed access to it.

Few nonmasonic admissions to lodges of the seventeenth century are as well documented as that of Moray. Most lodges give us only the names of these nonoperatives, as they became known, and little else about them. At best, as with the records left by the lodge in Dundee, we can observe a pattern, both in the circumstances of these admissions and in the effect the new brothers gradually had on the lodges. Very slowly and fitfully, the craft or guild evolved into "a society," which retained something of the old while adding the interests and values of the higher classes of men who had now been recruited and who would eventually come to dominate.

The Lodge in Dundee

By the 1690s, if not earlier, the Dundee lodge had fallen on hard times. Out of economic necessity, it began quite straightforwardly to admit noncraftsmen to membership. That process was undoubtedly related to what happened as the town sank from a once prosperous east coast shipping port to an increasingly impoverished community, threatened with civil disturbance.[53] Its decline accelerated with the sacking of Dundee by a parliamentary army in 1651 and continued throughout the last decades of the seventeenth century as the Atlantic trade and the western ports grew in importance. In the 1690s famine hit the area. The pattern of decline was reversed only slowly in the last decades of the eighteenth century with the growth of the linen and clothing industry. Thus, in the period where we can observe firsthand the transformation of a trade guild into a gentlemen's fraternity, all but the richest of Dundee's inhabitants negotiated with poverty and with "ye decaying state of ye Burgh."[54]

A town with a declining population of approximately six thousand, Dundee possessed about a dozen guilds of tradesmen, all strictly arranged by rank and status. The cloth dyers were last in social rank; the masons, coopers, barbers, wrights, and periwig makers were considered sufficiently skilled to be organized in a cooperative association separate from the other, less skilled trades. By the 1690s none of these craftsmen could have been significantly prosperous. Local merchants were also organized in their own guild, which enjoyed near monopolistic political power in the town. By the 1720s the masons contributed to it without being permitted to join.[55] In 1749 a mason applied for admission to the merchants' guild, but "he was objected to because as exercising a handycraft, he cannot be admitted a member of the Guildry, except he give over working as a tradesman, being contrary to several Acts of Parliament."[56] Ironically that same tradesman would have socialized with merchants in his lodge by this date. In the world of any eighteenth-century European town or city, rank or status was everywhere palpable. As they evolved in Britain, the masonic lodges of this period reflected those realities, in one sense mitigating them, in another, through conviviality and the rhetoric of harmony and fraternity, obscuring, and hence reinforcing them. This happened in Dundee, and, it will be argued, everywhere else that lodges came to exist.[57] Yet it is worth remembering that social differences in Britain were not as rigidly codified and protected by law as they were in many parts of Continental Europe.

In the Dundee masons' guild we can observe some of the circumstances under which nonmasons were admitted to the craft of working masons. This entry dated 1700 links the dues to be collected from "strangers" to the needs of "decayed brethren" and their widows:

> Dundee, the 17th of November, 1700: The which day the Mason Craft being convened and meet together as usually and taking to their serious consideration that their publick stock being but very low for the support of our decayed brethren, poor widows, and distressed stranger brethren who may need their supply of what our common stock can allow, therefore make and ordain every stranger that wants the benefit of our freedom shall pay ten pounds Scots money when they are to be booked . . . subscribed by a good part of our fraternity and in name of our absent brothers.[58]

Clearly by this year, and probably somewhat before it, the guild had come to a financial impasse. One solution was to admit masons from outside the burgh, or possibly nonmasons, depending on how we interpret the reference to "strangers" in the records of the fraternity. Other lodges in Scotland and England had, of course, also admitted nonmasons intermittently throughout the seventeenth century. Indeed, the decision in Dundee was only in keeping with what was by 1700 a fairly commonplace solution to the economic problems then experienced by all craft guilds.[59] This process was affecting merchants as well as skilled workers. In 1713 the Dundee Town Council, "taking to consideration the great decay of the burgh and houses within the same for want of inhabitants, and for encouraging strangers to come and live among us," decided that anyone marrying a woman whose father had guild privileges could enjoy "the privilege of a guild brother."[60] Thus even the merchants' guild had to admit some nonmerchants provided they were of sufficiently high social status. In some senses the social life of all the trade and professional associations was being altered under the impact of market forces; all were losing their "work" in the traditional meaning of the word. Only the masons found other ways of expressing their new identity, and throughout the eighteenth century freemasons of vastly different occupations continued to speak of their "work," with the term becoming symbolic for the life and practices of the lodge.

As nonmasons were being admitted to the Dundee lodge it continued to believe that its "freedom and privileges" within the town were worth a reasonable sum. The 10 pounds (Scots) membership fee requested was still less than the 16 pounds paid by a working journeyman to procure his "privileges" and status as a master in the lodge.[61] Entry fees were not always uniformly applied and in no sense at this moment could the humble craft of Dundee masons be imagined as an elite organization. All of that would gradually change.

The records are clear that preference for admission of noncraftsmen was to be given to relatives of actually "operative" masons. There was a predictably large number of such sons and sons-in-law admitted to the guild during the eighteenth century. They could be of any occupation. By far the largest number of new members who are not practicing masons, but who tell us their occupations, are described as merchants, and also as a clock- and watchmaker, a draper, a wright, a maltman, an officer of the excise (1721), a surgeon, and, finally in the 1730s, a supervisor of the excise, a doctor of medicine, a shipmaster, a clerk of the customs, and, most significantly, landed gentlemen of the county who bear the appellation denoting their gentry origin, "honourable." They received the same "freedom"—now uniformly described as "libertys"—and "privileges." These admissions are by far the most interesting from the point of view of subsequent masonic history. Yet the Dundee records, which at least tell of who and when, are silent about why a man was admitted. We might legitimately ask why this moment and this particular craft? Why did the transition not occur among, let us say, the periwig makers? Given the destruction of the English records we will never really know if the process we are seeing in early eighteenth-century Dundee was indigenous to the Scottish situation or an attempt to catch up with a trend being exported from England. For our purposes it is enough to know that the evolution from craft to lodge occurred, and that in the process the everyday practices of a craft guild spread far and away from the working men who invented them.

The "liberty" now accorded to gentlemen, merchants, and minor officials recalls the distinction, of medieval origin, between the "liberty" of buying and selling in the burgh, once given to burgesses who were also merchants, and the term "freedom," generally accorded to those who were now free to work at their hand trade.[62] Amid these distinctions, now imposed within their midst, a significant number of operative masons continued in the Dundee lodge. It struggled throughout the century, as did the other crafts, to protect and control the labor of their working members, often against the practices employed by local merchants, and to ensure that members would employ only craftsmen duly admitted to the guild. Yet there is also some evidence of tension within the lodge between the working men and their "betters."[63] By contrast we can compare the Dundee lodge with one that met in London in the 1730s. With over one hundred members, not one was a working mason and the vast majority were mercantile by trade.[64] Indeed, most English lodges became purely "nonmasonic."

One of the perennial effects of Dundee's poverty was the absence of sufficient funds to repair public works, as well as a dearth of capital to repair "ruinous properties . . . owing to the poverty of the owners."[65] Clearly it was in the interests of the lodge to find ways to foster such improvements. In addition, there was the problem of vagrancy and begging, in other words, of social control. These social and economic problems occurred, however, within a distinct political culture. As the Whig ministry in London led by Walpole came to control Scottish political life, much patronage came under its purview and under the skillful manipulation of its man in Scotland, the Earl of Ilay. No office, no agency of revenue collection, from salt to the excise, was small enough to escape Whig attention.[66] Concomitant with, and indeed augmenting, this consolidation of power was a policy of "improvements," which established commissions to improve fisheries and manufacturing and to encourage agricultural experimentation and innovation.

By the 1730s the local masons are actively involved in promoting public works projects, contributing generously in 1739 to a fund for building a workhouse for beggars and other poor. In 1730 guildsmen and burgesses had joined in petitioning the magistrates to build a new prison, with a local mason promptly volunteering to take down the old one for a modest fee.[67] Culture was also imported into the town, and in 1734 freemasons paraded to the local theater to see a production brought in specially from Edinburgh.[68] Of all the local guilds the masons were most active in a process of "improvement" that is visible in Dundee by the 1730s, despite its chronic economic problems. Even the appearance of famine in the vicinity in 1741 did not stop the Town Council two years later from putting up the money to hire a "professor of mathematics and book keeping" for the local public school.[69] This is not to say that the freemasons in Dundee were necessarily Whigs, but it is to say that they promoted the political culture of improvement associated with the Whig ascendancy.[70] It is also worth noting, if only in passing, that the habit of clubbing was more pronounced among late seventeenth-century Whigs in London than it was among their Tory rivals.[71]

More than civic involvement and a renewed interest in improvement came with the transformation of the lodge from what masonic histories like to call operative to speculative freemasonry. What is striking about the process that accompanies the admission of increasingly elite "brothers" is revealed in the new language gradually replacing the traditional guild terminology. In the seventeenth century guildsmen spoke more often of their statutes and ordinances, not frequently of their laws, and generally the brethren gave "their consent" to the admission of a new member or to the "selection" of their officers.[72] Occasionally, "the mason trade in Dundee being met together have made and constituted" a master to his "privileges."[73] These consisted of the right to regulate wages, to settle disputes among members, and to be consulted about taxes by the local magistrates.[74] They were the privilege to exercise authority and control in the lodge and in the community, but not to govern. That was the work of local magistrates.

Quite noticeably, and within less than ten years after the admission of merchants and the sellers of commodities, the language of parliamentary procedure and town government makes its appearance. An officer "was by plurality of votes chosen."[75] By 1718 "the members of the mason craft being convened did unanimously elect and choise" their officers, and in 1734 a quorum was fixed. By the 1730s the "freedom" of the guildsman, traditionally the freedom, upon admission, to practice his craft in the town, had been transformed into the "libertys of the craft." At that same moment (1732) "members [were] unanimously admitted and received into the Society [sic] of master masons." This "fraternity" of guildsmen has become a "society" of gentlemen and merchants, now styled as master masons, who vote and elect, who possess their liberty just as craftsmen once possessed their freedom. Merchants were used to having a role in town government. Kirk sessions and the higher church courts also set quorums; town councils could and did elect. These same men would also almost certainly have been voters; they elected the local MP, a right that was perceived as constitutionally guaranteed. The formal language of governance, as well as the habit of government, both local and especially national, came with these sellers, traders, and professional men.[76]

In 1734 the transformation was ensured. The power to govern decisively was placed in the hands of the gentlemen freemasons. The occasion for this shift of authority over the "government" of the lodge involved both money and labor. Money had been inappropriately lent without proper security. Craftsmen not belonging to the guild had been employed, while the quality of craftsmanship of some operative members was deemed inadequate. At the annual meeting of 1734 the gentlemen of substance were elected as the officers.[77] The Hon. John, Master of Gray, was chosen as master of the lodge, and he was also a local agricultural improver.[78] Suddenly language employed by London freemasons and first displayed in Anderson's 1723 *Constitutions* is used in full force. Terms appear that are not to be found in the records of the Dundee operative masons: "the Society of Free and Accepted Masons," the "Hon. Society of the Antient Lodge," "Laws and Regulations for the better and orderly Government of the respective Brethren." Brothers are charged with the task of assembling "to consider of such Laws and Regulations as shall seem most proper and requisite for the better Government of the Society . . . with full power to them to make and enact in the locked book of the Society such laws as shall seem best for preserving order and unanimity among the Brethren . . . and punishing delinquents of whatever Rank or Degree." A committee was established to do just that.[79]

For the first time in these 70 and more years of records reference is made to the "secret mysteries of Masonry." It shall no longer be "lawful by any and or number of the brethren of the lodge of this place to initiate or enter any person or persons of what ever degree or quality as they may have access to the knowledge of the antient and secret mysteries of masonry without first apprising the worshipfull, the master of the lodge with whose consent and approbation" a man may be admitted.[80] In this context the secrets refer to the traditional skills of craftsmen as well as to signs and words used by properly initiated guild masons to signal to one another their status, and hence their right to work in the vicinity.

It is significant that only now does emphasis on the "secrets" of freemasonry appear. Signs and tokens of membership were the everyday manner of communicating among guild craftsmen. They have now become symbolic of devotion to the fraternity, loyalty, and probity. The ability to keep the secrets of masonry—rather than the practice of those mysteries—became the only means of identifying a true brother. This social cement was mystical only insofar as it was language memorized out of its original context; it now became words and signs used in the bonding of men who were different from one another in nearly every aspect of their lives, save their membership in a constitutionally governed private society. Eventually the "secrets" of freemasonry will acquire a metaphoric meaning as brothers rise by degrees toward a veiled, yet constantly unfolding, wisdom and enlightenment. Accompanying this process will be ever more elaborate ceremonies conferring status and honor within the lodge.

This process of elaboration that we have witnessed at work in Dundee by the mid-1730s occurred elsewhere in the Scottish, as well as English, lodges. Gentlemen were admitted and elected "masters" of the lodge. Suddenly whole initiation ceremonies were created to install the master in his "chair," with overtones of ceremonies used to initiate men into the aristocratic and kingly orders, such as the Order of the Garter, or indeed with intimations of royal coronations and court ceremonial. In the 1730s, following the practice in England, Scottish lodges instituted "degrees" by which practicing, that is, operative, and nonpracticing members could be distinguished one from another.[81] Not least, in 1736, the thirty-three Scottish lodges, Dundee among them, sent representatives to an assembly that created the Grand Lodge of Scotland, which in turn elected a gentleman Grand Master, only, incidentally, after he had renounced any hereditary claims on the office.[82] The national government of Scottish freemasonry could now be said to have been put in place. One of its first acts may have been to give constitutional authorization to a foreign lodge that had appealed to it. The lodge was in Amsterdam and its master was Jean Rousset de Missy (see p. 105).[83]

The records in Dundee also indicate that in the 1730s the lodge officers further enhanced their authority. In that transformation officers were not only to be nominated and elected, but they were also given the power of oversight in all aspects of craft activity. Nominations were now to be held for "the Election" of officers who would have the power and authority to appoint a quorum "of the Operative Brethren not exceeding five in number . . . to visit and inspect" the work done by other masons. By 1737 "rolls [were] being called and votes marked" and elections were "carried by a plurality."[84]

In every sense power has decidedly shifted into the hands of the gentlemen freemasons, who will oversee the work of their operative brethren. Yet in this instance, and in contrast with the hostility shown to the protective practices of the working masons described in the 1723 *Constitutions,* the gentlemen freemasons of Dundee did continue to protect the "freedom" of their working brethren by permitting only initiated masons to work in the town. Throughout the rest of the century some efforts were made intermittently to restrict the practice of the craft to members of the lodge. The charitable obligations of the lodge also continued to be important,[85] and it proudly maintained its locked pew in the local church. Yet increasingly its records speak of the "liberty" of the freemason as more and more gentlemen, as well as relatives of practicing masons, are admitted to the society.

From the early eighteenth century the signs of increasing literacy also become more frequent. The marks and rough, uncertain scrawl by which the majority of brethren signed their names in the seventeenth century give way and eventually by the 1750s all but disappear—even among the craftsmen who remain.

In the 1650s masons spoke of "the blessings of God" and "the better ordering of our Comonwill," and they made reference to their craft as "the calling."[86] In Dundee these same craftsmen invoked the Trinity, opening their lodge in 1659 with words taken from the so-called Old Charges, rules widely practiced by lodges throughout England: "The might of the father of heaven with the Wisdom of the glorious sone and the grace and goodnes of the holie gost be with us at our beginning."[87]

Concomitant with evidence of increasing literacy, and fewer operatives, the old religious language all but disappears. In its place stands reference solely to the Grand Architect of the Universe. In the 1740s prospective candidates for admission as operatives were tested by "an Essay of an Architecture," now, however, requiring an arithmetic knowledge of Ionic proportions.[88] The imposition of order, always one of the goals of a guild or lodge, has been extended to include a simplified conception of the deity as well as sound fiscal management of the lodge. Lodge discipline also included correct social behavior, as well as the professionalism of skills—all now being adjudicated by the gentlemanly leadership of the lodge. Fines were occasionally extracted for infringements of the rules concerning employment. By the same token money was also lent at interest to assist in business ventures with the lodge operating at moments like a bank, an institution that did not come to Dundee until the 1760s.[89]

In this fascinating instance the consolidation of elite culture, a process historians have traced as under way from well back in the seventeenth century,[90] included the assimilation and transformation of one of the most representative institutions of early modern European popular culture. The guild, complete with its myths and rituals, has been embraced only to be transformed. And its most binding and potentially subversive practice, secrecy, has been given new meaning. Knowledge of the secrets delineated brothers by their degrees; it also enveloped their private association and made it special. For others, in a different setting, it may also have made it suspect.

A direct evolution out of its seventeenth-century predecessor, the lodge in Dundee might easily be imagined as vastly different from its Continental counterparts of the 1730s and beyond. Indeed in some respects it differed from many London and provincial lodges because of the large number of operative masons remaining in its ranks. Yet after 1734, at their core, the practices and ideals of this private society in Dundee—as revealed in the language it employed—were not fundamentally different from those elaborated upon by the London *Constitutions* (1723) and in turn imitated with greater and lesser degrees of imagination by countless European lodges.

The importance of the Dundee lodge is that it permits us to watch the unfolding from guild to fraternity. It also teaches us a lesson about eighteenth-century British society and about freemasonry in relation to it. The members of the political nation brought their constitutional and social values, as well as their habits of governance, to the lodge and then imposed them upon it. They managed also to integrate those values and the authority that went with them in ways that imitated their place in the larger society. Yet in this instance a necessary accommodation was also made to the interests of the wage laborer, albeit within the context of an essentially, and deepening, market relationship. All of these relationships of power and authority were negotiated under the mantle of a rhetoric of order, fraternity, and harmony that was deemed to be ancient, yet capable of adaptation. In hindsight we may find little in common between the liberties of a gentleman and the freedom of a stonecutter to sell and also to protect his labor. Yet clearly, in this new formulation, this freedom and that liberty were meant to be equated.[91] We may find this fraternity of medical doctors, gentlemen, excise officers, merchants, master masons, and journeymen stonecutters an improbable locus of "equality"—a term these Dundee records do not use, but do imply. Yet contemporaneous masonic rhetoric latched onto the term to describe the ideal private society where "all brothers meet upon the level," where each possessed a vote, and where any could be chosen, at least in theory, to be officers.

Originally the guild had been a social setting that controlled economic life. Within that context by 1700 nonmasons in Dundee were admitted by masters and freemen "to all our privileges as free as we are ourselves."[92] In the actual world of local politics that freedom possessed a political meaning to which tradesmen might aspire only if they ceased entirely to be handworkers, no longer to exercise "a handycraft." Dundee was no different from any other town or city in western Europe during the eighteenth century. Social place determined access to political influence and power. The rhetoric of liberalism and constitutionalism developed in seventeenth-century England blurred that inequitous reality, while at the same time offering an ideological challenge to it. How fitting that a guild, as transformed by gentlemen and highly literate professionals, became one of the first institutions wherein the rhetoric of liberalism was used to bind men of diverse social rank and hence of disparate power.

Fraternal binding also obscured the social divisions and the inequities of rank and degree endemic to the lives of the men who embraced "equality" and "liberty." In making social divisions less obvious the idealism of freemasonry ironically served to reinforce them. As tradesmen and gentlemen, doctors and merchants, broke bread together and practiced fraternity, they obfuscated the real divisions of wealth, education, and social place that existed between them. As one sociologist put it, freemasonry "contained a critique of individualism and antidote to it as well as an affirmation of it."[93] The guild had always been an institution that enabled men to negotiate in a market context. As transformed by merchants and gentlemen the new freemasonry became a place to celebrate the equality newly discovered in political and economic life. The fraternal bond also offered a hedge against the market, a locus for charity given to brothers in need.

The records in Dundee give substance to the rhetorical formulations about fraternity and harmony, the stuff of masonic idealism, and that rhetoric turns up in countless lodge sermons, speeches, songs, and treatises throughout the eighteenth century. Published orations in Britain also speak a language that was essentially Augustan, that is, court and Whig, and remarkably self-satisfied and complacent about the joys of order and harmony. Yet masonic rhetoric could also reveal the tensions within that liberal and constitutional order, particularly as these surfaced in the 1760s with the agitation led by John Wilkes against the power and influence of the court oligarchy. His movement appealed particularly to the less affluent among the middling ranks. In the next chapter we will observe the concern expressed by masonic officers that the lodges not become infected with the social radicalism of the Wilkite movement. Try as they may to avoid them, the lodges' pursuit of private social harmony possessed public implications.

What is true of the British rhetoric will remain true for eighteenth-century European freemasonry in general, however vastly different its forms and aspirations. In the pursuit of social harmony the lodge made porous the boundary between the private and the public. Men of a variety of ranks, and eventually some women, could experience a rarefied and idealized version of society within the confines of a private society. Not surprisingly, European freemasons, speaking a variety of European languages, were remarkably consistent in referring to the public realm when speaking within the confines of their private rhetorical universes.

The Political and Social Content of British Freemasonry

The suspicions that the fraternity aroused on the Continent from the 1730s on cannot be explained solely by reference to its foreign and British associations. But they do account partially for the hostility. This British export also possessed distinctive characteristics of a civic, or political, nature intimately related to its development in a specific political and social context, to the values and mores shaped by the English Revolution. With markedly political language the *Constitutions* praises the reign of the Roman emperor Augustus, using a contemporary parlance that signaled an identification with the Hanoverian and Whig regime, which had ascended to political dominance in 1714.[94] Predictably the earliest British leadership of the Grand Lodge founded in London in 1717 tended to be "court"-variety Whigs, that is, supporters of strong ministerial government and by their own definition the heirs of the Revolution of 1688–89. First and foremost, the new Grand Lodge sought to live by a constitution, or "constitutions," that is, statutes and rules first published in 1723, and intended to govern the behavior of all lodges.[95]

These small private societies came to be seen as organized around a constitution in the post-1688, or parliamentary, sense of that term. The goal of government by consent within the context of subordination to "legitimate" authority was vigorously pursued by the Grand Lodge of London and was demanded of all lodges affiliated with it. Records of lodges throughout the first half of the century, from London and the provinces, attest to the seriousness with which they were to "keep all and every rules, orders and regulations contained in the Book of Constitutions (except such as have been revoked or altered at any quarterly communication or other general meeting). And also all such other orders, regulations and instructions as shall from time to time be transmitted by us . . . our deputy for the time being or by any of our successors, Grand Masters or his deputy"[96] The day-to-day working of this constitutional order meant elections by ballot; majority rule (except for unanimous vote for admission to a lodge); in all matters, one man one vote; taxes in the form of dues; registration of membership; and, not least, rules of social behavior, of civility, and of decorum, to prevent anyone bringing "scandal upon the Society." Discipline was enforced through man-made rules and regulations, as well as by social pressure within the lodge, which included fines for drunkenness and swearing "or giving abusive language." All lodges were expected to give allegiance to the Grand Lodge of London, and hence to its Grand Master, as well as to the elected officers of each lodge, beginning with the Master. Places in a lodge were assigned according to seniority of admission ("Masters and Officers excepted"). Brothers asked permission of the Master before speaking at formal meetings, and dues had to be paid regularly.

Commonplace rhetoric among British freemasons always spoke of their being "free and accepted." As one master informed a provincial lodge, "you Voluntary and at your own Request enter into, calling God and the Members then present to witness, that you will never disclose or make known the Secret or Secrets that are then or hereafter shall be discovered to you." Bound together by the secret signs and rituals inherited from guild practice, the brothers, now from a variety of social ranks, in some instances from gentry to tradesmen, were asked to embrace a common moral code. They were admonished always to practice

> good morals. Such as to give to every one his due, to perform to God ourselves and the whole world, whatsoever is owing from the state of our nature and circumstances wherein we are placed. A Freemason should exercise himself in all those humane virtues, which consist in the Dominion of his Reason over his sensative passions and appetites. Such as Patience, Meekness, Temperance, and Chastity; He must be faithful to his promises, sincere in his professions, just and honest in all his dealings.[97]

The obligations of subjects, superiors, fathers, children, husbands, masters, and servants were then simply and straightforwardly asserted. In this rhetoric we find an almost effortless blending of traditional patriarchal values with the new language of constitutionalism and the older traditions of charity and friendship associated with voluntary associations. And should the bylaws of these new lodges "prove insufficient to keep up and support the good government and prosperity of this society then at all times it shall be in the power of the majority of the whole members of this lodge to make and add from time to time all such further and other good and wholesome laws and orders as shall be thought necessary and conducive thereunto."[98] The implication here is that laws and societies—not just the lodge—are human institutions and they can be altered by the will of the majority.

Although entirely private and avoiding any discussion of religion or politics, the typical eighteenth-century British masonic lodge was in effect a microcosm of the ideal civil polity. With an almost utopian sense of what is possible (discussed further in the next chapter), the lodges sought to make a better society through the virtue of each brother practiced within a constitutional setting. "The natural consequence of such excellent virtues," it was believed, "is promoting the interest of each other."[99] Within this context of order and harmony, self-interest will flourish. In masonic rhetoric behavior, not birth, ultimately determined the character and virtue of a brother. By implication even hierarchy is a man-made invention. Within this sociable meritocracy lies the first self-conscious attempt to create societies governed by the abstract principles of British constitutionalism.

Predictably, the lodges required literacy of their members; but, perhaps most important, relative affluence was necessary to pay the dues: a few pounds at initiation, and then a few shillings each month.[100] In addition, the membership records from the earliest official London lodges are noticeably high in fellows of the Royal Society, government ministers, Whig aristocrats, journalists, and, of interest for the Continental story recounted in chapter 3, Huguenot refugees with journalistic or political connections.[101] At a time when the political nation would be defined as the one out of five males who held sufficient property to vote, as well as those literate enough to follow the pamphlets that parliamentary politics encouraged, membership in eighteenth-century lodges tended to be confined to such men.

The emergence of this particular private society modeled on—indeed deriving from—the masonic guilds of medieval origin should be understood in relation to an important moment in the history of European political development. For much of European urban history guilds of craftsmen, and even of merchants, provided, as one historian aptly describes it, "the counter-culture to civil society."[102] The guilds were vital participants in town and city life; they functioned to protect their members from the power of the great magistrates, lay and ecclesiastical. Their understanding of freedom and equality was more protectionist and collective than it was individual and purely market. Yet with these qualifications the guilds also played a regulatory role in the commercial life of any city, operating both protectively and coercively in ways that have been described as "ideal . . . to police the workforce."[103] The guilds regulated who might practice "his mystery," that is, the skills of a particular craft, at any given moment and place. The relationship between the guild and the free merchant was partly adversarial, partly collaborative. But their relation to actual governmental authority in urban settings was significantly different. Guilds might administer the policies of local magistrates, but they did not make these policies, although they might indeed be carefully consulted.

In early eighteenth-century Britain there was, in one sense, nothing "counterculture" about the new speculative lodges. They embraced the rhetoric of constitutional authority, of the magistrates seated in parliament. The emergence of these private societies suggests a new political mentality striving for expression. We have arrived at that moment when a political nation exists within one of the European national states. This entity, in possession of voting rights, governed in tandem and in self-confidence with an older aristocracy and a constitutionally limited monarchy. In the cities the mercantile elite no longer needed guilds for their protection; in the countryside, the landed gentry expressed their political interests through parliamentary elections. In town and city the power of the old guilds to regulate wages and labor had now been broken. But the collectivist definition of liberty and equality inherent in guild culture—complete with the ambiguities that Continental and antirepublican opponents of freemasonry were quick to seize upon—could be given new meaning. It could now pertain to the aspirations of the political nation. Voters and magistrates could now meet within the shell provided by the guild. In the new masonic lodges they could practice conviviality and civility while giving expression to a commonly held social vision of their own liberty and equality.

As in all things new, elements from the past, from that once vital guild tradition, are also clearly present. There is the characteristic concern for the moral betterment of all brothers,[104] as well as an emphasis on charity for members fallen on hard times. This charitable element will remain present in the lodges throughout the century and beyond. In the 1780s the Grand Lodge of France had a committee of brothers devoted to adjudicating and distributing weekly and monthly charity to brothers who petitioned for it (see p. 211).

As far as can be determined, the old guild ceremonies of initiation and the ritual associated with festivals and feast days were retained by the British lodges, but vastly elaborated upon. Yet the original purpose of the guild, which was to confer on its members the "freedom and privileges" of practicing their craft, to protect wages, and to confer status and establish place within the larger community, is gradually replaced and a new language is directly substituted for the old. Increasingly the records speak of the "liberty" of the brothers, or lay emphasis on the older term, "fraternity," or, in seeking to describe the relationship between all brothers, speak of "equality." Within the confines of this egalitarian vision the working mason is still expected "to hew Stone and Raise Perpendiculars," but the new "Gentleman Mason" must practice "Secrecy, Morality and good Fellowship."[105] In this fascinating instance the medieval guild is reshaped to give expression to the aspirations of the modern, constitutionally governed polity. Gentlemen freemasons could retain the obligations and privileges granted by their social rank; they could also bond with lesser, but literate and reasonably affluent men, and jointly practice secrecy and fellowship. Within the new British lodges gentlemen, and even aristocrats, expressed their political hegemony while "laboring" to create among themselves an egalitarian culture. This civility emerged within the confines of an ideology espousing merit and equality.

But discrete words are derived from language spoken in a particular context. Early eighteenth-century masonic rhetoric was first articulated in the context of postrevolutionary English and Scottish society. This permitted its ideals to be prescribed for, and identified with, a larger society where, it could be imagined, good order and government prevailed. The "libertys and privileges" bestowed by this fraternal society were no longer conceived as guarantees against encroachments from the governing civil authorities, nor were they intended as protection against market forces. Rather they were seen to be the natural complement of constitutionally governed behavior, the reward for practicing the principles, it was believed, that should govern the civil polity. In this instance, it could be said, the public gave birth to the private, the political permitted the social and the cultural.

In eighteenth-century masonic sociability—more so than in any other versions of the new, and related, sociability—we find a consuming identification with laws and regulations that will ensure order and good government. It is undoubtedly true that the new individualism sanctioned by the seventeenth-century revolution "relegated . . . the practical utility and moral legitimacy of corporations, whether towns or guilds, . . . to the shadows.[106] Yet from those shadows emerged a new private society with which mercantile and literate elites could identify. The guild as it evolved into "an honourable fraternity" inspired a new —at moments quasi-religious—form of corporatism, complete with oaths, rituals, regalia, and "secret" truths. As the British *Constitutions* (1723) made clear, the lodges of "free and accepted" masons specifically renounced any "confederacy of their working brethren" that attempted to fix "work but at their own price and wages."[107]

By the 1720s the power of the craft guilds had been almost entirely broken by free-market economic pressures in England and Scotland. Out of their shell emerged a form of sociability suited to a new political nation, and this new society proved remarkably exportable. By 1750 it was estimated by a leading Amsterdam freemason and Huguenot refugee, Rousset de Missy, that some fifty thousand men belonged to masonic lodges flourishing in every major European city, in many towns, and in the various European colonies. By the 1780s there would be about thirty-five thousand freemasons in France alone.

In the creation of this new form of European sociability we have discerned the moment when increasingly large numbers of literate laymen (and as we shall see some women) could imagine the principles governing the constitutional state as something they could replicate in their own lives, at their leisure. They could recreate its ideal form and live by a constitution, if only playfully. They paid substantial dues for the privilege of doing so, and they were playfully serious about the meaning of this sociability in their own lives. This private polity could reinforce their identity with the "real" state. It could also—and this was the dangerous quality about masonic sociability in the context of any ancien régime—make men restless when their idealism ran counter to the dictum implicit in absolutism or in oligarchy, namely, that identification with the state was reserved to those chosen by a select few to serve it.

Medieval corporatism may in some attenuated sense bear relation to the late eighteenth-century emergence of trade unionism.[108] By contrast and earlier, elite sociability in the eighteenth-century masonic form signaled the birth of relative affluence and high literacy as the characteristics of those embracing the polity as their own. We may be startled by the willingness of gentlemen to embrace a craft guild, but not by the transformations wrought within that institution as a result. The new and nonartisanal brothers of the craft obviously believed that they had the right to alter it, and radically if necessary, should it fail to respond to their identification and their idealism.

Eighteenth-century urban gentlemen, so often the buyers and sellers of commodities by virtue of their occupations and leisure, expressed their identification with the civil polity through the form provided by an originally craft, urban institution created by the sellers of labor. Yet this was surely a more fitting form of voluntary association than models that could have been adopted out of mores, fraternal orders, or institutions found among the economically protected estates, the traditional clergy, or the aristocracy.

The experience of this new fraternity occasionally set men to thinking about the larger society as they sought to perfect their own private sociability. They would wax, often eloquently, about the joys of order and harmony, about the sociable virtues prescribed now for all men. Much of eighteenth-century British masonic literature officially published by the lodges has a decidedly utopian cast about it. In surveying that literature we may better understand why Continental reformers and visionaries could also find in their lodges a particular kind of social experience which, in certain circumstances, could create a dissonance between their personal experience of constitutionalism and the larger civil polity.

Whether we are examining the literature of British freemasonry, as we will in the next chapter, or entering individual lodges on the Continent, as we will in subsequent chapters, one major point needs to be stressed: These were political societies, not in a party or faction sense of the term but in a larger connotation. Within the framework of civility and in the service of an imagined social cohesion, the lodges practiced a civil administration, derived from British political practice and tradition. Predictably in a British context lodges were, on the whole, remarkably supportive of established institutions, of church and state.[109] Yet they could also house divisive, or oppositional, political perspectives. They could be loyalist to the Hanoverian and Whig order, yet they could also at moments show affiliation with radical interests, whether republican or Jacobite, and, possibly by the end of the century, Jacobin.[110]

Whatever the political affiliations of their members, the eighteenth-century masonic lodges were at the heart of a new secular culture, created in that century and fashioned to operate within the confines of its social ranks, privileges, and degrees. First articulated in postrevolutionary Britain, this new culture and ideology were sufficiently malleable, however, to be capable of exportation and transformation. In Europe we will observe lodges far removed from Dundee, practicing rituals utterly foreign to the tradesmen of Dundee. But they would have recognized the ideals described in Continental masonic literature, French or Dutch. They may also by the late eighteenth century have recognized, although not necessarily approved, that their sociability had been adapted or used in new and divisive ways. The form of the lodge became one of the many channels that transmitted a new political culture, based upon constitutionalism, which gradually turned against traditional privileges and established, hierarchical authority. That culture was in turn bequeathed to the modern era by the Continental revolutions of the 1780s and 1790s. We need to acquaint ourselves further with British freemasonry before we can appreciate what may have been its appeal both at home and on the Continent.

2

Temples of Virtue, Palaces of Splendor: British Masonic Visions

After the founding of the Grand Lodge in London in 1717, hundreds of lodges sprang up there and in the provinces. As in the case of the Dundee lodge, some had evolved out of local guilds and in their early years mixed gentlemen, merchants, and workers of various crafts and practicing masons. But increasingly, most lodges were totally "speculative," that is, no members were "operative," practicing masons. The distinction was noted throughout the century by masonic orators and commented upon favorably. "Freemasonry . . . is now advanced to a far higher degree of perfection than it could boast upon its first institution," a masonic preacher of 1777, speaking in the Anglican church in Colchester, informed his fellow lodge members. "Formerly it was only operative, confined to manual labor, and studied only the improvement of art." Gradually, however, workers were displaced from the lodges. "As morals, learning, and religion advanced in the world, so Masonry then became speculative, and attended to the cultivation of the mind." With this attentiveness came "an earnest desire to promote the good and happiness of [our] fellow creatures."[1] Once entirely divorced from its practical and manual functions, and in most lodges from workers themselves, the British masonic imagination took flight. It became not just speculative but frequently utopian.

Rather than approach this world of private sociability through a single lodge, I have chosen instead to survey the extensive published literature produced by the many lodges, which by 1740 numbered over 180. These sermons or orations were first preached before the assembled brothers, who in turn deemed them worthy of publication. Whether published or unpublished, masonic orations expressed the highest ideals of this private society, and throughout this book I rely heavily upon them. When combined with other types of masonic publications, they can tell us a great deal about the ideals of this new form of sociability as they were being developed, not by guildsmen, but by gentlemen, merchants, professional men, the literate and reasonably affluent who flocked to the new lodges. These men were participants in what British historians have now come to see as a "leisure revolution" that brought with it in the eighteenth century revitalized towns, unprecedented luxury, and an elite culture based upon affluence and luxury.[2] All of that is reflected and indeed glorified in masonic literature.

In its essential optimism masonic literature is utopian; it looks to the secular and social order for perfectibility. But in so looking it exhibits a distinctly practical attitude. Although concerned with the coherence and rationality of the ideal society, British masonic utopian literature imagines that such an order is in some sense possible. Historians who have looked at enlightened utopias have tended recently to discount their worldliness, their actual interest in the incarnation of their dreams.[3] Such a dismissal does not work for the British masonic and utopian impulse. Rightly or wrongly, brothers believed that they had taken one important step toward the perfectibility of the human order within their own lodges. Benighted we might say, but not irrevelant. The European political order would be transformed by the revolutions late in the century. We should listen to the dreamers across the Channel first and then see if what they were saying bears any relation to the course of European political development in the late eighteenth century. I am not suggesting that Continental freemasons simply borrowed the language of their English brothers. Rather lodges in both places were spaces in a new zone of civil society wherein aspects of the larger political and social order were mirrored and mimicked, yet also and simultaneously opened to scrutiny and criticism.

Predictably, British utopians were at moments troubled. In the British context—the century of government by oligarcy—their utopianism came in tandem with an underlying concern for decadence and corruption. The eighteenth century cast up many versions of the ancien régime, many forms of social privilege and exclusive access to political power besides those we associate with absolutism on the Continent. Concern about corruption and the tyranny associated with it expressed itself in Britain through the politics and philosophy of government known as the "country" opposition. Juxtaposed against the largely Whig oligarchy—the "court"—which controlled the offices of government, opposition sentiment could turn up in the politics of either party, Whigs or Tories. But increasingly after the Hanoverian Succession in 1714 the rhetoric of the country belonged to segments of the Tory party.

The ideological roots of the country lay, however, not in the Toryism of the late seventeenth century, but in the republicanism of the midcentury English Revolution. The point about the country was not its party affiliations, which could shift, but rather, given its origins, its potential radicalism. Increasingly, the view from the country claimed to represent "lesser" men, not the great landed gentry, not their placemen in the sinews of government employment. It became the voice of small merchants, shopkeepers, even artisans. They openly attacked what they described as the corruption of oligarchic ministers who had become, by appropriation, the actual heirs of the liberties and privileges believed to be confirmed by the Revolution Settlement, by the defeat of absolutism and arbitrary government in 1689. In the 1690s this country opposition percolated on the fringes of the Whig party. Its most representative exponents, politicians and freethinkers like John Toland and Anthony

Collins, saw themselves as the heirs of the Commonwealth tradition, of the midcentury republicanism of James Harrington or John Milton. By the 1760s the country opposition had come to mean angry crowds and tumultuous assemblies in support of the radical parliamentarian John Wilkes. Once again radicalism surfaced in British politics, and although its public face was Whig, some of its proponents could once have been country Tories.

The tension between "court" and "country" is one of the central motifs of eighteenth-century British politics. From its very inception, at the founding of the Grand Lodge of London, freemasonry expressed the ideological tension between court and country; its literature, sermons, and orations are permeated with it. In masonic thought the desire to emulate the luxury and order associated with court and oligarchy expressed itself concurrently with the fear that luxury bred corruption. In general, published British masonic rhetoric had a distinctively "court" air about it. It identified with oligarchy and monarchy, as bound by the constitution and the Revolution Settlement. When the discussion turned to corruption it was being held among the relatively affluent who are drawn to, and glory in, the pleasures and privileges derived from stable government, yet who are also troubled by the consequences. This is also a private discussion, where, in contrast to its public counterpart, other values, more enlightened than traditional, could be affirmed within the lodges.[4] In addition, it must not be forgotten that some masonic lodges had the air of the Jacobite hanging about them.[5] But nostalgia for the exiled Stuarts could easily be seen as treasonable in Britain, not the sort of thing that lodges would see into print. Although British Jacobites made their mark in Continental lodges, there is no published masonic literature in English that is Jacobite.

Masonic oratory extolled religious toleration, reason, and science, as well as discipline and order, within lodges possessing a constitutional government. In sermons as well as in constitutions, these principles are seen as the foundation of true masonry. Within each lodge brothers are exhorted to build the perfectly harmonious society. The masonic utopia can exist only in secular time, among the prosperous, the meritorious, and the educated; the *Constitutions* of 1723 specifically mandated that lodges must admit only "men free-born, of mature and discreet age, no bondsmen, no women, no immoral or scandalous" persons. In practice this excluded male servants, and increasingly the illiterate. Promotion within the lodge was to be grounded upon "real worth and personal merit only." The title of Grand Master, over all of British freemasonry, was to be given to a former master, "nobly born, or a Gentleman of the best fashion, or some eminent Scholar, or some curious Architect, or other Artist." Eventually those excluded from the lodges were designated as "strangers" from whose "malicious ridicule" the freemason should maintain a meticulous silence.[6] Eventually, on the Continent these strangers became known as "the profane." Such men—and initially all women—were incapable, it was argued, of embracing either the wisdom found in the masonic mysteries or the convivial egalitarianism of the lodge. They were excluded from the social affirmation of commonly held beliefs and values which, it was believed, could be given expression only through fraternal unity. The civil society created by the lodge was to be a carefully circumscribed space.

The masonic vision of true wisdom also excluded, by definition, the private illuminations of the saint or the mystic. For the freemason knowledge must be achieved socially. Yet the members of this society must be carefully chosen so as to permit it to maintain its "secrets." Within this homogeneous system of values, the unique insights proclaimed by the religious enthusiast as a result of his or her special communication with God are simply irrelevant to the fraternal experience and discipline of the lodge. There is no body of eighteenth-century literature more systematically at odds with the religiosity of the seventeenth-century Protestant sects, or with the piety of traditional Catholicism, or with the new Methodism, than that of freemasonry. In the British context this secular stance was noticeable enough. In the midst of Continental Calvinism or Catholicism, masonic religiosity could easily give offense. As we saw in chapter 1, the first narrative history of freemasonry in French (1738) allied the order with the English Revolution, but it specifically condemned the "enthusiastic sects" of the 1650s.

If we survey the religious landscape of eighteenth-century Britain we begin to see the distinctive quality of masonic religiosity. After the Act of Toleration (1689) there still existed legal discrimination against non-Anglican Protestants; Catholics and anti-Trinitarians, as well as atheists, had never been covered by the act. Among Protestant Dissenters, sectarian and even enthusiastic religious movements remained commonplace enough. Not least, from the late 1730s on, Methodism made many converts among men and women disaffected from the perceived laxity and worldliness of the established Anglican Church. In this context the masonic insistence upon religious toleration—"a mason is obliged . . . to that Religion in which all men agree, leaving their particular opinions to themselves."[7]—stood in bold contrast to the discrimination imposed against Protestant Dissenters, Catholics, and anti-Trinitarians by law and custom.

We do not know if Dissenters were particularly attracted to the lodges because of their relative tolerance, but French Huguenots seem exceptionally commonplace, particularly in the London lodges. Yet the ethos of freemasonry could not be further removed from the intense piety, even revivalism, of the sectarian or the Methodist. Anglican piety also never abandoned belief in the natural depravity of humankind, in the inability of human beings to merit salvation.[8] The masonic emphasis on the perfectibility of the human condition, on the ideals of harmony, order, and merit, if only in the lodge, set forth a secular oasis. It was a distinctively optimistic place by comparison with any of the human conditions described by the varieties of English Protestantism. Yet masonry could also have an openly Christian face; as one orator put it in 1737: "The Church of Christ is a Society of spiritual Masonry, select from the World, corresponding by outward signs."[9]

The abandonment of the millenarian and the sectarian occurred within high culture primarily in the 1690s after the establishment in 1689 of constitutional monarchy and parliamentary government. In that decade both Whigs and Tories who accepted the Settlement did so with the self-confidence of knowing that parliamentary rights had been secured without social upheaval or reform, without "turning the world upside down." Such turning had long been associated with the millenarian dreams of the radical sectaries of the 1650s, with what early modern

Europeans right up to 1789 called enthusiasm (p. 213). The demise of lower-class radicalism consigned the millennial dream, once fashionable even in reformist Anglican circles, to the fantasies of the discontented and the disenfranchised.

The secular could not be safely enjoyed by its beneficiaries. Yet the fact remained that this secular order had been secured through revolution. The seventeenth-century revolutions had been against the abuses of monarchy, against "the court." The revolutionaries had claimed to speak for the "country." Long after Parliament secured its right to govern with king and court, that rhetorical dichotomy remained. The court symbolized power monopolized at the center, enjoyed by an oligarchy. The country stood for virtue, in opposition to an imagined decadence.

The attempt to construct a harmonious society naturally put the freemason on the side of virtue, as opponent of corruption. The problem, however, was never quite that simple. The constitutional order that permitted men to even imagine such earthly perfection was appropriated after 1689 by a landed and commercial oligarchy that identified with the court, with its patronage and placemen. Eighteenth-century British freemasons were caught in a cultural, and hence a rhetorical dilemma. They identified with the ideals of the country, but their leadership lived, for the most part, like the court. As a result the lodges never posed—nor were they seen to pose—a threat to the state. However disturbed by doubt the British freemason might be, however country his sentiments might at moments turn, he extolled loyalty and patriotism to country. There is considerable national sentiment to be found in the British masonic impulse.[10] But those same ideals, preached in a different national setting, might turn patriots into opponents.[11]

When masonic literature extolled the status quo, it began by singing the praises of fraternity, conviviality, and mutual benevolence. All encourage virtue. Within this context merit should be the sole criterion for status within the lodge. Orators then went on, rather contradictorily, to allude frequently to the large number of gentlemen and aristocrats, even kings, who proudly shared in the masonic mysteries. This sharing of values should occur only in privacy and secrecy. Emphasis should also be placed within the lodges on the liberal arts and sciences, particularly geometry, which improve and civilize mankind.[12] Uniformly these writers claim to represent an ancient, generally Egyptian and Hermetic wisdom, rediscovered and augmented by the new useful learning of their age. With supreme optimism freemasons always find knowledge to be beneficial and progressive. The lodges eschew bigotry and superstition, yet they take care to exclude those whom masonic literature and ritual describe as "the prophane." And while also excluding women, the English freemason, although increasingly less committed to sexual exclusivity in the lodge as the century wears on, glories in the joys of family and domestic life.

On the pleasures of social harmony masonic rhetoric could embrace as its model the universe proclaimed by Newtonian science. In 1779, for example, the Kent vicar and freemason James Smith, preaching before his lodge, employed language drawn from the Newtonian tradition to illustrate the necessity and power of benevolence: "Attraction binds the universe as benevolence binds men," he confidently asserted.[13] In similar language and in the same period, Daniel Turner, an Anglican minister in Norwich, urged his brothers to practice philanthropy which "is not confined to name or sect. Like the power of attraction, which reaches from the largest to the smallest bodies in the universe, it unites men from the throne to the cottage."[14]

The early Newtonians laid great emphasis upon order, stability, and the rule of law. The belief in the order proclaimed by science in turn encouraged masonic fantasies about the possibility of creating perfect harmony in human society, if only within the confines of the lodge. Yet the Newtonian model also explicitly proclaimed a rigid spiritual hierarchy within nature, and by implication within society: spiritual forces, "active principles," rules over "brute and stupid" matter. Not surprisingly, masonic aspirations for stability and perfectibility were not always compatible. Masonic idealism carried within its boundaries an inherent tension: harmony required perfectibility. Even if this could be achieved within the lodge, could it ever (indeed should it ever) be sealed off from the larger society? Little wonder that in the 1760s, when agitation for reform, led by Wilkes, threatened to destablize society and government, the masonic orators acutely reflected both the agitation of the country and the stability symbolized by the court.

For most of the century, however, masonic orators dwelt upon their utopian vision. They savored certain especially pleasing and salutary aspects of their benevolent, progressive, and, as they imagined it, ancient creed. One of the most commonplace expressions of that sentiment appeared in the standard almanac used year in and year out by the practicing freemason. *The Free Mason's Pocket Companion* first appeared in 1735, and it was followed by a multitude of editions and translations. (On the Continent these companions were sometimes called "catechisms.") Each copy contained a reprint of the 1723 *Constitutions,* lists and addresses of known lodges in London and the environs, masonic feast dates, songs, and a short, largely mythical history of the progress bestowed upon humanity by the fraternity. *The Companion* informed its possessor that the growth of freemasonry augurs "the pleasing Prospect of having even in our own Days the Arts of the fam'd Augustan Age revive amongst us."[15]

In this credo the easy equation is made between the building of public, and especially domestic, mansions and the revival of learning. Indeed the ancient Romans had enjoyed such a revival, but it was destroyed by the Goths, who "with very little knowledge of geometry" gave us the ugliness of the Gothic. The Renaissance in Italy, "more especially the great Palladio," revived the Augustan style of architecture and Inigo Jones, the great court architect of the early seventeenth century, brought it to England. Masonic architects are portrayed at every turn as the harbingers of cultural revival, which is symbolized totally by the splendid Palladian mansions of the new oligarchy (the Earl of Burlington is mentioned by name). The freemasons gloried in the transformation of the royal style of the seventeenth century into the court, and hence oligarchic, style of the eighteenth.

We may find the interiors of these surviving mansions garish; this was not the judgment of contemporaries, who identified with the cultural values they proclaimed. In urging him to identify with the opulence of the court style, the pocket *Companion* told the freemason that places like Houghton Hall, in Norfolk, built by the great Whig oligarch and prime minister Sir Robert Walpole, was in itself a sure sign of cultural vitality. The Palladian style as it appeared in the new mansions of the oligarchs thrilled the masonic imagination. It was pagan and ancient, ornate yet symmetrical. Most of all, these huge edifices and landscaped gardens surrounded by vast landed estates symbolized the private and domestic realm of patronage, prosperity, and power. Out of these private enclaves came the foundations of an order and a stability imitating the cosmic order decreed by providence and confirmed by scientific observation. A masonic poet of 1739, with more enthusiasm than literary talent, rejoiced:

> But Order and Simplicity alone,
> Which in fair nature's works so fair are shown,
> Which now the schemes of Architecture fill,
> Can claim just wonder, or display just skill.
> By these old Greece and Rome their schemes did raise,
> And shone the patterns of succeeding days:
> By these their gen'rous modern sons are known
> A Kent, a Flitcroft, and a Burlington.[16]

Other masonic literature is even more explicit in this glorification of the lavishly domestic. An early anonymous masonic tract, like many others, accepted an essentially Hobbesian view of the brutality of the original human condition, and mitigated it not by the establishment of a contract but rather by the institution of civilizing domestic units built by masons:

> The race of man in full possession of wild and savage liberty, sullen and solitary, mutually offending and afraid of each other; hid themselves in thickets of the woods, or dens and caves of the earth. In these murky recesses, these cumbrous solitudes, the Almighty Architect directed Masonry to find them out and pitying their forlorn and destitute condition, instructed them to build houses, for convenience, defence and comfort.[17]

The construction of homes is only the beginning of human progress as measured in masonic terms; a plenitude of riches is the ideal—the heart of the utopian fantasy. That same anonymous writer continues:

> Some of our brethren from their exalted situation in life, rolling in their chariots at ease, and enjoying every luxury, pleasure and comfort, may with strict propriety be considered as standing on the basis of earthly bliss, emblematic of the greater square, which subtends the right angle. Others whom Providence hath blessed with means to tread on the flowery meads of affluence, are descriptive of the squares which stand on the sides which form the right angle.[18]

But what of those who cannot hope to achieve such extraordinary wealth in their lifetimes as to stand as squares supporting the masonic edifice—are they to be banished from the masonic paradise? While exulting in the splendor of his oligarchic betters, our early masonic writer reserved a special place for the commercially industrious:

> Those, who by application to peculiar arts, manufactures, and commerce, from their several productions not only add to the wealth of the nation, and to the happiness of

> the exalted, but have the heartfelt satisfaction of administering to the wants of the indigent and industrious, may with strict justice, be compared to the angles which surround and support the figure.[19]

The lodge differs from the domestic unit only in that it admits men of a variety of ranks, from the exalted to the industrious and even occasionally to the now "indigent," once "industrious." All may join in the intimacy of its secret proceedings. Indeed, just as the domestic sphere teaches obedience to authority, order, and charity, so too the masonic lodge, in the words of one its founders, seeks to civilize, "to subdue the passions, to promote morality, charity, good fellowship, good nature, and humanity."[20] The lodge is to the cultivation of social virtue as the home is to private virtue. The Reverend R. Green, a masonic preacher from Durham lecturing in 1776 in Newcastle, summed up the meaning of the lodge succinctly: It is "a place of safe retirement where we may securely enjoy generous freedom, innocent mirth, social friendship, and useful instruction."[21] Because of these advantages the freemason distinguishes himself from the rest of humanity by his gentle manner and moderate language, by his dedication to the work ethic and to the cultivation of the mind.[22] As the 1759 edition of the *Pocket Companion* remarked, the freemason is also a model citizen because he is "submissive to superiors, courteous and affable to equals, kind and condescending to Inferiors."[23] As the masonic philosophizer Wellins Calcott put it, "No one contends for superiority; here emulation is only with a view to please . . . and what may seem surprising among such a variety of characters, haughtiness or servility, never appear. The greatest admit of a social familiarity; the inferior is elevated and instructed, constantly maintaining by these means a beneficent equality."[24] The masonic emphasis on charity and benevolence fits in with a larger social movement commonplace in midcentury London, and presumably elsewhere. Philanthrophy, it was believed, would promote virtue among the givers and industry among the receivers. Domestic order and international competitiveness would be naturally enhanced. These charitable impulses were partly inspired by the realization that the new prosperity had had little impact on the chronically poor.[25]

But the placid assessment of virtues and benefits derived from masonic membership, its promotion of true citizenship, benevolence, and class harmony, masked the dissension that had developed by the 1740s within the masonic lodges over the issue of fraternal equality. Brothers had begun to criticize the social exclusivity of some lodges and to demand a more genuine egalitarianism. The resulting schism and the emergence of "antient" or, as it is sometimes called, "Scottish" freemasonry had little to do directly with Scotland, and it was new, rather than old. Its appearance at midcentury signaled, however, a split within the order that left traces on both sides of the Channel. By the 1760s most lodges in the American colonies belonged to the "antient" version of freemasonry; hence they were no longer officially tied to the Grand Lodge in London.[26] These new lodges proclaimed a more egalitarian ambience. Their literature suggests that these democratic tendencies, at least in the English-speaking world, included a dedication to ideals like virtue and merit, coupled with attention to the evils of corruption—all were themes dear to the country perspective. On the Continent, interestingly enough, the first known lodge to admit men and women as equal members and officers met in The

Hague in 1751, and its records make specific reference to "Scottish" freemasonry (see p. 131). In one sense this is not surprising because the issue that divided the "antients" from the "moderns," as they dubbed the Grand Lodge, was the egalitarian nature of true masonry.

The Ancients

The taking over of the old masonry of the operatives by gentlemen, and even nobles, produced a reaction from lesser men. The ensuing schism and debate pitted the newly risen men of artisan background against what they believed to be the decadence into which many of the London lodges had fallen. Their most eloquent spokesman was Lawrence Dermott, an Irish immigrant and artisan, who had risen to be a wine merchant in London. His popular tract, with the curious title *Ahiman Rezon,* began by reminding the brethren of the many ancient and biblical figures who had risen to fame from the most humble of backgrounds. After citing John Bunyan on the spiritualizing of the Temple of Solomon and giving mention to John Milton, Dermott mocked Anderson's mythical and official history of 1723 with its glorification of the Augustan. He also attacked those "that have been preferr'd to Places as Offices of great Trust, and dignified with Titles of Honour, without having the least claim to Courage, Wit, Learning, or Honesty."[27] Dermott glorifies the builders as opposed to the architects of Solomon's Temple—a favorite edifice of masonic lore—and claims for them a secret, cabalistic wisdom, transmitted through the original guild and embodied in the "old" regulations, or "charges." Dermott also castigated "the irreligious Paths of the unhappy Libertine [and] the arrogant professors of atheism and deism."

This assault on the fashionable religiosity of the English Enlightenment was not, however, accompanied with a total retreat from its principles: Superstition is denounced and "the Liberty of embracing what Faith he shall think proper" affirmed. "We only pursue the universal Religion, or the Religion of Nature."[28] The most telling assault on "the moderns" occurs in the proclamation that the freemason should "treat his inferiors as he would have his superiors deal with him, wisely considering that the original of mankind is the same."[29] The mason is a "lover of quiet" and is always subject to the civil powers, provided "they do not infringe upon the limited bounds of religion and reason."[30] The references to Bunyan and Milton suggest an affiliation with men of non-Anglican origins who may have had a sympathy with the Puritan tradition.

The egalitarianism was, however, very finely honed. It is not intended for the "miserable wretches of Low-life" or for women, to whom Dermott makes constant reference.[31] Equality is the prerogative of men of real worth and personal merit, not of seniority. This lionizing of tradesmen and small merchants is a constant theme in the literature of the "antients." It is accompanied, on the one hand, with sentiments of deference to the court, to monarchy and church—to which a lodge is compared—and, on the other, with country disdain for placemen and privilege. The sons of Noah, as masons are described, lay emphasis now on merit and virtue as the criteria for preferment, and on sober striving. The lodge is to be a place where the virtues of middling men are practiced and rewarded. This is a revolt of lesser men against their betters, and one which prefigures in tone and language the Wilkite agitation of the 1760s. It is also interesting for its obsessive concern about the relationship of this male fraternity to women, a topic to which we shall return.

In 1751, when the schism between the ancients and moderns occurred, the lectures and songs found in a reprint of the official *Constitutions*—parts of which the ancients had repudiated—acknowledge "the Contentions amongst Men" and beg the brethren "to avoid all discourse that may divide you into parties." The Hermetic tradition, with its pantheistic and cabalist associations, is, nevertheless, praised at great length, and one overtly anticlerical song is presented. Another "New Song" for the year intones,

> For Truth's sake a Lord is of Equal Degree,
> With a man that is own'd for Mason and Free.[32]

There is other evidence for the emergence of country radicalism among the ancients. In 1751 someone issued an anonymous English translation of a curious work by John Toland, his *Pantheisticon,* originally published in Latin in 1720. By midcentury Continental readers of the book, such as the friends of Rousset de Missy, associated it with freemasonry. They described the ritual given in the text as nothing other than freemasonry under a different name.[33] Toland's book purported to describe a meeting of his "Socratic Brotherhood" and its ritualistic invocation of nature—in other words, its highly heretical pantheism. The English translation of 1751 made specific reference to freemasonry in the margin of the text. Whether issued by friend or foe, this attempt to associate Toland's heresy with the fraternity seems too contemporaneous with the schism of the ancients to be unrelated to it. Someone like Dermott would have been uncomfortable with Toland's extreme pantheism, as it is sprinkled throughout the *Pantheisticon,* but not with its glorification of egalitarian fraternizing, complete with rituals. By 1751 it appears that some lodges had become battlegrounds where the meaning of equality, as well as the claim to possess the true, ancient constitution, was being adjudicated. In 1759 the official *Companion* uncharacteristically remarked that "the great part of mankind is not fit to be members."[34] In the American colonies the split between ancients and moderns led to the demise of the latter. By the 1790s in Pennsylvania the moderns had largely disappeared.[35] In Britain the breach was partially healed only in the early nineteenth century; it remains to this day a subject for masonic discussion, if not dissension.

In general, the impulse of the ancients was decidedly reformist. Once freed from the discipline imposed by the Grand Lodge, ancient lodges also experimented in new rituals and degrees. To add an air of respectability to these innovations, they were described as "Scottish." There is little or no evidence, however, for this supposed geographic origin. But the propensity of adopting these rites could signal a more general discontent. In 1759 a utopian fantasy entitled *The Temple of Virtue: A Dream* employed obviously "Scottish" rite language to elucidate its moral message. Written by David Fordyce, this dream vision takes the reader on an imaginary journey to the "temple of virtue." Lodges employing the Scottish rite would sometimes call their meeting place just that (see p. 134). En route there is a cautionary side trip into the "land of vice wherein could be found the cave of poverty, inhabited by its mistress accompanied by a set of dismal figures, dejection, lamentation, meanspiritedness, suspicion, dishonesty, and despair."[36] The escape from the cave of poverty is made possible through contemplation and work taking the wayfarer along "a secret path" into the temple of virtue "built of a transparent stone . . . of a quadrangular form . . . its portal supported by a double row of pillars of the Dorick order."[37] Both men and women are admitted into this temple. Their virtues, represented symbolically in the temple by deities such as the gods of Industry and Commerce, include domesticity and modesty (especially, but not exclusively, for women), a willingness to protect the modest "against the oppressor's Wrong," and scientific acumen.[38] By the end of the treatise the virtue celebrated is patently country in its ideological association, and the journey ends with a thinly disguised paean of praise for Pitt and "his most ardent love of liberty."[39]

This is a somewhat impatient tract. The search for virtue is encumbered by court corruption, luxury, greed, and tumult. The successful pilgrim who has finally been permitted to join "virtue's priests" has become increasingly alarmed along the way by the behavior of those inhabitants of "the mansions of luxury." However Palladian their taste, and no matter how much their circumstances differ from those found in "the cave of poverty," the behavior of the rich and powerful is dangerously distracting from the search for true virtue. The secret path to virtue has disclosed that the corrupt and the decadent can be banished only through concrete political reform.

The Impulse to Reform

The social turmoil caused in the 1760s by Wilkes and his followers, not a few of whom were freemasons,[40] sent the masonic leadership scrambling for the lecterns to remind the faithful that perfection within the lodge requires order and stability. In 1763 Thomas Edmondes, Esq., addressed his fellow masons in the old and prestigious Horn Tavern Lodge to which Montesquieu had once belonged. Here he praised his brothers for standing above "the turbulent disquietudes, and vitiated principles of most of the unselected and uncivilized part of mankind."[41] Two years later in Taunton, John Whitmarsh reminded brothers that "there are two grand pillars of the masonic art . . . its professed design to promote civilization and to adorn human life with every scientific and moral accomplishment." To achieve these goals, however, the freemason must honor God and King and be subordinate to his superiors.[42] In the same decade a masonic orator in Newcastle assured his listeners that "riot and disorder cannot correct errors that arise in government."[43] In 1764 an anonymous Grand Master lecturing near Birmingham admitted that "in all ages of the World, we find a record of unruly Members of every State; grasping at Power to which their virtues or abilities were by no means equal, and which too often overthrew the Constitution they attempted to defend. . . . This Observation affords a moral lesson to members of private societies, as well as Kingdoms and States." He asserted, however, that "Masons have ever made faith to the government."[44] In 1764 the Reverend Davenport, also lecturing in Birmingham, warned masons to be careful whom they admit to the society; "there was never a time when our fences needed to be more strictly guarded."[45] It is not accidental that these sermons were given in a city where Wilkite agitation was particularly intense.

Yet in that same sermon and almost as if some safe concession must be made to the ideal of equality, the Reverend Davenport called for the admission of women into the lodges, or at least for the creation of lodges for women, which existed, he claimed, in Germany and France.[46] Indeed, the very sermons from this later period which exalt order and hierarchy also most clearly demonstrate the tensions inevitably produced by masonic idealism with its utopian vision of equality and harmony for all and the need to preserve the status quo. An anonymous oration of 1772 demanding that freemasons never "poison their minds with Republican Principles" nevertheless warns of the dangers of corruption in a language that clearly implies the need for some kind of reform:

> When [the law] is dispensed with at Pleasure, when it is pressed against its true Intention into the service of prerogative on the one hand, or privilege on the other; when magistrates are put into office to serve a party by the partial administration of it . . . in a word when an honest cause is overturn'd by artifice, the torturing of witnesses, the disguising of truth . . . then the law . . . loses its nature and efficacy.[47]

This speaker is sure, he says, that these abuses would never happen in England. Many of his fellow orators, however, were not so sure about how well the larger society measured up, or could measure up, against the demands of masonic idealism. Indeed, by the 1770s the lodge is increasingly offered as the ideal society, so much so that some of its spokesmen denied its artisanal origins. The masonic philosopher William Hutchinson argued "that this society was never formed for, or of, a set of working architects or masons; but as a religious, social, and charitable establishment, and never were embodied or exhibited to the world as builders, save only under Moses and at the Temple at Jerusalem."[48] And to prove the merit of such an ancient society "derived from the Druids . . . from Phythagoras . . . [and] from Egypt," Hutchinson enlisted the late seventeenth-century political theorist John Locke.[49]

Locke had come back in fashion among British freemasons as early as 1753 when the popular *Gentleman's Magazine* printed a letter purportedly by him and sent to the freethinker Anthony Collins. In it Locke claimed to have discovered an old manuscript that extolled the masons as "the teachers of mankind," and he affirmed his desire to join the fraternity. The letters was a forgery but that was not, for the most part, known in the eighteenth century. For the pious freemason John Locke had been initiated into the fraternity.

Locke was hardly a favorite author in oligarchic Whig circles. Despite his popularity in the Colonies, and among Continental reformers and radicals, as we shall see in chapter 4, Locke was an author more to be remembered in passing than to be read, throughout much of the century of oligarchy. The revival of his name in masonic circles increasingly during the 1770s signals a willingness to invoke an author associated with republican conspiracy and the justification of revolution, as his *Two Treatises of Government* (1690) was believed to have offered. Masonic writers asserted, on the basis of weak, if not spurious evidence, that Locke had been initiated as a freemason and "that the favourable opinion this philosopher conceived of the society of masons before his admission, was sufficiently confirmed after his initiation."[50] Locke's devotion was repeatedly cited by revolutionary American freemasons. They listed him within an ideological trajectory that began with the Druids, went to the ancient Saxons, and ended with the formation of the new Grand Lodge in Boston in 1777.[51] However untrue, Locke's supposed membership in the fraternity also raised the issue of its allegiance to his political principles as contemporaries understood, or construed them.

In 1770 John Codrington, preaching in Exeter, reminded his brothers that they must never be involved in plots and conspiracies. But he tempers that obligation with the assertion of cherished masonic ideals: Men of merit even "of the most indigent circumstance . . . we rank as brethren on a level" and freemasons must free themselves of bigoted notions about religion—"humanity is the soul of all religions."[52] Indeed, the divisions between men are wholly artificial and Codrington proclaimed:

> The whole world is but one great republic, of which every nation is a family and every particular person is a child. To revive and spread abroad those ancient maxims drawn from the nature of man, is one of the ends of our establishment. We wish to unite all men of an agreeable humour and enlightened understanding, not only by the love of the polite arts but still more by the great principles of virtue; and from such a union, the interest of the fraternity becomes that of all mankind.[53]

Yet it should be noted that in the same sermon Codrington cautioned against admitting women, "not that we do not pay a natural and due regard to that most beauteous part of the creation . . . but because their presence might insensibly alter the purity of our maxims and our manners . . . we are afraid . . . that love would enter with them." For Codrington women represented to men only the emotional and the personal; the lodge is a public place, formal, a space filled by "maxims and manners." There is a division in the masonic mind between the personal and the public which we shall see reflected even in the midcentury Continental lodges intended for women (see pp. 134–35).

In the 1770s freemasonry in Britain, as on the Continent, became increasingly concerned with public issues. At the height of the American Revolution, the Reverend James Smith lecturing in Kent proclaimed that

> by nature the whole race of mankind however different they may be in their modes of living, in their size, or their complexions, from the most polished courtier down to the savage Caffer . . . from the fair Dane to the sooty Negroe . . . however unlike these are to each other, however unknown, still they are brethren . . . as all men are by nature brethren, so consequently all men are by nature equal.[54]

This man of democratic sentiment, whom we met earlier through his use of Newtonian imagery in this sermon, speaks not only of the force of attraction binding the universe and the need for order and harmony, but also of the equality of all men, attempting somewhat frantically to hold these notions in an increasingly fragile equilibrium: "A good Mason . . . is properly said to live upon the level with all men. Yet Freemasons are by no means Levellers . . . order and subordination . . . are requisite for the welfare of every society."[55]

Spoken but a few years before the outbreak of the first of a wave of democratic revolutions on the Continent, this sort of masonic rhetoric, which offered the private lodge as the cosmopolitan ideal for society as a whole, simply restated boldly what had always been at the heart of the masonic utopia. In tandem with the proclamation of luxury and affluence as ideals came the almost naive belief that the meritorious actually deserved to prosper. To say, so simply and so straightforwardly, as Codrington did in 1770, that "we are all upon a level, and . . . merit is the only just distinction" may well have encouraged those who regarded themselves as meritorious and who resented the distinctions and prejudices that inhibited their progress. Such utopian sentiments could justify demands for concrete social reforms, for the translation of that private masonic ideal into public action: the abolition of privilege and corruption, the institution of true fraternity and equality for all men, even for all women and also for slaves. The masonic presence in these revolutions, however moderate and undoubtedly nonconspiratorial it may have been, must be understood by reference to this utopian rhetoric, and hence in relation to the legacy of the English Revolution in all of its phases.

Order, Luxury, and Harmony

The reforming and utopian tendencies within eighteenth-century British freemasonry generally never obscured the more typical and widespread masonic dedication to harmony, moderation, conviviality, and social cohesion within the lodge. This stoical, even complacent serenity (however epicurean might be the fraternizing that accompanied it) directly imitated the harmony and order of the universe as revealed, of course, by science. In a well-known piece of masonic propaganda intended for a French audience, but of English origin and possibly even translated by the Newtonian scientist Jean Desaguliers, this harmonic and microcosmic relationship of the lodge to the larger macrocosm is developed at some length.[56] This is a particularly forceful piece of masonic propaganda written after a series of police raids on lodge meetings in Paris and in the wake of the papal condemnation of 1738.

The *Relation apologique et historique de la société des Franc-Maçons* argues that nature itself authorizes the masonic lodge, and it in turn is the place where science is learned under the guidance of Isis or Minerva, and where nature is mastered. Scientific lessons are actually given at the lodge meetings; "in many cases a discovery about nature or a demonstration of one of her phenomena has been more delicious than the best wine. The gaiety [however] never exceeds the bounds of reason, politeness and modesty."[57] There is scattered evidence mainly from the early decades of speculative freemasonry that scientific lectures were given. The value of science, rather than its content, was certainly a common theme in masonic literature. The origin impulse for the promotion of science within the lodges was English and Newtonian.

Although forced to compete with feasting and conviviality, science does manage to teach the freemason a lesson that is the essence of his religiosity: The universe is composed of many things, yet there is a unity amid this multiplicity. That unity "is God, eternal, immense and wise. . . . He is the All of which each being is a product."[58] Science sanctions theism, nothing more and hopefully nothing less. This defense intended for a Continental and largely Catholic audience, like so many other pieces of masonic literature, calls forth a single creed, one that could be embraced by a variety of Christians, as well as by Mohammedans and Jews.[59] As another tract put it, only within freemasonry can that creed be practiced; this society alone "redounds to the honour of the great parent of nature, and architect of the universe . . . worthy . . . of man whose greatest happiness is society, whose supreme dignity is humanity."[60] This universalism makes sense not only as propaganda but also as a true reflection of early masonic history.

In those years pantheists like John Toland, whom we shall meet in greater detail at the end of the next chapter, played a real, and complex, role in the spread of freemasonry onto the Continent. Toland's advocacy of an almost complete religious toleration derived not from any sort of Christian charity but rather from an extreme heterodoxy. In 1714 he praised the Jews because they "honor one supreme being, or First Cause, and obey the Law of Nature."[61] As one of the first eighteenth-century writers to take up the cause of religious toleration for the Jews, Toland is resuming a campaign that, as Christopher Hill showed, must be associated with the utopian yet millenarian impulse of the seventeenth-century revolution.[62] In Toland's hands the cause finds a new advocate and one who, as a pantheist, deified nature and hence the world of ordinary mortals. Toland had no need of an apocalyptic moment to justify, or to permit, his radical reforms. However, he did require a new religiosity, possibly even a new, civil, religion. As he proclaimed in the *Pantheisticon* (1720), which included the ritual for his followers, he was seeking a religion "more mild, more pure and more free." In the tradition of Milton, Toland also proclaimed himself one of those who "study the safety of the republick."[63]

That curious ritual devised by Toland for his Socratic Brotherhood was sent by him to The Netherlands as early as 1711. It was then probably published in Latin in 1720 as part of his *Pantheisticon.* Although official freemasonry never adopted it, we can see its appeal to liberal men (and even women) of a variety of religious backgrounds. Indeed, its philosophical assumptions depart so far from Judeo-Christian orthodoxy as to praise "the male and female Votaries of Truth."[64] Toland had sought to revive a universal religion more akin to ancient paganism than to any modern sect. Decades after Toland published we can find French freemasons writing learned treatises on the Druids—they had been among Toland's favorite pagans—because of the supposed universalism of their religion. We do not know if Toland's ideas directly influenced masonic interest in the original European pagans. What we do know is that later in the century French freemasons could argue that the religion and government of the ancient Celtic (and Gaulic) priests resembled masonic religion and government.[65]

The tradition of religious toleration and heterodoxy so much a part of masonic idealism may well have derived in large measure from pantheists and republicans like Toland, whose links with the order have now been reasonably well established.

Although Jewish membership in masonic lodges was always quite small, in 1731 we can identify a London lodge where six out of twenty-nine members were in all probability Jewish.[66] The records of Amsterdam freemasonry, where a pantheist and hence a follower of John Toland served for many years as Master of its main lodge, also contain names that are almost certainly Jewish.

The conviviality of brothers drawn from different ranks in society, as well as from different religions, preoccupied masonic publicists. As their literature makes abundantly clear, wine, song, and great culinary feasts occupy a central place in every masonic evening. One of the first identifiably masonic tracts is Henri Sallengre's amusing *Essay in Praise of Drunkenness,* written in The Hague and translated from the French by the freemason Robert Samber; it was dedicated by him in 1723 to the London freemasons, whom Samber includes, among others, in a list of great tipplers. That sort of celebration of overindulgence was counterbalanced by other literature advocating moderation, which almost obsessively discusses the acceptable limits to be observed by the imbiber.[67]

Fed by the unprecedented affluence and prosperity to be found among the eighteenth-century English middle and upper classes, the masonic affection for private luxury also induced a certain discomfort among its very participants. This is not to say that in general we find in this literature anything like the sustained attack on decadence and corruption, on greed and commercial interests, that was so much at the heart of country sensibility. Indeed, the masonic acceptance of commerce and glorification of the industrious and prosperous entrepreneur permitted only the occasional reflection on the dangers of luxury and overindulgence. The freemason coveted affluence; he wanted prosperity, but without decadence. His is the conscience of those Whig gentlemen who wanted to live like the court and reap its benefits, while managing somehow to avoid the inevitable slide into licentiousness and corruption. So the masonic publicists emphasize the ritualistic and fraternal aspects of food, drink, and song, seeking to make them into symbolic expressions of masonic unity, harmony, and moderation.

Yet the drinking songs sung in the lodges give ample evidence that the bacchanalian thrived and may even have provided an occasion for the safe expression of dissident ideas, which in that context were rendered harmless. Take, for example, this verse:

> Let Monarchs run mad after riches and power,
> Fat Gown-men be dull, and Philosophers sour,
> While the Claret goes round, and the company sings,
> We're wiser than Sages, and greater than Kings.[68]

In contrast to that harmless ribaldry, most masonic literature places great emphasis on decorum, civility, and table manners, literally on forks, plates, and napkins.[69] One of the primary functions of the lodge was to make all its members, regardless of birth, into well-mannered gentlemen who help instill public order. For the freemason society alone is the source of man's greatest happiness, and, as a result, he has a particular obligation to foster socially acceptable virtues.[70]

There is limited evidence that membership in the London lodges did modify the public behavior of brothers and hence contribute to the increasingly orderly forms of public recreation that became common in the latter decades of the eighteenth century. For instance, the epilogues and prologues given in London playhouses and specially intended for masonic audiences frequently refer to the virtuous and peaceful behavior of the assembled lodge members. Their deportment was apparently in noticeable contrast to the near riotous assemblies for which the everyday audiences of the playhouses were well known.[71]

Those masonic evenings in the London theaters were frequently accompanied by a special charity collection for a brother or his widow fallen on hard times. Charity to the deserving poor or the needy brother formed an important part of masonic ideology, if not practice. In advertising the benefits of membership to a Continental audience, that anonymous French tract of English origin mentioned earlier claimed that the order always took care of its own, even to the point of providing free medical care for members when a lodge was lucky enough to possess a fraternal doctor. There may be some truth to these charitable claims, and the available evidence suggests that lodges functioned as a hedge against the uncertainties and insecurities of an increasingly pervasive market society. Certainly masonic loyalty could be tangible. It could extend even to the victims of crime if their assailants were masonic and if, as I suspect, the good name of the order was threatened. In the 1730s members of the Horn Tavern Lodge gave assistance to a woman who had been raped by one of their members, yet they did not abandon him even after he was imprisoned for the crime.[72] For political crimes such as fomenting revolution, the *Constitutions* (1723) specifically forbade expulsion of a brother, although it did insist that "the loyal Brotherhood must and ought to disown his rebellion."

Eighteenth-century masonic literature, both British and Continental, offered the lodge as the foundation for earthly happiness. It provided an ethical system that emphasized fraternity and equality, as well as the value of liberty. It could also furnish a sufficiently broad religiosity to accommodate both the Christian and the heterodox or the anticlerical, yet it never encouraged social alienation. In general, masonic writers urged ordinary men to identify with the great and the prosperous, to emulate their comforts and luxuries yet never to forget the necessity for industry, virtue, and learning. An extremely popular fraternal song, first published in 1763 but almost certainly older, summed up, in three-part harmony, the essence of this idealism:

> Comus, away, with all thy revel train
> Begone ye loud, ye wanton and ye vain
> Come pensive Science, come pensive science
> Bring with thee Commerce and Arts, Commerce and Arts
>   Commerce and Arts and Industry
> Come Patriot virtue, Patriot virtue, also bring
>   and Loyalty who loves his king. . . .

Of freemasonry, it proclaimed:

> Thy social influence extends beyond the narrow sphere of Friends
> Thy Harmony and Truth improve the Earth our universal love.[73]

Late in the century as an expression of that universalism, some Continental lodges, as we shall see, actually began to admit women. The first one we can document met in The Hague in 1751, and then most frequently such lodges are found in France during the 1770s and 1780s. The egalitarian ideology of freemasonry possessed an inexorable logic. In that sense the utopian impulse led to social and possibly political reformism, however much the gentleman freemason, satiated by drink and conviviality, might want to avoid such troublesome exertions.

Radical Impulses

Given masonic rhetoric, it should come as no surprise that early in masonic history we can detect a politically radical underside, one which is particularly evident on the Continent later in the century. But before turning to Continental freemasonry, its mores as well as its origins, we should ask if the reforming impulse we have found in British freemasonry derived from sources other than the legacy of country ideology. There is some evidence, tantalizing although by no means conclusive, that also links masonic fraternizing with habits and behavior found in politically subversive groups, or at least with Whig party socializing both before and after the Revolution of 1689. This evidence needs rehearsing for the links it provides between the seventeenth-century revolutionary tradition and freemasonry, as well as its help in explaining eighteenth-century masonic beliefs about the origins of the fraternity and its mythical relation to Cromwell and English revolutionary traditions in general.

Social clubs were commonplace enough in late seventeenth-century England. Within political society, however, they were to be found more among Whigs than among Tories. Indeed, the relative lack of private clubs among Tories has been offered as one explanation of their relatively less organized political base in the decades after 1689.[74] By contrast, Whig fraternizing dated back to the 1680s when the Whigs were the party of opposition, even of subversion. Not least, Whig clubs often display in their records a markedly anticlerical, or even libertine character. The notorious Calves' Head Club donned "Priest-vestments" for their ritual pope burning; the Kit-Cat Club of the 1690s reveled in the impious and irreverent.[75] The club called its members knights and had a "president" who taught "What faith the priests of all Religions hold . . . ," as its manuscript remains report. (We should not forget that Toland's Socratic Brotherhood was also convened in the *Pantheisticon* by its president.) Similarly, a libertine group that met in The Hague, of which Toland had kept one of its handwritten minutes, called its members "knights" as well as "brothers" (see p. 91). By contrast, Tory clubs toasted church and monarch, or reserved the right "to silence any Brother who shall in his Liquor or any otherwise talk anything that shall ridicule the Holy Scripture or religion."[76] Yet both political parties assisted in the formation of civil society, in a new zone of social experience.

Such behavior—overtly political or simply convivial and leisured—as now was found among merchants and tradesmen had little in common with the traditional and protective fraternizing of the guilds. Yet this new sociability, characterized by an affluence that made feasting and drinking into affordable pastimes, might easily be grafted onto the practices of a guild, and might in turn transform it into a voluntary society of gentlemen. Not surprisingly, where we find the first, somewhat circumstantial evidence for the existence of a purely speculative lodge in England, it appears to have been established among London gentlemen of decidedly Whiggish inclinations who had friendly relations with the city's Company of Masons.

Eighteenth-century British freemasons said that the first speculative lodge was headed by Sir Robert Clayton, lord mayor of London, scrivener, and an extreme Whig.[77] In 1693 Clayton "procured an occasional lodge of masters to meet at St. Thomas' hospital . . . near which a stated lodge continued long afterwards."[78] His friends in that period included John Wildman, the former Leveller, and John Toland,[79] who, as we shall see in the next chapter, made much out of secret fraternizing, and hence out of what he may have learned from Clayton. In the 1670s Clayton had used his political influence as a London alderman to recommend to the Lord Mayor and Court of Aldermen that the "present charter" of the Company of Masons be extended seven miles around the city as "an advantage" to it.[80] This willingness to offer protection to the masons' guild may explain why masonic legend has it that Clayton was admitted to membership.

The seventeenth-century contacts between guildsmen and merchants, such as Clayton or the tradesmen of Dundee, hardly prepare us for the suspicions that the new fraternity aroused. Yet the Whig filiations of some of its members and some of its ritual practices help to explain the undercurrent of suspicion that runs through the society's earliest history. Throughout the early eighteenth century hostile accounts of the freemasons associated them, rightly or wrongly, with the libertine and the irreligious. A pamphlet of 1696 accused the masons of being "the anti-Christ" and warned Londoners to "mingle not among this corrupt People lest you be found so at the World's Conflagration."[81] In 1737 the leading Tory newspaper railed that "no government ought to suffer such dark and clandestine Assemblies" because they may plot against the state, and because they admit "Turks, Jews, Infidels, Papists, and Nonjurers."[82] Other accounts elaborated upon such charges, adding drunkenness and sodomy most frequently. In addition, the lodges were seen as places where government positions might be secured.[83] Given the relatively large number of court Whigs who can be identified in the lodges of the 1730s, the insight held some substance. Clearly the guild has been transformed, almost beyond recognition, and in its place stands a new sociability, disdainful of religious divisions, worldly in its embrace of affluence and civility, mercantile in its occupations and interests.[84]

Such a sociability would appear to have been more compatible with Whig than Tory political culture and ideology. Unique among nonaristocratic Europeans, Whig gentlemen, like Clayton, who were the beneficiaries of the Revolution Settlement, possessed unprecedented access to political power through parliament and the press. They had established the means by which their power, and the polity, might be rendered both permanent and stable. That political stability, upon which material progress might rest, was partially made possible by the clear subordination of church to state. After 1689 the commands of heaven, as understood by their leading clerical interpreters, implored the gentlemen of land, finance, and commerce, as well as all lesser folk, to bend their self-interest in the service of religion and society, but never to abandon it. Their worldly occupations received affirmation from the reasonableness of liberal or latitudinarian Christianity. Whether they bothered to listen or not to this newly subordinate and acquiescent clergy, secular-minded men, like Clayton, could comfortably imagine themselves the creators, the priests if you like, of a new social order wherein the civil society fashioned by the literate and enfranchised might flourish.

Late seventeenth-century Whiggery also possessed a radical underside with intellectual roots in the revolutionary and republican tradition of the Civil Wars and Interregnum. The political and highly secular philosophy that legitimated the Revolution Settlement to the enfranchised of town or shire always carried with it the possibility of further transformations, the reform of existing institutions, however glorious and legitimate their settlement might once have been. And in the eighteenth century that language of reform would never entirely lose its revolutionary associations, its republican tendencies, that echo heard long after the late 1640s and the 1650s when the language justifying revolution and regicide had first been spoken on the streets, in the taverns and the alehouses.

Throughout the eighteenth century oligarchic Whigs sought to disown this radical inheritance; but it kept coming back to haunt them—in the 1690s and well into the reign of Anne, in the 1760s and the Wilkite agitation, in the 1790s among the supporters of the continental revolutions, to be found in Derbyshire as well as in London. At every turn the clerical and social institutions of the various anciens régimes frustrated even the most harmless desire for social equality based upon merit or the institution of a religion of humanity. Yet the emphasis on education, personal virtue, and decorum within the lodge must have given dedicated brothers a sense of their own worth and ability, a sense further reinforced by the hierarchy based upon merit established among themselves, and by the claim that freemasons had a unique purchase on ancient wisdom. Given the opportunity, some men might indeed try to transform those private utopian impulses, however rhetorical and secretive their original expression may have been, into a concrete social reality. In the 1770s and again in the 1790s a few taverns associated with English lodges were used as places to discuss "a Republican Congress for New Modelling of the Constitution," voting rights for women, the American Revolution, and then the French Revolution.[85]

Such extraordinary transformations would inevitably entail a massive reform and alteration of the old order, a break with the past so abrupt as to constitute a new and secular form of apocalyptic action. On the Continent the break took the form of a series of revolutions which masonic rhetoric and idealism, with its British and utopian associations, may have at moments made seem more plausible. In their country of origin, however, most masonic orators encouraged order and stability, an accommodation to the social and political status quo. Indeed the lodges were an important vehicle for inculcating loyalism to king and government.[86] Only in the area of religious belief was the emphasis on toleration and "the religion upon which all men agree" radically out of step with the prevailing values and mores of British, indeed of every European society. This was a rhetoric more Whig than Tory, more court than country, although, as we have seen, not without radical associations.

Thus in the first instance the force and challenge inherent in British masonic idealism lay in the area of religious values, beliefs, and mores. Freemasonry exported onto the Continent a peculiarly English religiosity, the legacy of liberal

Protestantism with its emphasis on natural religion. It had been forged by nearly a half-century of revolution and under the impact of the new science.[87] Yet it could and did travel and translate as attractive across the Channel, much to the concern of police and clergy.

When we enter into these fraternal gatherings on the Continent we are observing a cultural transformation. British ceremonies, rituals, and language are being translated in new cultural settings, utterly specific to their time, place, and language. Rituals created among working men are now being used to express dedication to originally British laws and constitutions. Much of the ritual will be reworked and elaborated upon by Continental lodges. Yet the core of the idealism just outlined, with its utopian cast, will remain recognizable in various European languages, well into the 1780s, and it will continue to attract men of the middling ranks, as well as the aristocracy. But in the chapters ahead the original guild moorings of the lodges will be left behind in Scotland and England, as will the Parliament and Constitution within which the gentlemen of the original lodges, drawn from a variety of religious backgrounds, enjoyed their liberties and privileges.

3

Cultural Encounters: Freemasonry on the Continent

By the mid-eighteenth century freemasonry existed in most western European countries.[1] Its cultural migration was a complex process, to this day only partially understood. We will return to the chronology of the process and attempt to make sense out of the Channel crossing that accompanied it, but only after we have examined the tension that arose around the first Continental lodges. These were to be found by the mid-1730s in towns and cities of northern and western Europe, in that densely urban corridor from Amsterdam to Paris. With the lodges came the anonymous literary exposures, offering rituals and myths, not least, as we have seen, claiming Cromwell's association with the fraternity (see pp. 27–28). In this chapter we examine not the myths, but the realities, the actual beliefs of some of the earliest lodges, and, just as important, the official and unofficial responses to them in various European countries.

In the first instance the lodges on the Continent represented the foreign and the unknown. They also embodied British cultural values associated with the potentially subversive: religious toleration, relaxed fraternizing among men of mixed, and widely disparate, social backgrounds, an ideology of work and merit, and, not least, government by constitutions and elections. By the 1730s all these values were the prized ideals of an international cultural movement that laid claim to the secular and the modern, that came to be called the Enlightenment. And if that association were not enough, the lodges called attention to themselves by their secrecy.

The tension freemasonry aroused infected civil magistrates as well as clergy. In Paris lodge meetings were raided by the police (p. 27); in Portugal a freemason, John Coustos, a member of a London lodge, was arrested and tortured in 1743. The authorities claimed that he and his brothers had been publicly rowdy in violation of the Lenten season. The papal condemnation had been in 1738. In the 1740s freemasonry was regarded with suspicion in Austrian territories.[2] Their pious queen, Maria

Theresa, fostered that response, both in the Low Countries and in Vienna. One of the earliest Continental manuscript "Books of Constitutions"—this one from Lausanne, Switzerland, written in 1741—speaks of the "ignorance and maliciousness with which men judge things about which they have no idea," and notes that the freemasons have suffered as a result.[3] Indeed, from the mid-1730s the ecclesiastical authorities everywhere in Europe were alarmed about the fraternity.[4]

In Protestant Europe during the first half of the century, the lodges fared only slightly better than they did where papal authority was respected. The States of Holland condemned the freemasons in 1735, and from that time until well in the 1750s the lodges in the Dutch Republic grew at their peril. They were systematically attacked as being dangerous to the tranquillity of the Republic right into the 1770s.[5] Generally speaking, however, freemasonry grew more, and found greater acceptance, in Protestant rather than Catholic Europe.[6] Yet its popularity in upper bourgeois and aristocratic French society must not be forgotten (see pp. 184–85). It has been estimated that by the 1770s there were 10,000 freemasons in Paris, a city with a population between 500,000 and 600,000.[7] Daniel Roche has further estimated that 10 percent of all eighteenth-century French authors were masonic.[8]

Why did this imported form of socializing provoke the kind of profound hostility evinced by police raids and official condemnations? I will try to reconstruct what contemporaries believed was at stake when they condemned the masonic order and, just as important, I want to determine the motivations and ideals of the men who joined the earliest lodges under these circumstances. We shall travel to at least one town in northern and western Europe where masonry had spread, and where, in what was a generally hostile context at the best of times, the tension actually boiled to the surface and left traces in the historical records. By looking at an incident in the Dutch Republic where a new masonic lodge provoked clerical opposition, we do not have to rely solely upon police records or official proclamations to tell us what it was that contemporaries, both masons and their detractors, perceived as being at issue.

The Dutch at Midcentury

In approaching the Dutch Republic at midcentury, we can imagine ourselves as a British masonic visitor, a merchant or a sea captain, traveling abroad, and as a result leaving the relative safety of the British lodges. It was often the custom for traveling freemasons to visit foreign lodges, to spend a sociable evening, and to sign the visitors' book.[9] If we invent one such traveler—let us say our sea captain from the lodge in Dundee—we can imagine him making his way through The Netherlands in the early 1750s. Not least, we can attempt to recreate the discussions he might have heard among his Dutch brothers. In those discussions we can hear the tension between the imported and the indigenous, between the masonic and the traditional, between the new secularism freemasonry represented and the older values it seemed to repudiate.

Almost certainly a British masonic visitor would have been shocked by the accusations leveled against his honorable fraternity in the Republic. Like any imported cultural artifact, freemasonry required integration and adaptation. But this artifact was more than simply a book or an idea. It demanded a social experience of lodge governance and fraternizing, and with that came an idealized ethical system with implications that went beyond the lodge and its brothers. In Britain controversy about freemasonry largely occurred within the fraternity itself, for example, between the ancients and moderns about the true meaning of their mutual dedication to "all brothers meeting upon the level." By midcentury one would be hard-pressed to find in Britain any public expression of antimasonic sentiment.[10]

The Dutch Republic was the first Continental country where the freemasonry of the Grand Lodge of London was self-consciously exported in 1731 and officially established in 1734 in The Hague and the following year in Amsterdam.[11] The organizer of the Amsterdam lodge was the Huguenot refugee Jean Rousset de Missy. Prior to that, around 1721 a lodge of English and Scottish merchants existed in Rotterdam, and in 1710, again at The Hague, a group of Huguenot journalists and local publishers made merry in a private society that adopted most of the aspects of the new speculative masonry.[12] In December 1735 the States of Holland closed down the lodges in The Hague and Amsterdam, calling them "an improper gathering . . . an unseemly conventicle."

The masonic "disturbers of the peace" appear to have aroused the authorities because of the Orangist and British affiliations of the lodges, hence the association, which was real, with British policy toward the Low Countries.[13] Certainly that was the verdict of a sympathetic contemporary observer: "The leading men at this place, mostly spawn of the De Wit faction [i.e., anti-stadtholder] . . . have issued strict orders, whereby all Assemblies, and private meetings whatsoever are forbid, under the severest Penalties, lest Parties might be formed, to remove the Power, which they exercise in a most arbitrary manner, out of their hands and invest it [in] the Prince . . . the Brethren that composed the Lodge, were persons of honour, and of unblemisht reputation." As part of the same crackdown the theater in The Hague was restricted because it was an object of the stadtholder's patronage.[14] Also in December 1735 a mob attacked a lodge meeting. Here is how a British newspaper reported on the attack: "The vice, which raged in Holland about two years ago [i.e., homosexuality] came so strongly into the people's heads that they would certainly have made work for masonry and pulled the house over their ears, had not the peace officers in good time prevented the effect of their fury."[15] It was only after the Revolution of 1747, which restored the Orangist stadtholder, William IV, in the provinces of Holland, Zeeland, and Utrecht, that we again find clear evidence of masonic lodges in the Republic. For example, in 1749 a lodge was opened in the southern garrison town of Nijmegen. Its master was the governor of the garrison, Ludwig Friedrich, prince of Saksen-Hildburgshausen, a minor German aristocrat in the service of the Hapsburg emperor.[16] His garrison was but one link in the chain of fortresses manned by the Anglo-Austrian alliance against France, to which the Dutch Republic supposedly gave its allegiance.

In a town of comparable size in Britain, for example, in Dundee, the local lodge owned a church pew, which its officers occupied on a regular basis. By contrast, in Nijmegen in 1752 two freemasons were denied membership in the Dutch Reformed Church. In both places the churches were Protestant in a Calvinist tradition. In Nijmegen, however, the confrontation between clergy and fraternity brought to the surface the political and religious meaning that could be associated with the new enlightened culture. Clearly Nijmegen was a long way from Dundee.

More precisely, on a southwest journey from the coastal town of Dundee, Nijmegen is about five hundred miles away. Crossing the North Sea, then journeying inland and south of Amsterdam, a masonic visitor would have come to an area of the Republic that was also heavily Catholic, where French was still occasionally spoken. Nijmegen, a town of some eleven thousand souls,[17] was an entire culture away, a language and history away from mid–eighteenth-century Scotland. As one Scottish visitor of the period noted, however, there was a remarkable order and hence surface similarity among the many Dutch towns and cities: "The houses are charmingly neat both within and without. The description of one house or one town will answer to all the houses and all the towns that I have seen. The dress of the inhabitants of both sexes admits of the same similarity."[18] Given this apparent homogeneity, perhaps we should not be surprised that masonic fraternizing created such an uproar.

Both Dundee and Nijmegen were towns in essentially Protestant countries which enjoyed two of the highest literary rates in western Europe. And there were other similarities between the elite culture of mid–eighteenth-century Scotland and The Netherlands. The universities in Leiden and Edinburgh were also closely tied through their medical faculties, with the Dutch university having inspired much of the medical curriculum in Edinburgh. Indeed, Scottish students often studied at Leiden, its costs being less than staying at home and its Protestantism being regarded as safe for young minds.[19] Our seafaring freemason and his Dutch hosts would have communicated in French, the international language of the eighteenth century. French was so commonplace in the Dutch lodges that the first lodge in The Hague kept its records in both languages well into the 1750s. One elite lodge in Middleburg in Zeeland kept them in French right into the 1780s.

Rather quickly our visitor would have discovered that the controversy engendered in Nijmegen by the exclusion of two freemasons from the local church was no tempest in a provincial teapot.[20] The exclusion from the Calvinist church of F. C. Merkes and L. A. Merkes, brothers by birth as well as by fraternizing, was the subject of masonic discussion all over the Dutch Republic. Indeed, the Dominus Haverkamp, local Calvinist minister, had ensured that this would be the case. He had spoken from the pulpit against the fraternity, accusing it of "godlessness," of putting the church in danger, of also endangering the state, and even, by its exclusion of women, of the darkest of debauchery, in all probability implying sodomy. In particular he also had accused the fraternity of playing a card game, called in Dutch "Duyvelskaarten"—Devils' Cards—an eighteenth-century version of tarot.

These were quite serious and specific accusations. The mention of the Devils' Cards conjured up fortunetelling, magic, and anticlericalism. The cards had been attacked frequently by both Protestant and Catholic clergy because the power attributed to them implied that fate and fortune, not divine providence, ruled over human affairs. Not least they were frequently decorated with anticlerical, or sometimes lewd, pictures. In the 1750s one Amsterdam lodge imposed fines against excessive card playing (p. 159). We do not know if the masons played with Devil's Cards; what is important is that the clergy thought they did. These rather remarkable accusations were advanced by a minister educated in Leiden, and they were targeted against known and, there is no evidence to doubt, respected members of the community. The Merkes brothers were the sons of the town's rent collector, and they were also in state service.[21]

We are fortunate to be able to recreate something of the atmosphere of the ensuing controversy. Pamphlets were published by both sides, and petitions to the civil and ecclesiastical authorities were filed by the freemasons and their clerical detractors. In nearby Arnhem a female cousin of the excluded brothers privately appealed to one of them not to continue in this struggle with the local clergy, because, as her manuscript letter explains, only he would be the loser. Luckily this personal plea has been preserved. It tells us a great deal about what it must have felt like to live in one of these towns and to be in the eye of the storm between traditional religiosity and this new, and imported, secular society. The cousin writes, "The whole country is full of it. Yesterday I was in the shop near us. Oh! it was the freemasons, now; and the freemasons, once again . . . the old women who sits there in the shop says there was nothing else to talk about."[22] Clearly this strange import, not simply from abroad but also by 1750 from enlightened circles within the Republic, violated everyday assumptions about how men should behave.

We get an inkling of what was being said about the freemasons from hearing the charges repeated by this concerned, and by no means naive, relative. She has no illusions about the clergy, and she notes that the Dominus is "too clever for you; and he has money like water . . . he must have a hundred thousand guilders and he lives like a bishop."[23] In short, the clergy are very powerful, and, she tells her cousin, you are placed in an untenable position "if you have the dominee around your throat, and pulling on your ears." This scandal, she continues, will hurt your chances of marrying, and of becoming an officer. Those who do not respect God and his law can have neither luck nor blessings. Among the interesting rumors that have spread about the freemasons is the luxury of their meals, here in the letter associated with French manners, which "spoil the wallet and the stomach."[24] What this upright cousin could not have known was that other women at this time shared her concern; indeed French women, in this instance living in the southeastern province of Alsace, refused to marry men unless they renounced their freemasonry.[25] We do not know the reasons for their refusal. But we can reconstruct the thinking of one Dutch Protestant woman at midcentury as it related to this new, and almost inexplicable, fraternity.

The luxury of masonic manners primarily concerned our Francophone cousin. She says it is rumored that the masons eat as if they were at a wedding or a synod (a clerical gathering). The association with conspicuous and excessive consumption, which we have seen before in the comments of British freemasons about themselves, should remind us that in most parts of western Europe lodge meetings were gatherings of elites with some surplus income, like the military officers who frequented the lodge in the garrison town of Nijmegen. But this did not prevent, and perhaps it encouraged, wild rumors to circulate, hence the accusations recounted in this letter: the freemasons engaged in "cursed idol worship" ("vervloekte afgoderijen"), they pray to animals, they even can fly. This might provoke an ironic chuckle, "cousin, please don't learn to fly!" Yet the irony did not stop this young relative from briefly recounting a story told by a minister about someone in a local church so possessed by the spirit that he hung in midair "between heaven and earth."[26]

However naive at moments, this cousin possessed no illusions about the clergy: "When the dominees start they will not stop for a long time. They play a dirty game and they will ruin you. Watch out; they will try to prevent you from getting a lawyer to write something for you and they will attack them too. What to do then! And try to get close to 'the gentlemen' [*de Heeren*]," that is, to the members of the local municipal government.[27] In supplicating her Nijmegen cousin to leave the freemasons, our anonymous writer then adds, "From where I sit and write, I would also like to become one. But if it were evil, I would like to stop. But the women do not have a place in this and as I rethink [the matter], it would be no good, that someone else would hear this; for surely the Dominee would visit me, and that would be the end of me."[28] Places where women could not go or were not welcome were hardly new. From the tone of the discussion, however, what most disturbs this woman is that the masonic lodge is profoundly different from anything else around it.

Yet clearly her cousin was committed deeply enough to the fraternity that he was prepared to risk his reputation and to stand up to the local minister. We know this resolve from the petitions the Merkes brothers went on to file with the local secular authorities. They appealed to the assembly (Landsdag) of regents, who were an authority separate from the consistory of the Calvinist church, and, in theory, more powerful than it, but only in purely secular matters. Clearly the Merkes brothers were not about to take a rejection at the hands of Dominees Broen and Haverkamp. The magistrates seemed favorably disposed, but the ministers opposed the petition. Eventually the stalemate was solved only when the Merkes brothers found another minister from outside of Nijmegen who admitted them to the Reformed church. They also went on to become officers in the Nijmegen lodge.[29] But the damage had been done, and the incident had become news all over the Republic.

We need now to explore what it was that so compelled these Nijmegen freemasons that they were prepared to challenge the local clergy and to provoke the concomitant concern of their family. As we have seen, membership in the first, and recently opened, lodge in Nijmegen could result in scorn and insult on a scale, and of a specifically religious kind, that was probably not as likely, or at least as serious, in the much larger city of Amsterdam, or certainly in Paris, in this period.[30] Yet in those places the lodges were also controversial. We can infer the charges leveled against the Dutch lodges from the defenses published at the time by freemasons in Nijmegen and Amsterdam. These reveal a great deal about the intellectual posture that the fraternity could assume in its new cultural setting, and also its relationship to contemporary Dutch culture. The masonic defenses of the 1750s will also eventually bring us back to the origins of Continental freemasonry, to the problem of exactly how, why, and by whom freemasonry was transmitted to the Dutch Republic, and what else, besides its rules and rituals, came with it. But that question of origins must continue to wait until we have explored the posture taken by this new society in the Republic, until we have tried to determine exactly what has been imported.

The guilds out of which freemasonry emerged in Scotland and England have been left behind. Although back in the seventeenth century an English gentleman mason may have been admitted to the guild of practicing masons in the Dutch city of Maastricht, that event, if it occurred, initiated no transformation in the admission practices of the Dutch stonemasons.[31] The Dutch guilds possessed a long and honorable history, and in some industries they were still forces to be reckoned with well into the eighteenth century.[32] But throughout Continental Europe, where guilds continued to flourish in many countries, the imported society of freemasons will not include hand workers. In The Netherlands, as elsewhere, the lodges became societies of the mercantile, the educated, the wellborn or newly risen, in short, of men, and eventually some women, of the professions, both civil and military, and, not least, of the aristocratic and the leisured. Yet even among men of high birth their membership in the fraternity could arouse deep hostility, even within their own families. The aristocratic Grand Master for the whole of Dutch masonry wrote to his brothers in 1761 to explain, "It will not be possible for me to take advantage of your gracious invitation . . . I will be staying with some relatives who have not been initiated in our sublime mysteries, and who even have terrible ideas about them."[33] Next we will try to figure out what some of those ideas might have been.

As they embraced a new sociability, these relatively elite brothers found themselves at odds with the upholders of other values, cultural but also, as the Nijmegen controversy reveals, political. Forced to defend themselves, the Nijmegen freemasons responded boldly to their accusers. Repeatedly they reiterated "their love and respectful awe for the Divinity,"[34] which is not the same thing, they observed, "as banishing all religion and daring to speak neither of God nor of the Commandments." Clearly it would appear they have been accused of doing just that. They defended their good manners against, it would seem, charges of excess, noting that "in all states, communities and assemblies" one can find the good and the bad.

But the freemasons also went after their attackers in language that reflected their own cultural and political values. They accused the consistory of the local church of acting, in effect, in an absolutist fashion, of "an usurpation of the legislative power," and of "laying the foundations of hierarchy and the Inquisition,"[35] both of which, in a clear reference to the revolution against Spain, their ancestors had struggled to shake off. They further accused the ministers of having a curious delicacy of conscience that would exclude the brothers Merkes from the local church but that could find nothing wrong with "the participants of the East and West Indies Companies who have a rapport with the slave trade."[36] This is a rare reference, however obliquely negative, to the slave trade, a topic seldom mentioned in Dutch publications of the period.

As for the danger supposedly presented to the state, the freemasons reiterated their loyalty. But then they asked their detractors to consider the true nature of the relationship between the polity and the governed. Is it not the case that the freemasons believe that subjects themselves decide the laws, bearing in mind that there must be a proper submission of inferiors to superiors? If there be doubt about the relationship between the governed and the well-ordered polity, "it is true, that the Revolutions in England have on more than one occasion shown this" to be the case.[37] This reference to the English revolutions, written by an anonymous hand, tied masonic beliefs and practices specifically to an English and revolutionary tradition.

By contrast, and in a reference to the recent revolution in 1747 in The

Netherlands, the freemasons accuse the Calvinist minister of having spoken of the restored stadtholder as a king, and having predicted the demise of the polity on the basis of an apocalyptic passage in the Bible.[38] These political beliefs, labeled authoritarian and reactionary, are linked by the masonic polemic to a local event, one particularly "incomprehensible and notorious." In 1716 a Jew in Nijmegen was accused of drinking the blood of a Christian child. The masonic rebuttal associates this bizarre calumny with the views of the Calvinist ministry,[39] who, in their ignorance and implied superstition, are the same people who dare to describe the freemasons as "atheists," "spinozists," and so forth.

This is a bold and self-confident polemic which sought to label the Calvinist ministry as the purveyors of popular superstition and absolutist politics. But in this polemic, the alternative form of political organization, implied to be government by contract between subjects and the state, is explicitly linked to the post-1689 constitutional order in England. Implicitly, the English system of centralized government is being preferred. Yet republican government is not repudiated. In the constant assertion that there is nothing in freemasonry contrary to "goede Politie" or "religie" or "goede Zeden" (good government, religion, and good morals), the freemasons were in fact articulating how they believed a "republican regime" (*republicainsche regeering*) should be governed. Freedom and the rule of law are the most prized masonic values; so, too, are the harmony and friendship of all men from a variety of ranks, both high and low, who assemble in the lodge. Once again, as in the British context, the government and society of the lodge are exalted as the model for good government and society.

This model of an ideal polity was being put forward, however, at a time of great anxiety in the Republic. By the 1750s it was plain for anyone to see that the former prosperity and "greatness" enjoyed by previous generations had all but disappeared among large sections of the population. The restoration of the stadtholder, William IV (d. 1751), as the result of a revolution in 1747, which in turn had been provoked by the French invasion of Zeeland, had done nothing to reverse the decline. Nor had the revolution significantly weakened the power of the oligarchy that controlled local and national government. In this context the masonic vision of good government could be inherently problematical, if not inherently reformist.

The controversy in Nijmegen was taken up by the Amsterdam freemasons. Indeed, the leading freemason of that city, Rousset, followed it with great interest.[40] In Amsterdam, however, issues of greater historical significance than simply the reputation of the Merkes brothers, or of the fraternity, are raised in the course of the polemic. As a result of the revolution in the Republic in 1747, the main lodge in Amsterdam had been closed down by the authorities. Some of its members had been infected by the radical democratic movement, which, in the wake of the revolution, had dominated the politics of the city, and which had as one of its leaders Jean Rousset de Missy, the master of that lodge.[41] Indeed, when the Amsterdam freemasons became involved in the Nijmegen controversy there was no official lodge in the city. Whether justly or unjustly, freemasonry in Amsterdam had been implicated in radical political agitation, if not in revolutionary upheaval.

In the confrontation of 1752 the Amsterdam freemasons were already politically suspect. But to those suspicions were added new ones, points of contention that

DE VRYE METSELAAR.

Uit het Hoogduits vertaalt.

TE DORDREGT,

BY ABRAHAM BLUSSÉ,

MDCCLIV.

FIG. 3. Title page from a Dutch masonic publication of 1754 illustrating the masonic use of female iconography. In this instance Minerva and the muses are invoked to illustrate masonic wisdom and enlightenment; Minerva is also a symbol of the Republic.

seemed to embrace most aspects of everyday life. Now the freemasons had also to deal with the specific accusation of freethinking and heresy—not necessarily because they were freethinkers, but because that charge seemed to be leveled against any foray into the civil, and hence the secular, that occurred outside the traditional local institutions of government.[42] A new manner of secular fraternizing, especially one that met in secret and that was organized around constitutional principles and egalitarian ideals, suggested an embrace of new values and beliefs, religious, political, and as we shall see, ethical.

We know about these suspicions and contentions between the Dutch freemasons and their critics only because of the denials published by the Amsterdam freemasons. They depicted their detractors as gripped by passions and prejudice, as overbearing and proud. In the masonic mind the detractors represent "the world," and its attempt to brand the ceremonies and secrets of freemasonry as childish and senseless, as "magical" and "talmudic."[43] From that quarter even more sinister accusations depict the brotherhood as wallowing in luxury and sensuality, claiming that "their stomachs are their God."

At issue between the detractors of freemasonry and its defenders, in the first instance, is worldliness. The freemasons denounce their accusers as blinded by the world, but by this they mean by ignorance. They depict themselves as healthy in relation to it, neither sheltered from it nor afraid to use the passions in the service of hard work or to address the needs of society.[44] We may deduce that these detractors are conventionally religious and puritanical, we are asked to believe, about their bodies. In a most telling phrase the difference between the freemason and people around him is described as being like the speaking of a different language.[45] This is not a quarrel about an abstract set of ideas, about "The Enlightenment" per se. This is a dispute about how to live in the world. This new and foreign form of sociability appears to have satisfied the need for a different set of ethical norms. The heart of the quarrel is with traditional values, in particular with traditional religiosity, in short with the values, mores, and beliefs of Dutch Calvinism.[46]

But more is in contention than lifestyles in the world, accepted in masonic rhetoric as problematic, as requiring thought to strike the right balance between body and soul, between reason and passion. One of the accusations against the freemasons is nothing less than that they have formed "a conspiracy of a Party"; they have threatened "civil unity."[47] Consonant with their treason they are atheists, naturalists, indifferentists, and guilty of one other "ism," too dangerous, or too embarrassing, to be named by the freemasons in their defense, and thus left simply as ". . . isten." Given what we know about Rousset de Missy's lifelong dedication to pantheism, could it be that? We will never know. But what we do know is either that these anonymous detractors have assigned the Amsterdam freemasons to the camp of the freethinkers, or that the freemasons themselves, in mentioning these particular forms of free thought, recognize the intellectual lineage of the ethical posture they have been accused of affecting. Other more sympathetic witnesses to the reputation of the fraternity at this time in the Republic tell us it was believed that this "philosophical company, at the same time religious . . . held . . . to a purified Deism."[48]

There are two most remarkable references to historical personages—given the time, place, and language—made by these Amsterdam freemasons as they attempt to ward off their detractors. In their defense they deny that they are denizens of "de sluypwinkels" (the back rooms) inhabited by the detractors of the Bible. They are not the followers of Matthew Tindal (d. 1733).[49] Nor, in matters of state policy, are they the followers of Alberto Radicati di Passerano (d. 1737). Both were notorious freethinkers of the early eighteenth century. The first was English, and never, as far as is known, even a visitor to the Republic. Yet a manuscript French translation of his famous book of Christianity, *Christianity as old as creation* (London, 1730), did circulate. A copy is to be found among the private papers of a close friend of Rousset de Missy, the journalist and encyclopedist Prosper Marchand.[50] The second name disavowed belonged to a radical Italian nobleman who died in The Hague.

In this masonic defense we have discovered two extraordinary references, names presumably known to both defenders and detractors, that take us directly back to the most radical elements in eighteenth-century political and religious culture. In the 1690s in London Tindal was a denizen of Toland's radical Whig coterie, and Toland later acquired something of a pan-European reputation as the infamous and deistical author who sought to reduce Christianity to the shape and form of a natural religion. Some of his deistic writing had been published in Dutch.[51] How much was known about Tindal's connections with the more famous (or infamous) Toland cannot be determined.

Radicati was a Italian naturalist and a materialist in matters religious. He had also been a virulent opponent of the Inquisition who had tried to convince the King of Sardinia to abolish it.[52] Finding himself in personal danger as a result of his political activities in Italy, in particular his advocacy of secular control over ecclesiastical affairs, Radicati fled to London around 1730. There he published outrageously pantheistic books for which he was arrested and imprisoned. All his London associations were with radical Whigs of republican inclination. Eventually, after being bailed out of jail, Radicati fled to The Hague only to die there in penury. But he did not lapse into quiet obscurity; his writings were well known and he was the object of gossip and attack. He supposedly made a deathbed recantation of his pantheism and died a member of the Walloon church. Dutch followers of the gossip that swirled around the freethinking coteries of this earlier period would have known about his irreligion and his political stance extolling civil religion and a strong central government capable of undermining the power of the clergy.[53] What is remarkable is the staying power of these reputations, well into the 1750s. Here we find them invoked in the next generation of polemics concerning the nature and meaning of the new secular and urban culture we now, in retrospect, describe as enlightened, and which was also, in this instance, masonic.

Having been tarred with the brush of freethinking and irreligion of a very specific historical variety, as well as with civil disorder, the Amsterdam freemasons offered a carefully worded, and overtly pious, defense. They respond that while they do not need theologians to discuss matters of religion, they also carefully avoid religious differences among themselves. "The Freemasons are not men . . . who seek to undermine the Christian religion and to bring Naturalism into the world. They have a very clear insight into the limitations of the Light of Nature."[54] They then indicate their agreement with the religious neutrality of the scientific societies in London, Berlin, Paris, and Rome, although they are quick to point out that they are not the same thing.[55] Instead their purpose is essentially ethical; it concerns how to live in the world. The Amsterdam freemasons recognized something about their sociability that we need to keep in mind. It was similar to the goals of the scientific and philosophical societies and yet it was different; it embraced the whole human being.

The Amsterdam freemasons characterize their detractors by using the mechanical analogy to a spring in a clock. Their pious opponents hold their bodies in check like a spring wound so tightly that the wheels and cylinders bend out of shape. Eventually they become like windmills with gears so tight that they ignite under the pressure of their furious rotation. By comparison, the freemason holds his body as a real part of his humanity; he loves himself wholly, he beautifies his body without disturbing his soul. Out of this self-love comes a love for humanity—for society—and in social experience lies the root of ethnical conduct.

The freemason does not count among his friends those who talk of humanity but do nothing for it; the goal of masonic fraternizing is service to humanity. The results of this idealism are palpable: The world is becoming a better place, more perfect, enhanced by new knowledge, new discoveries, new arts, and learning for which the freemasons are partly responsible. With this posture in the world we avoid pedantry and quackery.[56] With this posture, with this cultural stance, the freemasons believed that they served the general welfare of the Republic.

This was the rhetoric that Amsterdam freemasons employed in 1752 to justify themselves against their detractors. They saw their sociability in civic terms. Clearly the lodges are intended to be far more than drinking clubs, or centers for convivial conversation, although they were certainly those things as well. These justifications also show the seriousness with which the Dutch freemasons regarded their organization. The dues they paid, which were not insubstantial (see p. 137), the monthly or even biweekly meetings, the many publications and elaborate records and rituals should attest to that seriousness of purpose, but so too, and most important, should the language they used about themselves. In their communications among themselves, freemasons referred to their lodges as "enlightened," their order as "illustrious," and a master was "venerable."[57] They were being more than self-congratulatory.

To be serious about the cultivation of virtue and civic duty, or about progress toward human betterment, is not quite the same thing as seriousness about one's own governance, about the nature of political organization. The masonic impulse as transmitted from Britain to the Continent might have been idealist, even utopian, solely about the joys of sociability or the possibility of human progress, without necessarily, in this new setting, encompassing a search for the ideal civil polity. But as we shall see, Dutch freemasons took up that search. They concerned themselves with legitimacy in relation to the British Grand Lodge, as well as with their own lodges, and not least with the search for the harmony that stands as the model for the true civic polity. Within the confines of the Dutch lodges, which were no different from the other lodges of western Europe, proper governance, adherence to the constitution, to legitimate authority, to rules of order as well as deportment—these often dominated the proceedings. In this context the political meant the organization and legitimacy of this private polity, its civic life, and within it the living out and perfecting of a disciplined and improving social order.

This microcosmic relationship to the institutions of government, to the official polity, is explicitly stated in a manuscript history of the fraternity in The Netherlands that late eighteenth-century Dutch freemasons possessed. Their historian was Alexandre de Vignoles, by no means an ordinary brother. He had been a Deputy Grand Master in England, a signatory of a new copy of the *Constitutions* sent in 1770 by the British Grand Lodge to its Dutch brethren, and an extremely active brother in

The Netherlands who also traveled extensively in Germany and Italy on behalf of the order. He wrote interesting manuscript histories of freemasonry in Naples, Berlin, and Sweden, and the Neapolitan text is complete with lists of brothers and their occupations. His manuscript history of Dutch freemasonry, written in 1778, begins with a statement that directly relates its spirit, its search for wisdom, to the spirit that lies at the foundation of the main legislative body of the Dutch Republic, the Estates General: "The Royal Art of Masonry should rightly be an analogue to the spirit of sweetness and wisdom which stands at the base of the government of the Estates General of the United Provinces, for, victorious after [overcoming] the first obstacles, freemasonry has rapidly prospered."[58] Dutch freemasons self-consciously came to see their organization as analogous to the civil polity, as practicing the same virtues that rest as the foundation of its main legislative body, the Estates General. That was what de Vignoles said in his history. We might imagine that his meaning was metaphorical, that his hyperbole got the better of him. But we have evidence that de Vignoles meant exactly what he said.

When Dutch freemasons organized their national system of authority and governance, the Grand Lodge of The Netherlands established in The Hague in 1756, they adopted "the form" of the Estates General of the Republic. This body "forms the sovereign tribunal of the Nation," and it permits a degree of sovereignty and independence to the provinces that send representatives to it. These are the words of de Vignoles writing in his capacity as Provincial Grand Master in London, and attempting to deal with a rebellious lodge in Berlin in 1774. To encourage the members' obedience and their conformity with the Grand Lodge of Prussia, and hence with the London Grand Lodge, de Vignoles cited the older Dutch system of masonic governance as a model: "This wise republic took this form for the administration of the society."[59] Because Dutch freemasons were jealous of their "liberty," "all the states" assembled in 1756 and adopted this structure. In the masonic system of government, as described by de Vignoles, each lodge is a state within the masonic nation.

Perhaps we can now better understand the hostility with which the establishment of freemasonry was greeted in the 1730s by one of the provincial legislative bodies (the States of Holland). To be sure, the local legislators could not imagine that in 1756 this new society aspired to an organization intended to imitate a national representative assembly for the Republic, one that would be organized by province, or "state," yet a body that would be halfway between the older model of a Estates General, intended to represent provinces, and the classes within each province, and a newer, national assembly. Neither their opponents of the 1730s nor the first Dutch freemasons were clairvoyant. But they were shrewd enough to see that this originally British society brought with it a new political culture, one not very desirable from the opponents' point of view. It was a culture that sought to create representative institutions which could operate on a national level among men who believed themselves to be equals and who sought to practice virtues relevant to the needs and interests of the state. In 1778 de Vignoles told his brothers that freemasons are now established in the Republic and "all the lodges have only in their heart the interest of the state." Another Amsterdam orator made the same claim, adding only that this was because so many freemasons were in fact men who occupied high offices in the government of the Republic.[60] We can only wonder what would happen if men skilled in the private practice of self-government, not to mention politically skilled in general, chose not to give their allegiance to this state or any other.

As de Vignoles's history indicates, the successful establishment of freemasonry in the Republic had been a slow process. Even after the protection offered by the restored stadtholder, William IV, and under the leadership of the Baron van Wassenaer, who, as this history mentions, sought to institute lodges for both men and women (see chapter 5), the state viewed the fraternity with suspicion. At one point, presumably in the early 1750s, "some goods and books" (*des meubles et des livres*) belonging to the order were confiscated. Yet, for reasons that are not made clear, the prohibition against freemasonry was never enforced with rigor. Encouragement continued to come from the Grand Lodges in London and in Scotland. Slowly the Dutch lodges multiplied. Various Dutch aristocrats assumed leadership of the lodges, among them Count Bentinck, a prominent Orangist active in the revolution of 1747 (see pp. 129–30). In their search to give stability to society the freemasons, we are told, "hold equally dear a brother who is zealous, and distinguished in the republic by the illustriousness of his birth and by the credit that is assured him by his virtues."[61] As de Vignoles makes clear, the links with British freemasonry remained strong, but by the late 1750s an indigenous institution has come into being. In 1756 the British Grand Master, the Marquis of Carnarvan, "authorized them [the Dutch lodges] to form and establish at The Hague a National Grand Lodge for the Estates General of the United Provinces generally and the dependent colonies."[62]

Once the government of Dutch freemasonry was put in place, eventually all lodges—although, as we shall see (p. 101), not without some negotiation and dissension—recognized the sovereignty of the national Grand Lodge. To do so members placed their hands on a book that included either "the constitutions of the society or the principles of the right of Nature."[63] In effect they entered into a contract with the Grand Lodge. Meetings of this new Grand Lodge opened with brothers saluting the Estates General and the hereditary stadtholder.[64]

Despite opposition, of both a political and religious origin, this new and secular form of civil society was firmly established in the Republic by the late 1750s. By the early 1760s it was beginning to speak about itself within a "national" context governed by its own constitution or by the rights of nature. Yet in some quarters freemasons continued to be attacked as "deists," or "atheists," and as "rebels" (*oproermaakers*).[65] The lodges were seen as training grounds (*een kweekschool*) for heresy and tumult. There was nothing particularly new in these accusations. What is interesting is their staying power and what they tell us about how the pious may have viewed these secular festivities well into the 1780s.

Language about "the nation" and "the rights of nature," found in masonic minutes and records, was, however, new to its age. In these private societies the words were applied to an operative system of civil governance. At the monthly proceedings of the main Amsterdam lodge, which resumed in 1754 and continued throughout the century, we shall see that system in operation, and I shall suggest that its form owed something to Rousset's midcentury reading of John Locke (see chapter 4). Given the implications of such language and behavior for the subsequent development of Western theories and practices of government, perhaps before we visit individual lodges, we need now, finally, to take one more look at the origins of these small private societies in Continental Europe.

The Matter of Continental Origins

Freemasonry in Continental Europe evoked the specter of freethinking, of atheism and pantheism. We must remember that these accusations were always quite serious, not just in The Netherlands but in any European country. Positions in the professions, in teaching, or in government service were lost if an officeholder was suspected of extreme heterodoxy. This was the fate of a teacher in the academy at Deventer, a town in the Dutch Republic, in the second decade of the century.[66] Indeed, in the 1780s as part of the "enlightened" reforms enacted by Joseph II in the Austrian territories, among them the southern Netherlands, the punishment for deism was either deportation or flogging.[67] By comparison to its southern neighbor, the Dutch Republic was relatively tolerant. We should hardly be surprised to find that it is no easy matter to recover the history of such beliefs. Even where the Inquisition did not exist, these were still private matters.

If we were to look at the "official" histories of European freemasonry, largely written in this century, no mention is made of such heterodox elements being present in the early, or even subsequent, history of eighteenth-century freemasonry. Those histories, quite rightly, follow the extant documentation that is available in the records of the lodges themselves. These refer to meetings, elections, dues, and so forth; they make no reference to religious doctrines or debates. The *Constitutions* of 1723 specified only that if a freemason "rightly understands the Art, he will never be a stupid Atheist, nor an irreligious Libertine." Yet it also asked that a freemason subscribe "to that Religion in which all men agree, leaving their particular opinions to themselves." With these ambiguous statements the Grand Lodge of London left the matter of religious beliefs. Meeting records from both Britain and the Continent are silent on the subject, making only occasional reference to the "Grand Architect of the Universe."

In Britain the official records begin with the founding in London of the Grand Lodge in 1717, born out of four London lodges that in turn owe their origin to the masons' guild in that city. Official masonic English (but not Scottish) history begins with that date. The history of the actual transition in England to speculative freemasonry, the society of London gentlemen documented in Anderson's *Constitutions* (1723), appears lost forever. The English guild records simply have not survived. What remains of the seventeenth-century English history of freemasonry resides in manuscript fragments, at least one of which has only recently turned up.[68]

This early English masonic document dates from 1659 and can be found in the library of the Royal Society in London. Given what I discussed in chapter 1 about the links between the masonic guilds and early fellows of the Society, the manuscript's location should not surprise us. It contains a long rendition of the various signs and words used by practicing masons by which they could identify one another. But mixed into the account is the text of the mason's oath which requires that a brother "keep all that we or your attenders shall be you keep secret, from Man, Woman, or Child, Stock or Stone, and never reveal it but to a Brother or in a Lodge of free mason, and truly observe the Charges in the Constitution." These working masons make mention of their constitution and then recount a fanciful history of their governance that goes back to medieval times when they had an assembly or parliament. Their ancient status and respectability, it is claimed, derive from their knowledge of geometry, the chief of all the liberal sciences, a knowledge which can be traced back to Hermes, the ancient "father of wisdom." Also, in medieval times the lodges were given a charter by the king and his "counsell," which is here identified as a parliament. Masons were then also paid real wages. This manuscript perhaps tells us more about the 1650s, the rise of parliament, and the prevalence of wage earning, than it does about the medieval origins of the freemasons. What is important about it lies in the early references to forms of political governance that we associate with the seventeenth-century revolution.

By contrast to documents such as the Royal Society manuscript stands Anderson's 1723 account of the transition from operative to speculative freemasonry—an account which is sketchy and terse. Based on this, masonic histories have tended to focus on certain benchmarks which, it is claimed, denote the appearance of true speculative freemasonry. Among them, and most important, is the use of certain terms, particularly "constitutions" and "Grand Master." These appear first, it is argued, only in 1717. Prior to that date, masonry, again argued from Anderson, was essentially artisanal or operative and had nothing to do with constitutionalism. Any society or coterie using such terms could not, therefore, be masonic in the eighteenth-century meaning of that term. What is usually missed in the discussion is the obvious: Early eighteenth-century English masonic usage of the term "constitution," was uniquely modern because it derived from the seventeenth-century revolution.[69] As the 1659 document illustrates, by that time the constitution had come to mean the laws and customs by which a community agrees to be governed. That modern usage is what the English lodges meant by their 1723 constitutions and that is what was transmitted to the Continent.

The contentions in official histories about every masonic term and its possible use before 1717 (and the circuitous logic they employ), would be solely of antiquarian interest were it not for the problem of trying to piece together how, and by whom, freemasonry was transmitted to the European Continent. Knowing all the agents involved in this transmission would help to clarify what other British "heresies," aside from constitutional and representative government, might also have been transmitted in the earliest lodges. English, that is, Newtonian, science might have been among the values transmitted by brothers such as the Newtonian experimenter, Jean Desaguliers.[70] In the 1730s when he was active on the Continent most literate people were Cartesians, if they were adherents at all of the new science. Similarly, before Voltaire became famous in the 1730s as the great heretic and deist that he was, the most important variety of irreligion, aside from spinozism, was what contemporaries in the first decades of the century called English freethinking, or English deism. Could the lodges, or early Continental societies that imitated them, have been places where men discussed such forbidden ideas?

The problem of origins is germane to the story unfolding here and in the chapters ahead, because the issue of heterodox religious beliefs and values makes its appearance early in Continental masonic history, so early as to suggest the presence of tendencies toward the heretical. It was also a charge that would never go away. We now know that the ethical values espoused by freemasons were at moments actually different, not just perceived as being different, from those held by other, more traditional, elements in any eighteenth-century society. Talk about merit, about the light of Nature, about natural rights, about the rights of the governed was not idle. It was part of a new culture that originated in Britain. We return to the question: Who brought it to the Continent?

There is every reason to accept the assertion that the first fully formed lodge in Continental Europe met in Rotterdam as early as 1721. We know about it because as a result of the 1735 prohibition against freemasonry, issued by the States of Holland, five Rotterdam freemasons, "all persons from the English and Scottish nation," came forward and testified that their lodge had been in existence for some fourteen years, hence 1721 or 1722.[71] Almost certainly these men were merchants given the close trading ties that existed in this period between Rotterdam and Scotland.[72] There is no evidence, however, that this lodge transcended its foreign origins and set down roots in the Dutch community by initiating Dutch members. Its existence is important because it pushes back the date for the appearance of this British export. It also suggests the distinct possibility of informal, or not officially affiliated, masonic gatherings in Continental Europe prior to the 1730s. For example, the official establishment of freemasonry in the Austrian Netherlands (i.e., Belgium) occurs in the second half of the century. But we know that there were unofficial lodges in Brussels, or, at least, freemasons there, from a much earlier date.[73] In 1756 Rousset de Missy stated that there had been lodges in Brussels ("it was considerable and had been established—the Duke of Ursel was master"), Liège, and Antwerp.[74]

The association of the Duke of Ursel with freemasonry makes sense. He had had contact with the English alliance against France through his service with the Austrians. As governor in Namur in the 1730s he challenged the authority of the local nobility and clergy. In short, by the standards of the day he was a reformer.[75] In Liège in 1744 a local curé wrote anxiously to Rome to signal that freemasons had appeared in the town and to ask what he should do about it. The lodge may very well have been a military one composed of French soldiers who were in occupation at that moment. German lodges date from the late 1730s and the 1740s, while in Catholic Europe, after the papal condemnation of 1738, the development of masonic socializing was real, although fitful and easily curtailed.[76] In short, early masonic history is no straightforward matter.

As the evidence now stands, we know more about the Rotterdam lodge of 1721 than we do about one that supposedly existed in Paris around the same time. Composed of English and Irish followers of the Stuart cause, the Paris lodge dating from 1725 or 1726 may be the first of a long line of French lodges where Jacobite exiles became prominent.[77] Indeed, the association of Jacobitism hangs about the earliest known French lodges, as does the contradictory association, that of sponsorship by the highest levels of official British, and hence Whig, representation in Paris, in particular Lord Waldegrave, ambassador in the 1730s.[78] In the 1730s and

1740s French Jacobite freemasons were active on behalf of the Stuart pretender, a fact known to the governments on both sides of the Channel.[79] Obviously there were reasons why freemasons in Paris or elsewhere on the Continent, particularly in these early years, might want to maintain a low profile. Finally, to complicate the origins of Continental freemasonry even further and to illustrate the danger of relying on "official" masonic history, we have testimony from the next generation of British masonic officers, the historian de Vignoles, introduced earlier in this chapter, that there were lodges in Saxony in 1729 and Russia in 1731.[80]

We can say with confidence only that enough evidence exists to suggest that by the 1730s masonic lodges were popping up all over western Europe, often sponsored by official representatives of the British government or by their Jacobite opponents. Hanoverian Britons were especially active in the Low Countries; the Jacobites seem more prominent in Catholic Europe. All carried with them British political culture and mores, and in the Low Countries the earliest lodges tended to be pro-British or at least supportive of the Anglo-Austrian alliance.

Waldegrave was not the only Whig involved in the Continental establishment of freemasonry. The first official lodge on the Continent, which opened at The Hague in 1731, included Lord Chesterfield, the British ambassador, as well as the ubiquitous Newtonian lecturer and liberal churchman, Jean Desaguliers.[81] These were court placemen, Whigs identified with the Hanoverian Succession and the Walpolean ministry. What they had in common with Jacobite exiles, even newly converted ones like Lord Wharton in Paris (he had once been a Whig and the London Grand Master), was their dedication to political causes, however fundamentally different. These were men with political agendas and, in the case of Desaguliers, with cultural ones as well. In public lectures he transmitted Newtonian mechanics as part of a cultural package that included its application to industry. He self-consciously aimed his lectures at the genteel and leisured, who subscribed to them in numerous Dutch cities.[82] He was also possibly the first person to articulate the relationship among applied mechanics, labor-saving devices, and profit.[83] With this progressive package came a dedication to various Whig aristocrats and the Hanoverian cause, as well as a fervent commitment to freemasonry that especially included an eagerness to initiate men of high birth into the order. On the Continent attraction to this particular society with these political and cultural associations implied an openness to mixing with men of different religions, probably an interest in the new science, and, in a Dutch context, possibly a certain discontent with local magistrates or regents. They were seen to be pro-French and anti-Orangist or, at best, neutral to the alliance between Britain and the Low Countries which after 1714 included the Austrians and the maintenance, at no small expense, of the barrier fortresses intended to protect the Low Countries from French invasion. At the first official lodge meeting on the Continent to be recognized by the Grand Lodge—in 1731 at The Hague—Francis, duke of Lorraine, royal representative of the Austrian Hapsburgs, was initiated. In the same year he was supposedly introduced to masonry at the home of Walpole, Houghton Hall.[84]

Ever since the Revolution of 1688–89 and the crowning of the Dutch stadtholder, William of Orange, British interests on the Continent saw the Low Countries as critical. To preserve that interest various agents and spies had represented one ministry or another, with members of the Whig party, particularly drawn from its radical and deeply anti-French fringe, often recruited or self-appointed to the task of preserving and strengthening the alliance. One such unofficial envoy was the English freethinker of republican inclinations, John Toland.

With him and his kind the Continental story of freemasonry starts to get both complicated and intriguing. Toland (1670–1722) was as extraordinary as he was controversial. He was one of the most heretical thinkers of his age, and although erratic, he established quite a reputation in his time and well beyond. In the Dutch Republic a gossipy and somewhat outrageous journal of the period made reference to him as if he were a household name.[85] Toland left behind in his papers a curious document, handwritten in French and dated "The Hague, 1710." Mercifully, it is also signed. Quite simply it is a two-page meeting record of "an order" that called itself the Knights of Jubilation (as written in the text, "Chapitre General des Chevaliers de la Jubilation"). This order, clearly libertine and playful, also possessed "tres gaillardes et joyeuses *Constitutions*"—meaning "the statutes and rules of our order"—called its members "brothers," and was headed by a "Grand Master."[86] These are most unusual terms to be found together in 1710 in any language, but especially in French, and not least in The Hague, among a group of men the majority of whom were French Huguenot refugees.[87]

The use of the term "constitutions," although written in French, was intended in this context to carry the British meaning of rules for an organization. The document is written in the hand of one of the refugees and signers, Prosper Marchand. Clearly he and his other brothers, as they called themselves, had learned a new meaning for "constitutions." Since to the best of our knowledge none of them had ever been to England, how then did they learn that meaning? Other letters from members of this group have been preserved in Dutch libraries and these indicate that they also belonged to another little club—or at least some of them did—that guarded what it called "the Secret." As this linguistic plot thickens, keep in mind that the earliest translations of "lodge" into French used the words "l'ordre" or "société."[88]

Manuscripts like the one Toland left behind in his papers turn up only rarely in historical research. They are rare because they contradict an accepted story line. They are anomalous; they do not "fit" anywhere and not surprisingly they become the subject of historical controversy. When I first published the manuscript some years ago as an appendix to *The Radical Enlightenment* (1981) I argued that freemasonry offered the best explanation of what was going on at the meeting held by the Knights. A few historians disagreed; others just did not know what to do with the problem; still others agreed. Without dwelling unduly on all the arguments, I will summarize what can now best be said about the meaning of Toland's private record keeping.

The language employed in the document Toland preserved is masonic. There is simply no other explanation for this cluster of terms to appear in what is clearly a meeting record. Of course, the problem with asserting the masonic character of the text is that it presumes that prior to 1717 there were London gentlemen and their associates who were familiar with the transformation occurring within the old guilds. They had begun to use terms like "constitutions" and "grand master" prior to that language being put into print by Anderson in 1723. And not least, through various English travelers—in this instance probably Toland himself—they had exported their knowledge onto the Continent. Existing evidence supports this set of circumstances explaining the masonic nature of the Knights of Jubilation, bearing in mind that they may not have fully realized all of its cultural antecedents.

One very rare version of the masonic *Constitutions,* printed by a London Whig publisher, stated in passing that the "Orders and Constitutions" had been agreed upon in 1663.[89] Still other of the earliest English publications about the freemasons, but not put out by the official Grand Lodge, claimed that "no Constituted Lodges or Quarterly Communications were heard of till 1691, when Lords and Dukes, Lawyers and Shopkeepers, and other inferior Tradesmen, Porters not excepted, were admitted into this Mystery."[90] And there is other evidence for English (as opposed to Scottish) activity earlier than 1717 including the involvement of the architect and fellow of the Royal Society, Christopher Wren. In 1774 the historian de Vignoles informed a rebellious lodge in Berlin about the early history of the London Grand Lodge. He stated that

> Sir Christopher Wren, famous architect, keeper of the king's fortresses, member of Parliament, had been elected in 1710 for the second time Grand Master of the Society. He held the chair until 1716. At that time the brothers realised that at the age of 88 [Wren was born in 1632 and would in fact have been 84] he was not able to oversee their conduct. They resolved to unify themselves and to give him a successor. One only found four regular [lodges] in London; they assembled and represented brother Wren by the Master of the oldest lodge.[91]

If de Vignoles gave an accurate account, and he is quite self-conscious in the letter about saying that this information extends Anderson's history, then we can push the establishment of the London Grand Lodge back to at least 1710, if not earlier. Decades before de Vignoles wrote to Berlin, a Deputy Grand Master in London wrote almost casually in 1757 to a Dutch officer and mentioned Wren as the predecessor to the first Grand Master listed in Anderson's official history.[92]

Thus it would seem that we can date the beginning of organized English freemasonry to sometime during the reign of Anne (d. 1714). That may be mildly interesting to lovers of dates, but there is more at stake here than a date. Knowing the dates and the people involved helps us uncover an aspect of early Enlightenment culture both in Britain and on the Continent. We should focus for a moment on the relationship between the beliefs and practices of a radical freethinker like Toland and the beliefs and practices that could find expression in the new sociability. Toland searched all his life for an alternative to the Christianity of his day. He also possessed an interest in rituals of all kinds (in 1711 he claimed to a Continental correspondent in The Hague that he himself was devising a "new" ritual). It would now appear that his interest extended to the new masonic lodges.

Toland was an inventor of rituals for what he called his "Socratic Brotherhood." These were what he sent to The Hague, if not elsewhere. He was a known visitor in the Dutch Republic, and even before being translated into French, his deistic writings were available in Dutch as early as 1710.[93] He also knew and spoke French. We know that in London Toland associated with the Whig politician Sir Robert Clayton, who, it is believed, had masonic affiliations. From him Toland could easily enough have learned about masonic practices and terminology. There may also have been other sources for Toland's fanciful excursions into the creation of fraternal rituals. In Whig circles various private clubs with ritualistic and libertine overtones were fashionable, particularly after 1689 (see p. 69). The Kit-Cat Club called its members "Knights" and had a "president" who taught "What faith the priests of all Religions hold."[94] In 1711 it sponsored a large public procession through the streets of London that culminated in the burning of an effigy of the pope.[95]

All of these experiences could have been sources for the imported terminology employed by the Knights of Jubilation. And if the document from The Hague found in Toland's possession were dated twenty years later, say 1730, we would also have no trouble connecting the men at this meeting with early and official Dutch freemasonry. The writer of the meeting record, Prosper Marchand, was a long-time and intimate friend of Rousset de Missy, the master of the Amsterdam lodge La Bien Aimée. Rousset's name appears in the official roster of brothers in 1734. He was one of the principal architects of the movement, becoming the master of La Bien Aimée before its disbanding in 1749 (see chapter 4). Thus the link between Toland and the Knights of Jubilation leads from Marchand to Rousset, and hence to the earliest official history of freemasonry in Continental Europe. Indeed, one of Rousset's first publications was a translation of freethinking works by Collins and Toland.

The link between the Knights and organized freemasonry, and one of its main Continental leaders, Rousset, rests on a variety of evidence, both personal and intellectual. By the 1750s Rousset and Marchand were old men, and the original members of the Knights of Jubilation were long dispersed. Toward the end of their lives, Rousset wrote with affection and candor to Marchand about the religion of Nature, or as Rousset called it in the letter, his "pantheism." But the open use of the word, with its blatantly atheistic associations, was rare as well as it is historically important. The word "belonged" to Toland. He had first used it in 1705 to describe his creed, and few would openly acknowledge their allegiance to such a secular and heretical creed unless they were conversing privately with someone deeply sympathetic, if not converted. In their last years Rousset also asked Marchand to salute a mutual friend "by the fraternal number," that is, in the ritual masonic manner of a triple embrace. This was the same form of address Rousset used in his correspondence with his lodge brothers, and from it we can conclude that Marchand, once a playful Knight in 1710, had somewhere along the way become a faithful brother.[96]

The fact that the leading freemason in Amsterdam was also a self-described pantheist shows his deep familiarity with English freethinking as transmitted by John Toland. Freemasonry originated in England, and so too did freethinking as the term was used in the early eighteenth century to describe Toland, Tindal, and their associate Anthony Collins, who popularized it in *A Discourse of Freethinking* (1713). Toland knew the Knights—how else did he get their private meeting record and leave it among his manuscripts—and Rousset embraced a religion of Nature which Toland had made famous or, more precisely, infamous.

What conclusions can we now draw from these rather remarkable connections? Should we, for instance, argue that all the lodges in Rotterdam and The Hague in the 1720s and 1730s sprang from the Knights, hence from a milieu deeply heretical, not to mention, because of Toland's radical Whiggery, deeply political? The available evidence does not warrant such a conclusion. But it does permit us to say that the most important Dutch freemason of midcentury, Rousset, learned his freethinking—more precisely his pantheism—and probably his dedication to Whig causes from a particularly subversive English source. The term "pantheism" was unique to Toland and, when using it, Rousset described his own deeply held convictions.

The associations between the Knights of Jubilation, Toland and Rousset, once uncovered, make the linguistic detective work worthwhile. They enable us to illustrate subversive aspects of eighteenth-century sociability in its masonic form that might otherwise have remained obscure. At its origins Continental freemasonry possessed associations with a new secular culture, one tied completely to this world with only a passing interest, if even a belief, in the next. Let us be clear. By no means would all, or even most, European freemasons ever deal with the full implications of their secularism, or probably even realize that it could take its followers to the point of believing, as did Rousset, that death was merely a "falling asleep."[97] These were metaphysically extreme positions, generally articulated only by men with philosophical interests and abilities, by those whom the age deemed philosophes. Yet holding to them entailed a certain hypocrisy if one sat in a church pew. Meeting for fellowship in one of the new masonic lodges would have entailed far less discomfort. There is a streak of freethinking or deism that turns up at moments in the history of Continental freemasonry right into, and especially during the 1790s (see p. 174). We now know that this tendency had its origins in the British political culture out of which masonic sociability emerged.

For most men the lodges were simply centers of conviviality and fellowship, places of order and decorum, where profound social differences were mediated, allowed for, and even accorded deference, where men were rewarded for virtue, and their supposed equality was justified by an ideology of merit. On the Continent these were private societies creating a different kind of public space from that found in the guild hall, or the Estates, or at court, or in the town councils, or in the chambers of a king's representative. Of course frequenters of all those places could be found in one or another European lodge. The social and historical origins of their masonic behavior came, however, not from family life or churches, but rather from the guild practices of protective craft communities as transformed by English and Scottish gentlemen accustomed to elections and constitutions.

But the intellectual origins of their behavior, whether even known or acknowledged, had roots just as subversive that stretched back to the philosophical naturalism unleashed by the intellectual revolution of the seventeenth century. Published in Amsterdam in the 1740s and dedicated to the English freethinker Anthony Collins, an atheistic tract called *Le Philosophe* drew out the most extreme implications of that earlier philosophical revolution. Atheists, it claimed, now see "the existence of God [as] the most widespread and deeply engrained of all the prejudices." In its place the enlightened man, the philosophe, puts civil society, "[as] the only divinity that he will recognize on earth."[98] The message in this clandestine tract was blatantly materialist, or pantheist, if we prefer Toland's word. By the time it was published its subversive message and the accompanying metaphysics imbued literate culture in western Europe.[99] In the 1750s a masonic orator, himself a French philosophe, the abbé Claude Yvon (see p. 159) called upon his brothers in Amsterdam to become "philosophes." If they ever did so in the subversive way the anonymous *Philosophe* meant, they embraced what the more radical of the English freethinkers preached. The historian Franco Venturi described the spirit of the English Revolution as transmitted by the freethinkers: It was "lived again in non-mysterious Christianity, in pantheism, in free-thinking, in a whole series of attempts to renew on a different plane the 'Good Old Cause' as the English Commonwealthmen like Toland and Collins called the republican ideals of the Revolution."[100]

Probably our Nijmegen freemasons had no idea that they were doing anything so heady as worshiping a new god, or as subversive as embracing the cause of a distant, century-old revolution. Yet in their ceremonies mention of the old god is noticeably absent. And when pressed by the clergy even the Nijmegen freemasons could display a disturbing hostility toward established authority. In the place of traditional pieties, freemasons throughout Europe placed emphasis on dedication to society and on being sociable men.[101] In place of the word 'God' they put the Grand Architect of the Universe, and his main task was to be invoked formally, and infrequently. Originally he had been an imported deity, of English and Newtonian origin, but his purpose was easily reconciled to that assigned the godhead by Continental spinozism or by deism as popularized in the writings of Voltaire. Perhaps we can now better understand the trials and tribulations of the Nijmegen brothers. We now understand why almost instinctually a local Calvinist minister, spying the new fraternity in his precinct, charged the followers of its new deity, however unfairly in this instance, with "godlessness."

4

Creating Constitutional Societies

The early years of the masonic fraternity on the Continent were plagued by disputes engendered largely by ecclesiastical authorities, both Protestant, as was the case in Nijmegen, and Catholic. But controversy was never solely the work of antimasonic publicists external to the lodges. The task of establishing these new, constitutionally governed societies also brought with it crises over legitimacy and authority, and not least, over national identity as the fraternity spread far and away from the London Grand Lodge. The records of Dutch freemasonry, once again, richly illustrate this phenomenon. They permit us to watch the tensions and uncertainties of the fraternal participants in this new and unique form of social and political behavior. As one example, we shall focus on the disagreements that arose between the most historically important Dutch lodge, located in Amsterdam and called (after 1754) La Bien Aimée, and the national Grand Lodge in The Hague.

Woven into their disputes were issues about the nature of true masonic government and, more precisely, about the validity or legitimacy of the masonic constitution. Amid these disputes we can also witness some of the first efforts made on the Continent—if only in a private, voluntary setting—to exercise a form of self-government. Within the confines of private sociability the abstractions found in some of the favorite texts of the Enlightenment, from Locke through Montesquieu, and not least Voltaire—who praised all things English—may take on for us a more textured meaning, one lived as well as read. In this chapter and in subsequent ones we look to the Enlightenment as it was lived in the new Continental lodges.

The new lodges, both in Britain and on the Continent, were never simply private fraternal societies; they were also, as we saw in chapter 1 in the case of the Dundee lodge, constitutionally governed and legitimized civic societies. Predictably, within their private deliberations can also be found overtones of larger national and international issues about which brothers appear to have had deep disagreement. In the microcosmic polity constituted by a lodge, values and issues drawn from the larger society were debated and negotiated, social place and rank were adjudicated, and the nature of authority was questioned and resolved. In the Dutch lodges, events in the political experience of the Republic at midcentury played into, exacerbated, and possibly even at moments caused this atmosphere of internal controversy. The records of La Bien Aimée, as well as other Dutch lodges, permit us to reconstruct the fluidity between the private and the public, just as they also reveal the tension between the desire for orderly masonic government and the autonomy of individual lodges, between obedience to the national authority of the Grand Lodge and rebellion against it.

Two events in the history of the Dutch Republic provide the background: the Revolution of 1747–48, which restored the stadtholderate, and the so-called Diplomatic Revolution of 1756, which broke the historic alliance between the Republic and its British and Austrian allies, leading the Austrians into an alliance with France. In that same year Dutch freemasons established their independence from the Grand Lodge of London, creating a "national" Grand Lodge in The Hague. Similarly, the Revolution of 1747–48 directly involved the leading freemason of Amsterdam, Jean Rousset de Missy, and his lodge La Bien Aimée.

Only one national state—as distinct from city or colony—experienced a revolution in the long century between 1689 in England and the outbreak of revolutions in 1787 and then 1789 in western Europe. The Dutch Revolution of 1747 not only restored the stadtholderate, but it also extended to radical protests against the corruption of the Republic. These protests were most pronounced and violent in Amsterdam in 1748. One of the leaders of the radical movement, called the Doelistenbeweging, was Rousset de Missy, the founder of freemasonry in Amsterdam in 1735. He began his public political involvement in the Revolution of 1747 as a publicist and official historian for the Orangist cause and the new stadtholder, William IV.[1] In this political role, Rousset most often followed directions from William Bentinck, a key advisor to William IV and himself a freemason.

In response to the confusion provoked by the French invasion of Zeeland, which, in turn, prompted the sudden restoration of the stadtholderate, Rousset, working in the service of Bentinck, briefly contemplated in 1748 bringing out a new edition of the French text of John Locke's *Two Treatises of Government.*[2] Presumably the edition was meant to justify the revolution just as, it was believed, Locke's text had justified the Revolution of 1688 over a half-century earlier, in England. But in 1748 the project came to naught. However, I shall be arguing later in this chapter that Locke's ideas on government may have been put to other uses by Rousset and his masonic brothers when in 1755–56 they attempted to reconstitute and revitalize their lodge. In that same year Rousset, and his publisher and masonic brother Johan Schreuder, finally brought out the new, and slightly altered, edition of the French version of the *Two Treatises.*[3] The one project fed into the other. Rousset's dedication to an idealized version of English constitutional government found expression both in his work as a journalist, translator, and editor and in his leadership of the lodge.

In 1749 Rousset's lodge (named at that time Lodge de la Paix) had been closed down by the authorities. Their action cannot be separated from the events of the previous two years. By 1748 Rousset had become an agent out of control. He allied himself with rebellious artisans and small shopkeepers in Amsterdam who believed that the revolution had not gone far enough. Their demands ranged from an abolition of various privileges and monopolistic practices of the oligarchic regents to an assault on other monopolistic economic practices, namely, the privileges of the guilds.[4] On this last point, the movement was by no means united. What evidence we have suggests that Rousset sided with the more radical fringe of the Doelisten, with the advocates of a free market in wages as well as offices. Among the more radical demands of the Doelisten that command our attention are their "progressive" advocacy of free-market principles; industry (not simply trade) as the basis of economic life; the application of mechanical principles and practices to manufacturing; and the harnessing of scientific knowledge as promoted in the scientific academies.[5]

In the mid-eighteenth century the linking of these causes to political agitation, petition, riot, and open defiance was strikingly new in Continental Europe. Predictably the authorities were alarmed and moved quickly to exploit differences among the radicals, as well as to liberalize access to office holding, particularly in Amsterdam.[6] The Doelisten were outmaneuvered and defeated; for his part in their activities, Rousset was exiled in 1749. But the memory of the radicalism that surfaced in 1747–48 continued to haunt Dutch politics in the 1750s, if not beyond. The masonic lodge of which Rousset had been master and founder—for which, as he boasted, many other Dutch lodges derived—had also been deeply troubled by the revolution. As its records reveal, "The *burgerlijke* unrest in 1748 had influenced our lodge. Some of our brothers were susceptible to it, others were offended by it and most were indignant about it."[7]

This is the background for the reconstitution of La Bien Aimée in 1755 and for the political thought woven into its history. In that year its leading spokesman was a publisher and friend of Rousset, Johan Schreuder. At the moment they produced the new edition of Locke, they were also struggling to reestablish the order and government of their lodge. That fact, coupled with La Bien Aimée's "rebellious" posture in relation to the authority of the new Grand Lodge, permits us to argue for a correlation between masonic political behavior and the liberal political theory embedded in Locke's treatise and championed by so many eighteenth-century Continental reformers.

La Bien Aimée in 1755

In 1755 Rousset's lodge saw itself as persecuted by the larger society, by "a slanderous public, evil-minded hypocrites, prejudiced writers, frightened rulers, cursed Inquisition, thundering Vaticans, and booming Preachers."[8] In the history of "our days," as Johan Schreuder lectured to his brothers on the annual feast day in late 1755, could be added the "blackened reputations of the Vatican and the Inquisition, the names of the cities of Amsterdam and Nijmegen." In the past few years, since its closing, he continued, the lodge has been like a "hunted bird [*verjaagd vogeltje*]." Our only joy comes from the contemplation of ourselves. Only recently, he continued, the brothers had been "like sheep without a shepherd," but now "after receiving proper and legal authority," we joyfully reopened our lodge as "legal members of a legal lodge."[9]

Schreuder's obsessive concern is to assert "the legal"—to use his own words—existence of his reconstituted lodge, and to affirm its legality by pointing to the growth in membership and, more important, to the fact that other lodges recognize it. Indeed, even freemasons from other countries visit the lodge and sign its visitors' book. Legality and hence legitimization, he asserts, are provided by "the representatives" of other lodges, and these in turn receive a "legal reception" from La Bien Aimée.[10] The law that Schreuder refers to here has nothing to do with the laws of the country. These are laws and legality being created in the private realm by men for other men, by the lodges themselves.

Masonic law was taken most seriously by the brothers. In 1756 when the reconstituted lodge was quarreling with the Grand Lodge in The Hague over allegiance to it, what was at stake between them were what they described as legitimization and sovereignty, the rule of laws and the nature of duly constituted authority. In this instance, the legitimization of the lodge, of this new civil society, depends more upon its legality than upon its traditions, or upon the quality and birthright of its masters. By the 1760s the Grand Lodge would extend its legal prerogatives nationally and assume the power to adjudicate between "plaintiffs" and "defendants," even awarding damages to the defendant when he was absolved "of the accusations against his person."[11]

The 1755 minutes of La Bien Aimée's meetings bear out the relevance of Schreuder's oration about legitimacy. In late 1754 members of the disbanded lodge met, "consulted and deliberated with each other," and decided "to request . . . that the Very Venerable Master, Brother Rousset de Missy, out of his power and authority, by an authentic document (or certificate), would grant and authorize them to form a regular lodge . . . and would, for his part, appoint a Brother . . . in his name and for his part, to reopen the closed lodge, to form the brothers into a legal lodge and, in person, to act as their Venerable and Master."[12] Accordingly, Schreuder wrote to Rousset, still exiled in a small town outside of Utrecht, and asked his permission to reopen the lodge. He responded with "a true joy": "We approve thus the proposition that he [Schreuder] has made for your part and we consent very willingly to the request of our Honorable Brothers." Rousset then named Pierre Bunel as the master of the lodge, at the same time urging his brothers not to permit "the pernicious innovations which false brothers seek to introduce." He begged them to attach themselves to "the English Constitutions": "We recommend you to its paternal care."[13] Rousset railed, in particular, against what he called "*galanterie*," which he equated with French excesses. In the rules adopted by the lodge in 1756, the term appears, along with religion and politics (*staatkunde*), as specifically forbidden to be discussed.[14] In the years these discussions are taking place the term could mean sexual license; it could also imply frivolity, a lack of seriousness of purpose.[15] In this masonic context Rousset juxtaposed galantry as the antithesis of a modest or virtuous lifestyle.[16]

But the legitimacy of the reconstituted lodge rested on more than its probity. It depended on various factors. Rousset's permission and approval are seen as essential. He is still their master, and this passing on of legitimacy lies in his person, just as the care and protection of the English *Constitutions* of 1723 are "paternal." In the minutes of another lodge from exactly the same period we can hear how this personal, yet constitutional, understanding of authority was expressed. The master of the lodge presented his successor to his brothers who had elected him with these words: "Receive then from my hands by the consent of all our brother members, the signs of our new dignity . . . and my very dear brothers! receive your very venerable master! have for him all the love and devotion that he merits."[17] This election has been made possible "by the faculty that we have been given by the Constitution."[18] At this moment of presentation the master is a figure as traditional as he is modern. Authority is being passed to him out of the hands of his predecessor; he has also been chosen by "a public suffrage," by the unanimous consent of the members. We may associate his legitimacy with theories of governance that are traditional and patriarchal—hereditary even—as well as they are modern, and, in a Lockean sense, contractual and elective. Not least the brothers are asked to accept the result of their "public vote," to bear witness to it "publicly." In the lodge at this moment the private has become the public.[19]

In every lodge, and La Bien Aimée is no exception, the brothers constituted the lodge for themselves and then submitted willingly to the authority of the master, who was expected to govern with the care shown by a "tender father." Thus in La Bien Aimée the brothers requested the reestablishment of the lodge. Once it was reestablished, they were dutifully attentive to Rousset's instructions, incorporating them into the elaborate set of "household" rules used to guide the behavior of all brothers. Yet, within two years, the brothers, now over fifty strong, declared that they did not regard the old *Constitutions* and rules of England "as fixed and the unchanging basis of their work and behavior . . . but regard them as good helping aids to be used when necessary as a first point of deliberation and then to use them as far as the character of business agrees with the Constitution of the Order in this Country as well as with the respective lodges in particular."[20] This flexibility appears to have been a response to the increasingly national character of freemasonry within the Republic. By contrast, however, and over the years, Rousset's lodge would tend to support the preservation of the English rituals and oppose departures from this "ancient orthodoxy" initiated by the Grand Lodge.[21] It would also demand the right to enter into "opposition" and to protest if changes were too hurriedly adopted.

In 1756 the main and oldest lodge in The Hague had established itself as the National Grand Lodge. The terms "national" and "the Nation" begin to appear routinely now in masonic discussions. The establishment was an event of capital importance to its contemporary supporters. In masonic documents lodges that affiliated with the new national polity spoke of "their great satisfaction at having been informed of the happy Revolution that arrived at the end of the year 1756 when all the lodges of Holland assembled, having reestablished a very Respectable Grand Lodge."[22] To describe this establishment as a "happy Revolution" was to conjure up language both historical and political: English Whigs often referred to 1688–89 as the "late, happy Revolution." We are reminded of the French exposé that had the masonic lodges in England being established in 1691, in direct response to that revolution (see p. 28). Could it be that the Dutch freemasons were attempting to create their national polity in self-conscious imitation of the spirit of that revolution?

Is this a parliamentary and constitutional system being established in the new masonic nation?

As extraordinary as it may seem, the answer to these questions must be affirmative. The very next statement by the lodge La Philanthrope, in the city of Middleburg, the capital of the southern province of Zeeland, provides the clue. Although welcoming the establishment of the Grand Lodge as a "Happy Revolution," the Zeeland lodge, composed of some of the most elite men in the city, noted that it had not participated at the founding. The reason for this reluctance sprang from its own sovereignty:

> The Province of Zeeland has been separate from the others, and [given the fact] that this Province made a Sovereignty apart, the Brothers, who reside here, in order to participate in the happy Union of their Neighboring Brothers, see the need to recognize and to unite themselves especially to the Very Respectable Grand Lodge, which came to be constituted in Holland, in order that by their participation they render complete its spread over all of the Republic.[23]

Thus the recognition given by individual lodges to the Grand Lodge was hard won and sometimes grudgingly given. The rights of sovereignty had to be weighed against the need for social recognition on a national scale and legitimization. A major portion of the discussions in The Hague between the Grand Lodge and the other lodges concerns their adherence to the authority of the national Grand Lodge and its rules.[24] Where that authority was actually accepted, representatives of the Grand Lodge made "inspection visits" to individual lodges.[25] La Bien Aimée was, however, most noticeable among those lodges that obstinately resisted its authority. When the Grand Lodge could win the allegiance of a lodge, as it did in the case of the Middleburg lodge, the reward was a new constitution along with "the faculty" to hold elections within the lodge.[26] Adherence to the masonic nation brought with it a legitimacy that was constitutionally established and expressed through open elections. The impulse at work in the formation of the national Grand Lodge was deeply idealistic. As one orator told his brothers in 1751: "Against human instinct we should seek to unite, to unify their hearts and souls, in order to improve themselves, and in order to form an entirely spiritual nation."[27] That oration was a direct translation of a printed oration given in Paris in 1737 by a leading masonic orator and eventual master, the Chevalier Ramsay (see p. 7). What is happening in the Dutch Republic among freemasons of the 1750s will be repeated throughout western Europe as national grand lodges are formed, as schisms erupt, as men (and perhaps some women) attempt to think through the meaning of living under their constitutions.

The Zeeland lodge's new allegiance to this spiritual nation did not obscure its recognition of the rights of the local, and actual, political authorities, "des seigneurs Etats de cette Province."[28] They had imposed a stamp tax on all official documents. The master of the lodge informed his brothers "that the principal duties of Masonry consist in the obedience to its sovereign, and in the exact observation of the law which conduces to the benefit of the whole society." The lodge then deliberated as to whether or not it should use the stamps for all of its documents. It agreed to thank the master unanimously and "to show their zeal for the public good and their submission to their legitimate sovereigns," and, not least, to pay the tax.[29] These Dutch freemasons, like their European counterparts, were good burgers, drawn, in this instance, from the most elite ranks of local society. Doctors, lawyers, military officers, merchants, government officials, a director of the East India Company are commonplace occupations given in the records of Middleburg lodge. In their "enlightened deliberations," to use the phrase that these and other masonic records repeatedly used (see p. 45), they sought no undoing of the existing social and political order. They were too closely identified with it. Yet faced with issues of sovereignty and legitimacy they proved to be remarkably self-willed, to discuss and to vote, before giving their consent. On occasion they could also withhold their consent, as did the Amsterdam lodge when faced with the claims to authority proposed by the Grand Lodge in The Hague.

Operating with quite a different perspective on the obedience owed the new Grand Lodge, and refusing to give it, La Bien Aimée struggled to impose order on its members, levying fines for violations, requiring the dues to be paid by all brothers or, in their words, that they be "taxed."[30] In the earliest records of the reconstituted lodge, the concern is more with legitimacy than with behavior, with distancing the lodge from "clandestine lodges" in the city that were without any legitimate standing. We know little about such groups, although one was "a certain Jewish lodge" in Amsterdam.[31] To ensure its legitimacy, and hence to separate itself from these lodges, La Bien Aimée established contact with other Dutch lodges and with foreign lodges, such as Minerva zum Zirkel in Leipzig, a contact made by Schreuder, who as a publisher journeyed frequently to that city. There he was received with all solemnity by his foreign brothers, and representatives or "envoys" from the Leipzig lodge visited the lodge in Amsterdam.[32] The Dutch brothers praised their German colleagues for their continual conquest of "profanism," and they sent songs to augment the festivities at their "enlightened assemblies."[33] When in turn a German lodge found its legitimacy threatened by a "clandestine lodge" in the same city, the Amsterdam brothers offered to help: "If you want our judgment, please send us copies of the acts on which you base your rights and legitimacy."[34] The contacts of La Bien Aimée routinely extended to "sister" lodges in Amsterdam and throughout western Europe,[35] as in Stockholm, where it received a gold medal as a token of friendship; they also reached Nantes, La Rochelle, and even the Dutch colonies, in particular Curaçao. There merchant travelers, former members of the Amsterdam lodge—their "mother" lodge, as they put it—established their own lodge, and promptly sought "an ample and perfect constitution" from the Grand Lodge in The Hague. Concern for constitutional legitimacy was not unique to La Bien Aimée. In 1755 its sister lodge, Concordia vincit Animos, would not recognize another lodge in the city until it produced copies of its original constitutions from France.[36] It also would not allow the physical removal from the lodge of its own constitution, and it insisted that at the elections for a National Grand Master in 1756 the papers of every lodge be carefully scrutinized.[37]

Although the Dutch merchants met in the Curaçao lodge with "some English brothers," their legitimacy was sought from The Hague, now that a Grand Lodge existed there, and not from the Grand Lodge in either Paris or London. As the letter to their Amsterdam brothers makes clear, a new lodge, however distant, could be established at will, with brothers filling the offices by a simple election. But the legitimacy of the lodge—a matter separate from its creation—required recognition from other, constitutionally established lodges.[38] It is worth noting, if only in passing, that the establishment of the lodge in Curaçao was not without controversy. The description of that process makes reference to "the slander through Sex" that threatened to embitter the opening of "our temple of decent amusement."[39] As we saw in chapter 3 with the lodge in Nijmegen, the slander suggests the possibility of accusations of sodomy against this exclusively male fraternity. The topic must await a fuller discussion in chapter 5, but the reference, once again, reminds us of the range of social tensions that masonic fraternity could arouse.

To prevent these tensions spilling into the lodge in Amsterdam, as elsewhere, new brothers were admitted by "election," but with an overwhelming majority, near unanimity, required for admission.[40] The process was profoundly social and personal. Candidates for admission were invariably described as "honest men, possessing the character, and the morals and the discretion of which there can be no reproach, such that they may aspire to the advantage of being initiated into our mysteries."[41] Men had to be local, or known well by brothers who were local. Men could be, and were, rejected.[42] As the orator said, the principles of our institution, "the Philantrophy, the charity, and the sweet primitive equality of all men, which is the foundation of our Art, . . . [is what] we seek to reestablish in our hearts and well as in our assemblies."[43] In the new public space which the lodge created, brothers "promised unanimously to correct our conduct." "The public" outside the lodge judges morality only "by appearances"; the world is a place of "prejudice" and "caprice." But freemasons know that morality is inseparable from virtue, and "the good company of my brothers is always the necessary condition for morality; you dictate in detail the duties of society."[44] Morality and virtue are inseparable from social experience; they *are* social experience. As Schreuder put it, the external displays of civility, so important in the lodges, reveal "the internal civility" of a man. Charity is at the heart of civility, a personal caring of each brother one for the other.[45] And the lodge permits that experience among men carefully chosen by their peers, governed strictly by the rules of the order, sequestered from the world, obedient to their master as "friends, citizens and as brothers."[46] In the sacred temple of freemasonry brothers will find "a true liberty . . . a true peace." Brothers are united "in order to give an example to all the world which will see us as being in the process of making our superb edifice the high point of perfection."[47] They will stand firm against "the unfounded slander of the blind common people."[48] Such important work required brothers carefully chosen, with similar values and mores. Only near unanimity would suffice. Other matters required only a simple majority of voting brothers.

As the "household rules" of La Bien Aimée make clear, once admitted, brothers were required to be punctual, and attendance was rigorously demanded, with fines imposed for absence. When the fines proved controversial and threatened to impair the harmony of the lodge, they were removed and an annual fee of 24 guilders was put in their place.[49] Eventually in place of a system of black and white "beans" used for voting "by ballot," a system using coins, probably imitative of the practices of the old local guilds, was adopted.[50] Moreover, in at least one other lodge, fines were also imposed for "immoral" behavior, excessive card playing, sleeping away from home in places of ill repute (see p. 159), and lingering at the lodge after it was formally closed. The beneficiaries of immorality were to be the poor into whose "box" the fines were put. Some time in the nineteenth century Dutch freemasons went through their old records and came up with a list of men who had been excluded from all the eighteenth-century lodges and the reasons for the exclusion. Tantalizingly brief, they include "outrageous behavior" and "unruly behavior," as well as dereliction in dues payment. Dozens of men were banned or excluded from the 1750s to the 1790s.[51]

By the late 1750s, the legitimacy, as well as the discipline, of La Bien Aimée was firmly reestablished. In addition, Dutch freemasonry in general had begun to assume a national identity. Its Grand Master could now speak of "les frères deputés des loges respectives qui ont assistés à l'assembleé Nationale tenue à la Haye."[52] At these national assemblies held in The Hague, the ceremonies placed brothers standing in rows, first symbolizing the "Staten van Holland," that is, the States of Holland, the body that had once condemned the order, and which could be described as the legislative body of the province. Behind them stood other brothers described as representing the National Grand Master. Finally, standing in back of them, were the officers of the lodge, visitors, and all the other brothers—all of whom then joined in the communal singing that was so much a part of masonic ritual.[53]

This identity was clearly civic, governmental, and by the late 1750s, increasingly Dutch and national. By that time, it was as if the national polity could be symbolically located within the lodges. Any doubts we may have about this nationalist meaning are dispelled by the fact that in 1758 English brothers, who want to establish their own lodge in Amsterdam, appeal to rebellious La Bien Aimée, not to the Grand Lodge in The Hague, for the recognition that brought legitimacy with it. Both dissident groups, for very different reasons, are having a dispute with the national Grand Lodge in The Hague. But the English brothers are seceding from the Dutch Grand Lodge because they do not share its national political identity. The following letter, from an English freemason—replete with nationalist and rebellious sentiments—is an extraordinary document. If it had been written in, let us say, Boston in 1777 (when the Massachusetts lodges did secede from the London Grand Lodge),[54] we would explain it by reference to a new and emerging national identity. A similar interpretation seems appropriate to this text:

> January 13, 1758
> The Right Worshipful and Honorable Lodge, La Bien Aimée
>
> We George Smith A.B. & Lect. Math. G[rand] M[aster] of masons by a Constitution granted solely unto us by James Brydges, Duke of Chandos, Earl of Carnarvan . . . of the Antient and honourable Fraternity of Free and Accepted Masons.
>
> Being willing and desirous together with several other worthy Brothers, to have a communication and correspondence with your Right Worshipful Lodge; further craving your assistance and advice, in regard to a derision and misunderstanding between the English and Dutch Members of our Lodge, the purport of which is.

> We the English, provided with the above Constitution, actually will not be subservient to either the Laws or Demands of the present National G[rand] M[aster], neither are we willing to receive a National Constitution or be Dependent therefrom; which is what our Dutch Brothers insists upon.
>
> We therefore think proper to establish a lodge entirely English, by the Name of Concordia, and shall therefore desire, as by these present admittance into your Right Worshipfull Fraternity of Masons, and from thence to be favored with your right worshipfulls, Wardens, Officers and Members Advice, for the promotion and propogation of Masonry and the Craft in general. We therefore salute you by three times three.[55]

In these records we have come upon the private socializing of middling men of considerable literacy and sophistication who define themselves as adherents of a constitution, and laws, which permit them to defy other, also self-defined, legitimate authorities. George Smith, for instance, was a teacher of mathematics and Newtonian mechanics. The defiant tone of Smith's letter reveals his own sense of English national identity, one that is now in reaction to the formation of the Grand Lodge of The Netherlands in 1756. Like the records of La Bien Aimée, the letter reveals the obsessive masonic concern for the legitimacy of these private polities, a status achieved only through a social act, by the recognition accorded a lodge by other lodges. But what if legitimacy were to be denied, and recognition withheld? While the brothers in La Bien Aimée refused to follow Smith in his rebellion,[56] they had constitutional and procedural problems of their own with the new national Grand Lodge.

At the founding of the first official Dutch lodge in 1735 no terms such as "national" or "the nation" appear in the records. Until the 1750s lodges functioned with a remarkable degree of local autonomy, so much, in fact, that when Rousset set up his lodge he secured its legitimacy through the assistance of a lodge master in the northern Dutch town of Leeuwarden, one Hendrik Lijnslager, a sea captain closely involved in the entourage of Prince William IV. For reasons that remain unclear, Rousset apparently appealed to the Grand Lodge of Scotland for a constitution for the new Amsterdam lodge.[57] At least this was Rousset's memory of his lodge's establishment when he was asked about it twenty years later during the process of reconstitution in 1755. In the same year, another newly established Amsterdam lodge also appealed to the Grand Lodge in Edinburgh for its constitution.[58]

There is an interesting and, it would seem, new masonic element revealed in Rousset's account of the original founding of his lodge. Anderson's *Constitutions* (1723) was an amalgam of the rules, some derived from the "old charges" of guild masonry, which were to guide the new speculative freemasonry. Allegiance to that text and to the Grand Lodge of London ensured the legitimacy of a British lodge. But as Anderson's document came to be understood on the Continent, "the constitution" of a lodge refers not only to the text, but also to a formal declaration of legitimacy that had to come from an already established and hence legitimate lodge. The term "constitutions" begins to take on the meaning—and increasingly it is used in the singular—that we associate with British political culture and late eighteenth-century European constitutionalism. In the Dutch as well as the French-language texts routinely found in Continental freemasonry by the 1750s, if not earlier, the constitution of a lodge has come to mean those customary laws by which the lodge is governed, by which its legitimacy is established.[59]

Why in 1735 Rousset's lodge chose a process of legitimization through the Grand Lodge of Scotland we will never know. Indeed, it is not even clear when, or if, Rousset was made a freemason by the first Dutch lodge in The Hague. Its records list his initiation in 1735, but his name was added to that date in a different hand and ink. There was never any question, then or now, that he was a most dedicated freemason. Yet given what we know about his early contacts with Whig circles representing British interests in the Republic, it just may be that he was initiated by these foreign brothers and not by the first Dutch lodge.[60] As a result, his name was only belatedly added to the Dutch list. This is important because later in 1756 Rousset's lodge sought clarification about its constitution, which had apparently been lost. The most immediate place to search for this clarification was in the archives of the earliest official Dutch lodge in The Hague. And with that request for information, controversy erupted.

Up until that moment the legitimacy of the Amsterdam lodge, or any other for that matter, had possessed an autonomous quality. Once acknowledged, however informally, autonomy had never been questioned. Once conferred, legitimacy seemed to reside in the person of the master, and it could be passed on from one duly elected master to the next. This personal and autonomous quality of a lodge, coupled with its elective character, gave the early lodges a curiously hybrid form of private government. This can be seen in Rousset's own governance when master of his lodge. The records describe him as having brought to it "an industry, a dignity, and a didacticism, of which one could find few other examples."[61] In 1755 his personal approval was seen as essential for the reconstituting of the lodge. However, at the same moment, the new national Grand Lodge in The Hague was beginning to define its authority as a sovereign body, demanding, in effect, a new oath of allegiance to it by which the legitimacy of all the Dutch lodges would have to be reaffirmed.

In 1756 the Grand Lodge in The Hague claimed to have no record that Rousset's lodge (de la Paix) had ever existed, or that he had been present in The Hague in 1748 at the inauguration of a new Grand Master. He and his lodge had been lost, or removed, from the official memory of Dutch freemasonry.[62] The Grand Master who disclosed this disturbing news to Schreuder was Louis Dagran, a prosperous cloth merchant in The Hague. Officially Dagran was only acting Grand Master, having stepped onto the "throne," as the chair of the Grand Master was called, when its incumbent, Juste Gerard, baron van Wassenaer, had stepped down in 1752 apparently for reasons of health. As we shall see in the next chapter, Wassenaer had been a masonic innovator who in 1751 introduced lodges for both men and women. More important for the story we are about to tell now, Wassenaer was a nobleman, as were most Grand Masters. Dagran clearly was not, and his correspondence reveals an obsessive concern that his authority as acting Grand Master be respected. The tone of his letters also suggests a somewhat arrogant and petulant man, but this does not explain the willingness of his brothers, and most of the other Dutch lodges, to embrace his national vision of Dutch freemasonry.

The dispute with La Bien Aimée concerned more than the constitutional status of Rousset's lodge. Dagran regarded the lodge in The Hague, and hence himself as the acting Grand Master in The Netherlands, as an entity independent from the London Grand Lodge. He saw his lodge, to use the language that it began to employ, as a "national" Grand Lodge for the Republic. In the words of Dagran: "Thus do not forget, that as a Great Power we are independent of other Great Powers and in the face of that [let us] open the eyes of the Amsterdam Brothers."[63] The Amsterdam brothers would not, however, acknowledge the independence of the new Dutch Grand Lodge. For many years they had operated under constitutional authority conferred by a foreign power and administered through their master, the now banished Rousset de Missy. Dagran saw their posture as an affront to his personal authority. His rancor is evident in the tone his conversation takes.[64] The emotion displayed is a fitting reminder that the power and authority claimed by freemasons in their private society was personally felt and jealously guarded.

A "national assembly," as it was called by Dutch freemasons, was held in 1756. In place of Dagran a new and aristocratic Grand Master was elected. He came to preside over what was now referred to as the "national" Grand Lodge of The Netherlands and Its Provinces. Gradually the British Grand Lodge gave the Dutch body de facto recognition and still managed to maintain cordial relations with it.[65] In the case of La Bien Aimée, however, the bitterness toward the Grand Lodge in The Hague simmered on. Other lodges (in Rotterdam, for instance) also balked at having their constitutions reaffirmed by the Grand Lodge of The Netherlands. All the lodges quarreled about their "equality" in relation to one another, that is, their seniority based upon the longevity of a lodge. Apparently the rebelliousness of La Bien Aimée and some of the other lodges caused the Grand Lodge to pass a resolution in 1757 condemning with abhorrence "all kinds of rebellion." It went even further and broke with the longstanding rule, found in Anderson's *Constitutions,* "that if a Brother should be a rebel against the State, he is not to be countenanced in his rebellion . . . [yet] they cannot expell him from the Lodge, and his relation to it remains indefeasible."[66] The Grand Lodge of The Netherlands, and masters of various Dutch lodges, decided that for "*rebellie,*" of an unspecified nature, a brother should be "banned from all regular lodges in this country."[67] At the same meeting the "bad conduct" of La Bien Aimée was also condemned, and Schreuder was informed that he could not be the master of a regular lodge. If his brothers did not conform to the Grand Lodge within three months and profess their innocence, they were to be declared clandestine and irregular.[68] La Bien Aimée of course did not conform, and Schreuder stayed on as its master. In recognition of his services in this troubled period he was eventually made Honorary Master of the lodge.[69] Perhaps we can now understand how it was that this self-willed lodge was forced to protest that it had never formed "a Party."[70]

The use of the term "party" is significant. Brought into Dutch directly from English, it possessed an explicitly political meaning. The Dutch Grand Lodge consistently used it against rebellious lodges: They form a "party." In the 1760s the Grand Lodge, still quarreling with other lodges, accused a lodge in Utrecht (which Rousset had set up during his exile there in the early 1750s) of being a party.[71] By then, however, the dispute with the Amsterdam lodge had been settled. In 1759 with the election of a new Grand Master the dispute was buried, and a new constitution was granted to La Bien Aimée. It in turn directed its members "to forget and leave aside all events of the past as if they had never happened, to respect the Highly Noble and Respectable Grandmaster . . . and to consider all legitimate lodges of these countries as worthy fellow members of the same body."[72] A tenuous and fragile "unity" had been at least temporarily achieved.[73] The other lodges were now permitted to have "correspondence" with the forgiven rebels.[74] But Pierre Bunel, the old master Rousset had nominated as his replacement, still objected that the new leadership of La Bien Aimée was "illegitimate and usurping."[75] As late as the 1780s Bunel appeared in the lodge and somewhat mysteriously presented it with the missing document, the original Constitution, or a copy thereof, from the Grand Lodge of Scotland, dated 26 December 1755.[76] The lodge sealed it away in its archives.

Throughout the 1760s disputes over the legitimacy of one or another lodge, or over the right of a brother from one lodge to be admitted to another, continued to be commonplace.[77] At this distance the emotion generated by these disputes is hard to recreate: the threat to a lodge's "honor," the issue of obedience to duly constituted authority, the yearning for "harmony and respectability." These were real desires expressed in those words and emotively. When another lodge tried to settle the dispute between La Bien Aimée and the Grand Lodge, the mediator spoke about its desire "like in former times, to join hands and hearts fraternally together and to promote the construction of the respectable temple."[78]

It seems appropriate to relate these controversies of 1756, including the amnesia expressed toward Rousset and his lodge, to events in the larger society. In the mid-1750s the security of the Dutch Republic was deeply threatened by the specter of another French invasion. It became painfully clear, in the face of Dutch economic decline, that Dutch defenses were weak, and that the will to continue in the Triple Alliance with Britain and Austria was no longer there.[79] In the ensuing Anglo-French war on the Continent, the Dutch Republic opted for neutrality and the Alliance collapsed. That collapse is the background to the so-called Diplomatic Revolution of 1756, which brought forth the realignment of Austria with its old enemy, France. With regard to international alliances, the Republic was now adrift. Its regent oligarchy had once again chosen neutrality.

In opposition, increasingly nationalist voices could now be heard to speak of the Vaderland in terms of its corruption and decay. The decision to establish a "national" Grand Lodge also reflects a growing sense of national identity. Dagran's insistence that we are a "great power" echoes it, just as the decision may also reflect a loosening of the ties to the British alliance. This is not to suggest that in 1756 Dutch freemasonry lost its generally Orangist complexion. But Orangism, especially at midcentury, could also be strongly nationalist. Equally, and in contradiction, there were now elements within the fraternity that were less than eager to bow to the authorities in The Hague, however national their claims to legitimacy. The antagonism of the Amsterdam brothers may reflect the historic tension between Amsterdam and The Hague, but more likely it also signals a disillusionment with neutralism on the part of Schreuder, Rousset, and their brothers. They were no less identified with the Dutch Republic than were their brothers in the Grand Lodge. The fact that it now asked that all lodges keep their records in Dutch rather than in

French, which was fashionable in elite circles, could hardly have impressed the Amsterdam lodge. Unlike more elite lodges, it had been doing so since 1754. La Bien Aimée's dedication to what it called a pure, "English" type of freemasonry may also signal its concern over the foreign, noticeably French, influences found in other lodges, especially in the high society of The Hague.

The independence of La Bien Aimée also signals a tension with authority that in subsequent decades never disappeared. Its records for those decades document the tension.[80] As we shall see in chapter 7, in the 1770s and the 1780s the lodge's orators dwelt upon the meaning of republicanism, both in ancient Rome and in their own masonic system. In 1782 La Bien Aimée proposed that the Grand Lodge "conclude an alliance with the lodges of North America, now declared independent by this Republic." The Grand Lodge agreed but was careful, given its pro-British sentiments, to suggest that it simply recognized all masons spread over the surface of the earth.[81] In 1783 La Bien Aimée also welcomed a brother from Philadelphia and congratulated him on "his newly won freedom." From early in its history La Bien Aimée assumed a posture of opposition.

As we saw in chapter 3 from the historian de Vignoles's account of Dutch freemasonry written in the 1770s, which described the way the Dutch Grand Lodge was set up in 1756, every effort was made to recognize a degree of individual autonomy for the lodges. Hence the model of the Estates General was chosen as the system of representation for the masonic national government (see pp. 85–86). It may have been the case that the brothers in La Bien Aimée wanted more from the masonic polity than the imitation of an archaic representative institution which by the 1750s in the Republic functioned to legitimize neutrality and decentralization, both of which permitted the old oligarchy a free hand in foreign and domestic matters. Yet at the time the model also suited the rebellious instincts of the lodge.

It would be impossible to separate La Bien Aimée's "rebelliousness" toward the Grand Lodge from the profound disfavor into which Rousset de Missy had fallen in 1749, or from the fear of the radicalism he represented, to which a few of his brothers had been attracted. Clearly there were still men in the new lodge who, at the very least, would constitute a private governance for themselves. They were not unmindful of the need for legitimacy, which came only from other masonic societies. But they were capable of seeking that for themselves and of defying authority within the context of a fraternal organization dedicated to constitutional order and obedience to legitimate authority. Other lodges were also capable of "rebelling against the decisions" of the Grand Lodge, returning their constitution and seeking a new one from London.[82] By the same token, when the Grand Lodge acted internationally it concluded a "Treaty of Alliance" (with Prussia in 1778) in "the general interest of the two nations and traveling brothers in particular."[83]

Freemasons imitated, as well as defied, political authority with remarkable self-confidence. In the second part of this chapter we will speculate on what may have been one of the intellectual sources for the defiant mode. We will postulate that at least some of the Dutch brothers knew the political writings of the English philosopher John Locke. He seemed to prescribe the true principles around which a nation's government could best be organized. In the last decades of the eighteenth century Continental freemasons of a variety of ideological persuasions idealized the lodges as places where true patriotism and love of country could find expression. The discovery that what was true in the lodges of the Dutch Republic could be true in other parts of Europe, as we shall see in the concluding chapters, only reinforces the point about the lodges being philosophical societies for the mercantile and genteel, where within small and intimate settings all sorts of civic ideals could find expression.

The expression of those ideals grew louder, more widespread, and more disparate on the Continent by the latter decades of the century. A vast masonic literature from Prussian freemasons of the 1770s and beyond for example, saw the lodge as an analogue to a single nation, united in harmony, "a republic governed by wise and general rules."[84] This literature glorified the reign of Frederick the Great, even justified his conquest of Silesia, his seizure of it from Austria in 1740 (see p. 156). Such a glorification would have appalled freemasons like Rousset de Missy (d. 1762), who all their lives had been resolutely pro-Austrian.

Similarly in France all the lodges met in 1772 in "a National Lodge," represented by "deputies." At this assembly the deputies vowed never to allow anything "to destroy our primitive constitutions, to deprive us of the most sacred right [i.e., property] which had been recognized by civilized societies, to strip us of the prerogative which an entire free nation enjoys."[85] These "representatives" of all the French lodges imposed "the law" on themselves. They established a renewed "Gouvernement maçonnique dans les Provinces." Because self-imposed, it is most free, most natural, and "in consequence the most perfect of governments."[86] French masonic government would take many forms and express many, often conflicting, political impulses. By the 1780s these expressions begin to relate in interesting ways to the origins of the French Revolution, as we will see in chapter 9. Now we must look at the ways in which the masonic lodges transmitted to a European audience the theory, as well as the practice, of English constitutional government.

Locke's *Two Treatises* and the Crisis of 1755

If the authorities in The Hague, either masonic or governmental, had known what else Rousset and his brothers were up to in 1755, or of his close involvement with the reconstitution of his lodge, they might have taken action more serious than simply fussing with the lodge about its legitimacy. In the case of the actual government, it might have arrested him once again or banned the edition of John Locke that he was publishing with Schreuder, the orator and eventually master, of La Bien Aimée.[87] From the perspective of The Hague situated in "the richest and most beautiful part of the populous province of Holland"—or so a traveler in 1760 described it—the discontent coming from Amsterdam and elsewhere must have seemed irksome and possibly even irrelevant.

The Dutch provincial authorities who had the power to ban books, like subsequent historians, probably missed the fact that Rousset was the instigator of the new edition of the French translation of Locke's *Two Treatises,* complete with a new, and overtly political, preface. As was his habit when publishing clandestinely, Rousset camouflaged his identity on the title page by using only initials, "L.C.R.D.M.A.D.P." Astute followers of his literary career know that those initials, among other variations that he liked to use, identify "Le Chevalier Rousset de Missy, Academie du Plessis" (the school where he had studied).[88] In his private correspondence with Schreuder in early 1755 Rousset discussed the form that their reconstituted lodge should take, and in the same letters they also discussed the publication of a book by Rousset. Through another lodge brother, a Mr. Silo, Rousset received the proofs of his text from Schreuder and made various changes.[89] This was not their first publishing venture together. As early as 1725 Schreuder appears to have helped bring out Rousset's French translation of a political treatise by Johan de Wit, the great seventeenth-century Dutch statesman.[90] All of this evidence, which has been discussed in greater detail elsewhere,[91] permits us to identify Rousset as the editor of this text, and to fill in the masonic background for the 1755 edition of Locke.

Rousset was a profoundly political, highly educated man, who was immensely well read and prolific. His introduction and notes to Locke's text are insightful and original. They place Locke in a political tradition that Rousset identifies as republican. While present-day interpreters of Locke would almost universally deny him a place in that particular body of political thought, it is not so clear that eighteenth-century Continental reformers and opponents of absolutism would have agreed. For one thing, the French translation of Locke widely available on the Continent, which Rousset was simply reediting, translated the English words "commonwealth" and "community" as "république."[92] In the context of various Continental anciens régimes, Locke's text was associated with subversion. Consequently, the distinction between constitutionalism and republicanism was blurred, if not obliterated. It should also be remembered that from the 1750s on Locke had been widely claimed by English freemasons as one of their own (pp. 63–64).[93]

This set of circumstances now permits the 1755 edition of Locke to achieve a historical importance even beyond what it may have meant to Rousset and his brothers. For example, it was almost certainly the edition of Locke that the young Jean-Jacques Rousseau read, complete with Rousset's preface, which argued for Locke's relevance to a republic. In addition, the 1755 edition was the most widely reprinted edition of Locke in Continental Europe right up to, and during, the French Revolution.[94] What then, in 1755, did it also have to do with La Bien Aimée? And what did the edition have to do with the political situation prevailing in the Dutch Republic? An analysis of this French translation of Locke's text, as well as a look at Rousset's new preface and the notes to it, helps to provide answers to both those questions.

The original translation by the Huguenot refugee David Mazel was done in 1691 when England and the Dutch Republic were allied in war against France.[95] Mazel's French translation left out Locke's own preface, the whole of the *First Treatise,* and the opening chapter of the *Second;* also, all the chapters were renumbered. Mazel's translation wrought subtle, but important, alterations to the original language of Locke's text. In general they had the effect of somewhat radicalizing Locke's message. A few examples should suffice to illustrate this subtle transformation.

Where Locke says that the king "may do to all his subjects whatever he pleases," Mazel translated the passage and then added the following phrase (in italics here): "un seul homme peut faire à tous ses sujets tout ce qu'il lui plait, sans que une personne n'ait le droit de se plaindre de ceux qui exécutent ses volontés, *et de former aucune opposition.*" In a phrase added to the original Mazel has introduced the concept of an opposition. Elsewhere in the translation, Locke is made to be a much more overt opponent of absolutism of Louis XIV—when Mazel translates "the violence and oppression of this absolute Power" as "la violence et l'oppression due Gouverneur absolu," a personalizing of absolutism. In another alteration, Mazel translates "the consent of any number of freemen capable of a majority" as "le consentement d'un certain nombre d'hommes libres capable d'être représentez par le plus grand nombre d'eux." This points toward the type of representation found in various corporate bodies on the Continent, the still powerful guilds, the Calvinist churches, or the theory of an *états généraux,* namely, that individuals represent others in their estate or class and not simply themselves. Mazel is not making the alteration to vitiate Locke's emphasis on the legislature but rather to adopt it to the circumstances of Continental institutions. Similarly, Mazel translates "the subjects of that Commonwealth" as "sujets d'une certaine République et d'un certain Etat." The mention of a republic was inserted in the 1691 translation done by this Huguenot refugee at work in, and committed to the survival of, the Dutch Republic in opposition to the threat posed by French absolutism. Sixty years later, when the Huguenot Rousset took up Mazel's text for reediting, the same causes were still dear to him, just as they had been at the time of Rousset's own flight from France in 1704.

With Mazel's translation in hand, Rousset added a new preface, which proclaimed Locke as a commentator on the republic and the safety it offers free men:

> je n'ai eu en vûe, que ce que l'Auteur dit du Gouvernement Républicain, qui convient le plus aux Sociétés que forment des hommes libres pour mettre à couvert de toutes violences & leurs personnes & Leurs propriétés.

Having made Locke into a defender of republics, Rousset makes clear that his prescriptions for good government are especially needed at this moment. This edition is being published because

> Certaines circonstances dont le détail, ne serviroit ici de rien, aiant fait désirer à quelques Régens de nôtre République, que l'on répandit ce *Traité* de Mr. Locke dans la nation, ôu l'on n'est pas aussi instruit qu'il seroit à souhaiter de la Nature du Pouvoir Souverain, ni des Fins des Sociétés Civiles.

Certain regents of the Republic have suggested that this text will instruct the citizen as to the true nature of sovereignty and the purpose of civil society. To assist in this purpose, Rousset informs his readers that he has made many corrections, altered certain ambiguous phrases, and at other points in his notes directed the reader to different political theorists, such as Burlamaqui and Cumberland, who also explicate the principles of natural laws and natural, or primitive, rights.[96] All these theorists, Rousset claims, demonstrate "l'excellence de la Constitution Républiquaine telle que celle de notre Etat."

But with his recommendation Rousset adds an admonition. He warns that some citizens, who distinguish themselves by the title "Noble" in other republics such as Venice, Genoa, and Poland, enforce an unbearable slavery there. Of course, he then claims that "with us the nobles are citizens just like the rest of the inhabitants, and they do not have more to say than the magistrates established by the Constitution."[97] The message in this preface is clear enough, if somewhat disguised: Beware of the tyranny to which any oligarchy may subject its citizens. Rousset concludes that, according to the report of the ancient Roman historian Tacitus, the Dutch, even at that time, possessed a republican government. In 1755 this preface could be read as a call to preserve the historic opposition of the Republic to French absolutism, as well as to maintain its alliance with England, in its post-1688 form of society and government to which Locke's text, it was believed, originally spoke. In 1755, both the opposition to French absolutism and the alliance with England were perceived to be in jeopardy.

For decades Dutch opponents of the oligarchic abuses of the regents had championed the English alliance as the protection against French bellicosity, and had spoken in opposition to the neutrality often promoted by the great merchant traders. The Anglo-Dutch alliance had been strengthened in 1747 by the restoration of the stadtholder, William IV, only to be once again threatened by his untimely death in 1751 and by a subsequent drift in the management of the royal household under his widow Anna of Hanover, daughter of the English king.[98] In late 1754 the situation turned ominous. All astute political observers of the European scene then believed that the war raging between England and France in the New World would return to the European Continent. A French invasion of the Low Countries once again appeared imminent. In early 1755 near panic could be found in some quarters on both sides of the Channel as Dutch and English financiers and politicians realized that the French might—in the words of the Duke of Newcastle to William Bentinck—"take possession of the Low Countries, as a sort of deposit, till we had done them justice in North America."[99] In his private diary for March 1755, the Marquis d'Argenson, a former foreign minister and an astute observer of the French court, reported that Louis XV had warned the Dutch Republic that it should not behave as it had in the preceding war, that is, pretend to neutrality while in fact giving security to France's enemies.[100]

Rousset was deeply concerned by this situation, as his private letters in 1755 to the Austrian government indicate. In them he condemned what he described as the Republic being governed, once again, by special interests.[101] Comparing the situation to the crisis provoked by the danger of French invasion in 1672, Rousset lamented the self-interested stance of the regents. They are vehemently opposed to the stadtholder (and hence to the alliance), he says, and this is nowhere more the case than in Amsterdam.[102]

This is the divisive political atmosphere in which Rousset and Schreuder brought out their edition of Locke. As Rousset's dealings with the Austrians reveal, he was a strong supporter of the British-Austrian alliance, even at times serving as an agent, and possibly a spy, for the Austrian government.[103] The situation in 1755 called for strong and effective national leadership, in effect for constitutional reform, as Orangists such as William Bentinck had long advocated. At precisely the same moment, the promoters of the new edition of Locke also reconstituted their masonic lodge.

We should reflect on the tone and nature of Locke's magisterial *Two Treatises,* especially the version available to French readers of the eighteenth century. The emphasis throughout the *Second Treatise* is on the rule of law and on the legitimacy of duly constituted authority. Although in the eighteenth century the book was believed to have been a justification for the Revolution of 1688 (we now know that it was written before it), the text puts great emphasis on the power of legitimate legislative authority, on order in government, but also on the right of men to form a contract out of which duly constituted authority arises. The language of the text, as we read it today, is constitutional and not specifically republican as we now understand that term. But as late seventeenth-century English contemporaries would have understood republican discourse as found in the writings of the Renaissance humanists, or of the mid–seventeenth-century English theorists Harrington, Sidney, or even Milton, Locke could be read as essentially belonging to their side.[104]

Locke's treatise was never simply, nor even primarily, a call to arms, nor does it vest direct governing power with the "people," who do, according to Locke, possess ultimate sovereignty. All those "failings" to move in the direction of a more radically democratic concept of government undoubtedly struck Jean-Jacques Rousseau, among other readers, when in the mid-1750s he looked to Locke to justify, and elaborate upon, his own understanding of popular sovereignty. Perhaps Rousseau was even more disappointed with what he found in the 1755 edition of the Mazel translation—presuming that he did first encounter Locke in his 1755 version—because of its preface.[105] There he would have found language intended by Rousset de Missy to whet the republican appetite, but a text that failed to live up to what might be expected of all the citizens of a republic.

But there is plenty in Locke's text that was consonant with what other progressive, occasionally radical, reformers of the 1750s would have wanted. Certainly Rousset and Schreuder would have felt comfortable in advocating it. What they attempted to institute in their ideal civil society—their masonic lodge—has, it may be argued, a Lockean quality. The emphasis throughout the *Second Treatise* is on authority and governance, on the rule of law once sovereignty has been established. We may rightly think of the historical Locke of the 1680s as a radical; reading him without knowing that context allows us to see him as readers in the eighteenth century may have. Then he may have been read as an advocate of the rights of the people and their representatives, to whom he offered the prescription of strong government, legitimate, orderly, and dutifully obeyed.

In the "household" rules adopted by La Bien Aimée, to which all brothers give their consent, the emphasis in late 1754 is on obedience and order within the lodge. All brothers are expected to have a thorough grounding in the rules of the lodge, to put their signature to them, to make regular and substantial payments to the lodge, to give respect at all times to the master, who is permitted two votes on all matters, and to other elected officers.[106] They must not speak out of turn or raise contentious matters in "Godsdienst" (religion) or "Staatkunde" (statecraft). Officers, whose conduct is also strictly prescribed by the rules of the lodge, are responsible "that everything in the lodge be held in good order," that "deze subordinatie" remains in force.[107]

These rules conform to the spirit of Rousset's instructions to Schreuder. Create a lodge, he urged, that would repudiate "des nouveautés pernicieuses," that is, the pernicious French abuses that have crept into the lodges. And he begs that the new lodge be loyal to "une constitution anglaise,"[108] that it be, in effect, a constitutionally governed society. What Rousset wants is "a true and legitimate English lodge, exempt from all the impertinent French additions."[109] We are never fully informed as to what these corrupting additions may have been. The only one mentioned is excessive drinking, perhaps linked in Rousset's mind with the meaninglessness of what he calls *galanterie.* Yet by the 1770s that term, as used in French freemasonry, was associated with a willingness to endorse lodges for both men and women.[110] As we shall see in chapter 5, at least one mixed-gender lodge existed in The Hague in 1751. It is possible that in using the term Rousset had such lodges in mind; but if he does, they are associated with all sorts of other deviations from true English freemasonry. He sought to control the minute details of social behavior in the lodge, wishing, as he says in his letter to Schreuder, even to limit drinking to one bottle of wine per member per meeting.

Clearly the lodge, as a truly constitutional society, was not to be simply a place of order, harmony, and sobriety. It was also intended to teach civility and good manners, a code of conduct appropriate to men who associate freely and, as the constitutions say, "upon the level." In perhaps his most important instruction Rousset begs Schreuder to limit the lodge to about twenty-five members. Anything else is confusion, as was the case in the original pre-1749 lodge, which had swollen to ninety-three brothers.[111] We cannot help being reminded here of that timeless discussion in European political thought about the size permissible for the true republic.

In seeking to show the relationship between the orderly government sought for the lodge, and the spirit, if not the letter, of Locke's text, as it was presented in Rousset's edition, we should also look at the annotations he provided for it. These were learned references to Cumberland, Pufendorf, Burlamaqui, and Montesquieu, all regarded by the editor as natural law theorists. In one passage which speaks of the right in the state of nature to avenge a wrongdoing—"si quelqu'un répand le sang d'un homme, son sang sera aussi répandu par un homme"—Rousset adds a note explaining the biblical and mythical origin of that right: "ce sont les propres termes des ordres que Dieu a donné à Noé et sa famille, en sortant de l'Arche, ainsi c'est l'ordre du Maître de la Nature."[112] This reference to Noah and the Master of Nature is masonic language, hence relating Locke's ideas to the masonic myth of Noah. According to the 1738 edition of Anderson's *Constitutions,* the Noachidea, the sons of Noah, was the "first name of masons according to some old Traditions," and "a mason is obliged by his tenure to observe the moral law, as a true Noachidae." It is necessary that "all agree in the three great Articles of Noah, enough to preserve the Cement of the Lodge."[113] In the note affixed to Locke's discussion of self-preservation, Rousset endows the first masons, the sons of Noah, with an intuitive understanding of the necessity for the contract, an understanding given by "the master of nature." This note complements others which explain to the reader that passive obedience is not in the laws of nature, and that Locke never wished to abolish the right of resistance. And in yet another note of clarification—reminiscent of Rousset's almost obsessive concern to prevent "license" in his lodge—Rousset adds his approval of Locke's insistence that, to quote the English text, "freedom of men under government is to have a standing rule to live by, common to everyone of that Society, and made by the Legislative Power erected to it" (*Second Treatise,* chapter iv). Taking up Locke's condemnation of Filmer's definition of liberty, that it meant "everyone to do what he pleases," Rousset presents his understanding of the distinction between liberty and license: "C'est là plutôt la définition du *Libertinage* et de la *Licence*. La Liberté a des bornes, et c'est la saine Raison, que le Créateur a donnée à tous les hommes, qui les lui prescrit. Chacun end porte les Loix tracées dans son coeur, du doigt même de la Divinité." The concern to prevent *libertinage,* or similarly *galanterie,* was never simply the result of prudery or the desire to control. It also was linked, at least in Rousset's mind, with behavior appropriate to the liberty endowed men by the Master of Nature. His brothers might have said by the Grand Architect of the Universe.

Given the simultaneous appearance of the Locke edition and the reconstitution of La Bien Aimée, we can reasonably link the content of the first with the goals and ideals of the second. These were based upon an agreement of all brothers to submit to the rules of the lodge. These laws were enforced by duly elected and constitutionally sanctioned officers whose task was to preserve the peace and safety of their small, private society. The cherished Lockean ideal of the preservation of property is also not neglected in the rules of the new lodge. Many of them concern who shall have access to a treasury designed to give loans and to assist brothers who have fallen on hard times. Finally, there is a sense in which the rules of the lodge and the officers who enforce them, who seek to instill virtue and harmony within the lodge, begin to assume a tangible independence. The officers may be said to be supreme, to act with the supreme power Locke would give to his legitimately constituted legislature.

Certainly the desire to identify with legislative authority was a central part of the ideals of Continental freemasonry. As we already saw (p. 85), the government of all the Dutch lodges established in 1756 self-consciously imitated the governance exercised by the Estates General. We know this from comments made in the 1770s by the masonic historian de Vignoles. We also know it from the records made at the time. At their banquet in The Hague all the lodges first toasted the Estates General and then gave a second toast to the hereditary stadtholder.[114] They met on that occasion to create new national policies and to elect a new Grand Master to replace the controversial Dagran.

The appearance of Lockean ideals in Amsterdam during the crisis of 1755, their expression in a French text influential throughout the rest of the century, and then their possible embodiment within the confines of a private fraternity make the notion of a lived Enlightenment more palpable and understandable. That notion raises another significant historical issue. The political rhetoric of constitutionalism, and especially of republicanism, points forward to the late 1780s and the 1790s. The Continental revolutionaries of that era embraced that discourse. Their opponents blamed the revolutions on the Enlightenment; those given to conspiracy theories blamed the freemasons. The charge came as early as 1789 (p. 9). How then are we to make sense of this conundrum? We know there was no conspiracy; we know that the lodges were deeply imbued with the values and symbols of the old order, which the revolutions repudiated. Yet we also know, for instance, that in 1795 La Bien Aimée jubilantly greeted the officers of the invading French revolutionary army (see pp. 175–76) and changed their ceremonies to better proclaim the principles of the French Revolution. By no means did all Dutch or Belgian—or French—lodges embrace that revolutionary ardor, but some did. Thus a conspiracy theory arose to explain the supposedly causal link between freemasonry and the revolutions. Many of its disseminators knew far less about eighteenth-century freemasonry than we now do, but exponents of conspiracy theories are often not interested in facts.

The antimasonic literature, used cautiously, helps us understand what contemporaries perceived, however imperfectly, about the political meaning in masonic rhetoric and ritual. We can also now see after our discussion of Scottish, English, and Dutch freemasonry, the political and social meaning given to these new private fraternities by their members. For them, the lodges could function as idealized polities, civil yet private. In that idealization lay a tension, barely beneath the surface, between the private and the public. Some men probably never sought to apply what they learned about self-governance anywhere but in the lodges. Others could seek more and reason by analogy to the larger society. If the lodge constituted a new private space, located somewhere between the public and the strictly private, that is, the personal and domestic, might it not have become another kind of extended family?

The lodges might have evolved into the purely social and leisured, increasingly one of the many pastimes of the genteel and the educated. The admission of women into some of the lodges might indeed be said to signal just such a turn away from the civic and governmental. Or, as I shall next argue, the lodges for women and men, as well as masonic emphasis on the lodge as possessing a domestic life, permit us to gauge more closely and exactly how the lodges intertwined the private and the public. In so doing they gave enlightened idealism a personal, and hence more intense, meaning.

Particularly on the Continent, masonic rhetoric often referred to the activities of the lodges as "*domestique*,"[115] to authority as "paternal," to neighboring lodges as "sisters," to lodges from which they originated as "mothers."[116] The relationship between the master of a lodge and his brothers had emotional overtones that eighteenth-century men expressed through metaphors that were personal and domestic. A Dutch master of the 1760s addressed his brothers "from his heart . . . I recommend the interest of the lodge to you with ardor, and the paternal love for the brother members."[117] In the same period a grief-stricken brother wrote to his "mother" lodge at the death of his wife in childbirth and his ardent wish that the child, who had been saved, will "see the Light with you, my tenderly loved mother, La Bien Aimée." The lodge responded with compassion, referring to his deceased wife as "our sister," although she was almost certainly not the member of a women's lodge.[118] Later in the century an Amsterdam orator introduced his sons as candi-

FIG. 4. The female figure used by the Amsterdam lodge, La Bien Aimée, as its lodge symbol and adopted in 1754.

dates for admission with the moving story of how one of them had saved him from drowning. He knew of "no more appropriate way" to reward his valor than to offer them both membership as equals in his fraternity.[119] In this private realm men spoke with emotion about their devotion to the lodge and to one another. At their festivals masonic orators spoke of "the celebration which today reunites the immense family of masons."[120] One of the few excuses a member could offer for being negligent of his duties, or for requesting honorary membership, aside from travel abroad, was "family and domestic affairs."[121]

The ideal of the domestic was intimately connected to the ambience and values of the lodge, yet it was intended to be a separate sphere. Predictably, lodges often chose women as their symbols. Minerva was a favorite, and masonic iconography made much of her. She could be wisdom, or enlightenment; she could also symbolize a republic.[122] La Bien Aimée chose for its emblem "a woman, gray with old age, wearing a white veil." Her age was meant to symbolize "the antiquity of true friends and our noble order." Every item she wore, every posture and gesture of her hands, was endowed with a carefully described symbolism.[123] She was, among her many virtues, a faithful wife (see illustration above).

If the lodges were analogues to the home, intended to inculcate the virtues associated with domesticity—brotherly affection, fidelity, loyalty, devotion to work, and so forth—then why should this fraternity remain exclusively male? The question was asked early in the century, and by midcentury some lodges chose to respond to it by establishing lodges of both men and women. As we shall see in the next chapter, the earliest known records of such a lodge are dated 1751, and it met in The Hague. But almost certainly the mixed lodges, or lodges of adoption as they were somewhat inexplicably called, date from slightly earlier, probably the 1740s.

Creating new constitutional societies brought to the surface all the limitations of access imposed by birth or education which were inherent in the new constitutionalism. Those limitations now concern us. We have given a willing suspension of disbelief to these fraternal proceedings; we have approached them on their own terms. Yet, if we are at the historical moment when constitutional societies are being created, privately, and in almost every European country, then we may legitimately ask: For whom was the new civil society created? For men, the answer presents itself, who were highly literate, prosperous, usually from the skilled professions, and also in some cases wellborn and titled. Divisions of rank, birth, and wealth were never obliterated in the lodges, whatever their rhetoric and ideals. And women were simply excluded from this form of civil society. But as with all matters masonic, the answer to which we now turn was not quite that simple.

5

Freemasonry, Women, and the Paradox of the Enlightenment

> Sheltered from the sight of the profane and in the home of Brother P. Chevalier, the 23 of July 1755 . . . the lodge having been opened, the resignation of [three brothers, named] was accepted, as no brother within masonry objected to this . . . nevertheless there was unanimous regret on the part of all the brothers.[1]

Most masonic lodges did not meet in private homes. Yet the Amsterdam lodge Concordia vincit Animos did so on the occasion when it regretfully accepted the routine resignation of three brothers, out of the sight of the profane, in July 1755. What was important was that this gathering at the home of M. Chevalier not be "in the sight of the profane." We can only speculate as to where Mme. Chevalier may have been on the evening of 23 July. On another occasion when the lodge met in a private home it could not find "anywhere to retire"; consequently, the lodge was never formally opened.[2]

Perhaps on the evening in question Mme. Chevalier was in attendance at the local Walloon church; Pierre Chevalier was an official there, its reader. The lodge that met in his home had in it many men of French origin. There was also, however, a fair sample of Dutch surnames. We know some of them through the records, where they are described as a wine merchant, a watchmaker, a manufacturer of glass, a schoolmaster, a doctor, or, simply, as merchants.[3] Neither they nor the Dutch brothers could be described in social rank as anything other than comfortably bourgeois, literate, and prosperous enough to afford the dues. Although the lodge was visited from time to time by titled gentlemen—a Dutch baron, for instance—this was not a particularly elite gathering.

In retrospect, its most important, and unexpected, member was the noted French encyclopedist the abbé Claude Yvon (see pp. 158–59). One historian described him as the metaphysician of Diderot's great *Encyclopédie* (1751–1775).[4] He was in Amsterdam hiding from the Parisian authorities. They were after his traveling companion and close friend, the abbé de Prades, for blasphemy, among other charges.[5] As the loyal orator of his lodge, this self-exiled French abbé often spoke about masonic truths and about the need to exclude the profane. For instance, in August 1755 Yvon addressed his brothers to remind them that "this temple, erected [by the brothers] in common, remote from the Profanes, would appear to be one of virtue. A multitude of honest men have been eager to join it."[6] His orations will concern us in the next chapter; here I will concentrate on defining what he and his brothers meant by the profane.

In the early decades of European freemasonry, if we rely on the printed apologies, all women would have been, perforce, among the profane. Antimasonic writers of the 1740s seized upon their exclusion from the lodges, but did so in order to imply that there one found other, "criminal pleasures." And such writers, often adopting a misogynist tone, presumed that the lodges were centers for the bacchanalian, and that women were more than eager to join them. Only a "specious pretext of decency" kept them out.[7] From the perspective of the stereotypes offered by masons for why women were to be excluded, and by antimasons as to why they in fact were, there is not much from which to choose in trying to recreate all the purposes and meanings of women's exclusion. Our search, however, is for what the experience of freemasonry may have meant to those few women finally admitted to the lodges. To find this we also need to know the historical implications of their general exclusion, that is, what gender exclusion tells us about the nature of this new and enlightened fraternity.

But by the 1750s on the Continent gender exclusion within the fraternity had begun to break down. Certain lodges now began formally to admit women. We must search to find any clues that reveal the presence of women prior to that decade. One such clue, as we saw in the introduction, turned up in the Parisian police reports. Forced to meet in private, as opposed to public places, lodge brothers in the 1740s were arrested along with sisters. We have no sense that the women were present by contrivance, or as a foil. They probably lived there. Yet a reminiscence by a French brother of the 1760s who had been in the fraternity in the 1730s may provide the best clue to understanding the pressures that forced the lodges to bring women into their confidence. Lecturing in Strasbourg, he recounts how in "the time of Derwentwater"—that is, Lord Derwentwater, Grand Master until his resignation in 1738—and because of the papal condemnation, women were "used" as protectresses of the order. The brother is explicit about why their help was enlisted: Accusations of sexual license, in short, of sodomy, prompted the move.[8] Yet when the innuendo and pressure lifted, so too did the interest in women's participation. To better understand that reticence we need first to examine the masonic meaning of "the profane." That notion defined the borders of the masonic polity, and, predictably, those boundaries shifted, depending upon time, place, and circumstance. Who then, for Yvon and other mid–eighteenth-century freemasons, were the profane?

The term came into widespread use in Continental European freemasonry during the 1740s. It appears in various languages and its use could vary widely. It could, for instance, mean anyone outside the lodges, "du Prophane Vulgaire," who scorned the bad conduct of masons who belong to unofficial, or "clandestine," lodges. Such was the usage of the term in Paris in the 1740s and then, in a letter to the Amsterdam lodge La Bien Aimée from a lodge in Stockholm.[9] This usage conforms to other masonic language that expressed a tension with "the world" and presumed its hostility. As we saw in chapter 3 in Nijmegen and Amsterdam in the 1750s traditional Dutch Calvinist piety seemed to be embodied in the world, among the profane. Once adopted the term pervaded masonic discourse. By the 1770s French freemasons possessed a distinct understanding of time that depended upon their understanding of the profane. The common date was the "style vulgaire," whereas masonic time, which added four thousand years to any date (1773 becoming 5773), was "enlightened" time.[10] The custom of delineating the masonic time "of light" from vulgar time can be found in Amsterdam as early as the 1750s.[11]

In the 1770s French freemasons also began to delineate "the society of vulgar men, where there is idolatry and tyranny." By contrast, it was claimed that in the lodges could be found "this precious equality."[12] In the French lodges of the 1770s and 1780s the tension between the lodge and the profane is increasingly palpable. The lodges will "frighten the soul and imagination of the profane by substituting a regime made to please reason, made for the interior of our hearts, because such a society would affirm the exercise of social virtue, banish the prejudices which tyrannize the vulgar."[13] The profane should "only be admitted to our breast when brothers have tested the openness between them."[14] By the 1770s it was as if these lodges were at war with the profane. Clearly this originally imported term has been given a new and indigenous meaning. A French-language masonic almanac of 1773 declared that "banishing in our assemblies the *Sexe enchanteur,*" that is, women, shows that the joy and pleasure of the senses is not the point of our association. Women were but one example of the profane.[15] In the same period Dutch freemasons said that it was the vulgar, not the freemasons, who foment civil disorder.[16] And, they claimed, "the vulgar" are the same people who persecute the order.

The term derived conceptually from the English and Scottish guilds and had always embodied the notion of the outsider, among Scottish masons a "cowan." Originally the word had meant another craftsman who might be a competitor for wages and labor, but not a member of the local guild. In medieval times women could frequently be just such competitors, although their membership in certain guilds was also not unknown.[17] In the early eighteenth-century, however, the term lost all such practical and economic associations among freemasons. Its meaning was purely social and cultural. Where we can tease out its implications, we find that it distinguished masonic morality from the nonmasonic, the ideal from everyday reality embodied in the profane who practiced the antithesis of masonic virtues. As one English writer known to the Grand Lodge put it, the profane in early Christian times were those from whom the creed was hidden, having been rendered into a "secret note, mark, or token, by which the faithful in all parts of the world should interchangeably know and be known. The Creed was not to be prophaned, or divulged."[18]

The possession of secret signs delineated the righteous, or separated believers from the world. Masonic fraternalism always possessed a moral dimension, and among the most fundamental moral imperatives of early modern European society had been the rights and duties of the father. Patriarchal authority was taken, certainly by men, to be the basis of all order in society and government. Masonic fraternalism built upon that presumed truth, incorporating thereby gender as absolutely fundamental to determining who might be permitted to join the new fraternity.[19]

Almost invariably, masonic usage throughout Europe after midcentury also implied that the profane were not simply going about their business, however prejudiced and uninspired it may have been. Rather they were watching the brothers, commenting upon them, even condemning them. Yet in general terms, this hostility did not prevent the brothers from courting the profane. A popular French masonic song enticed the profane: "Less strange than zealous / Come! you can join with us."[20]

Yet despite the courtship, the condemnation of the profane increasingly identified them with the commonality of men and, at least in theory, all women. Increasingly the profane came to mean "the vile populace," the superstitious and uneducated, who thwart the fruits of masonic labor.[21] Against the "indiscreet attention" of the profane the freemason had no protection except in his "temple."[22] Although scorned, the profane were frequently addressed by masonic orators, as if they were present: "Profanes, open your eyes, leave your lethargy. The times have come to embrace the cause of virtue, to renounce error, and escape the yoke of prejudice, of which you have been for a long time slaves and victims."[23] Being profane became in masonic discourse a state of mind as well as a social category.

To pass out of the category of the profane required, therefore, special circumstances. In theory, any man could be a freemason. As Rousset de Missy put it in a letter to a close friend, "we are friends to all the world," but then he added, "except to the Jesuits, whom not one master of a lodge would receive in our order."[24] The *Constitutions* (1723) demanded literacy and excluded women and bondsmen, who were largely servants; moreover, every lodge imposed initiation fees and then regular dues.[25] A rite of initiation was also required, which presumed the prior approval of a vast majority of brothers. Until the moment of that approval the candidate seeking admission was called, significantly, "a profane." He both literally and symbolically knocked upon the door of the lodge, and sought the permission of its brothers to enter. This term was used in every initiation ritual to be found in every European country. Until the moment of admission the candidate was a profane. In some sense the profane lurked in every brother; only the power of his ritual initiation into the brotherhood freed him from its influence.

In a ritual recorded in Amsterdam in 1757 the candidate for the degree of entered apprentice is asked: "In what place was the first Lodge formed?" The answer followed: "Upon a Mountain inaccessible to the Profane, where a Cock was never heard to crow, a lion to roar, or a woman to babble! Otherways in a deep valley."[16] In the case of women the prohibition against entrance extended to them as a species, to the whole gender. One of the first printed defenses of that policy explained that "the essence of a society of women could never be that of men."

They can never have a role in true governance.[27] Special circumstances, it would seem, had to be present before they could be permitted passage to the light of freemasonry.

It might be presumed that where the fraternity felt less threatened, its understanding of the profane might become more malleable. However, this was never the case. In Britain the prohibition against women in the lodges remained throughout the eighteenth century, despite occasional calls for reform. It remains to this day. In the eighteenth century the explanation for this rigidity might rest on the weight of guild tradition, despite the fact that women in earlier times had been known to break through that tradition, at least in England if not in Scotland, and to be admitted to the guilds. It was in the Continental lodges that the exclusion of women broke down. The lodges for men and women came into existence by the second half of the eighteenth century, and we may legitimately ask about the circumstances of that reform.

What we find is that the acceptance of women into the fraternity required a particular set of circumstances which had less to do with the social rank of either the men or the women than it did with the economic situation of the women themselves, as well as with their willingness to embrace the masonic vision of enlightened culture. In addition, the evidence strongly suggests that the lodges for men and women laid emphasis on only certain aspects of masonic idealism, upon virtue in the polity, as distinct from its governance. The absence of language of governance within the proceedings of the women's lodges only reinforces the point that first and foremost the male lodges were schools of government.

But the admission of women does signal the desire to enlist their support in secular and civil society, possibly to encourage their ambivalence toward traditional culture or their own particularist needs. Certainly the historian Joan Landes has argued that the French salons, where women were quite prominent, emerged within an ideological framework that sought to "empty out the feminine connotations (and ultimately, the women as well) of absolutist public life."[28] The role of women in the lodges is, however, even more complex. The admission of women to eighteenth-century societies of "equals" gives us one of the first moments in Western culture when liberal idealism about merit and equality had to face the reality of socially constructed gender differences. Predictably the brothers and sisters expressed many and different reactions, ambiguities, and confusions when faced with the disparity between words and life.

In order to comprehend the strength of the prohibition against the profane, we need to examine it within a congenial setting. In some European countries there were lodges that felt little or no hostility from the civil and religious authorities. Indeed, of all the Continental countries with which I am familiar Sweden offered the most open and congenial environment for masonic fraternalism. By midcentury it was also governed by a limited monarchy; it was a parliamentary state. Yet there too the profane remained outside the lodges. In lodges composed of the most elite men, sanctioned by the approval of court and clergy, a profane could be a woman, or a man, even of noble rank, who was clearly an outsider. In every case, however, the distance between the safety and sanctity of the lodge and "the world" was palpable and its bridging unacceptable.

Just such an elitism characterized the lodges that met in the Royal Palace in

Stockholm in the 1750s.[29] We have a privileged view of their proceedings, and of one meeting in particular where "a profane" made herself privy to its assembly. The Swedish brothers wrote in fascinating detail to the Amsterdam lodge La Bien Aimée to describe the event. It is worth hearing the full account just as it was written:

Stockholm, 12 August 1757

> The 24 June or the day of St. Jean Baptist [the major masonic feast day] all the members of the three lodges turned out at the Church of Ladugårdsland to hear the sermon which was given by brother Halman, Doctor of Theology, and pastor of this church; after vocal and instrumental music, the sermon finished, all the brothers passed by the sacristy, in front of the door where there was a large basin, in which for the profit of the poor was placed 6000 Dal., intended for the Orphanage. After this, we departed for this house where we had all the children pass in review before us. And then we went in 70 carriages to the Palais Royal at Carlberg, which the King had given over to us for the day, with the promise that He himself would attend our Assembly, if the state of his health would permit.
>
> The shrubs and all the avenues of the garden were guarded by 27 men, and at first we were not allowed to enter without showing tickets or signs with which we were all provided. Having all arrived at the garden of this Chateau, the 3 Grand Masters invited their lodges to dine in the Orangerie, where we were seated at 3 in the afternoon, and we did not arise until 9 that evening. During this time the house was guarded by 27 men of the Artillery and 15 of the House. In the little garden of the Orangerie there were 6 trumpets of the Court and kettledrums which played at the changing of each course, seven in all, and a discharge of cannon. I must confess that in all my life I have never been at such a grand and agreeable company and such a great diversity of dishes. With regard to the Ceremonies, one observed those which are common to the Lodges of Table.
>
> During this time a lot of people [*une multitude de monde*] gathered about us, carried away with curiosity. Among others, the wife of the Spanish ambassador [*L'Ambassadrice d'Espagne*] asked through one of our members, for permission to see a gathering so splendid. Finally she was permitted. But before she entered, the Grand Masters asked us to cover ourselves by putting on our hats; not to look at the lady, in order to signal our disdain at all that is profane. And she entered and exited without anyone having looked at her or having given any attention to her.

But the account did not end there. This breach of a masonic feast by one of the profane led to consternation and accusations. The brother who observed the entire spectacle shrewdly remarked:

> It is remarkable that so many masons who formerly had been protective of their attire, never showing them to the profane, were on this day so wayward as to display them. And during the same meal, several got up from the table to promenade in the garden, all dressed up as they were. The meal ended; all three lodges promenaded in the garden, led by their grand masters, dressed, etc.

In that comfortable, luxurious setting of the Swedish court many brothers relaxed their prohibition about appearing before the world fully identified by their elaborate costumes. Accepted in the highest circles of the state, permitted to preach in a church of the established Lutheran faith, feted and entertained by the king, who in 1761 became Grand Master, their dedication to secrecy mellowed.[30] A woman of high rank, almost certainly from the Spanish nobility, was permitted to observe the proceedings. Forays were made out into the world wearing the decorous aprons, gloves, and sashes of the order. But, as our witness recounted, the fraternity paid a price for its indiscretion:

> Judge, if you will, the noise the Vulgar made about this—and it was a real pleasure to hear their reasonings. Some believed us to be the cause of various commotions with the ministry. Others, that we had the intention of rebuilding the Tower of Babylon, and begged God not to punish us, as he had punished . . . before. Still others imagined that our unique goal had been to enjoy the fair sex [*d'aimer le Sexe*], and to produce illegitimate children. And finally, others who were just lost in their speculations, etc.[31]

This account suggests that in Stockholm the profane suspected the freemasons of political intrigue, licentiousness, and perhaps most cynically, of siring illegitimate children to be provided for by charity. Charity had been central to Swedish freemasonry since its inception in the 1730s.[32] But the habit did not save the order from hostility. Hostile speculations directed against the freemasons also meant speculations against some of the most important elements in Swedish society and government. Despite this context where the rivalry between the two main political parties in Sweden also reflected social and cultural differences, the charges against the lodges were nevertheless similar to the kinds of accusations against the fraternity that occurred in almost every European country, time and time again. Sexual license appears almost invariably. That sort of innuendo is also reminiscent of the charges frequently leveled against the traditional clergy, and sometimes against the aristocracy. Masonic secrecy may have conjured up the same set of profound social and class resentments.

Although entertained beyond anything some of them had ever experienced, the gentlemen of the very elite Swedish lodges were not so intimidated by the possibility of innuendo that they refrained from rudely disdaining the wife of an ambassador, or from daring to appear in public in full regalia. The three lodges had over three hundred members; the officers were government officials, chancellors, the secretary to the king, his physician, a surgeon, the secretary of state (as Grand Master), officers of the army, the secretary to the royal archives, an iron merchant, magistrates of the city. On the occasion of this meeting in Stockholm the usual sense of the solemnity and importance of the proceedings was reinforced by the grandeur of the court. Between it and the speculations of the profane lay a gulf that defies easy explanation. It is not sufficient to say that the chasm between the Swedish lodges and the larger society was simply a reflection of the arrogance permitted noblemen and magistrates. There is every reason to believe that humbler brothers, in far less elevated or secure circumstances, would have behaved in exactly the same way.

When the prohibition against the profane was loosened or revoked, there must have been compelling reasons to do so. Exploring those reasons may tell us something about the boundaries of masonic culture, and hence the boundaries around the enclaves of the enlightened. We need now to inspect a moment when women were given citizenship (as distinct from salon membership) within the new, and enlightened, culture. Such a moment occurred in 1751 in The Hague: The Grand Master of The Netherlands, Juste Gerard, baron van Wassenaer, initiated a lodge for both men and women and signed its *Livre de Constitution*. Possibly in recognition of this unique break with tradition and the special patronage of the baron, the lodge took his Christian name as its own, La Loge de Juste.

This is the first known lodge of women and men anywhere in Europe. The Hague was not an inappropriate setting for such a cosmopolitan gathering.[33] With a population of no more than thirty-five thousand in the mid–eighteenth century, this medium-sized Dutch city was, in fact, one of the most cosmopolitan in western Europe. As a Scottish visitor put it, The Hague "is a charming agreeable place for one that wants to be in the world. It seems to be the center of Europe where you meet with people of rank from all countries. Here politeness cements them all together."[34] This ambience was created by the diplomatic corps, the vast publishing industry, the governmental institutions, and the theater-in-residence, the Comédie Française, which enjoyed a well-earned international reputation. The actresses and actors of the Comédie joined with William Bentinck and various other *haagse* gentlemen and one gentlewoman to create the first mixed lodge, or lodge of adoption, as lodges that admitted men and women as equal members came to be known. We can imagine that it may have taken a great deal of politeness to cement this experiment in sociability.

The origin of the term "adoption" to describe lodges for women is shrouded in mystery. Some clue may lie in the way the word was used as a verb. Brothers always referred to themselves as having been "made" freemasons, or as having been received into the order. In the few records we have from sisters where they reminisce about their initiation they speak of having been adopted.[35] The term may have been used purposefully to conjure up the adoption of children into a family where, by nature, they would not normally have been placed. Once again the term, whether purposefully or not, implied the domestic unit, in this instance held together by sentiment rather than by an accident of birth. However they got there, the sisters in La Loge de Juste are unique for the early and detailed records they left behind.

The manuscript records of de Juste have the lodge's constitution along with a complete membership list. They also provide a set of initiation rituals. The records are entirely in French, the spoken language of polite society in mid–eighteenth-century Holland. Perhaps appropriately, de Juste invented its own rituals so that the female and male members might express their equality, "fraternity," and mutual search for virtue and wisdom. Each initiation ceremony, for admission or for the various masonic degrees, brought the initiate closer to this virtue, which, as shown by one ritual, is equated with productivity and the discipline of industry.

Almost without exception, the language of the rituals is highly mystical and symbolic; squares, temples, symbolic fires, and secret words abound in the original texts. Some of this language derived from the alchemical tradition; all of it was intensely spiritual. Most important, it is new language not commonly found in other masonic texts from the same period. Its signal characteristic might best be described as a mystical striving, the search for perfect virtue. Generally we would not expect to find that kind of language in masonic circles so early in the century. By the 1770s, particularly in Germany, freemasonry had rediscovered the mystical and magical, the rosicrucian and alchemical, grafting that tradition onto its rituals and its ethos.[36] Similarly it begins to appear in records of Amsterdam lodges, also around the 1770s, possibly imported from their many ties with Germany and its cultural movements.

The use of the mystical and magical to express masonic ideals might be imagined as always present in the movement, the legacy of its links to Renaissance humanism and Hermeticism.[37] Yet both the British and Continental records of eighteenth-century freemasonry present a more complex picture. In the early part of the century the mystical and magical elements in the masonic legacy of the seventeenth century seem barely evident. Even the "pantheism" of Rousset has a rationalist quality about it, with no excursions into the mystical as a way of expressing belief in Nature as distinct from belief in the Judeo-Christian God. This rationalist tone fits well enough with the nearly universal repudiation of religious enthusiasm so characteristic of the early Enlightenment.

The appearance of mystical language in a midcentury lodge that was clearly engaged in a radical departure from acceptable, gender-exclusive freemasonry focuses our attention on the potential for innovation within this unique fraternity. Its links with the Platonic and Hermetic traditions of the Renaissance, however tenuous by that time, made available a philosophical idealism that emphasized the mind or intellect as the sole criterion for judging the worthiness of an individual's merit and the quest for secret truth known only to the initiated. This propensity toward the mystical within Continental freemasonry will surface increasingly during the second half of the eighteenth century. Out of this tendency came the mystical language of the radical Illuminati and other revolutionary secret societies modeled on the lodges. There are no known links between those revolutionary secret societies and the earlier lodges of adoption. That is not the point. What is important about masonic idealism and its propensity to search for mystical language was the power it gave to men and women to express dreams and fantasies, rooted in their contemporary circumstances as they imagined them transformed. In justifying this lodge, which met briefly in The Hague, brothers made reference to the myth of Plato's cave. In the eighteenth century feminist sentiments can also be found in other neo-Platonic circles.[38] The impulse to search for enlightenment could sometimes bring with it recourse to illumination, particularly when the ideal bore so little relation to the reality around it.

In La Loge de Juste, mystical language provided the means for expressing egalitarian social behavior, which, if lived out in the "real world" of any European society at the time, would have been highly subversive, if not incomprehensible. Yet all this striving to build "the temple of virtue" as prescribed by the ritual, complete with secret signs and passwords, disguised as much as it illuminated. "The primitive light" that shone in the temple to which women were suddenly being admitted was in fact concealing the obvious. Never once is it mentioned in the rituals that new, normally forbidden worshipers, until that moment universally defined as profane, have now been admitted. These mystical rituals never once explain why this singular breach with tradition has occurred.

We have to piece together the reasons for this event from a variety of other sources. Masonic reformers of the 1740s had demanded that women be admitted into the lodges on the grounds that sexual exclusivity contradicted their ideal of equality. In that decade, possibly in response to women having been admitted, French lodges specifically outlawed the practice, a prohibition not lifted officially until 1774. We need to consider the possibility that the Dutch lodges, familiar with the French masonic literature, could not effect the same prohibition because they were forced to respond to local pressures coming from outside the lodges. Certainly we have heard the hint of sexual slander in the attacks upon the order, particularly from the Calvinist ministry (see p. 76) in the Republic.

The Reformed ministers were the same group who led the assault against sodomy that erupted in The Netherlands in the early 1730s.[39] That persecution led to the execution of dozens of men accused of homosexuality, and it was widely commented upon in the European journals of the day. The degree of hatred directed against homosexuals in the 1730s and beyond appears to have been uniquely Dutch, and historians have connected it to a general crisis in the Republic. It coincided with a revulsion against foreign influences and the persecution of booksellers, the supposed purveyors of ideas that were libertine and unorthodox. Surely that homophobic and xenophobic episode would have been remembered in the early 1750s. The persecution of homosexuals in the Dutch cities did not end in the 1730s. Less serious persecutions occurred in 1764 and 1776. Although none of the masonic sources make mention of these events, we need to remember them, and to bear in mind that in 1735 rioters in The Hague did bring up the charge of homosexuality against the freemasons.[40] These charges do not adequately account for the decision in 1751 to step away from the male exclusivity of at least this one Dutch lodge, but they may have played a role.

Other factors appear more obviously to account for the existence of La Loge de Juste. The presence of William Bentinck as a sponsor of the lodge places it among the many projects of reform with which he can be associated. He was, of course, a key figure in the Revolution of 1748 that restored the stadtholderate. As a Dutch Whig—probably the best description of his political goals—Bentinck wanted to see British institutions exported to the Republic and, not least, he wanted to forge alliances among progressive groups sympathetic to the Anglo-Dutch alliance and the stadtholderate. He wrote to his mother that he was appalled by "our miserable constitution, without any executive power."[41] As curator of the University of Leiden, he took an interest in appointing liberal theologians within the faculty,[42] and he was a promoter of scientific inquiry. His liberal approach to freemasonry would be part of the same reforming mentality. In his way, Bentinck was a republican who wanted to see a strong central government develop in the Republic as the guarantor of the Anglo-Dutch alliance and in opposition to the corruption, as he imagined it, of the regents.

Thus Bentinck, along with his brother Charles, belonged to a small circle of midcentury reformers in the Republic. They read the writings of the French philosophes and even welcomed Rousseau and Diderot into their homes.[43] Diderot, for one, came away from his experiences in The Netherlands convinced that greater social equality existed there than in France.[44] As progressive aristocrats associated with the masonic lodges the Bentincks had social contact with groups normally excluded from the most elite circles in the Republic: merchants, minor government officials, publishers, Amsterdam Jews—the type of men who turn up in the membership records. Why not also women?

There is one other factor that plays into that question in ways that may never be fully understood. William Bentinck's marriage was notoriously troubled, and his wife understood their plight in terms larger than simply personal. It led her to speculate on the inequities between men and women, on the inferiority of her circumstances as a woman.[45] Bentinck could not have been unfamiliar with her analysis; it was well known to her confidants in The Netherlands and abroad. The equality espoused by La Loge de Juste defied the reality of women's circumstances in every European society. Might it not also have assuaged a conscience troubled by charges for which there was no obvious rebuttal?

Bentinck and his brothers played out this fantasy of gender equality with the educated and theatrically gifted women of the Comédie Française and with one or two Dutch ladies also drawn to the lodge. Its master was the Grand Master of The Netherlands, the Baron van Wassenaer; his deputy Grand Master was Henri du Sauzet, an Amsterdam publisher and an associate of Rousset de Missy. The Grand Mistress was an aristocratic woman of The Hague, Marianne, the baroness d'Honstein (d. 1762), the wife of Johannes, baron van Honstein, a lieutenant captain in the Grand Regiment of the Republic. Her broad signature rests directly across from van Wassenaer's in the *Livre de Constitution*. The Grand Mistress, as she was called, appears also to have been a Catholic; records in The Hague show that the family was baptized and held their children's weddings in the Catholic church. The family also had extensive property holdings in the city and made frequent recourse to notarized legal documents, which survive in the municipal archives.[46] Catholics, of whatever rank, were a disliked minority in many quarters of the Republic. Membership in masonic lodges may have been one means used by elites who were not from the religion of the majority to bridge the gap that separated them from their generally more influential counterparts.

The Baroness d'Honstein was, however, the only aristocratic woman among the female membership of the lodge. We have precious little historical evidence about the women from the Comédie. Most were foreign born; they lived and worked among themselves.[47] They had already, perforce, established a fairly close-knit community. Some of the "sisters" were married to their fraternal "brothers"; at least this is true for Mmes. Van der Kaa, Derosimond, and De Vos, while one sister, Marie Armand de Verteuil, was separated from her husband, and Mlle. Prevost was single at the time of her initiation. Her mother was also a lodge member. Of the nineteen sisters who made up the lodge, a few, such as Elizabeth Forest and Mlles. Julien, Emilie, and Le Blanc, all with the Comédie, made their permanent residence in Paris; two came from Nantes. Rosa Frazy (who signed her name Rosa Frazi) may have been Italian, but she made her permanent residence in London. As constant travelers, the actresses and actors may also have exported their egalitarian freemasonry to other European cities.

As theater people they may also have imported their particular form of gender-inclusive freemasonry from the subculture to which prejudice had so often consigned them, particularly in France. In the 1740s in Paris an actor in the Comédie Italienne was among those arrested in his lodge by the police (see p. 4). In that same decade the Comédie Française appears to have performed a play about the freemasons.[48] This dramatic interest continued and one of the major themes in French plays about the freemasons was the curiosity, titillation, and anger provoked in women by their exclusion from the lodges.[49] Some actors and actresses may have been parodying the familiar from the perspective of an insider.

Apart from the actors in The Hague, there was a significant number of local aristocrats among the thirty-one brothers in La Loge de Juste. All appear to have been native Dutch; some are described as living "on his estates and in The Hague." In addition, five gentlemen are listed with their military titles, as lieutenants or captains of the Guard. They remind us, once again, of the strong military presence in the lodges of Continental Europe. All these men had joined with this company of French-speaking actors and actresses who catered to the most refined dramatic tastes of their age, doing serious drama, some by the French philosophes, along with comedies and Italian operas. Both players and patrons, among whom we may count the aristocratic and military brothers, were fluent in the international language and enlightened culture of the century.

Among the signatories of the lodge's constitution were the husband and wife team of Jean and Françoise Gravillon Baptiste Anselme. In the 1750s Jean was director of the Comédie; in the 1760s his wife and daughter assumed that role. Mlle. Rosette Baptiste, the daughter, also exercised her independence in a more libertine fashion. She was widely regarded as the mistress of Jacques-Jean, comte de Wassenaer d'Opdam (1724–79), one of the brothers who in turn took a serious interest in the well-being of the Comédie. The Anselme family appears also to have been Catholic, at least to the extent of baptizing one of their children in the hidden Catholic church that flourished discreetly in The Hague.

The libertine reputation of Mlle. Anselme did not inhibit her fellow actors and actresses from joining with her in this lodge. The troupe had always suffered, as did actors and actresses in general in this century, from accusations of libertinism and immorality. Local clergy and scandal-mongers had frequently attacked it.[50] Yet from at least the late seventeenth century and the stadtholderate of William III, the company had enjoyed court patronage. It is just possible that its definitions of respectability also differed self-consciously from those that prevailed in the larger society. In such a small city this extraordinary and new form of socializing, with its British associations, could not have gone unnoticed, especially when it entailed so many prominent citizens.

The quasi-mystical ritual of the lodge may have been suggested to it by a British masonic reformer, William Mitchell (1724–92), an officer of the excise and a teacher of English who resided in The Hague. Mitchell had become enamored of the new "Scottish," or philosophical, freemasonry (see p. 59) found at midcentury in many British lodges that were critical of the London Grand Lodge. They had attacked the Grand Lodge for its social exclusivity and had revived what they claimed was an older, and truer, masonry. Among the innovations associated with

Scottish freemasonry were new grades or philosophical degrees with rituals that employed language more mystical than rationalist.[51] Official Scottish freemasons of the 1750s were quick to repudiate these innovations as "irregularities."[52] The records of La Loge de Juste include Mitchell's name and make specific reference to "a new masonry, under the title of Scottish masonry, divised in two grades, with the names of architect and grand architect." Within the first year of the lodge's existence this innovation in the social mores of The Hague came to the hostile attention of a visiting French abbé, who proceeded to write a satire against it. Once again, freemasonry had come to the attention of a profane—in this instance to the attention of a profane from France, where the social stigma attached to actresses was particularly intense.[53]

Without mentioning masonry by name, the abbé Coyer's attack makes specific reference to Captain Mitchell and "ses frères," to the English origin of their "frivolity," to their interest in mathematics, and then quite pointedly to what he calls the courtesans in their midst.[54] The thrust of the attack centers on the forms of socializing adopted by this coterie, on their imitation of aristocratic manners while at the same time valuing merit, not birth, among themselves. Indeed, the abbé argues, they have taken elegance of manners to the point of a religion and in their temple, while despising all other religions, they worship the sun and the moon. They have prohibited polygamy, but in fact they practice it, and in the process have made it possible for members of "the inferior sex" to lose their virtue with decency.[55] Coyer never mentions freemasonry by name, so we cannot be sure that the angry abbé had La Loge de Juste firmly in mind when he penned his attack, but it seems a distinct possibility. Certainly the description he gives fits quite neatly, and he was in The Hague in this period. Not least, he did know one prominent French freemason, the Chevalier Ramsay.[56] Predictably, of the many innovative customs adopted by the lodge—or by some similarly egalitarian group of brothers—the mixing of the sexes on an equal footing, even more than the apparent irreligion, gave Coyer the greatest offense.

The actors and actresses of the Comédie had managed to give offense in other quarters besides the clergy, and did so precisely because of their social behavior. One of them, or one of their supporters, publicly attacked the social prejudice that prevailed against actors and actresses, even claiming that snobbery was worse in The Hague than in Paris. Actors and actresses, he or she proclaimed, were as good as anybody else, "for anyone can have titles and riches, but talents are a gift from heaven and such gifts are always respectable."[57] This is language that has a masonic ring to it; it goes on to make the point that some people have "the arrogance to believe that Nature has put them above a Mason or a Baker."[58] This defiant defense was answered quickly, also anonymously: These actors and actresses think that merit and not birth should count in the eyes of society, and in so doing they threaten "the maintenance of law and public security. Despite the republican spirit and independence that reigns here," this detractor of the Comédie argues, "one is still strongly persuaded that subordination is necessary. Each citizen is useful and respectable in his place [*dans son état*]."[59]

This hostile critic may not have known about the masonic socializing of the actors and actresses who openly defended their talent and merit. They were meeting in secret as equals with some of the most elite elements in this cosmopolitan city. Yet there were other enlightened sources that may also have nurtured their sense of self-worth. The spirit behind the plays of the philosophes performed by the troupe complemented the lessons it learned in its secret fraternizing. Throughout his life Diderot argued for the theater as an agent of social change, as a podium for enlightened thinking as well as an occasion for emotional release.[60] It would rival the pulpit, indeed surpass its force, he said, by acting out ideals that contradicted those most commonly preached by the clergy.

Such enthusiasm for the educative value of the theater did not begin with eighteenth-century reformers. The historian of Renaissance neo-Platonism and Hermeticism, Frances Yates, found seventeenth-century actors and actresses who advocated Rosicrucianism and used the stage as a podium to spread that mystical gospel.[61] There exist intellectual links between the reforming zeal of that seventeenth-century movement, German and English at its origins, and freemasonry at its origins (see p. 36). Later, eighteenth-century freemasons, such as those who enacted the mystical rituals of La Loge de Juste, may have been recovering those supposed affinities. We may also reasonably imagine that actors and actresses of the mid-eighteenth century would have been aware of the reforming traditions in European theatrical history. Certainly this troupe was self-consciously hostile to the bigotry and ostracism commonly meted out to men, and especially women, of the theater.

Perhaps the passion to act out alternatives to social convention extended beyond those evenings on the stage when one had the opportunity to perform the new, philosophical plays emanating from Paris. Perhaps the actors and actresses also wanted to create for themselves an alternative fantasy of enlightenment that could at least have the illusion of reality. "Without distinction of birth," as the manuscript records of La Loge de Juste proclaim, "the brothers and sisters" will deport themselves "without vice, in order to augment the good manners of society and to dissipate the shadows that cover the eyes of the profane." They declare that the members will attempt to spread themselves "over the surface of the earth."[62] Yet the profane remained, despite, or perhaps because of, the tension created by the goal of universality.

Without detracting from the zeal and originality of the ideals proclaimed by this egalitarian lodge, some historical antecedents for this sort of egalitarian socializing should be acknowledged. These precedents are ones that the lodge itself had an interest in; it collected anecdotes and written "tableaux" about them. In the late seventeenth century The Hague had been a center for upper-class *préciosité,* a movement with feminist overtones led by French aristocratic women.[63] Also, within Dutch republican and bourgeois circles associated with Johan de Wit in the 1660s, at least one club with important intellectual interests had admitted men and women as equal members. Reference to that club is made in the manuscripts of La Loge de Juste, where an unknown writer attempts to patch together its history.[64] Another group, of eighteenth-century origins, is also mentioned in the historical jottings of the lodge: The Ordre de Mopses. It began in Austria in the late 1730s and may have been imitative of masonic practices. The order was more of a social club for women where "brothers" paid court in mock-heroic fashion to "sisters" who assumed titles: the married woman (*soeur aimable*), the frigid beauty (*soeur bril-*

lante), the lady of love and laughter (*soeur gracieuse*). La Loge de Juste appears to have been interested mainly in the order's initiation ceremony, yet none of the lodge's ceremonies appear similar to what can be pieced together about the mopses from their various eighteenth-century commentators.[65]

When all these antecedents are assessed the conclusion remains that La Loge de Juste was engaged in something new and unique. Its records betray a sense of that uniqueness and equally important, this lodge required both special ceremonies and protection. It was recognized and assisted financially by the Grand Lodge and its Grand Master. The constitution stated that relationship openly: "In the name of the Grand Architect of the Universe . . . under the most exalted and wise protection of the Baron Wassenaer," the lodge has been opened. Yet ultimate responsibility for its well-being lay with the Baroness d'Honstein. Her leadership is acknowledged, as is the importance of all the officers, women and men, whose titles are given in both the masculine and the feminine, for example, *député maitre* and *députée maitresse, un grand secrétaire* and *grande secrétaire,* and *un grand orateur* and *grande oratrice*. The annual elections to these offices were to be without "distinction of birth," and, most important, all rituals, and hence all offices, reflected an absolute gender equality.

In keeping with the Scottish form of the lodge, it also initiated its members in a special degree, the grade of architect. This appears to be a ceremony, and possibly a grade, unique to the lodge, and both women and men could be initiated into it. One had to have been a master or mistress of a lodge before rising to the special wisdom embodied in the degree. Its recipient, who had to be initiated by a member of the Grand Lodge, hence by a man, vowed to practice virtue: silence, charity, fidelity, and temperance. The mystical language of the degree permitted the women and men to become something other than they were, to reach out through gestures and words for an illumination of the spirit that would be individually experienced as well as socially recognized. The initiation rite to the degree closed with "the kiss of reason," and the degree carried with it a secret password, "Nejusrimatea," which permitted initiates to be known to one another. As the manuscript catechism that accompanies the degree ceremony explains, the word signified "production." The Venerable, representing the Grand Lodge, and one of the other officers were meant to chant out the meaning of that universal masonic "work" which begins and ends in the symbolic center of the lodge.[66]

At the center stands the temple of virtue, and in its center shines a primitive light, the light of reason. La Loge de Juste took a small animal, the ermine with its precious coat and fastidious manner, as a symbol of its proud and elegant search for virtue and reason. Adorning a pictorial representation of the animal was the motto "I would rather die than defile myself." In the ritual for the reception of a master and mistress the virtue sought is specifically identified as Christian, an identification that does not appear in other, exclusively male lodges from the same place and period. Yet in other parts of the records virtues are simply named, with a distinction being made solely between the nonmasons, "le prophane masculin, et feminin," and those initiated into "the light of all grades of the freemasonry of adoption."[67]

The overwhelming impression left by the records of de Juste concerns virtue. The ethos of this lodge centered on moral improvement, on reason and work as the means to self-knowledge and worth. Such sentiments were commonplace in other, exclusively male lodges from the period (see p. 159), but in those lodges virtue was more overtly linked to the well-being of society and, most important, to governance. The lodges for men and women only indirectly embraced a larger political reality. In the eighteenth century the constitutional ideal, the creation of constitutionally governed civil societies, was masculine work. The lodges of adoption provided access to that ideal inadvertently. They were primarily schools of manners and virtue. Yet their brothers had to acknowledge that while aspects of freemasonry remained purposefully hidden from their sisters, "this new association [of] men and women without number who in civil society scarcely have contact, are united together by the sweet bonds of fraternity."[68]

In the 1750s in Dutch freemasonry these new lodges were intended to be universal. The records of de Juste speak of "the lodges of adoption which will establish themselves in the United Provinces." There is no firm evidence that other such lodges were established in the 1750s, but the possibility was contemplated for a brief time. Intended for the use of all Dutch freemasons, the 1751 *Almanac* printed toasts by which sisters and brothers in such lodges might begin their "Fête de Table." "Drink to our amiable sisters, my brothers," proclaims the ritual, answered by "drink to our tender brothers." Very shortly (and probably with increasing gusto) all join in song, proclaiming "our perfect union."[69] In the same *Almanac* a Mlle. de Brouquère is listed as a "grand maitresse," but her name appears nowhere in the records of de Juste. It is just possible that at least one other lodge of adoption had been established in the Republic.

Equally interesting is the fact that members of La Loge de Juste turn up in a troupe of actors and actresses brought to Vienna in 1752.[70] Later in the 1760s the company had links with high Austrian officials known to be freemasons. Of course the world of Viennese masonry in the last quarter of the eighteenth century was one of the richest milieus ever graced by dramatists and composers. This was the world of Mozart. His masonic milieu may have been wider than the traditional male lodges usually studied would suggest. The rich masonic symbolism found in *The Magic Flute,* for example,[71] where it is gender specific—and what could be more gender specific than the evil Queen of the Night—may relate to many contemporary themes with which Mozart was familiar. If there were lodges of adoption in Vienna, we can only wonder what they would have made out of the evil personified by the Queen and her entourage. Equally we may ask, What were the reactions to female freemasonry to be found among Mozart and his brothers, and do any of those responses find their way into the portrait of Mozart's evil queen?[72] Did these lodges of adoption meet with hostility and resistance in Vienna, just as they did in The Hague? In the 1770s in Paris the proposal that one of the women's lodges be merged into a regular lodge evoked an outburst: "A vain sex, indiscreet and fickle . . . possessed of dangerous instincts . . . we know women, their foolish spirit, their inconsequential heart . . . inconstancy is her only element."[73]

Given the inferior status accorded women throughout eighteenth-century Europe, their removal from the ranks of the profane required explanation and justification. Their lack of freedom in marriage had been used to justify their exclusion from the lodges, which were to be composed of "beings, free and independent."[74] Put another way, "The first quality of a mason is to free, and liberty is never the allotment of women."[75] Unable to offer or extol liberty, the adoptive rituals offered the sisters and brothers the route to virtue, and implicitly to equality. But did the sisters, and especially the brothers, understand why they should undertake this particular journey jointly?

One oration that attempted to answer the question has survived in a very rare songbook dedicated to "the sisters of the fraternity spread over the surface of the earth." Aside from songs and melodies composed by two brothers of de Juste, the songbook published a preliminary discourse delivered by Saint-Etienne, a deputy master of the lodge.[76] He speaks to his brothers to convince them of the value of the new lodge of adoption. The passions, in particular vanity, ambition, and self-regard, he proclaims, have taken hold in the heart of man, and these are moderated only by "the sciences." The passions have produced "in various nations a profound ignorance," and that blindness has prevented thousands of men from seeing that women "have been formed to be [men's] faithful companions, sharing in the happiness, the pleasure of their actions." Women are "one of the most beautiful ornaments . . . in the order of nature's perfections."

The orator likens this widespread ignorance to that found in Plato's cave. As a result of its perpetuation for many centuries, "masons would not admit their wives into their lodges." This ignorance, he continues, must be dispelled, not just in faraway places where masons may be found, but rather "in their Republic." This lodge is the polity where a small group of citizens have escaped ignorance, and "they are distinguished and known under the name of masons, perfect friends, faithful compatriots and guardians of a temple of virtue and truth." By admitting women, these men alone "by their wise discretion, in the practice of their labors, have maintained the deference and affection which is due to the perfect companion of man." The metaphors are traditional; women are helpmates to men. But the message goes one step further.

Saint-Etienne manages a rhetorical exist from the gender exclusivity of the traditional lodges by claiming that "the light" has finally dispelled the darkness: "Our profound study in the art of masonry has enabled us to find a true method of perfecting our building [*nos édifices*]. It is by the assistance of our sisters." With them, he proclaims, we shall build "the school of manners, the temple of virtue." By 1751, as a result of the Orangist Revolution of 1747–48, freemasonry in the Republic had surfaced from under the weight of the prohibition placed on it by the States of Holland in 1735. The reformers of 1751, it would seem, now wanted to enlist women into their temples of virtue. The effort to include women, as we shall see, failed in the Republic, as in most other European countries. We can only imagine what the universal enactment of this fantasy might have created.

Saint-Etienne's brief discourse to his brothers gives us a powerful example of the resourcefulness of masonic rhetoric in justifying digressions from social convention or in articulating departures from conventional moral or religious wisdom. Once placed in the temple of virtue, compelled by "the primitive light," hermetically sealed from the ignorant and the profane, brothers could redefine the profane, and then join with sisters to seek the perfection of the masonic work. Paradoxically, mystical language permitted reason to be invoked in defiance of tradition and social convention. Once conjured up in the service of virtue, reason permitted masons to argue for the universal truth, and applicability, of their actions.

Yet barriers against other profanes remained. Masonic idealism bore little relation to the real barriers to membership that income or the absence of surplus wealth must have presented. Admission to La Loge de Juste was a costly matter, more costly than admission to most other lodges. Aside from the gold-plated jewelry depicting the sun and the moon that grand masters and mistresses wore, silk and taffeta accessories were also a part of a member's basic attire.[77] Like all European freemasons, the brothers and sisters embraced the symbols of the workman's uniform; but in rendering their aprons in taffeta and their gloves in silk they also symbolically repudiated the sweat, dirt, and hard work that is the lot of the worker. At the Comédie Française, where so many of the brothers and sisters were employed, a stagehand with some technical skill who arranged the scenery between acts was paid a little over 6 guilders a day for four days of work in 1752.[78] Since the company performed irregularly, that sum could not be expected on a daily basis. In the same year the best seat in the theater cost 3 guilders, although places were available for less than a guilder. In 1750 a worker in the shipbuilders' guild in Amsterdam, one of the most highly remunerated in the Republic, could hope to earn 1.4 guilders per day. Unfortunately, the actual income of any one of the actors or actresses cannot be determined from available records because they negotiated for space and other necessities as a company and then divided up the profits equally among themselves. We do know that the actors and actresses of this prestigious troupe lived well and kept servants, and at this time a good actor on the Amsterdam stage could earn up to 1,000 guilders a year.[79]

Membership expenses in La Loge de Juste were not affordable on the wages of a day laborer, or even an ordinary shopkeeper, but the lodge was open to the wellborn, highly remunerated professional classes, and prosperous merchants. All of these men and a very few women who might fit into these categories, could probably manage to find the money for a woman's taffeta apron at 5.5 guilders or a man's at 3, and a trowel at 1, to name only the most important items in the masonic wardrobe. But expenses only began there. The lodge required stationery, plates, and drinking cups, not to mention the services of cooks, waiters, and laundresses. There was, of course, an initiation fee that could run from the 21 guilders paid by Mr. van den Bergh (which was less than half of what a foreign worker paid to get into the Amsterdam shipbuilder's guild) to the 78 paid by M. and Mme. van Belle, who were incidentally prominent and respected Protestants, to the highest sum of 52 guilders paid by an individual, predictably by William Bentinck.[80] Not every brother or sister had to pay the initiation fee, suggesting that allowances were made for the difference in means among the members. The three boy servants who waited on the members at their meetings each received a guilder, or 3 guilders a month. Even the cook who prepared the Easter lamb in 1751 received a small compensation. Compared to other lodges, de Juste maintained an elegant, even sumptuous, style. The total cost for opening the new lodge came to 592.2 guilders, with its initial income equaling only 439.5 guilders. The Grand Lodge made up the difference.

Membership in de Juste was for the prosperous; it was costly, but not exorbitant, and within limits differing degrees of prosperity were accepted and contributions reduced accordingly. Knowing these social and economic boundaries permits us to say other things about the women who invested in the lodge and who, through its ceremonies, proclaimed their symbolic equality as *soeurs* and *maîtresses*. The actresses were working women living an unusually cosmopolitan and highly mobile lifestyle; they traveled extensively in France, Austria, and the Low Countries. In that sense they already lived as those citizens of the world proclaimed by the enlightened and philosophic literature. The Enlightenment promoted the cosmopolitan as the ideal; these women lived as cosmopolitans. All of them had to be shrewd businesswomen, and they possessed more than a passing familiarity with the literature of several languages and the arts. But most especially they were students of manners and dress. They were skilled at turning fantasy into reality.

The importance of the fact that so many members of de Juste were theatrical people cannot be overemphasized. It required no small imagination to create the equality of the sexes, and to act it out in new masonic rituals to be staged with serious and decorous formality. Yet does not the experience of the stage reveal, especially to the players and it is hoped to the audience, the relativity and historicity of mores, sexual and otherwise? A camaraderie and economic interdependence that already existed among the troupe could be given expression in these symbolic actions. Among men and woman who were socially marginal, an equality could be embraced that reflected an aspect of their private social and economic reality. At the moment of the ritual that equality could be proclaimed publicly as both social reality and social ideal.

As social beings the women of La Loge de Juste experienced the Enlightenment in secret. Yet theirs was still a more public version of it than was possible for most eighteenth-century women, for whom enlightenment was largely confined to the printed word read in the privacy of their homes. It is little wonder that feminist writers throughout the century, from Mary Astell to Mary Wollstonecraft, responded to enlightened culture with decided ambivalence. But we do not sense any of that discomfort or reservation in the elaborate rituals, songs, and catechism chanted by *les soeurs* with *les fréres*. The new lodges of adoption met in public yet discreetly concealed spaces often specially designed for them.[81] They were alternatives to the domestic and private sphere, without in any sense repudiating the values and ideals of domestic harmony and virtue. The lodges were as real as, and often more elegant and defined than the coffeehouses, the scientific societies, the meeting rooms of clubs and enlightened coteries, from which women were for the most part excluded.

There were moments in the eighteenth century, such as the one just described, when the Enlightenment endorsed a new social and economic reality that afforded greater freedom and equality to a very few women. By the 1780s their participation, particularly in French freemasonry, was increasingly commonplace. Yet, in actual numbers, few women outside of the salons experienced the social world of enlightened culture. Those who did found the Enlightenment in a different kind of privacy, in the secrecy of their lodges, and then within very restricted class boundaries. The extension of fraternity and equality into the lives of the mass of the people was perceived by enlightened men, and possibly also by enlightened women, as a process fraught with great danger.

The boundaries against the profane, certain men and all women, were seldom breached. Even La Loge de Juste, so seemingly harmless in its proceedings, was only an experiment; it ultimately failed to take hold on even a small scale in the Republic. We have no evidence that the lodge survived beyond 1751. A subsequent history of Dutch freemasonry, written by de Vignoles (see p. 85), said that the lodges of adoption were not well received. We know that in 1761 the brothers of the lodge formed a new lodge with the suggestive name L'Égalité des Frères, the equality of all brothers.[82] Its orator spoke pointedly against license, as opposed to liberty.[83] Other Dutch orators in the same decade lamented the many abuses to which freemasonry was subjected: "The joy and pleasures of the senses are not the purpose of our association." In 1760 the annual *Almanac* made it clear that "the amiable sex" is the object of tender love, and that "discourse walks with love." Only the friendship of men could, however, produce the harmony sought in masonic society.[84] At a meeting in 1778 of the Amsterdam lodge with radical associations, La Bien Aimée, the orator lectured on why women are excluded from its proceedings.[85] In the same year there appears, once again, some evidence of an adoptive lodge in The Hague. The official *Almanac* of 1780 printed the oration quoted earlier that designated freemasonry as one of the few forms of civil society where men and women have contact. The discourse was given in a lodge of adoption operating in The Hague in 1778. Yet well into the 1790s the Amsterdam lodge La Bien Aimée was explaining why women did not belong to it. Although by then, once again, they did belong to other lodges in the Republic.

In the Dutch Republic, just as elsewhere, the profane kept coming back. When in the early nineteenth century during the Napoleonic occupation, the occupiers tried to root out unconventional social gatherings and to return women to their "place" in the family, the lodges of adoption came under attack.[86] Clearly they had returned to the Republic in the 1790s, if not earlier, and their prevalence may owe something to the reforming zeal that dominated the Low Countries in that revolutionary decade. We can only conclude that lodges for women and men remained a subject of contention in France as well as the Dutch Republic. In 1779 French brothers objected to the Chamber of Administration of the Grand Lodge even examining "the work" of an adoptive lodge.[87]

Yet we must look to France for widespread evidence of lodges for both women and men. The French lodges of adoption of the 1780s were, as a Viennese brother described them, "without a doubt one of the most noteworthy new developments in the world of masonry."[88] The scholar who has written most about these lodges, Janet Burke, sees them as tied inextricably to French aristocratic society, and to women of high birth with a degree of economic independence and certainly great wealth.[89] They were particularly prevalent among the lesser nobility, among women whose husbands were minor government officials and also freemasons. Yet as we shall see in the case of Strasbourg, lodges for women could also be found among the highest nobility (chapter 8).

As in La Loge de Juste, the emphasis on virtue appears in the justifications published for the French lodges: "Masonry is the school, Of decency and virtue" said the words of one song sung for a newly initiated sister.[90] We will conduct ourselves "by Virtue, in the milieu of a temple consecrated to this goddess."[91] The lodges were more than simply centers for virtue or social influence, or places where the lesser nobility mixed with the greater. For the French women whom Janet Burke has studied freemasonry became a way of life. It provided a locus for their charitable activities and, most important, a center for female friendship and conviviality. The mysticism we noted at La Loge de Juste was widespread in the French lodges of adoption, which employed the rituals of the Scottish rite, often vastly elaborated upon. This mysticism was fueled by masonic theosophes active in the adoptive lodges, as well as by mesmerism, the cult of spiritual healing imported into France by the Austrian mystic Franz Anton Mesmer. Spiritualism appears to have added to the emotional force of the masonic ceremonies, which in adoptive freemasonry, as in the male lodges, emphasized not simply friendship but equality and fraternity. As one masonic song from 1775 put it, "Friendship among the common people is nothing more than a shadow, a disguise. Among us it is a sentiment, as solid as it is sincere."[92]

In the French aristocratic and adoptive lodges of the late eighteenth century elite women began to invent their own ceremonies.[93] Their equality among themselves increased as did their charity toward the profane. In their ceremonies the ritual language began to demand equality in knowledge, wealth, and influence. Women freemasons took up the educative ideals of the Enlightenment, and did so at a time when some of the Parisian salons of the great philosophes, the Baron d'Holbach's, for example, specifically excluded women from its proceedings.[94] They began to develop philosophical justifications for women's participation in all social institutions, and they lionized their ability to live out the most cherished masonic ideals.[95] Not least, they connected this newfound "honest liberty" with "the moment when the feudal tyranny lost its power in France, [it] was, without doubt, the epoch when women tasted the first fruits of liberty; the century of Louis the Great put the finishing touches to the light of justice."[96] Both France and the Enlightenment are credited with this "happy change in customs," this movement away from absolutism. When freemasons were persecuted in Italy, French women's lodges wrote to praise the queen of the Two Sicilies for her toleration.[97]

The idealism of the adoptive lodges coincided with the most turbulent period in eighteenth-century masonic development. By the 1780s masonic reformers and antimasonic opponents had questions: For whom was this equality meant? Should it not be extended socially? Does it not have specific political implications? The lodges of the late eighteenth century addressed these questions through discussion, exhortation, and rules of conduct seeking to clarify the meaning of freemasonry in the lives of their members. The lodges of adoption proved so controversial that in one hostile fantasy brothers first queried "profanes" on their attitude toward these mixed lodges, as part of the process for admission to a lodge.[98] The women in the mixed lodges knew that the men who joined them were different: "We have found just men who instead of offering us condescension . . . pride and superiority, present us with an association, a sharing."[99] To bind that association masonic ceremonies were modified; now a woman gave a pair of gloves to her husband at her initiation. She did so at a ceremony where the table contained a representation of the "tree of life" and the serpent.[100] Presumably the ceremony would rescue the woman from the curse of Eve's temptation. In Dijon, where the lodges of adoption were

FIG. 5. The biblical story of Adam and Eve, complete with all its ambiguity about women, was used as an engraving in a work intended for use in a French lodge for women; from *L'Adoption ou la Maçonnerie des Femmes, En trois Grades,* 1775.

quite popular, the woman orator especially recommended the virtues of charity, modesty, and discretion.[101]

In the 1780s, if not earlier, a few French women's lodges found a singularly radical voice. They spoke of the "tyranny" of men exercised through their knowledge of the sciences, the dignities and obligations of the state, and the bearing of arms. The response to such tyranny should entail on the part of women "the bearing of arms and the study of the sciences."[102] The result would be equality between "the Amazons" and the "Patriarchs." We do not know who wrote this poem about amazons and patriarchs, but it came out of a women's lodge.

Despite the lodges of adoption—whether radical or moderate—the prohibition against the rest of the profane was never dropped. The masonic polity remained right into the 1790s an exclusive space. Yet the masonic emphasis on self-knowledge, on virtue, both personal and civic, might mean that in certain circumstances sisters and brothers, such as the members of La Loge de Juste, might be better schooled at taking risks, at openly, no longer secretly, defying conventional prejudices and the prevailing social order.

6

Speaking the Language of Enlightenment

We will never know precisely what it was like to live a life attentive to enlightened ideals. Some European men and a few women sought to express those ideals sociably, within the perimeters set by private fraternizing. Within those limits the masonic lodges were by far the most cosmopolitan, and internationally connected, enclaves of the century. To know them and how their idealism related to the Enlightenment, we must go by what masonic orators said lodges and brothers should be, as well as by what letters, meeting records, and diaries may have to tell us. Vast reconstructions have been attempted for the much more public thought of the famous philosophes, the supposed originators of the Enlightenment: Voltaire, Rousseau, Diderot, and, in the American colonies, Franklin.

But they were the grand men of the Enlightenment, not the little men who so often admired them. Much has been made of the official academies, particularly in France, as the loci of the Enlightenment's followers. But as I make clear in the conclusion, the few thousand academicians familiar with the "the light" were also officially sponsored. In most European countries the lodges occupied a middle ground: a place where the occasional government official might be found, but one which was nevertheless officially suspect. In this chapter we will listen to the less famous, less official voices of the masonic brothers who addressed one another monthly, in various European countries and languages. I seek here to recapitulate and to generalize about masonic ideals as found throughout western Europe. In the process I do not want to render the Enlightenment into the property of the freemasons, but rather to show the brothers (and sisters) as its consumers, interpreters, and appliers.

In the next three chapters masonic idealism will be reconstructed in specific contexts, first within one Amsterdam lodge, and then within various French lodges. The records of the Amsterdam lodge (unlike almost any French lodge) are so

FIG. 6. Title page from published discourses delivered to brothers in various French lodges in the 1760s. The lodge is here referred to as a school. The place and date of publication are false.

abundant for the 1790s and earlier that they deserved a separate chapter. There we will observe the lodge La Bien Aimée as it lived through the revolutionary upheavals that affected western Europe in the 1780s and the 1790s. First in this chapter we will hear from as many European (and American) masonic voices as is feasible, to recapture the universality of masonic discourse within western Europe.

We will examine not only orations but also pocket-size almanacs, so popular and commonplace among the brothers. Because they were small and fragile, few of these masonic almanacs have survived. But in size and purpose they were the equivalent of our daily diaries and calendars. Their daily usefulness was matched only by their value as traveling companions. Sometimes they gave the locations of lodges all over western Europe; almost invariably they contained orations or songs that could help pass the time. The concession to publish them was highly prized among masonic publishers. In the publishing heartland of Europe, the Dutch Republic, Johan Schreuder, whom we met in chapter 4 as a leader in the 1750s of La Bien Aimée, was the official publisher of masonic almanacs in both Dutch and French texts; the business passed from him to the publisher Van Laak.[1] He incorporated material in the almanacs from England and France, and he sought to make them pleasing "to the lovers of music and poetry."[2] In Britain various publishers put the almanacs out, among them William Preston, who was also a masonic reformer and an officer in the Grand Lodge.[3] But The Netherlands was the main Continental publishing center for this ephemeral literature.

By casting a net so wide, into literature both lofty and mundane, we are seeking to recapture how men identified with the age of Enlightenment sought to articulate their prescriptions for living it. In addition, the discipline of the oration, or art of rhetoric, was particularly prized in all the enclaves of the new sociability. To recite a poem in the local literary society, to give the results of experimentation—however crude—in a philosophical society, and to exhort brothers in a lodge were all part of the training of men newly empowered to speak in private, if nowhere else. Within freemasonry the orators were the key figures; they must educate their brothers and sisters. Thus we will take seriously the words of a French orator of 1782: "The sanctuary of masonic friendship and fraternity . . . is consecrated by the voices of their orators."

Throughout the eighteenth century, especially from the 1740s on, European freemasons spoke of being enlightened. The term could have a variety of meanings, some vaguely intellectual, others symbolic, as was the use of metaphors about the light from the sun, or the many dramatic effects intended at lodge meetings by the elaborate use of candles. In French orations masters and brothers were routinely described and complemented as *éclairé*; in Dutch, as *verlichte;* in German, as *aufgeklärt*. In Britain one of the principal duties of a lodge was to "initiate the unenlightened."[4] Genevan masons described themselves as "true children of the light."[5] By midcentury French masonic ritual used to initiate an apprentice into a lodge asked what made him want to be released from his somber life. The answer given in the ritual was: "As the means to be enlightened I search the enlightened."[6] A French-language almanac of 1787 said, "We have given ourselves the title of children of the light."[7]

Within French lodges, or in any others, the search to be enlightened need not have entailed the irreligious. In masonic belief being enlightened was inextricably tied to morality, to virtue. In 1749 one orator spoke of the love of God and in the very next sentence of "the man Philosophe, that is to say the truly wise, finds that there can be enough good, enough beauty, but that there can never be enough virtue."[8] In Philadelphia revolutionary freemasons of the late 1770s spoke about the liberty sought by patriots; they also spoke piously about being "enlightened and enlivened by a Ray from Thee." They meant the deity; they also endorsed republicanism and revolution.[9] On other occasions American orators spoke of the Copernican sun that "unified and Enlightened" the universe and bound it together "by the powerfully attractive influence of the Divine Principle of Friendship, Affection and Knowledge."[10] Although mystical language about the sun was commonplace in masonic rhetoric, it was the Newtonian sun, the centerpiece of "the mechanism of the universe" placed there by the Grand Architect that was intended.[11] There is, however, also a small eighteenth-century literature that links freemasonry with the most extreme heresies of the Enlightenment and associates the lodges with materialism.[12] We do know that the lodges could provide refuge to pantheists like Rousset and to materialists like the French philosophe Helvetius. Yet in provincial lodges such as we find in Strasbourg funeral orators were particularly eager to make it clear that "our order is founded on wise principles and . . . rejects all materialism."[13] Only in the early nineteenth-century reaction against the French Revolution do we find masonic rhetoric that is aggressively Christian.[14]

One of the most distinctive characteristics of Continental freemasonry was its incessant creation of new degrees. Within French freemasonry, in particular, the custom of elaborate grades and degrees became commonplace. Yet rather than see the degrees as simply expressions of the mystical and romantic, which by the 1780s they could certainly be, we should also see them as capable of reflecting the ideal of becoming enlightened. In Paris in 1778 the lodge Amis Réunis practiced twelve degrees. Some, such as Le Chevalier de l'Orient (the Knight of the East), reflected aristocratic affects; others, like the seventh degree of the Rose-Croix (Rosicrucians), invoked a fashionable mysticism. Among the higher degrees came Le Philosophe Inconnu (the Unknown Philosopher) and still higher Le Sublime Philosophe.[15] In the same decade other French lodges created the degree of Symbolic Master. In representing this degree the brothers stood in silence, as a "lugubrious light enlightened us, and we are made to enlighten the Universe." The initiate "represented Solomon, who enlightened by a Divine wisdom . . . instructs his subjects."[16] In these ceremonies the Enlightenment is brought full circle: Having disdained traditional religion, it is being enlisted in the service of a new religiosity. As early as 1755 French freemasons said that "the true mason is not only virtuous, he is at the same time a philosophe," a word borrowed during the 1740s to mean an adherent of the secular and the freethinking. When used in the context of the Enlightenment the word meant not a philosopher in the sense of Descartes or Newton, but rather a man possessing particular characteristics: "reasonable, sociable, virtuous; he is perfect,"[17] as one orator put it.

With such sentiments about the capacities of enlightened men naturally came optimism. "I am truly persuaded," began an orator, "that in our time barbarity and superstition and ignorance are disappearing. . . . The illuminations of truth are penetrating all spirits, insinuating themselves into all hearts, eternalizing forever the masonic reign, because the [masonic] art speaks of reason, which must be actualized, of necessity, in this century of Philosophy."[18] Freemasonry is being presented as the embodiment of its age, a new movement with ancient roots, the harbinger of the age of reason. In Dutch lodges the newly elected master addressed his predecessor and begged him to "enlighten me with your profound illuminations."[19] When in 1760 a lodge was officially established in Utrecht (a university town) brothers wrote to it to offer congratulations: "We are charmed to see the light shine in a City where until now the thickness of darkness had not permitted even the tiniest sparkle to pierce the clouds of ignorance and prejudice."[20] Once in possession of these illuminations brothers believed that they could bring "their superb edifice to a higher point of perfection."[21]

Perfection never possessed other-worldly connotations in this new secularism. True fraternity and equality stood as the ideals sought by every lodge. Freemasons knew full well that in the larger society there were ranks and stations, but inside the lodges, "in the citizenry [of them] we are members of one body to which we all belong . . . in our society there is this equality wherein we know no station."[22] Even monarchs could espouse equality: Joseph II of Austria was said to hold equality at the very foundation of his conduct; thus he was "un roi philosophe."[23] Masonic rhetoric about equality tried to relate it to enlightenment, but always to defer to the inequality of the larger society. One of the earliest Continental *Constitutions,* dated 1741, Lausanne, Switzerland, made the paradox presented by the ideal of equality explicit: "The order of freemasons is a society of confraternity and equality, and to this end is represented under the emblem of a level . . . a brother renders to another brother the honor and deference that is justly due him in proportion to his rank in the civil society."[24] Worshiping in the new temple of the enlightened may have made the tensions and hostilities born of rank and birth—so endemic to eighteenth-century societies—more palatable. To imagine these sentiments as purely and simply democratic is to miss the contexts wherein they were spoken.

Within the masonic temple a new deity could be invoked. Among the achievements upon which the Enlightenment rested had been the new scientific cosmology. Freemasonry turned the vast and ordered universe of the new science and its Grand Architect into an object of worship; with that cosmology came the justification for being cosmopolitan. The universe as discovered by European exploration and by the new science stretched before only those who could appreciate the implications of its vastness and knowability. The cosmopolitanism preached by the Enlightenment, it was claimed by the orators, encouraged fraternal bonding.

The cosmopolitan ideal was frequently invoked among men who were less rooted in their local environment, hence, for example, among military men, who often had their own lodges.[25] Their wanderings in the service of the state could be justified, ironically, by their being cosmopolites: "Are we not members of the same family? Is the universe not the country to the masonic?", asked a military orator on the eve of the garrison's departure.[26] He concluded, somewhat ironically, with a nationalist and monarchist salute to Louis XVI. An orator in Liège could simultaneously praise Joseph II for his cosmopolitan vision and then remark that "the Glory of Joseph II is his own, the glory of Louis XIV was only the result of circumstances." The masonic vision wanted a European cosmopolitanism that would not interfere with national identity or monarchical glory.

Identification with the nation appears quite early in masonic rhetoric (see p. 7) and was invoked most frequently and simultaneously with cosmopolitanism: "The earth itself is only a great republic, of which each nation is a family, and each particular a child."[27] Within this rhetoric brotherhood took on a new meaning. The family became a metaphor for society and the nation; simultaneously the social

CHANSONS
DE LA
TRÈS-VENERABLE
CONFRAIRIE
DES
MAÇONS LIBRES.

A LA HAYE,
Aux depens du Sr. VINCENT LA CHAPELLE,
Maître de Loge.
Et ſe vend chez ANTOINE VAN DOLE,
Libraire.

M. DCCXXXV.

FIG. 7. Masonic imagery was frequently universalist, evoking common Enlightenment themes: science, and knowledge of the globe and the universe. Title page from an early masonic songbook in French probably used all over western Europe and published in French in The Hague in 1735. Vincent La Chapelle was one of the founders of Continental freemasonry.

became identified with the domestic and consanguineous. Within this new conceptualization of the social universe brotherhood came to denote devotion to one's country. Society and, by extension, the nation overshadowed and thus transformed the metaphors that described the traditional family and, most especially, the traditional father.

At moments the transformation toward the benign father sought by these new social brothers and articulated by a new ideology recommended for the family is made explicit: "The freemason is always the pleasure of his friends . . . tender father, amiable husband: the glory of his children and the triumph of his spouse; he carries the virtues of the lodge into the bosom of his family."[28] In a telling oration, read probably by hundreds, if not thousands, of brothers because it was printed in a French-language masonic almanac for 1774, an aristocratic father addressed his son who has now become his brother.[29] At his initiation the father lovingly exhorts him to make "this illustrious order . . . your second country. Recall that Brutus and Manlius had sacrificed their own children for the love of country, and that my duties to the order . . . are also sacred, also formidable for me." If the son will respond with a comparable devotion, this will be the source of great pleasure. For in becoming a brother, one truly becomes a man.[30] The implication here is that even fathers and sons can become equals, provided they attach their loyalty to their country. Similarly, a man seeking membership in a regular lodge, having been in one not officially recognized, refers to himself as abandoned, as illegitimate, "removed from maternal tenderness."[31] The use of family imagery was purposeful and intended to emphasize the seriousness of the public ethics being sanctioned by the new sociability. Not least, the monarch had always been described in paternal terms. In the 1780s masonic rhetoric took up the analogy but qualified it. "A new temple has been raised within our walls . . . under the sacred auspices of a sensible and virtuous prince which the family of reformed masons regard as their father."[32] Would this family have recognized the legitimate paternity of a tyrannical father? We cannot be so sure that it would. Certainly we saw in chapter 4 that freemasons were perfectly capable of rebelling against the "mother lodge." French freemasons in Strasbourg in 1764 acknowledged the Paris Grand Lodge in those maternal terms and then haughtily implored it "to avoid the pomp and tyranny that crushes its children."[33]

In laying emphasis on the public and hence the national—and yet rendering both in very personal terms—masonic rhetoric could still rise beyond its linguistic and geographic borders. Even after battle, military lodges were reminded, the prisoners are our brothers. One of the most frequent masonic phrases, so commonplace in the literature as to be almost taken for granted, referred to the lodges or to the order "spread over the surface of the earth," found in every corner of the globe. Masonic rhetoric captured the moment in the development of Western hegemony when European secular culture could be imagined as capable of being everywhere. Predictably, reference to the nation came in tandem with the evocation of the universal. In the 1790s when talk of the "fatherland" was commonplace amid the revolutions in France and the Low Countries, brothers who had "lived and worked" together in various countries, even in Africa (quite possibly in the slave trade as they were Dutch), found in an oration printed in their official almanac that "in whatever country, in whatever state I come, there freemasonry is for me a nation, and the bosom of friendship."[34] Perhaps we have to acknowledge that enlightened fraternizing made world travel and trade, in whatever commodity, easier and more acceptable.

The recognition that "all the nations will never be a single family" did not stop the masonic desire to create just that: Only "the spirit of masonry operates [to produce] this astonishing revolution." Speaking in the 1780s the French orator who sought this universal human community then went on to make the historically interesting observation—given the events of 1789 and beyond—that although the laws of masonry may do little to promote man's happiness in "the political state," they do add to his virtue and happiness in "the social state." "This sublime school" creates "the good father, the good son, the good citizen, the good friend." The Grand Lodge of France is invoked as the true masonic government. The orator admits that there are troubles in some lodges; equality should be measured less by the "differences in conditions" and more by the "principles of education, of sentiment, and social grace."[35] We are reminded of one of the earliest French orations given by the Chevalier Ramsay in the late 1730s and widely distributed: We seek "to form in the course of time a spiritual nation."[36] It is as if the social has become an essentially political experience, or at least the only sphere wherein it seems possible to negotiate the disparities of power between men. Speaking also in the politically troubled 1780s Dutch freemasons became more aggressive in asserting the order was "a happy and flourishing republic."[37]

One masonic thinker, also a major writer and intellectual of the century, spoke with a unique and insightful voice about the political meaning of the masonic search for a private harmony and equality. Gotthold Lessing lived in the state-sponsored Enlightenment promoted by Frederick the Great in Prussia. Freemasonry played a distinctive role in that setting; it aided and abetted the cult of monarchy (p. 192). But Lessing wanted more from the lodges. Indeed, Lessing the philosophe wanted more from humankind than he found in the mores of the time. As early as 1748 he was frequenting lodges in Berlin, and his masonic initiation appears to have been in 1751.[38] By the 1770s German freemasonry was in considerable turmoil with reformers such as Count Zinnendorf demanding that the lodges express an almost utopian search for perfection.

In an anonymous dialogue written precisely in the 1770s Lessing drew out the ethical implications of masonic secularism. If we know the freemason by his deeds, he argued, then he must leave his mark in the world.[39] From the world Lessing reasons immediately to the state. Do men exist to further the happiness of the state, or should the reverse not be the case? Indeed, the happiness of all its members is the happiness of the state. The state that subordinates the happiness of its people to its own interests possesses all the attributes of tyranny. The listener to these sentiments in the dialogue quickly responds, "You must not say that so loudly!" But the masonic speaker is unrelenting. Only in civic life, through political institutions, do men find the formula for happiness. His listener reminds him, however, that human beings are hopelessly divided, into many states and religions. Predictably the masonic voice has the cure: Freemasonry will unite humankind, its universalism offers the first step toward unity.[40] This was an uncharacteristically radical masonic text, but one that could not have gone unnoticed, if for no other reason than its resonance with arguments that were being put forward at that moment in the rebellious American colonies.

Up until the 1780s most masonic literature displays none of Lessing's impatience. More commonplace was a dedication to the state, whether monarchical or not. Yet simultaneously, even before the 1780s, masonic rhetoric gloried in republics. We would expect to find that rhetoric in the Dutch Republic, but it is universally present in Continental freemasonry, possibly a reflection of its English and Scottish origins.[41] Among the most frequently cited masonic heroes is the ancient Greek legislator Lycurgus.[42] Both he and Solon are models of wisdom and lawgiving. They are also invoked as legislators, participants in their own governance.

In the 1780s the Grand Lodge of Austria went even further and claimed that "every lodge is a democracy."[43] German freemasons of the same period identified "our freedom [as] the tradition of the British nation."[44] Danish freemasons of the 1760s praised the condition of "republican freedom" as a great good.[45] And of course there was the myth of Cromwell, which never went away. Masonic propagandists as late as 1776 were claiming that Cromwell founded the order, but that they were not republicans, nor was there anything "révoltante" about the society.[46] In 1779 the most intellectual lodge in Paris, the Nine Muses (or Sisters), entertained Benjamin Franklin, lavishly praising his virtues; it also described its members as "citizens of the Masonic Democracy."[47] By the 1780s the proceedings of the Nine Muses were printed far and wide in masonic almanacs. In a French-language almanac emanating from The Hague in 1784 the discourse included is openly political. The speaker, probably the Italian Count of Medini, a translator of Voltaire, says that he has been all over Europe, to Belgium, Germany, and France, always "enlightened by new lights." He has discovered that everyone is interested in freemasonry; only in masonry does the distance which nobility and civil titles give to an individual disappear. The unity of masonry gives it a solidity that even the Roman republic did not have.[48] The enlightenment he has found in his travels tells him to regard with a "philosophical eye all the revolutions in States; I find they are in the natural order of things." Their causes lie in the legislation, the government, the genius, mores, and passions of a nation.[49] And freemasonry sought to address all those aspects of the human condition. By the 1780s masonic speeches in some quarters of western Europe directly reflect a profound political discontent. By the 1790s in Germany we can find masonic literature that openly spoke the language of the French Revolution and violently condemned despotism and slavery.[50]

Alongside a republic as the ideal freemasons most frequently cited England by name as the country worthy of emulation. Anglophilia naturally accompanied these political sentiments and is readily found among French freemasons even after the American War for Independence, in which France had been an ally of the colonists. In the French lodges of the 1780s we can hear the orator proclaim: " The country of Europe that is regarded by almost everyone as the most wise, England, seems to possess the true and unique religion." French freemasons publicly longed for the same honor and distinction accorded the order there.[51] Regularly brothers were told in their almanacs, among other sources, that the "general principals of masonic government" come from England. It possesses the first national Grand Lodge as well as the system of nominations and elections which all provincial lodges now follow "within the limits of the political government of their respective states."[52]

At all times within freemasonry authority must descend from the Grand Lodge of a nation, even if the prince is the head of a lodge. The other prerogative of the legally constituted lodges is "liberty . . . this precious liberty which the Constitution of the order renders so admirable and which even a Monarch would not dare to destroy."[53] That statement occurred in a French-language almanac for 1776—in the history of republics, a significant year. In that same year the German almanac said that freemasonry "unites men and nations through the holy . . . bonds of virtue, brotherly love and charity . . . nations are enlightened, as it were unified through humane and social politics."[54] By 1781 lodges in France spoke of "Saint Liberty! . . . the oppressor be called the enemy of the republic of Masons."[55]

In this period there are even orations praising Voltaire for having seen the truth, for having been a republican (which he was not).[56] When dissension and schism occurred within the French Grand Lodge, as was the case in the 1770s, the choice seemed to be between being "a republic in which each individual participates equally in power; or finding only a despotism."[57] These seemed to be the only alternatives. The solution chosen under the regulations of 1774 proclaimed that the Grand Lodge "was only a body formed by the reunion of the free representatives of all the lodges."[58] In the autumn of 1789 we can find lodges writing openly to the Paris Grand Lodge in favor of the National Assembly and sending money to support its members. They acted "as citizens and as masons."[59] By no means did all French lodges contribute to or favor the Revolution, but all of them would have understood the meaning of being citizens and masons. At that same moment another lodge put it well: "In the civil order the deputies of a Province represent it to the general assemblies of the Nation; it is the same with the lodges."[60]

Of course by 1791 those hostile critics of freemasonry who had invented the myth of its conspiratorial role in the Revolution repeatedly attacked the fraternity for the subversive implications of its organizational structure (see p. 210). Entwined with politics was religion. Freemasonry was subversive because of its associations with England, with Cromwell, and also with the deists and atheists of the Enlightenment.[61] From as early as the 1730s not only were the political values disseminated by the republic of letters distrusted for their English and Dutch associations; the greatest fear they aroused centered on the subversion of traditional religiosity. These fears could only have been exacerbated by knowledge of the ritualistic and ceremonial side of freemasonry to which police spies as early as the 1740s alluded (p. 5).

The opponents of freemasonry were frequently the enemies of the Enlightenment. As one masonic orator shrewdly put it, "The churchman . . . only imagines that we profess an all new religion; yes, he says, . . . the thing is only too certain: the children of light shun the light." Our orator never denied the religious analogy, nor did he seem bothered by the condemnations he got from the clergy; he simply affirmed the secrecy within which freemasons hid their enlightenment.[62] At other lodges orators spoke about "the first apostles of the masonic religion who have invented these mysterious emblems intended to protect the truth, to hide from the contempt of the profane, from the persecution of the fanatic." In the 1760s Dutch brothers discussed a change in the "ancient" rituals in these terms: "It seems to us that some differences from one lodge to another should not be more interesting than the differences in customs of people who profess the same religion."[63] French freemasons of the late 1770s praised the newly reconstituted Grand Orient as the keeper of the "true masonic religion."[64] A decade earlier Strasbourg freemasons described a priest who wanted to join their lodge as "enlightened." But after he sought instruction in "our mysteries" without seeking membership he was regarded with great suspicion.[65] Yet many Catholic clergy did belong to lodges. Almost never is the masonic religion identified with Christianity. But then never is it described in language that would render freemasonry overtly hostile to the churches. Just as in Britain and Sweden, Protestant countries where freemasons assembled publicly in churches, Parisian freemasons assembled at least once a year at "a solemn mass."[66] Similarly, German freemasons as early as the 1740s hotly denied that they were in any way atheists, rebels, or "unmanly."[67] Clearly the charges of political subversion, irreligion, and sodomy were most commonly made against the society, and generally made in the same breath.

Particularly in Catholic countries such as France and Belgium, hostile critics might have been placated had they been privy to some of the masonic degrees. Certain of the higher degrees practiced in French freemasonry had Christian connotations, for example, the grade of Chevalier Elu (Elected Knight). At his initiation into the degree a brother promised "to adore God and to be faithful to my king and charitable toward my brothers and to defend the Christian religion with the last drop of my blood."[68] Other French masons tried to give the secular symbolism used in masonic art a Christian connotation. In these efforts, for example, the triangle became a symbol of the Trinity, the three persons of the divinity "who enlighten the vast universe."[69] As we shall see in the last two chapters, French freemasonry could be just as aristocratic and Christian as it was republican or deist. Occasionally pious German orators also spoke of the lodges as intended to make men "christlich."[70] And always the charge of impiety is refuted. Yet at other moments the ancient goddesses Isis and Minerva are named as patrons and "the religion of Noah and the Patriarchs" is invoked.[71] It was then up to each brother to determine what might be meant. In 1774 an orator in Brussels bluntly asked what the *Constitutions* of 1723 meant when it spoke about obeying the moral law, about the religion in which all men can agree.[72]

Among the conclusions at which a brother might arrive, if only fancifully, was that since masonry was as old as either Christianity or Judaism, as the almanacs told him, brothers might in fact be closer in their values to the ancient Romans. Masonic almanacs regularly gave a synopsis of each month which related that month to pagan mythology: "March, so named and consecrated to the god mars, by Romulus on the supposition that he was his son. The first month of the Roman year." And so the almanac went, month by month, at the same time giving the saints' name for each day along with the monthly phases of the moon.[73] Year after year these largely French-language almanacs gave a truncated history of the Roman republic and its gods. Sometimes they compared "this temple of equality" to the Roman Senate and found even the Romans less agreeable than this newly founded center of order and legality.[74] In 1793 we will find Amsterdam freemasons celebrating the Roman feast of Saturn on Christmas Day. Earlier French freemasons wrote treatises on the similarities between masonic morals, ceremonies, and customs and those of the ancient Druids of Gaul. Perhaps we can better understand why some historians have seen in the Enlightenment the rise of modern paganism.

Certainly by the second half of the century language about being enlightened—

at the same time secretive about the commitment to Enlightenment—was used self-consciously by freemasons to identify the society with the highest aspirations of the new secular culture, with what in 1784 Kant described as this age of Enlightenment. This identification, curiously we might find, only reinforced the masonic dedication to secrecy that was as much metaphorical as it was real. The belief that most people were incapable of, or hostile to, the new culture of Enlightenment was widespread both within and without the lodges. Indeed, Kant himself had carefully qualified his description of the age; as he ruefully observed, ours is not an enlightened age. All the more self-consciously did European freemasons commonly address one another as "enlightened." They believed themselves, and their masonic order, to be just that. And they cast a cold eye on the world outside their lodges. They condemned "the barbarity of the time, the ferocity of customs, the tyranny of the despots, the absurdity of cults"; they longed for a time when prejudice and fanaticism would be exterminated.[75] Indeed it was the Enlightenment itself that, they claimed, made them aware that "man is depraved . . . and society is the cause."[76] The true mason shuns ambition, vainglory, the passions, and self-interests. "The Child of light enjoys within himself a profound peace and the calmness of his passions." "Particular interests must give way to the general interest."[77] The German almanac for 1776 told the brothers that the true mason shuns the partisan and the self-interested.[78] A French oration of 1782 condemned "egotism, civil and political." In the masonic version of the Enlightenment it is intended as the antidote to rapacious greed, to ambition and self-interest, to the virtues associated with raw market competition; and to pride, the persona of the haughty. And in the masonic version, the Enlightenment was the culture of the few; the many were mired in superstition and ignorance. Most of the philosophes would have agreed.

Once the passions and egotism could be excised, the ideal of fraternity could be refined. The term possessed an ethical dimension from its earliest use and it always relied on metaphors of friendship and family. Some of this idealism can be traced back to the early eighteenth-century English philosopher Shaftesbury, whose writings on the social nature of the truly civilized man remained popular with freemasons right to the end of the century.[79] In certain instances the fraternal ideal was juxtaposed to an "egotism" believed to be rampant in the larger society, among the profane.[80] Philosophically conservative orators identified this rampant egotism with a fashionable atheism and materialism. And they gloried in male friendship in opposition to admitting women into the lodges.[81] Yet others proclaimed that in "this enlightened century . . . one has seen masons in France and England open their fraternal arms to the dear part of the human species . . . their lodges have been the first to introduce women in our temples."[82]

Masonic sociability assigned an ethical, or moralizing, dimension to the Enlightenment, even before Rousseau put pen to paper. As freemasons in Bordeaux wrote to their brothers in Amsterdam, "our work of 28 years . . . forms a hive of true friends and citizens characterized by the integrity of our candor and sociability."[83] Yet lodges could also use overtly anti-Semitic language to exclude Jews, "cette nation infirmé" as the lodge in Liège put it in 1774. There is other evidence from Dutch, German, and Swiss lodges of Jews and even Muslims being admitted freely into the lodges.[84] Particularly in Germany they have been found to be present but somewhat marginal in the lodges.

Within limits some masonic philosophizing about civil society could be openly Rousseauian. The purpose of masonic sociability was to restore men to their primitive goodness, to revive in their hearts the laws of nature.[85] The equality of all men is the first law, and only freemasonry understands this most fundamental—and by the 1760s some might say Rousseauian—lesson. The entire world is a republic, each nation is a family, every individual is a son.[86] All of these sentiments could be found earlier in the century in one form or another of masonic discourse, but by the 1760s the ideas of Rousseau were being fitted effortlessly into masonic idealism. For those unfortunates who are oppressed by power, calumny, and hatred, as this refined rhetoric would have it, the freemason offers a country, as well as brothers and protectors.[87] Recognizing that the only power such an idealized society possesses is moral, the Rousseauian freemason is self-conscious about the necessity of symbols and mysteries "which produce in the heart and spirit of the individual the sentiments capable of making them like their work and their duties. In effect symbols and mysteries are the principal nutrients of the human spirit."[88] Equality may be an unobtainable ideal given the inclination of men in society to oppress one another, but through charity and benevolence all men can become brothers.[89] All just and moderate government is founded on the principle of human liberty, and in France the freemasons have adopted the word "*franchise*" as the term which expresses "the liberty of the heart."[90] In 1773 the Grand Lodge of France called for "a general assembly where deputies from all parts of the kingdom would bring together their powers and illuminations."[91] From that time onward we can find orators claiming that brothers "were elevated by the most moderate form of government . . . [that they should] conserve this national freedom, the happy fruit of liberty."[92]

The Rousseauian version of freemasonry possessed a particular coherence. Rousseau's condemnation of French society resonated with masonic utopianism. His emphasis on the heart as the key to human progress appealed to the masonic love of ceremony and fraternal affection; it also humanized the Enlightenment for men who might strive to be reasonable but knew that they were driven by feelings and emotion. Now they could "form a just idea of freemasons, who are to be regarded as a society of symbolic philosophes . . . are constantly wise, cultivating the pleasures of society and the sweetness of friendship. The general character of these Philosophes is one of simplicity, moderation, sweetness and tranquility."[93] We may find it nothing short of extraordinary that men wedded to socializing and civility, some of it quite lavish and formal, could embrace Rousseau's call to return to the simplicity of nature. But the lodges had always been described as not quite of this world, separate, better, enriching. By the 1770s some brothers could imagine that Rousseau had summed up what they had always been searching for in masonic laws and practices. Indeed Rousseau received personal encouragement from two leaders of Dutch freemasonry, the brothers William and Charles Bentinck. They invited him to their home, and throughout his life Charles Bentinck thought that Rousseau had expressed the essence of Christianity, which is not dogmas but morality.[94] In the late 1760s Amsterdam freemasons were told by their orator "about the main reason why freemasonry was so well received by enlightened men: it restored men to their Natural State," we may call it a Rousseauian condition, a state of transparency, without disguise.[95]

In French lodges by the late 1770s Rousseauian rhetoric could become quite heated, and quite pointed. An orator in Grenoble in 1779 put it this way: Being more 'philosophe' than those who tediously parade and sterilely seek to display the sublime maxims [of the philosophes], the masons search modestly to put them into practice.[96] In ancient times "being a citizen was an important and noble matter, sufficient to satisfy all the desires of ambition. But in our modern institutions where the form of government is such that the majority of subjects must stay in the place assigned them by nature, how is it possible to contribute to the common good?"[97] The orator finds the answer in "feelings proud and republican" and contrasts them with the pride and arrogance displayed by cabals, factions, political assassinations, civil wars, by prohibitions that punish the love of one's country as if it were a revolt. An atmosphere of crisis is invoked, brought about by moral decay, by hereditary hatreds, jealousy, avarice, and cupidity. Predictably the answer to this impasse lies in the masonic temple, where morality and philosophy united seek to flourish, where in effect one can leave society, which is equated with the collision of interest and rivalry, both of which pose constant threats even to masonic idealism.[98] Like so many masonic orations, this one was never published; we do not know why. What is clear is that into the temple at Grenoble men have brought their growing impatience with contemporary social and political institutions.

But we should not imagine the voice that imitated and elaborated upon Rousseau as loud enough to muffle all the others. Every lodge in every town had an orator, and it was his task to make eloquent pronouncements on masonic ideals. Invariably a host of other sentiments, some far away from the masonic version of Rousseauian reform, got expressed. By midcentury, for instance, Prussian brothers believed that they already lived in an epoch that banished fanaticism, an era of Philosophy and Reason, and hence of the true happiness of man. They also gloried in the enlightened (and militaristic) prowess of Frederick the Great.[99] They proclaimed him a great hero and imagined themselves as living in a "golden age" governed by a "king more valiant than Alexander."[100] They celebrated his day of birth, his achievements, and even, by implication, his unprovoked seizure of Silesia in 1740.[101] He was described as a Hero Prince and a Philosophe, who in the "German Empire" assures the glory and longevity of freemasonry. He in turn responded by saying that "the society works only to germinate and fructify all sorts of virtues in my states."[102]

The masonic adoration of Frederick II, who was a freemason, was repeated outside of Germany. It even made its way into the pocket almanacs, usually published in French and carried by the most ordinary of brothers.[103] Modern-day masonic belief has it that Frederick invented the most famous, and last, of the masonic degrees, the thirty-third. Eighteenth-century masonic records do trace it back to the 1760s and attribute it to Frederick.[104] This was one of the most aristocratic and authoritarian of all the eighteenth-century degrees, claiming its mythic origin with the Knights Templars and designating its initiate as "Sovereign Grand Commander." If Frederick did invent the degree, it was the least he could have done given the adulation that the society heaped upon him. To the masonic orators of Berlin he was "the father of his subjects," an Achilles, Titus, and Solon all in one.[105]

But Frederick was not the only monarch to enjoy rapturous praise. At the low point of his popularity Louis XV of France was spoken of in glowing terms by at least one French lodge.[106] Decades later Louis XVI was venerated by men and women members of "la nation Maçonne" for his reforming instincts.[107] The French women's lodges of adoption, with their strongly aristocratic base, were especially appreciative of Louis XVI and careful to compare him to other monarchical reformers.[108] Dutch lodges were told by their master that "the principal duty of masonry consists in obedience to its Sovereigns, and in the exact observation of the laws."[109] In 1765 when a brother joined riots against the "civil and academic authority" in the university town of Leiden, he was expelled "to show how much freemasons . . . love . . . good order . . . [and] the duty of subjects to the government."[110] Even in the early 1790s, when the stadtholderate was being maintained by Prussian soldiers, masonic almanacs reprinted orations from an earlier era praising the hereditary stadtholderate.[111] The King of Sweden, whom we met earlier as he entertained the Stockholm lodges, received similar praise in the French-language almanacs.[112]

In the Austrian Netherlands the Hapsburg administration had early on allied itself with the Enlightenment. It was the stick with which to beat the clergy and to attack the privileges of the indigenous aristocracy. By the 1780s Belgian freemasonry was firmly in the camp of the monarch in Vienna, or at least so it seemed on the surface. Austrian lodges were particularly active in promoting the new science,[113] a favored cause of enlightened monarchs locked in struggles with their local clergies. In the Austrian colony of Belgium, Joseph II was loudly praised by the lodges as a reformer, a king whose glory exceeded even that of Louis XIV.[114] Then in late 1786 Joseph II tried to bring Belgian freemasonry under his control; he closed down all but three lodges, one in the capital city of each of the Belgian provinces. He did so in the name of order: "These assemblies abandoned entirely to themselves have taken off in every direction . . . and by a fanatical liaison, have not been conducive to the most perfect equity."[115] Most brothers docilely conformed, but a few did not. The very next year the same almanac that printed the decree, along with a damning comparison to the protection the order had enjoyed in Prussia, printed an oration that needs to be heard: "We wanted to imitate them; the Kings, the sovereigns, the magistrates who were established: but alas! the power is without boundary, the authority without limits, the slavery absolute; & the Mason generally only finds the happy alliance of sovereignty and liberty in his lodges."[116] In the same small book was printed another oration which exhorted: "The Mason must be a moral man, faithful to the government under which he has the happiness to live."[117] The choices seem fairly obvious: The enlightened freemason could either retreat into his lodge and contemplate the nature of the arbitrary power surrounding him or he could conform. It seems reasonable to argue that the emperor's move contributed to the discontent that made for revolution in the Austrian Netherlands in 1787.

The use of the lodges as places where praise of monarchs mixed with the Enlightenment was a heady and volatile mixture. Focusing on the person of the ruler might lead to focusing on the nation. Particularly in the German lodges, where the cult of monarchy was so pronounced, at least in Prussia, masonic thought took a distinctively nationalist turn. The same books of orations contain both sentiments.[118] Ironically the political uses to which the heads of the German states put some lodges may have contributed to the growth of a radicalized mutation of the masonic gene, the German Illuminati. Their history is in many ways quite separate from the mainstream lodges that concern us here, but it cannot be denied that once overtly political in their purpose, the lodges might turn in all sorts of directions.

Matching the cults of monarchs (sometimes even in the same oration) was the adulation accorded to some of the major philosophes: to Franklin, who brought freemasonry to the American colonies in 1735, but especially to Voltaire.[119] He was a masonic favorite, particularly after his initiation, late in life, into the lodge of the Nine Sisters in Paris. We can find eulogies at his death in many a French-speaking lodge. The praise began with his literary prowess and continued to extol "this indefatigable mason" for his struggle against ignorance, barbarity, and fanaticism. In particular his plays were praised for "the happy rapport of their maxims with ours: in effect, the fidelity to duty, the hatred of tyranny, the horror of superstition, the respect for the rights of man."[120] Voltaire's monarchism coupled with enlightenment especially pleased lodges of military men, who also used the occasion to glory in the achievement of Louis XVI.[121] The eulogy spoken for Voltaire at the Nine Sisters was widely circulated through the ubiquitous almanacs.[122] So too were the details of the elaborate ceremonies in his honor held at the Nine Sisters and witnessed by Franklin, Greuze (painter to the king), and many other luminaries.[123] In general the masonic interpretation of Voltaire placed him as a symbol of the toleration sought in the lodges and of anticlericalism.

Still other major philosophes can be found who were much more directly involved in the lodges. Among the exiled visitors to midcentury Amsterdam was a French philosophe of some considerable importance at the time, the abbé Claude Yvon. He quickly became a leader in a local lodge. Yvon had been a close associate of Diderot, and he wrote some of the most important articles in the famous *Encyclopédie*. His article on the soul was far too generous in recapitulating the arguments put forth by materialists against its existence. Already under suspicion because of his association with Diderot and with philosophical heresy, Yvon and his close friend the abbé de Prades were forced to flee Paris in 1752 under fear of arrest. De Prades had submitted a blatantly materialist thesis to the Sorbonne, and it had been carelessly passed.[124] When the authorities discovered they had been made to look foolish, the Parlement of Paris issued a warrant for his arrest.

In the company of de Prades, Yvon made his way first to Amsterdam. Like so many itinerant men of the eighteenth century, he then not simply joined but actually helped found a new masonic lodge, Concordia vincit Animos. Its proceedings, as we saw at the beginning of chapter 5, opened in 1755 in the home of one of the brothers. Sparse though they are, Concordia's minutes are invaluable because they provide us with the texts of orations that Yvon himself gave to his brothers.[125] Many such orations have been preserved, but in this instance we can actually listen to one of the philosophes at the very center of the midcentury movement for Enlightenment as he explained to his brothers his understanding of how freemasonry should transform them. Like so many orators in every Continental country, Yvon is conscious of "the public slander" directed against the Order: "The world . . . could not imagine that the rigorous order which ties our secret assemblies together and cuts off entry to all profanes could be innocent. . . . In the same way, in former times, the pagan Corruption blamed emerging Christianity for crimes that it wanted to cure itself of and extirpate entirely."[126] Having made the analogy to Christianity the exiled abbé locates freemasonry as "the temple of Virtue. . . . Yes, my brothers, it is a temple that we are building dedicated to Virtue. Its foundations are laid down in our hearts. Moral and civil virtues are its Decorations. . . . We ourselves are, my brothers, the living stones of this Temple."[127]

The virtue proclaimed by Yvon is meant to be both private and public. We should not think this to be idle rhetoric. At the same lodge meeting where Yvon spoke, the master, with the consent of the brothers, imposed penalties to assist in the search for private virtue: Monetary donations were to be given to the poor box of the lodge by men "convicted of playing cards in the morning before noon . . . and . . . after midnight or [those] who pass the night at the game, as well as those who do not sleep at home, either at the 'Musicos' or in other improper places." And lest the self-policing being advocated should fail, "those among the brothers who will know but not denounce the one who is guilty, if they are convicted of this, will pay the double penalty."[128] The somewhat obscure term "Musicos" implied more than a cabaret, and the rest of the sentence clearly implies a house of prostitution.[129] Neighboring lodges also had elaborate rules of conduct that prohibited cursing, or discussions of "statecraft," and insisted upon "good order" and "subordination" of brothers toward their officers.[130]

For Yvon and his brothers the temple of virtue was a rigorously demanding place. The obligations of freemasonry are, as he explained, "geared toward the perfection of human nature."[131] If this be the case, why then are "lessons . . . so useful for the world's happiness . . . not spread far and wide" instead of being hidden from the profane by a "religious silence"?[132] The Enlightenment provides the rhetorical answer: "To sample our lessons, my dear brothers, one must have a mind prepared by long instructions, one must rise above popular prejudice, one must even be a philosophe up to a certain point. Thus all of this requires a kind of initiation and consequently a separation from profanes."[133] For those who would become philosophes, Yvon offers a promise of transcendence, by degrees: "We will only make the veil before your eyes drop little by little. . . . Your eyes might be hurt by the glare by which the light shines, the light our mysteries hide inside." At first through emblems and allegories this light will be unveiled. Truth and virtue must be approached slowly by men who have been corrupted, who have been "born in the midst of despotism; only knowing liberty by name, you will find her in our meetings."[134] These were strong words and the reference to despotism was unmistakably political. The intention of this striving is to "make a man transcend himself . . . this is the most beautiful lot of humanity."[135]

During the second half of the century national states could be seen as potential agents for the promotion of the enlightenment of which Yvon spoke. Earlier in the century masonic rhetoric tended to be less nationally focused, and it was commonplace to speak of all humankind: "The earth itself is only a great republic."[136] As we have seen, it became commonplace for freemasons to refer to "la République Maçonne." In it "les classes particulières" evince a love for the public good.[137] This universalist rhetoric was never entirely abandoned. In the almanac of 1772 brothers were reminded that the greatest achievements of the mason builders had been "public edifices," particularly in the republican style of Vitruvius and Palladio (see p. 57).[138]

By the 1770s some lodges abandoned the terminology of the "degrees" or "grades" and instituted instead a system of "classes" through which a brother might rise. This interesting choice of words was intended to enhance masonic equality.[139] While making a distinction between civil and masonic society, these innovative lodges did believe that in both places membership in different classes should not detract from equality, not permit some men to have greater "rights in the Society."[140] The French lodge that was making these innovations was self-described as descended from the Jacobites, the followers of James II and from there to King Charles I of England. Yet its antirevolutionary antiquity could be renounced in at least one respect: The introduction of classes for brothers could not claim, and did not seek to make, any pretension at antiquity.[141] The necessity for reform within the lodge required innovation, and the new classes were symbolized by medals and sashes. All of this masonic regalia was costly, and thus we can assume the members of this lodge to have been prosperous, if not aristocratic.

We need to be absolutely clear that prior to 1789 in France nothing subversive of established authority was ever intended by this rhetoric. Whether speaking in the Dutch Republic or the Austrian Netherlands, in the French monarchy or Vienna and Berlin, freemasons in the first instance identified with power. The "most wonderful quality of the mason is to be a citizen." In the 1780s French lodges spoke of making voluntary contributions to the king "to repair a momentary disaster."[142] In 1789 some of the lodges did just that. But in so doing they now allied themselves with the new National Assembly and cast their fate with the Revolution.[143]

By the very end of the century, as a result of the democratic revolutions, freemasonry achieved a reputation that it would never subsequently shed. It was reputed to be where liberal reformers gathered, especially in those countries where the Enlightenment had only dimly penetrated. In the Austrian land of Moravia lodges were central to the late eighteenth-century transmission of enlightened culture.[144] This would also seem to be the case in Italy. Lecturing to his brothers in Milan in the year 1800 the masonic lecturer could describe the lodges as a refuge in a turbulent world. He then went on to give a rather recognizable intellectual history of the previous century. Its sense of the perfectibility of humankind "to which we are susceptible" owes much to the immortal Newton, in other words, to the new science.[145] The ancient Egyptians, Greeks, and Romans are another source of human wisdom, and of freemasonry. Not, he assured his listeners, the Crusades, because they must be associated with fanaticism, which could not have been at the origin of freemasonry. At another moment praise is heaped upon Rousseau for having seen the corruption of morals which results from civilization. "If only the unfortunate Rousseau could have known our august assemblies; if only you had enjoyed the sweetness of the union that reigns among us."[146] Nature shows man the most simple and most beautiful religion. Our Milanese lecturer, who is speaking in French, then catalogues of evils of religion and juxtaposes them to the reasonableness of freemasonry. Another lecturer in the same place praised republican Rome of the ancients, and then went on to eulogize the French, beginning with Descartes and Voltaire. Speaking at length on the Newtonian laws, this orator then described the order and harmony that pervades nature.[147] With this natural religion men will temper their fanaticism. In these orations the Enlightenment faith of the eighteenth century is being transmitted and lionized. There is not a negative word spoken about its principles or those of the revolutions that have made the world in 1800 such a turbulent place.

We need to know how an institution of private sociability so intimately bound up with ancien régime society, with status, respectability, rank, and order, could also be porous enough to allow other impulses, dissonant, reforming, and hostile to tradition, gain expression amid its assemblies. Asking that question of freemasonry also permits us to ask it of the Enlightenment. Or put another, more commonplace, way: What did the Enlightenment have to do with the democratic revolutions at the end of the eighteenth century, in America, Belgium, the Dutch Republic, and France? We cannot hope to address that question for every country or for most lodges. But we can, and will in the next chapter, show how one lodge in a major European city, Amsterdam, lived through the 1780s and 1790s, providing for its brothers a setting in which to imagine and discuss reform and then revolution. It might be argued that the Dutch Republic is exceptional in European history with a tradition of freedom that excluded it from the abuses of the old order. Dutch patriots of the 1780s or Dutch Jacobins of the 1790s would not have agreed.

7

Living the Enlightenment: Cosmopolitan Reformers and Amsterdam Brothers

By all accounts eighteenth-century Amsterdam was one of the most cosmopolitan places in Europe. Although by the last quarter of the century London had replaced it as the banking capital of Europe, Amsterdam remained a city, however economically troubled, that was tied to international commerce. Also by tradition as well as by the circumstances of decline, Amsterdam was not noticeably happy with the Orangist government in The Hague. In 1760 a British merchant wrote home the following account of the profound discontent and seditious fraternizing about which he had been told:

> Their greatest grievance was to see their country enslaved by their own countrymen—by the very representatives who were chosen to protect their liberties and privileges. Why to procure the liberty to send over their just complaint to England a deputation of the richest merchants in Amsterdam danced attendance for three weeks at the Hague before they could be heard . . . and yet Amsterdam alone pays fifty-eight [percent] out of one hundred [percent] of the whole public revenue. Nay they were so free to assure us that the principal people in Amsterdam formed an association to shake off every connection with the rest of the provinces and they did not doubt but it would soon come to this.[1]

In 1760 the formation of an association to promote Amsterdam's secession from the Republic may have been coffeehouse boasting. By the 1780s, however, there were political associations up and down the country. Their goal was not secession; rather it was a thorough reform of the institutions of government. By the 1790s throughout western Europe voluntary associations had come to provide one of the contexts for revolutionary ardor, a republican ardor that eventually also seized the brothers of La Bien Aimée.

Amsterdam is one of the few cities in the Low Countries to have escaped the destruction wrought by modern warfare. Thus complementing its present-day beauty is the richness of its archives. There are few places in the corridor from Amsterdam to Paris where we can find a complete set of monthly lodge meetings that permit us to listen to the same masonic orators, literally month by month, as they commented upon the world around them and sought to make sense out of it. To the best of my knowledge only one lodge in western Europe, La Bien Aimée in Amsterdam, left such a complete record, an inventory of its minutes, correspondence, and orations, month by month from its reconstituting in 1754 into the 1790s, and indeed beyond. Recently three years of records for a lodge in Bordeaux were discovered, and their editor asserts that these are extremely rare.[2] In this chapter we will be concerned with the proceedings of La Bien Aimée from the 1760s to the 1790s, at the time when the Dutch came face to face with the fact of their economic decline and simultaneously sought to transform their system of government.

In chapter 4 we met La Bien Aimée along with its founder, Rousset de Missy; we learned of its disbanding in 1749 after the Revolution of 1747, and we followed its reconstitution in 1754. It and the new Grand Lodge of The Netherlands then quarreled bitterly over its legality, and the dispute simmered until 1760. In other words, this was a lodge that historically, at the very least, had its own mind, and at the most might be a haven for the malcontent, the factious, and the rebellious.[3] We know from its records that in the 1780s and 1790s the lodge had more than its fair share of *patriotten* (patriots), the name assumed by opponents of the stadtholder and ruling oligarchy he was seen to protect. Indeed, in 1787 the lodge chose as its orator J. A. Craÿenschot, a publisher of radical anti-Orangist pamphlets who would shortly be forced into exile. Put another way, this was a lodge with a long history of attracting merchants (many of them with international businesses), sea captains, bankers, publishers, surgeons, professors of anatomy and surgery, jurists, musicians, and painters—professional men from Amsterdam (and abroad), as well as a few Dutch barons, who had intellectual interests and who tended, as the minutes will reveal, to gradually cast a cold eye on the prevailing social and political order in the troubled Republic.[4] Nothing about these men, however, suggests that they were marginal; comfort, if not opulence, pervaded their proceedings.

La Bien Aimée cannot be imagined as standing for all lodges, but then neither was it aberrant. Many of the themes we encounter in its records were standard to the Enlightenment and, as we saw in the previous chapter, standard to European freemasonry. Not least, we have the lodge's visitors' book, which shows the vast international contacts that a lodge in Amsterdam could have.[5] Not every European lodge got to entertain the then unknown Jean Paul Marat and the soon to be infamous Casanova.[6] The masonic sources of Marat's political rhetoric have been acknowledged elsewhere.[7] The importance of masonry in the life of Casanova can be demonstrated from his memoirs. We have no evidence from any quarter that what these famous as well as obscure visitors experienced in Amsterdam was different from what they knew and expected in other lodges.

Over the decades every secretary of La Bien Aimée left us a precious, if maddeningly terse, record of how this lodge experienced the late Enlightenment and the revolutions. We must recall that the Low Countries, both the Dutch Republic and Belgium, revolted for different reasons and in different ways in the 1780s before the 1789 upheaval in Paris. In all three countries the 1790s were turbulent. In all three places, as we saw in previous chapters and will see in our discussion of the French lodges in chapters 8 and 9, the lodges reflected upon the public order, mirrored it, recoiled from it, and in the case of La Bien Aimée ultimately embraced the revolutionary principles of the French. The Enlightenment in all three places, now understood as a social experience, permitted those reflections within the civil society created by the lodges.

Of the many leaders of the Dutch *patriotten* movement who were freemasons—and one historian has estimated that by 1795 the majority were—none was more important by the 1790s than Johan Valckenaer.[8] A regent in his native Friesland and a professor of law, Valckenaer appears in the minutes of La Bien Aimée as an active member right up until 1787, when his name disappears. The mystery is easily solved when we realize that in that year, after the invasion of The Netherlands by Prussian troops who restored the stadtholder to power, Valckenaer, like hundreds of Dutch patriots, fled to France and threw themselves on the mercy of the French king. Proudly they maintained that they were continuing the struggle in exile. In the case of Valckenaer exile permitted him to witness the French Revolution firsthand. He became its ardent supporter, seeing in it a continuation of *patriotten* causes and interests. When he returned to Amsterdam in 1795, and to his lodge, he had become a dedicated Jacobin, a seasoned political radical, and eventually an educational reformer of considerable stature. We should bear in mind that up until his exile Valckenaer heard most if not all of the orations and discussions in La Bien Aimée recounted in this chapter.

In the first decade of its reconstituting most of La Bien Aimée's time was spent in dealing with the problems of its legality and organization. In 1754 the brothers, some twenty-two in all, were without their master. Rousset was in exile and they were "scattered sheep without a shepherd."[9] They asked him by "his power and authority, by an authentic document, to authorize them to form a regular lodge."[10] This he did with alacrity, naming Pierre Bunel as the new master. Thus began the makings of a major quarrel with the new Grand Lodge of the Republic, which would not acknowledge the legality of Rousset's old lodge. We dealt with that quarrel at some length, and indeed will return to the phenomenon of these internecine quarrels, which were commonplace throughout European freemasonry (see chapter 8). Here it is the lodge's sense of self that concerns us, the contours of its secular conscience.

Among La Bien Aimée's first acts was to reach out to foreign lodges for recognition. When an envoy turned up from the intellectually prominent lodge in Leipzig, Minerva zum Zirkel, Bunel sent brothers off immediately in a rented coach to bid him their respects. More was at stake here than civility and cosmopolitanism, although both were important. La Bien Aimée desperately needed the recognition of other lodges in order to establish its legitimacy (see p. 99). And these two lodges were to remain in regular communication throughout the rest of the century. They communicated in French, and, using it in the envoy's presence, the orator thanked the German lodge for its "friendship and respect."[11] Respect was central to what lodges gave one another and members also gave each other. Seldom was a meeting held without reading to the brothers a flattering letter from a foreign lodge; in October 1758 the correspondent was the lodge La Concorde in Strasbourg.[12] A few years later it was yet another Strasbourg lodge, La Candeur, this one engaged in a bitter quarrel with the French Grand Lodge and seeking recognition from the Dutch Grand Lodge.[13] Over and over we will find the Amsterdam lodge, and all others, speaking of their honor and glory; brothers are "honorable and enlightened."

Honor had once been the prerogative of the landed estate, of the aristocracy even in the mercantile Dutch republic. The men of La Bien Aimée, the majority not being from the aristocracy, nevertheless assume honor to be their right; much of the civility of a lodge is taken up in telling members and visitors how honorable, enlightened, and worthy they are. The lodge's furniture and silver decorations, its "throne" for the master, its brother servants, the orchestra that played on special occasions—all were intended to create an aura of splendor and opulence. For these rich merchants, doctors, lawyers, and a few men of baronial title, the Enlightenment only reinforced this sense of specialness, otherness. Thus much of the lodge's activities in the 1750s, when it was not fighting with the Grand Lodge, concerned putting these symbols in place.[14] Also put in place were elaborate rules governing every office in the lodge, specifying the duties of officers and of brothers, their places in order of rank and subordination, even in processions, right down to the furnishings and ceremonial vestments of each officer, who, wearing their swords, carried a copy of the *Constitutions*. In the search for order and decorum very little was left to chance.[15] By 1765 the lodge had grown to sixty-six members.

Central to the ordering process was the building of a strong treasury for the lodge; this, it was believed, would guarantee the harmony and the welfare of all brothers.[16] The vagaries and uncertainties of market life were never far from day-to-day concerns. Although the lodge prospered, it also had a poor box for the relief of brothers who regularly appealed to it. Men gave to the treasury at their initiation into the order, with the conferring of a new degree, or if they were chronically late or absent. This treasury was in turn invested at interest.[17] Ordinary brothers also gave money to the brother servants for the new year. These were men of the servant class, sometimes servants in the home of the masonic master, who although sometimes initiated, stood back in the proceedings of their "equals" and waited upon them. The lodge as a whole, like others, also contributed to a school for poor children.[18] Eventually money took on symbolic value. The old voting system of casting black and white beans, one probably taken from the guilds, was replaced; voters now cast pieces of money.[19] This sense of the reality of economic life may have fueled a sentiment that turns up repeatedly in the orations. Life's circumstances are forever changing; time can sometimes reduce all to a pitiful state. There is a mutability in all things.[20] References to the "troubles and persecutions" that have besieged the order in the Dutch Republic never entirely disappear from its monthly deliberations.[21] Yet the lodge continued to prosper.

Throughout the process of building, annual elections for officers and new members continued. No other business was more solemn in the life of the lodge. Orators regularly spoke about the "original laws and foundations of freemasonry," or on "the true and moral duties of an upright mason,"[22] but on the occasion of an election special orations were given before the voting.[23] By the 1760s these classically educated men increasingly made an analogy between masonic elections and the solemnities enacted by the ancient Romans during elections and then inaugurations of their magistrates.[24] Elections proceeded after the master had stepped down from "his throne" and placed his mallet on the Constitution Book of the lodge.[25] He would then leave the room purposefully, even if reassured that his departure was not necessary, so as not to unduly influence the freedom of the voting.[26] When a master resigned his office he separated himself from its symbols, taking off his special attire and handing over the staff.[27] Newly elected officers were in turn instructed about the importance of their duties, and they then paraded "together with their swords drawn to the throne of Lights where the venerable master had them take the customary oaths." On the occasions of the elections brothers were exhorted to identify themselves with the virtues associated with the Romans, or to ponder the causes of the decline of ancient Rome. Their actions in this private forum self-consciously imitated the ancient civic rights of the Roman republic. Yet they were also intensely personal; always the master exhorted his brothers about "the love and intense devotion," the "brotherly love" they should have for the lodge.[28] Similarly the Roman dedication to civic duty was depicted as personal and manly, analogous to the rituals performed by fathers when their sons reached their maturity.[29] Masonic duty is similar to both civic and domestic duty; yet it should also come before public duties. Fraternity is a living creed that bridges the space between the public and the private.[30]

The identification with the ancient world was easily made among these Dutch brothers whose formal education remained distinctively classical and humanistic. There was also the shared belief that the freemasons had inherited the traditions of the original masons, skilled in "the art of building among all people and places, beginning with Solomon's Temple to that of the Roman, Greek and other learned emperors . . . [being] well known as architects and mathematicians."[31] This lore formed the subject of orations and also the content of the masonic "catechism" on which new members were quizzed before the assembled brothers. The masonic identification was ultimately not with the ruled but with the rulers. King Solomon ruled Israel according to masonic virtues that were not inherited by his successors.[32]

Yet other virtues more modern than ancient in their historical importance were routinely discussed, among them "freedom." Without it there is no unity. Freedom cannot exist without virtue expressed by good laws.[33] It is invoked most frequently in discussions of elections but also simply to describe the Dutch: They are freedom-loving. It is a characteristic that freemasonry claimed to reinforce. By the mid-1760s the masonic virtues are being equated with the restoration of man's natural state: "The orator exhorted about the main reason why Freemasonry was so well received among the enlightened: the Natural State of humanity is therein restored perfectly, no disguise will be tolerated among them."[34] The sentiments being expressed might be classified as Rousseauian; but should we not reverse the order of influence? As part of his genius Rousseau provided a vocabulary for sentiments that predated him. We should remember here that Rousset de Missy, the founder of the original lodge in 1735 and its master into the 1750s, was a self-described pantheist and a republican. Not least the Dutch Republic possessed a tradition of opposition to absolute authority. When celebrating the two hundredth anniversary of Leiden University—created during the late sixteenth-century revolt against Spain in thanksgiving for Leiden's having resisted a long and desperate siege by the Spanish—the brothers in La Bien Aimée reminded themselves of their brave ancestors.[35]

In the private enclave of sociability provided by the lodge, primitive states of virtue could be imaged and contrasted with the social state that surrounded the brothers, with the universe of the profane. The world (not the lodge) is an unstable place, the orator warned; care must be taken in electing leaders within the fraternity.[36] Decency must always be practiced precisely so that the profane do not misconstrue the meaning of freemasonry. The men who are creating these virtuous enclaves, at least in this instance, were neither primitive nor rebellious. Within the lodge they debated change with deep reservations. One such debate has been preserved. Although we do not know the change that is being contemplated, we know the reactions: "Innovation" was distrusted and should be undertaken only if it leads to improvement for "the [masonic] order in general." Theirs was the "royal science," and change required "research and experiment" before it was embraced.[37] These cautious voices belonged to elite elements in Amsterdam society—not the great regents, the actual oligarchy, but to men of wealth, education, reputation, and substance. In the private enclave of the lodge they were swordbearers, as well as self-fashioned ancient electors of the Roman "*burgermeesters.*" "Through Nature," they said, men were made devoted freemasons with true friendship and charity being their most signal characteristics.[38] And the continuing practice of these virtues, they believed, would lead to even greater perfection. These were also men with rather considerable self-confidence. They were doers endowed with civility: "A good freemason shows by his deeds his good taste."[39] And despite his affluence he is meant not to judge by a man's external appearances.

The distrust of external appearances extended to the trappings of birth: "No one has more right to pride himself on coming from old noble and famous lineage than the people who have a virtuous man as an ancestor."[40] Increasingly La Bien Aimée's discussions turn to true virtue and the need for no outward ornaments; only the masonic symbols are necessary.[41] Men are naturally sociable, but reason must be cultivated; without it virtue is impossible. The society of the lodge is thus necessary to inculcate reason, its ultimate purpose.[42] The search for reason, which is the building of the lodge, requires work. The work ethic never ceases to be praised in the proceedings of this lodge and many others. A favorite masonic symbol was the beehive; these Dutch brothers refer to the lodge as the "Republic of the honeybees." Beelike industry and cooperation are the ideal, and everyone can "make themselves skilled by assiduous attention to the Arts and the Sciences."[43] Time must always be used well and appropriately.[44] Similarly, charity should be dispensed only to the deserving, who are in need through no fault of their own. Letters from brothers pleading for assistance contain litanies of misfortunes, bombing in wars, flight from religious persecution, and affirmations of a lifetime of devotion to freemasonry.[45] Exactly the same tone is struck in letters asking for charity sent to the French Grand Lodge in the 1780s.

In the 1770s serious efforts were made to unify Dutch freemasonry. Officers from The Hague paid cordial visits to the lodges and observed ceremonies and orations. La Bien Aimée was no exception.[46] These visitations seem to have resulted in an increasing emphasis on systematic charity: "The love of human beings shows that it is not enough to have assisted and helped the needy on some occasions, rather it is desirable that the Brother Freemasons in this country would imitate the examples of some of our foreign brothers by designing a permanent setting for mutilated, old and tired sailors who 'til now have risked their lives to the benefit and advantages of our city and have no place to go in their old age."[47]

In this effort to assist the worthy poor, that is, those who were impoverished through no fault of their own, various impulses are present. The definition of those worthy of charity is completely consonant with the masonic emphasis on a work ethic. It also signals a willingness to address the needs of the larger community, in this instance the city of Amsterdam. There is also a growing emphasis on the Enlightenment applied, on usefulness, on "the usefulness of the Arts and Sciences." In the turn toward the useful, freemasons were participating in a general movement evident in Dutch sociability in the 1770s and 1780s. The leading historian of this phenomenon, W. Mijnhardt, had described these "useful societies" as the last and most nationalist generation of old-regime sociability.[48] In the masonic case the ideology of charity, coupled with a nationalist rhetoric, was already present; it simply had to be activated. Possibly La Bien Aimée was experiencing competition for membership from the new and aggressive advocates of application and usefulness.[49] Certainly the orator of 1773 was willing to assert, somewhat defensively, the order's superiority to all other "knightly orders." In the masonic version of usefulness even its celebrations and feast days became useful.[50]

As sociability became fashionable in the Dutch Republic, also in France and the Austrian Netherlands, Dutch freemasons may have been at a disadvantage. In the Republic more than elsewhere, the accusation of immorality had hung about them and would not quite go away. The tension, as Dutch freemasons interpreted it, was between the commonfolk (*het gemeen*)—perhaps the most literate and certainly the most urbanized on the Continent—and the elite. For reasons we can only guess, 1773 was a particularly difficult year for the Amsterdam lodge. Once again the brothers found themselves on the defensive against "slander." Their orator of the year, and many more, was Cornelis Jacob van den Lijn. He was particularly gifted as a speaker and hence a printed copy of one of his orations for that year has survived. He was also an important merchant and international speculator; within the year he became master of the lodge. His printed oration of 1773 advocated a "paternal" kindness in the face of slander, an attempt through sympathetic understanding to achieve true friendship.[51] The records of La Bien Aimée reveal that for reasons we cannot determine even the Grand Master of the entire Republic was under attack.[52] Once again we hear about the precariousness of life, about vulnerability.[53] Simultaneously the value of self-knowledge and human dependency on one another is emphasized, as is constancy, particularly to newly initiated brothers.[54] Caution is also advocated; so too is reason.[55]

Van den Lijn's remarks were highly emotional on what he saw as the most serious, and most unjust, of the accusations against the order: that it is a training school for atheism and civil disorder, that the brothers are lovers of unbridled pleasure. We have heard these charges before (p. 82). In defense he cites the first article of Anderson's 1723 *Constitutions:* A freemason can never be "a stupid atheist or an ungodly freethinker." On the matter of the order's relationship to the government van den Lijn was blunt: "Do not the mean and low, the common people, play the main role" in these unjust accusations?[56] He asks, how could the freemasons be against the government when so many men in high governmental office belong to the lodges? As for pleasure, are not women excluded from the lodges? Van den Lijn has given us as frank a statement as we are likely to find in confirmation of the rupture to be seen everywhere else in eighteenth-century western Europe between the culture of the people and the culture of the enlightened.

Yet among the enlightened quarreling remained endemic. In 1776 La Bien Aimée would not permit other brothers from Amsterdam simply to visit the lodge without prior permission, and the master also warned the brothers against arrogance.[57] Brotherly love and secrecy are once again advocated. Clearly something is troubling this lodge, but it is never precisely defined. Instead there are attacks on glory received without true merit, and not least on the decline of Rome from its splendor and greatness.[58] The origin of "the knightly orders" is traced to the "loftiness of virtue" and the bravery of one of the Knights of St. John (the masonic patron saint) at the recapture of Jerusalem during the Crusades. Loyalty and constancy are once again invoked, as is freedom at the moment of an election.[59] The laws of the ancient Egyptians are praised and compared to those of the masonic order. This is a theme that will recur, and it suggests an identification with the search for a civil religiosity. Cryptically in 1779 the minutes tell us that there are things beyond the control of the lodge that sometimes need its attention.[60] Once again the theme of utility emerges in the lodge's discourse, in particular the usefulness of the sciences.[61] This was a common theme among Dutch reformers of the period, who believed, with considerable justification, that the Republic had fallen into decline in part because of the superiority of its neighbors in applied mechanical science.[62] Within the year the brothers are told that all useful societies need laws; at the new year of 1780 the master gave his blessing to the lodge and expressed his concern "in relation to the recent precarious epoch of our beloved Nation and its high government."[63]

It seems reasonable to relate these remarks of the late 1770s to the deepening economic crisis in the Republic, to its quarrel with Britain because of Dutch trade with the American colonies and the impending Anglo-Dutch war. This was the moment when Dutch reformers began to sense that something had gone very wrong and to question the competence of the stadtholder and his government. Within a few months the orator will praise the brothers for being "Dutch [and] freedom loving."[64] The themes of light and enlightenment are renewed in these discourses; the master is compared to "the glowing light in the West." Once again the lodge disputes with the Grand Lodge, this time about La Bien Aimée's reluctance to send representatives to an international meeting in Frankfurt to consult about the interests and concerns of the Order. Prussia incidentally was a British ally. Finally, by the end of the year the orator tells his brothers of their love "for our dear fatherland in a time when proud and useless lust for power, as well as abominable egoism, intend its downfall. The love we received by drinking the milk of childhood, showed itself in full force, that is, our affection for the distinguished Government of the Country as well as for dutiful subjection to its administration, its cautious and wise decrees, present sound evidence that real freemasons are good friends and loyal Patriots."[65]

These are loyalist sentiments expressed in wartime. They are best interpreted as still vaguely Orangist, yet there is a concession intended by the reference to *patriotten;* it would seem that there are reformers (often of that name) also present in this lodge.[66] What is also clear is that the lodge is in debt. These were economically very troubled times and the lodge is having trouble raising its monthly and annual dues.[67] What is needed, the master says, is "a contract" from each brother.

The lodge, although increasingly concerned for its survival, is not preoccupied to the exclusion of the world around it. Yet for economic reasons the number of visitors from Amsterdam must be limited at any one meeting. These troubles could have been seen as analogous to those of the larger society. "The pillars of a [small] society consist in observing good order, maintaining the constitution, and a reasonable freedom; following these pillars results in the growth of that society, while neglect inevitably causes downfall [or decay]."[68] Decline can occur in any society, that is the message to be drawn from the remarks of the master. In the same year the orator explains that work produces unity in the lodges. But is work enough?

The masonic order, the brothers are reminded, originated in "the superstitious centuries [and was then] transmitted to our better enlightened times." Every effort is made to be joyful, a general hospitality pervades the meeting and we are told that the Master is "filled with patriotic, disinterested and freedom loving feelings [even] in this time of unrelenting attack, lustful oppression and the violation of the most holy alliances of our neighbors."[69] Although vague as recorded, the remarks tell us that the events of the moment pervaded the proceedings. In this instance the lodge was hailed as a refuge from the world, a place of friendship and hospitality. At the next meeting concerns about the political and economic situation in the Republic become more explicit: "The welfare of the people is at its greatest low." Then there is a discussion of the three known forms of government without a preference expressed in the minutes. Did some brothers favor monarchy, or aristocracy, or democracy? Perhaps there were voices raised for all three. At the very next meeting in 1782 a proposal comes from the Grand Lodge in The Hague to conclude an "alliance with the freedom loving and now independent Lodges of the Great East, of North America."[70] In these troubled times the Dutch had supported the American colonies against their commercial rival across the Channel. Critics of the stadtholder had been particularly avid for the American cause, for which loans were raised in *patriotten* circles in Amsterdam.[71] Also in 1782 a treaty was concluded between the two nations. In concluding the masonic alliance with the American brothers our Amsterdam lodge was now open to American visitors. Within a few months a brother arrives from a lodge in Pennsylvania to effect "this alliance and correspondence with the free brothers of North America."

The visitors from America arrived at a good moment, amidst discussions that were going on in the lodge about the nature of government, about the best form it should now take. If men were discussing the forms of known government, and deeply distressed about the condition of the people, they might have much to learn from discussions with Americans recently successful in their search for freedom and independence.[72] And with that success in Pennsylvania had come a major expansion of freemasonry in the new state.[73] In 1778 the Grand Lodge of Pennsylvania had made a firm commitment to the revolutionary cause. Historians of Dutch and

Anglo-American republicanism are beginning to recognize that despite their different languages, Dutch and American republicans shared a conceptual universe that decried tyranny and the decadence of entrenched interests, and that looked to the Romans and to the more recent republicans of the seventeenth and eighteenth centuries for guidance.[74] Conversations such as the ones that went on in the La Bien Aimée may have facilitated the forging of a transatlantic republican consciousness.

What the Pennsylvania brother saw must have been impressive. New furnishings had been purchased and the display was such that brothers when they first saw it "were besides themselves and were silent for a long time, not able to express in words what they saw."[75] Standing in a circle the brothers ceremonially inaugurated the new furnishings. We cannot miss the quasi-religious tone of these proceedings, this celebration of the mundane: "The procession started, very stately without any confusion in spite of the large number of Brothers, accompanied by the customary music. After it the enlightened master of the [visiting] lodge, La Charité, expressed his profound pleasure in our work, and thus the lodge was closed."[76] We know from other meetings in the 1780s that La Bien Aimée was in serious debt, but we do not sense a scaling down of its protocol or festivities. Indeed, by 1784 its membership had risen to eighty-one brothers. Orations at this moment make frequent reference to "the excellence of harmony."[77] Or they condemn "the conceit" and the hypocrisy of men and comment upon the harmful and horrible nature of wrath. These are sentiments that almost never appear in masonic literature. All this at a time when there is evidence of renewed quarreling between lodges.

Yet the "work" of the lodge continued. Elections were held regularly; feasts were enjoyed "with all loving harmony." In early 1787, at the height of a crisis provoked by *patriotten* unrest, the orator calls for "self-knowledge which is founded on the power of reason, the law and conscience." He tells his brothers that freemasonry needs a constitutional restoration (*grondwettige herstelling*), and that this would be easier to achieve than a restoration of statecraft.[78] The choice of terms is important. One of the most famous *patriotten* pamphlets of the day, *The Constitutional Restoration of the Dutch State* (*Grondwettige Herstelling van Nederlands Staatswezen,* 1784–86), argued for sovereignty in the people but through the maintenance of elite leadership. It was an argument that had little populist appeal, but it would have struck the men of La Bien Aimée as making good sense. Perhaps the orator is suggesting that the lodge is an easier place to achieve constitutional reform than is the state.

In early 1787 the master, because he has allowed the election to be free, in effect gives his brothers in this lodge an "unlimited freedom" to hold an election.[79] Out of it the patriot publisher Craÿenschot was made the lodge's orator. At this same moment some patriots were calling for the creation of a national assembly in the republic. In his first speech Craÿenschot exhorted his brothers to study "the histories, foremost those concerning freemasonry; [he] showed again new signs of his excellent ingenuity and unlimited knowledge of Antiquity." Did he want them to think about its English origins? Did he believe that in its fundamental principles the masonic order offered a model of good government? We will never know for sure, but we might reasonably imagine that he did.

The turning point in the confrontation between patriots and Orangists was 1787.

Both sides were armed and civil disturbances occurred in nearly every town or city of any importance. By the summer of that year it was clear that the stadtholder had lost control over the Republic, yet it was also clear that support for the patriots was neither firm enough nor unified enough to ensure their ability to seize control of the institutions of local and national government. In so many cities the old oligarchy remained strong. At the same time patriotic rhetoric was becoming increasingly democratic; the patriots claimed to speak "for the people." The specter of the Revolution of 1747 haunted these proceedings; on that occasion the "little people" of Amsterdam led by Van Gimnig and Rousset de Missy had for a brief time refused to be governed. In 1787 there were demands for a National Assembly, with the purpose of dismantling the Estates General, which was in any event hopelessly deadlocked. So similar are many of the moves made by the patriots to what eventually unfolded in Paris in 1789 that some historians have imagined the Republic in 1787 as a "rehearsal" for the French Revolution. It is better to see both phenomena as part of a larger movement for reform and then revolution that erupted, for different and yet similar reasons, in the late 1780s in the Low Countries and France. But in The Hague in 1787, as opposed to Versailles in 1791, the stadtholder had a trump card. In the autumn of 1787 the Prussian army, allies of the stadtholder, William V, and of the British, invaded the Republic and before long even Amsterdam surrendered. As one patriot put it, "The English . . . endeavor to enslave everyone and keep themselves free."[80] Thus began years of repression, of officially sponsored violence against the patriots, many of whom now fled south to Brussels and Paris. Yet the traffic was not all one way; a new member from Brussels is initiated in the Amsterdam lodge in 1794.

The minutes of La Bien Aimée are eerie in their silence for much of 1787. When they resume in 1788 membership has fallen from the high of eighty-one in 1785 to forty-three, and eventually to twenty-two in 1792. The master urges his brothers to recommence "our work with new zeal, after an extraordinary quiet, not caused by the sound of the hammer of discord striking in our temple, but by the unfortunate circumstances of the times outside."[81] Private enlightened sociability always possessed the capability to look inward, toward self-knowledge and improvement. The formula was classical and stoic in origin, and its adherents believed that private virtue cultivated in society would serve the state. Now the brothers are urged to "renounce oneself [and of] necessity to control one's temper," or they are reminded about "the goal of our order being to make a freemason humane, reasonable and virtuous."[82] Times are hard and as winter sets in they become even harder. The winter of 1788–89 was one of the worst on record throughout western Europe; the orator "gave a moving speech about the destitutions of the present incessant, severe winter, and recommended liberal compassion for his fellow brothers and equal human beings."[83] The patriot ideology of equality gave added meaning to the hardship of that winter, which would be seen in retrospect to have boded so ill for the kings of Europe. With hardship the lodge's debt only mounted.

In the early 1790s the lodge almost totally disintegrated. The exiling of some of its members, the death of its master of ten years, and the burden of debt effectively closed it down. For different reasons we can see a similar pattern in the French lodges of precisely these years (p. 213). Yet some brothers remained intensely loyal;

Craÿenschot (back from exile) is once again, but only briefly, orator (1793) and a new master is elected. There is an emotional intensity in the records of the 1790s; brothers about to be admitted are called children. There are "the usual formalities in a generous, merry, enthusiastic and friendly way . . . after which the brothers went home pleased and content in order to have their freemason wives share in their joy and contentment."[84] Brothers are exhorted to promote the true happiness and prosperity of each other. "Just as a father cannot leave his children a better inheritance than a good upbringing, freemasonry also leaves to the disposal of its practitioners virtue and good morals as its enduring legacy."[85] Given the financial problems, new servants are brought into the lodge because a servant of the new master has volunteered to donate his labor; he is deemed "a suitable object."[86] There is a drawing together evident in these records. It is tied not to cosmopolitanism, but as we are about to see, to an incipient nationalism, to a sense that specific peoples must belong to specific nations. The impulse is toward homogeneity of a people, not simply toward the love of the fatherland.

One of the hallmarks of Amsterdam cosmopolitanism was the relatively high degree of integration accorded to its Jewish population. At the very beginning of Dutch freemasonry in 1735 there was at least one known member who was Jewish. Yet we know that there was also a "clandestine" Jewish lodge in the city (p. 102). For decades the records of Dutch freemasonry are silent about the religions, and even sometimes about the national origins, of its members. Yet in 1793 the subjects of religion and nation are now on the minds of the brothers. Jacob Salomon de Jong has applied for membership but had not "yet come to terms with himself . . . to make this important step; instead he wanted to confront his conscience once more with the laws given to the progeny of Israel by Moses." The request for time while this Jewish visitor ponders the rules of the masonic creed in relation to those of his birth could not be denied "in accordance with the general laws of our Royal Order." Perhaps de Jong decided that there would be better fellowship in numbers; suddenly La Bien Aimée is approached for membership by "nine former members" of another lodge all "of the Jewish Nation and Religion." This at a time when Jewish emancipation has been enacted in France (1790–91) and the implications of equality are everywhere being discussed.

The answer given by the lodge to these prospective Jewish members is stunning in its departure from any other formula for membership found in the minutes or the Constitutions. La Bien Aimée agrees to approve as members the

> nine gentlemen of the Jewish Nation and Religion who have a blameless reputation, under the following condition: [. . .] that [they] are entitled to all prerogatives and liberties to which all other effective members of our lodge are entitled [with] this express condition and stipulation that none of these Gentlemen of the Jewish Nation and Religion who will be received as effective members of our lodge now or consequently will ever be able or permitted to be nominated, elected and even less appointed to any administration of the lodge.[87]

Clearly this is an attempt to keep leadership in the much smaller lodge totally in the hands of the "Dutch" brothers. As Lessing had pointed out decades earlier (p. 150), nations and religions ultimately have little to do with the brotherhood of all men. It was not a lesson to be heard, however, amid the new, and in the Dutch case frustrated, nationalism of the early 1790s.

At this moment to the south the French Revolution had taken a radical and Jacobin turn. At first very little of those events seems to filter into the proceedings of the lodge—a myopia that other historians also have noted in the Dutch-language press, as opposed to the French-language press in the Republic, as well as in the Dutch pamphlets of the time.[88] Instead the concern is with virtue, which "if we would all exercise . . . [, we would] avert much of the slander that the blind world maliciously spreads about us."[89] Again in late 1793 the ancient Romans are invoked, as were the ancient Egyptian priests at an earlier meeting. The Roman feast mentioned is that of the god Saturn.[90] Only two years later will Saturn once again be celebrated; those minutes contain the key to the allusion. It is a celebration of the banishment of "the tyrant Tarquin and his damnable wife Tullia." We may speculate that the celebration of virtual tyrannicide in late 1793 could not fail to have noticed, with approval, the execution in that year of the French king, Louis XVI, and his wife, Marie Antoinette. It may also signal a willingness to banish the stadtholder.

Paganism is once again fashionable in the lodge: "Our brother orator ascended the chair and entertained us with the customs of the ancient Egyptian Priests to transmit the heroic deeds or the histories of the country to posterity by way of metaphoric symbols . . . which makes us notice how necessary is silence, virtue and the sociable love of mankind."[91] Once again we find approval being voiced for a civil religion, with pagan connotations; in the early 1780s patriots had already celebrated with feasts held in their "temple of virtue."[92] Almost every eighteenth-century state outlawed deism and atheism; they were associated with the subversion of both church and state. They were distinctively human creeds, easily adaptable, as the English freethinkers were the first to point out, to the needs of a purely secular set of social and political priorities. In the 1790s deism became the civil religion of revolutionaries all over western Europe. In these temples, as our Amsterdam orator put it, men could imitate "the practice and custom of Egyptian Priests to sketch the Histories or commemorable events of the country in hieroglyphic signs on commemorative columns or obelisks as well as on the walls of their temples and in particular the way in which they accepted the philosophers Plato and Pythagoras as members of their Order."[93] No one has ever worked out in detail the masonic contribution to the Cult of Reason in revolutionary France or to the new secular religiosity found throughout Europe and America in the 1790s. Yet the evidence so far assembled suggests that there was such a contribution.

By late in 1794 the unmistakable language of the democratic revolutions, French but also Dutch, found its way into this lodge: "The most important requirements which promote the prosperity and durability of societies in general and of freemasonry in particular [are shown] by our worthy mentor; how strongly fraternal unanimity, Freedom and Equality contribute to this, and finally which advantages have been ours because of this."[94] Note also that the master has become a "mentor."

We have come a long way from the late seventeenth century when, under the impact of the English Revolution, the freedom of Scottish and English stonemasons became the liberty of gentlemen freemasons. At each moment in this process these words existed in profoundly different contexts, and had, as a result, profoundly different meanings. But we must not exaggerate the differences. Freemasonry was one of the social practices that transmitted onto the Continent a vocabulary that put freedom and equality central on the word list. Without these linguistic resources it would have been harder for some men, and some women, to speak and understand those same words in the 1790s (or for that matter in the 1990s). In 1790 one Dutch patriot wrote to his English friend James Watt (the inventor of the steam engine): "The French go on softly but surely, and if you will examine without prejudice, the very most sound and manly advices and resolutions, that are given and taken by the National Assembly [in Paris,] you shall admire them and confess that they have now far outrun their instructors the English."[95] For many Dutch republicans of the 1790s the French were their "deliverers." Throughout western Europe the events of the later 1780s were also seen to bear relation to English principles.

By mid-January 1795 the French army invaded the Dutch Republic and routed the Prussian (and by their consent British) occupiers and counterrevolutionaries. Amsterdam patriots and republicans in turn rose in rebellion and proclaimed a new Batavian Revolution. Other cities quickly followed, but nowhere was the enthusiasm greater for the new, and long-frustrated revolution than in Amsterdam. On 24 January La Bien Aimée met "in the first year of Batavian Freedom." Within less than a month the lodge itself puts into effect its understanding of this internationally established set of revolutionary principles. The minutes of the day open with the slogan, in Dutch, "liberty, fraternity, equality," and then:

> Before opening the lodge our beloved chairman congratulated the assembled fraternity on the long hoped for revolution in our dear country, because of which liberty, fraternity and equality had now become the motto of our days, and furthermore announced to the brothers that from now on all honorary titles were held to be abolished among us.[96]

Overnight the master has become a chairman; brothers have lost their aristocratic titles within the confines of the lodge, and the motto of the French Revolution, first coined in the Dutch Republic, has been adopted. Exiled brothers have come streaming back to the lodge, "those who had been oppressed, chased, even exiled by our former rulers, were welcomed most appropriately and movingly."

But the revolution did not end there; once again a revolution in the public order has come to transform the private. Before their eyes the brothers disassembled their traditional rituals and with them the symbols of the order, status, and hierarchy at the heart of the old regime. An entirely new ceremony is observed at the feast "because all distinctions, breaking equality, have been abolished unless they are associated with a necessary order." The singing of masonic songs is now preceded by the singing of the hymn to the French republic, "La Marseillaise." The Grand Master from The Hague is present, once the Baron van Boetzelaar, he has become "burger" (citizen) Boetzelaar. Exiled brothers are embraced for having advocated "the three rights of the people." Not least, the servant J. Voogt, who might have been one of those who had donated his labor because his master in life was also master of the lodge, and the other servants were finally bid "to enter as they belonged to this 'degree' on the grounds of equality and thus qualifying them as members as of the Order." Voogt is thanked particularly, "it being wished that the knot of alliance between the French and Batavian Commonwealths which he had wished for so industriously, may hold out without ever untying."[97] Support for the patriot cause and the revolution extended deeply into Dutch society (just as did Orangism), to servants and artisans. The problem with words like "equality" is not that they simply float in the air but rather that they are possessed by people who oftentimes begin to believe that they apply to themselves.

In the masonic temple the fantasy of equality could be given a verbal reality so actually impossible anywhere else. The orator now routinely refers to "the equality of the people."[98] New members are routinely introduced as "citizens," and the master, orator, and at least one other member of the lodge were also members of the new revolutionary council that governed in Amsterdam.[99]

Rather than imagining that all lodges flourished in the new atmosphere of equality and fraternity, the reverse appears to be true. Just as in France, where some brothers were too busy with the revolution to go to their lodges or, as we shall see in the last chapter, lodges had become suspect during the Terror, so too in The Netherlands the sociability born in more peaceful times seemed to languish in the 1790s. A larger and more pressing civil society was coming into existence and needed tending. National meetings of all the lodges failed to materialize,[100] but in La Bien Aimée elections continued, as did the annual, but very secular, Christmas festivities. On Christmas day the feast of Saturn was once again celebrated, "at which occasion the Tyrant Tarquin and his damnable wife Tullia and various of their horrid supporters were chased from Rome, and [this] was applied to the present circumstances in general and consequently in particular to the Origin of our [masonic] festival of St. John."[101] The rewriting of masonic mythology, this time the origin of its major festival, parallels the creation of the Cromwell myth. The masonic creed with its deistic tendencies could encompass just about any human, historical experience and render it into the narrative of a new mythology. Interesting for the mythologies and continuities of the early modern European revolutions, the masonic tendency to create secular myths generally worked in favor of tyrannicides or mere tyrant-chasers.

This lodge of "free Batavians" continued its identification with rulers right to the last years of the century. "The Order of Freemasons descends in a straight line from the Lords of the Temple [i.e., Solomon's] who originated from the Knights of St. John, so that the celebration of the festival of St. John by the brothers is most praiseworthy and reasonable."[102] Here the mythology of the festival that connects the lodge to the destruction of tyranny is also given a comfortably aristocratic rendering among the citizen brothers. The idealism of 1795 begins, once again, to give way to the reality of the social order in the Republic. This was a reality that was being self-consciously negotiated through symbolic representations; "the brother orator . . . gave an excellent treatise about the power of symbolic representations for the exercise of moral duties."[103] Interesting in this respect is the leadership that the lodge now begins to assume on the national masonic scene. After decades of quarreling off and on with the Grand Lodge, La Bien Aimée is now working for greater national cooperation, and for greater homogeneity of rules and practices.[104] It is also interested in finding ways of having the antimasonic laws that have been passed over the years by various local and national governments removed from the books. This process of rationalization and legitimization should be seen as part of the larger impulse for reform that swept the Republic after the Batavian Revolution and extended to education, industry, agriculture, and even the introduction of the metric system. These impulses for orderly reform, although they included the education of female children in the Republic, only selectively applied to women. La Bien Aimée, for instance, reiterated its ban on women in the lodge, the master spoke about it and the brothers cheered upon the completion of his speech.[105]

As La Bien Aimée prepares to welcome in the new century, the minutes reflect a sense of business as usual. The heady and emotional rhetoric of the earlier 1790s gives way to charitable collections in 1799 for those afflicted by the serious floods of that year, and to the ongoing project of codification and unification. Progress is made with the national assembly of "the Batavian people" in gaining legal recognition for the Dutch lodges,[106] something that had never been possible before the revolution no matter how many distinguished men joined the lodges. If the people still objected to their secretive ways, or imagined the lodges as centers for the libertine, their objections go unrecorded amid proceedings which in the past had been sensitive to any and all "slanders." In the face of poor attendance new fines are imposed with officers now subject to higher penalties than members. Procedures for elections are changed to "ensure that free elections not in appearance but in reality" are allowed to occur.[107] If these brothers felt the profound disillusionment that many a Dutch republican came to feel in relation to their French occupiers, the minutes at least up to 1800 are silent. For better or for worse this was a new order that too many brothers had worked to assist into being. The general principles of the Batavian Republic were closer to their ideals than the regime it had so suddenly and irretrievably replaced.

Dutch freemasonry began officially in the 1730s with a distinctively Orangist cast that it would never lose. Some lodges, in Middelburg, for example, were heavily oligarchic in their composition and utterly resisted the lure of both the late eighteenth-century Dutch revolutions.[108] In that town, built up originally on the wealth of the Atlantic trade, the homes of patriots were plundered. In the slaveholding colonies whole lodges were composed of the leaders of the Dutch East India Company; in Surinam the first lodge opened in 1773; that in Curaçao earlier, in 1757. Indeed, Dutch republicanism, although influenced by late Enlightenment arguments against slavery, never aspired to its actual abolition in the Dutch colonies.[109] The system was just too profitable, and the fear of slave rebellion, such as had occurred in the brutal slave colony of Surinam in the 1770s, was too fresh.[110] Patriots occasionally condemned slavery or sought the "natural rights" of Dutch citizens governed by the harsh trading companies, but the Dutch revolution never went as far as the French in proclaiming the rights of all men.

Amsterdam also never occupied the same national role or importance as Paris. We can find strongholds of *patriotten* in many of the smaller towns and cities as early, if not earlier, than in Amsterdam. In that sense we might also expect that there were many Dutch lodges that mirrored patriot values and rhetoric in the 1780s and

1790s. In the old port town of Deventer in Overijssel, for example, the lodge founded in 1784 had a decidedly *patriotten* cast.[111] The local regents banned it in 1787, so the lodge simply met elsewhere. But the Deventer records are not so rich that we can trace what participation in the new revolutionary culture the lodge's ceremonies and orations provided. In a town of eight thousand, as was Deventer, feasts in honor of Saturn might not have gone unnoticed. Similarly in Nijmegen, where back in the 1750s the brothers Merkes, whom we met in chapter 3, had been given such a hard time by the local clergy, a new and anti-Orange lodge was founded in the 1780s. The old lodge apparently remained loyal to its Orangist roots.[112] Both are part of the history of the Batavian Revolution in a town where we know that the locals tended to notice just about everything. In Amsterdam the activities of La Bien Aimée would have been lost in the general commotion of the times in which it participated.

To the revolutionary era of the late eighteenth century, some lodges contributed a privatized version of republican and revolutionary culture, both new and inherited, once English, now French and Dutch. What began on the Continent as constitutionally governed societies for gentlemen offered by the second half of the century an alternative model, a microcosm of a new secular and civic, yet quasi-religious, political order we have now come to know simply as the modern world.

8

Dissension and Reform in the New "Civil Society": The Strasbourg Lodges of the Late Eighteenth Century

More than in any other place examined in this book, in France prior to the Revolution of 1789 freemasonry betrayed the nature of ancien régime society and culture. The lodges mirrored the social tensions and antagonisms of the old regime, while at the same time offering the alternative inherent in the new political culture of the Enlightenment: a public forum where individuals contested for power, voted and elected their representatives, found identity in a polity separate from the communal identity offered by kin, church, and estate. Of course many forms of eighteenth-century sociability helped to create the new public space. Some historians have even argued that in France the corporate bodies, guilds, estates, and academies could inculcate ostensibly "modern" forms of social and political experience.[1] None of them, however, offered a kind of political experience so intense that after the events of 1789 and beyond they could still be remembered, as were the lodges, as bearing relation to the new social and political reality initiated by the French Revolution.

In this chapter we will try to recreate the experience of certain French lodges in the 1770s and 1780s, particularly lodges in Strasbourg on the French–German border. In the next and last chapter we will look at the workings of the French freemasonry as established after 1773 on a national level. For it we will rely upon the voluminous records of the Grand Lodge of France, made available to scholars only after World War II. After falling into hostile hands during the war, the records finally made their way into the Bibliothèque Nationale in Paris. For Strasbourg in the eastern province of Alsace the evidence also comes from rich masonic records preserved in private hands but now to be found in the municipal archives of the city. They provide us with everything from correspondence and orations to detailed descriptions of rituals and ceremonies.

The Strasbourg records of the 1770s and 1780s amply document that French lodges permitted men to speak and act in reforming as well as in deeply conservative ways. Both impulses subsequently surfaced in the revolutionary and anti-revolutionary culture created in 1789. The reforming discourse found in the lodges of the 1780s (and elsewhere), once made legal a decade later, would come to be described as revolutionary. Yet throughout this story it must be remembered that the men and some women who created the new cultural forum offered by the lodges did so often without the slightest interest in, or desire for revolution. They participated in a new zone, what I have been calling civil society, without any notion that what they were doing could rightly be seen in hindsight as the invention of a new political culture, which in its turn permitted the events of 1789. We must be careful about causation here; culture permits—it does not determine. On the Continent the culture of sociability, especially when divorced from official sanctions and functions, permitted a new and mature civil society to emerge, beneath the mantle of the old order, shaded and protected by it, but not the offspring of its originally feudal religious and political culture. In this respect the lodges and philosophical societies were different from the guilds, confraternities, and various legally constituted and privileged corporations, whether lay or clerical, just as the Enlightenment was different from traditional culture. Not surprisingly, the lodges could take on many personae, from the republican to the conservative, at moments even to the mystical—although in the service of the secular. Predictably, they were often deeply troubled places.

Two phenomena were most visible in the lodges of late eighteenth-century provincial France, and Strasbourg freemasonry during the 1770s and 1780s illustrates both. First and more noticeable were the dissensions, bordering on internecine struggles, within and between lodges. These generated anger and hostility far beyond what the circumstances seemed to require. Some of the emotion was local in origin, but a major source of irritation emanated from the actions taken by the Grand Lodge in Paris. The anger and hostility was particularly evident after 1773 and the formation of the new national Grand Lodge, the so-called Grand Orient. Through renewed centralization, which we will examine in greater detail in the next chapter, it sought to impose order and social hierarchy within the masonic "nation." In the process it ran afoul of many lodges, among them some of those we are about to visit in Strasbourg.

The second of the phenomena visible in Strasbourg freemasonry in this period was a new and strident rhetoric—much of it published by anonymous brothers—which voiced profound and general social discontent and proclaimed a radically reformist approach to the meaning and purpose of the masonic state. In its most applied form, the new approach found in some Strasbourg lodges spurred them to create societies or clubs intended to apply masonic wisdom to societal ills.

But there were distinct limits to the movement for reform. For the most part the discontent and impatient impulses remained confined to the sermons of the Strasbourg orators, or to new societies created by the lodges and demanding noticeably high membership fees. Note, for instance, the tone of one orator: "The light of this century has revealed to us that man is depraved and it is society alone that is the source [of this depravity]." Put another way, "Man is exhausted by the fetters of high society and searches for particular associations, to enjoy there the charms of liberty and virtue." The mason is a freeman, proclaimed this orator, and he sacrifices a portion of his indefeasible condition (*propriété impréscriptible*) in order to obtain the advantages of reunion with his brothers. Anyone who would exercise "a despotism in the midst of this liberty, would be an evil brother; encroaching upon the liberty of the mason, [and in the process] depriving him of a sacred patrimony."[2]

These fiery sentiments were being expressed in a provincial city. Strasbourg was hardly Paris. Fortunately, the documentation left by its masonic lodges reveals a great deal about the values and beliefs of a variety of provincial men (and some women) from different classes or estates, and with different, although no less reformist, visions about what the light of the century prescribed. Speaking in the same lodge the Strasbourg orator of 1777, whom we just heard, explained that freemasonry had arisen in the East where despotism, "born in a climate hot and effeminate," had also been nurtured. Freemasonry was its antidote. The disease to be cured, despotism, was here associated with the "effeminate," and with medieval feudalism.[3]

Even within the Christianized freemasonry so commonplace in the more socially conservative of Strasbourg's lodges, reformist and anti-authoritarian rhetoric held pride of place. Goodness, it was argued, resided not simply in actions, in the appearances of virtue, but in the inner intentions. True masonry resided in the heart, not in the decorative dress or degrees of a brother. And in the eyes of God all men are equal. This approach to the meaning of freemasonry could take on a variety of social and political postures. Always reformist, it could call for a renewed spirituality led by a pious and meritorious aristocracy; or it could take a democratic turn as we heard in the Parisian orations in honor of Benjamin Franklin recounted in chapter 6 and as we will hear in the orations given by bourgeois brothers in Strasbourg. But the impulse to reform should not be confused with the prevalence of unity and harmony.

To appreciate the sources of the dissension within the Strasbourg lodges, and thus the context of these fiery orations, we need to know more about the city and its lodges. On the French–German border, Strasbourg, with a population of fifty thousand, had about twenty-nine lodges in the period from 1763 to 1789; their total membership approximated fifteen hundred. In Strasbourg we find French, German, and foreign nationals tied by the world of international commerce in which the city, by virtue of being situated on the Rhine, had an important stake. Predictably in this international milieu French was the language of choice; it was also the language of elite culture in Alsace, where the local dialect, closer to German, was more commonly spoken (and can still be heard).[4]

Despite their international and commercial setting, the Strasbourg lodges were among the most stratified and disparate of any in France. Rather than mirroring social harmony and equality, the lodges reflected deep social and religious divisions. In Strasbourg there were purely aristocratic lodges, La Candeur for example (which was majority Catholic, but with a noticeable Protestant minority), as well as another lodge composed almost entirely of merchants (called St. Geneviève), yet another for musicians, one for actors and servants, still another for doctors and medical men (Les Beaux Arts); in addition, there were Protestant lodges and Catho-

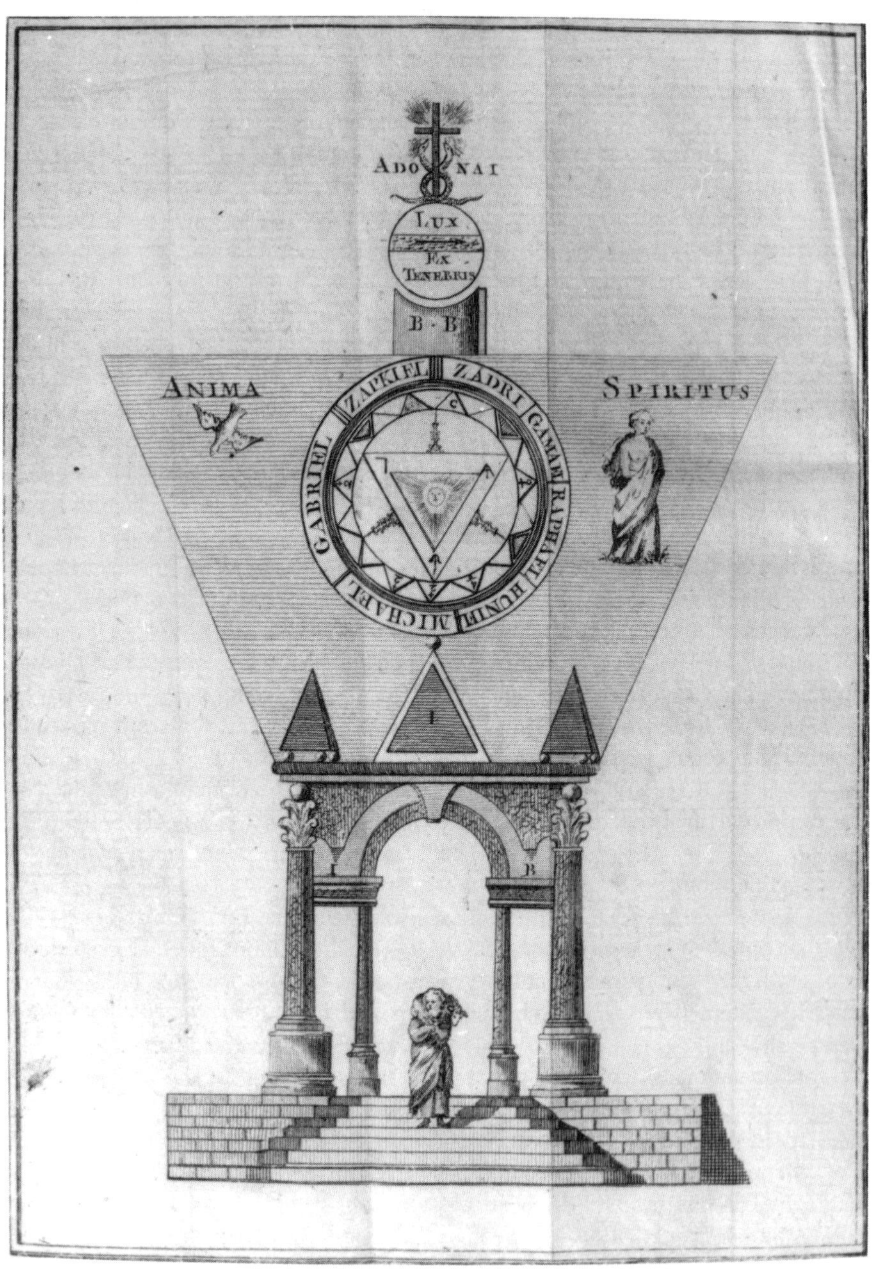

FIG. 8. Masonic symbolism, particularly in Catholic countries, could also be religious and mystical. Engraving from yet another anonymous work probably of French origin, *Les plus secrets mysteres des hauts grades de la Maçonnerie dévoilés ou Le vrai Rose-Croix,* Jerusalem [a false imprint] 1768.

lic lodges. As in the Paris lodges of the 1740s discussed in the introduction, most Strasbourg brothers were young men largely in their twenties and thirties.[5] Among them the political culture of French civil society was probably the most bifurcated to be found in western Europe.

Recent studies have shown how closed the Alsatian aristocracy had become; it almost never accepted marriage with a bourgeois. Yet a number of men were "ennobled" in the region, particularly during the second half of the century. One could acquire an aristocratic title through service as an officer in the army, occasionally through industry—particularly arms manufacturing—and of course primarily in the royal bureaucracy. A man paid the king handsomely, even exorbitantly, for a title and the feudal holdings that came with it. The total cost could range from 12,000 to 330,000 livres. But that brought status and relief from certain direct taxes.[6] Nevertheless, many of the old Alsatian nobility were deeply in debt, a pattern common in eighteenth-century France. Most noblemen in Alsace paid an annual poll tax of between 30 and 50 livres; by comparison masonic dues were more noticeable and could average 10 livres a month. An Alsatian domestic servant might hope for an annual income of about 300 livres. To illustrate the vast distances between the simplicity of the lowly and the grandeur of the great, La Candeur could spend nearly 100 livres on an evening's reception of a new apprentice at which probably no more than thirty men might be present.[7]

Strasbourg also housed a respectable university; the German poet Goethe graduated from it in 1771. The university even sported a lodge of aristocratic students, but many locally renowned intellectuals were notably absent from the lodges. In short, by midcentury, enclaves of the new enlightened culture did reside within Strasbourg's walls, nurtured in part by its publishing industry and its geography. The new scientific society of the 1760s contained men who would later appear in masonic ranks (not least the young Goethe).[8] Yet amid enlightenment there remained a palpable tension between Strasbourg's Catholic and Protestant populations, a tension that only certain forms of sociability managed to transcend. Among them were the lodges, although interestingly enough the founders of Strasbourg freemasonry were Catholic, as was the vast majority of the brothers. The first lodge created by a Protestant was founded in 1779.[9] Both the culture of the old order, with its divisions by confession and kinship, and the new culture of enlightenment,with its emphasis on worldly ethics and the transcendence of rank and estate, were vividly present in Strasbourg freemasonry. This is the nature of any mature civil society. It creates a zone of social interaction where people meet somewhat formally as individuals. They reflect existing power relations and conflicting value systems just as they attempt to mediate them. The dangerous part arises when civil society offers a more accurate reflection of power and greater opportunity to address it than does the established political order.

The tensions within the Strasbourg lodges may be particularly related to the controversial history of the order within this provincial setting. In the 1740s and later, the hostile Catholic clergy of Strasbourg refused absolution to freemasons in the town and at the same time the brothers were accused of homosexuality. Possibly with memory of these events, in 1763 a lodge was established for women and a woman was chosen as the patron for the essentially aristocratic La Candeur. In La

Candeur, probably one of the most conservative lodges to be found in France, we find strongly Christian tendencies with various Catholic reformers of the 1780s active, among them Cagliostro, a mystical freemason and Catholic. He and Cardinal Rohan held "seances" in the lodges to search for "regeneration." Protestant freemasons—Strasbourg had a large Protestant population—were predictably suspicious of these activities, regarding them as the old Counter-Reformation in new garb.[10] By contrast, lodges in other provincial centers surrounded by rich agricultural land, in Burgundy, for instance, had privileged membership, which nevertheless mixed nobles with lawyers and some important wine growers and merchants.[11]

In the Strasbourg lodges French society of the old order looked like a series of granite pillars of vastly uneven heights upon which the state, both civil and masonic, rested. Predictably the masonic state so built possessed serious instabilities. One historian of French freemasonry has simply described them as the "traditional masonic conflicts."[12] To give but a few examples, a lodge in Strasbourg composed primarily of German merchants and practicing the masonic rituals of Berlin only reluctantly sought affiliation with the French lodges. In that instance differences in language and traditions undoubtedly played an understandable role. But language had nothing to do with the bitter quarrel between the aristocratic lodge La Candeur and the Paris Grand Lodge. It occurred because an officer in Paris, deemed by the Strasbourg lodge to be of inferior social status—more precisely, a valet in the service of a local provincial official—had been assigned the task of dealing with its application for a constitution.[13] For a time La Candeur simply seceded. It reconciled with the Grand Lodge only in 1773, at its renewal under aristocratic leadership. "Under the authorization of our superiors, the lodges are reunited no longer having to fear either the conspiracies of ambition, or the enterprises of despotism, or the irregularities introduced by Cupidity." So spoke the obviously self-satisfied orator of La Candeur in that year. Our order is the cult of virtue, he concluded.[14]

The great nineteenth-century French historian Alexis de Tocqueville was the first commentator to offer an explanation that may help us understand French society as witnessed in the Strasbourg lodges and elsewhere: "In no period of French history was it so easy to acquire a title as in 1789, yet never had the gap between the middle class and the nobility been so great . . . the bourgeois was almost as aloof from the 'common people' as the noble from the bourgeois."[15] The lodges had come to mirror the breakdown of social relations, which de Tocqueville was the first to analyze. In seeing the lodges as loci of the new civil society we do not suppose that they somehow escaped their time and place. Quite the reverse is true: They mirrored their time while also providing a new space wherein its predicaments and tensions could be given verbal expression and reflection, and wherein alternative visions could also be articulated. The strident idealism of late eighteenth-century French freemasonry existed not in spite of, but because of, the deep social divisions fostered by the ancien régime.

And it should be borne in mind that this sort of quarreling was not unique to Strasbourg. We find the pattern repeated over and over again elsewhere. In Toulouse in the 1780s two lodges quarreled, again bitterly, because men of high station in one lodge appeared in their masonic regalia at a ball, thus in the eyes of their critics exposing the order to public "derision." In Limoges lodges experienced internal crises which their historian has, once again, related to issues of class and estate.[16] Another historian who has worked extensively on urban culture and sociability in the west of France found barely a city there where local lodges were not at one moment or another racked "by an often virulent polemic."[17] Meanwhile, the quarreling in Strasbourg was so extreme that the lodge in Lyon, hardly a sanctuary itself, described the Alsatian disputes as "political enterprises and outrageous excesses."[18] What emerges from the evidence provided by the French lodges, in Strasbourg and elsewhere, is the picture of a society riddled by social tensions and hatreds that were more pronounced and visible than what can be seen in the other western European societies to which the microcosm of the masonic lodge has provided an entrée.

The records in Strasbourg permit us to relate masonic feuding more concretely than has been done before to the larger society or, more precisely, to the tensions between and among the three estates. La Candeur left a splendid set of records, almost as detailed in some years as what we have for the Amsterdam lodge La Bien Aimée. The French records offer no support for the image that the lodges were consciously attempting to create democratic forums. Nothing could have been further from the interests of the Strasbourg lodges. Nor should we see them as mirroring a hegemonic ideology from which one dissented at one's peril—that interpretation, as noted in the introduction, has been offered by a few present-day historians. By contrast, we are about to witness dissension around almost every conceivable issue.[19]

As early as the 1760s the Strasbourg lodge La Candeur quarreled with the Paris leadership, which it viewed as too lax for permitting men of inferior social status to exercise authority. In 1763 it castigated the Grand Lodge by noting, in contrast, that "La Candeur was composed of the most grand nobility." From that posture it objected to the status of the brother whom the Paris lodge had assigned to deal with the Constitution for La Candeur. Indignantly the Grand Lodge was accused of "plunging masonry into degradation."[20] In 1763, at its founding, La Candeur had been quite clear that it would follow only the strictest form of freemasonry. Self-consciously La Candeur stood in reaction to "the Dutch and English" practices of too frequent elections.[21] In this reformist posture it described French freemasonry as "an object of amusement," admitting men who by their estate and by their mores "should not be members of this grand republic."[22] Breaking for a time with the Paris Grand Lodge, La Candeur even briefly sought affiliation with the London Grand Lodge and with the Amsterdam lodges. La Bien Aimée reminded the Strasbourg brothers that it had a Grand Master and referred them back to the Count of Clermont. The reforming posture and seriousness of La Candeur has been described as prefiguring the reforms initiated a decade later by the new Grand Orient in Paris. It too was led by aristocrats and, as we shall see in the next chapter, sought to impose order and government, only now on a national scale.

When the new Parisian Grand Lodge (also called the Grand Orient) was formed in 1773 it in turn quarreled with various lodges because of their social composition. As more and more "marginal" men joined the lodges, actors and servants, for example, the Grand Orient in Paris, with its aristocratic leadership, reacted sharply.

A Strasbourg lodge of servants and actors was simply suspended for a time by it. In the same year (1779) a merchant wrote incredulously to the Grand Orient: Someone "has objected to me about my civil estate? The master [of this lodge] . . . is a merchant like me. . . . I dare to respond that I am a respectable man and so recognized by all my colleagues in commerce. I am [also] regarded as a good father of my family."[23] While at one time La Candeur may have looked down upon the Grand Lodge, after its reorganization aristocratic values were very much in evidence. Unimpressed by the protests coming from indignant merchants, the Grand Orient objected to another Strasbourg lodge because it had too many merchants in it.[24] It also did not like the fact that its orator was an actor. The pressure within the leadership of French freemasonry was toward greater exclusivity; the response from the rank-and-file membership was decidedly ambivalent.

In general, however, the Strasbourg lodges, like many others in France, chose to widen the gap between the elite and the popular and also between the military and the civilian.[25] Lodges had always existed for military men (as we saw in Nijmegen), but in late eighteenth-century France military lodges, often composed of minor aristocrats, seem greater in number and more segregated from civilian society. This may be a statistical illusion brought about by new and better record keeping. One of the innovations imposed by the Grand Orient in the 1770s was a membership form for every brother, listing side by side "civil qualities" and "masonic qualities," for example "surgeon" and "orator," as well as age, place of birth, address, and signature. We might find these lists preserved in Strasbourg and elsewhere invaluable for the demography of the lodges. Their original purpose had been to keep track of social hierarchy, to make sure that enough "honorable" men could be found in any given lodge.

The tensions within the Strasbourg lodges were expressed in discussions that concerned the meaning of social hierarchy in relation to the goal of moral perfectibility, of virtue. In the socially segregated lodges in Strasbourg, we can find men speaking frankly about their betters as well as their lessers. There the most socially elevated, and thus, by virtue of their birth, supposedly civilized brothers sustained their own, separate civil society, their closed temple. Of the 110 old Alsatian noble families, 37 were represented in the lodge La Candeur. Their statutes expressed their major concerns; charity was seen as a central duty. Admission had to be by unanimous approval and was clearly very selective; initiation dues were very high, 129 livres.[26] The purpose of this lodge was to be simultaneously closed and exclusive while liberal toward the needs of the lesser society.

Given the border location, lodges like La Candeur were also close to the German influences at work in central European freemasonry. Strasbourg was something of an entrepôt between the masonry we associate with Paris and Amsterdam and the more mystical versions to be found in Berlin and Vienna. Perhaps the best illustration of the Strasbourg version of Enlightenment culture, as supported by La Candeur, lies in two societies, both with masonic foundations and ambience. Such societies, of which there were many founded by lodges throughout Continental Europe, are often described in retrospect as quasi- or para-masonic. In them the idealists of the lodges could recruit nonmasons and engage in specific projects for social reform and utility; these were the goals of similar societies set up in the west of France. Indeed, the phenomenon resembles a similar turn toward the practical that has been found in the Dutch societies—by no means necessarily masonic—of the 1780s. In eastern France the Strasbourg Society of Philanthropy and the Harmonious Society of Reunited Friends, both with strong associations with La Candeur, were the local version of the Enlightenment applied. The Strasbourg philanthropic society, in its own words, "is a confederation by which generous and sensible men, brought together by the charms of friendship and the attraction of a perfect equality, can impose upon themselves the constant exercise of social virtue, benevolence, a reasonable tolerance, a profound respect for the Divinity, a culture of the arts and the useful sciences, and the sincere vow to enlighten and relieve men, insofar as it is in their power. . . . [This society] seeks a nation of practical philosophes."[27]

Amid the aristocratic Strasbourgian version of the practical, often including the same organizers and joiners, can be found what in hindsight we would also describe as the mystical. The Harmonious Society of Reunited Friends founded in the 1780s was medical and mesmerist. Through medicine and magic in the form of "animal magnetism" it sought the transformation of the human condition. These were the followers of Franz Anton Mesmer, the Viennese doctor who traveled in aristocratic circles in central and western Europe during the 1780s and claimed to possess the power, through electricity, to heal and cure. Not only was the aristocratic lodge La Candeur well represented in both the philanthropic and the mesmerist society, so too were lodges whose membership included doctors and men of the liberal professions. Women also found a place in these societies. There, as they said in their correspondence to the societies, a woman could express her zeal for "the utmost happiness [*le premier bonheur*] of humanity."[28]

The ambience in both societies, as we shall see, was simultaneously rationalist and theosophic. The light that shone in their midst cast its rays into realms strange as well as familiar to students of the European Enlightenment. Rather than separating these impulses into enlightened and its antithesis, romantic, I shall see them as complementary and profoundly social as well as civic. Rather than arguing for these impulses as simply representing the "end" of the Enlightenment, I shall consider them inextricably bound up with its civic culture created by the mores of elite civility and sociability. The mystical could express concrete social and ideological postures; in whatever guise, however, it was not ideologically neutral. Hence mesmerism could be both radical and conservative in the postures it assumed toward established authority.[29] Not least, in mesmerism and freemasonry we have another place where women's participation in the Enlightenment could find expression. These societies admitted elite women, indeed encouraged their participation. We should remember that at this time it was still commonplace in the Alsatian Catholic churches for men and women to be segregated from each other, even in the face of protests, in one instance from the wife of a local tax farmer.[30]

The tensions within French society, which de Tocqueville noted well over a century ago, created ostensibly strange alliances, or generated impulses that appear difficult to understand, if only in retrospect. Among these we may put the aristocratic reformism of the 1770s and 1780s. The tensions between the needs and interests of the monarchy and the French aristocracy, itself disparate and divided by conflicting claims to antiquity and status of birth, create one of the great themes of early modern French political history. It would be almost unimaginable that these tensions would not be present within the French lodges. In lodges particularly from the 1760s on aristocrats gave leadership as elected officers who mingled freely—at the weekly or monthly meetings—with the men of the third (and sometimes first) estate who had elected them. They made substantial financial contributions to the lodges, even, in Strasbourg, lending the lodge money when needed. But behind the door of the temple peace and harmony among the orders and estates was often fragile; aristocratic leadership was not always a given. Where it was firmly established, for example, in La Candeur, aristocrats sought to impose their vision of order and reform on the other lodges. Where the aristocracy was excluded, bourgeois brothers took the opportunity to express their hostility and resentment.

In the early years of French freemasonry, as we saw in the introduction, the concern for degrees and hierarchy within and between lodges must have seemed a remote issue by comparison to the struggle to establish respectability. Certainly that seems to have been the case in Strasbourg. All evidence suggests that there were a few lodges in the town as early as 1743, and in the following year—just as in Paris—the magistrates issued an interdict against them. The clergy were also not pleased by their presence, and it is not until late in the 1750s that we can begin the history of the Strasbourg lodges with any confidence. Interestingly, but typically, the lodge granted a constitution in 1757, La Loge de Saint Jean d'Hérédon de Sainte Geneviève (we shall call it St. Geneviève), was at first filled with more marginal men, actors and musicians, and then gradually became overwhelmingly bourgeois, only to remain so for some decades. Its printed membership list from the early 1780s is a picture of remarkable segregation: twenty men, the vast majority of whom were *négociants* (merchants). In an interesting observation on the changing attitudes of the authorities, one other was a secretary to the police; there was also an artist, a dyer, a watchmaker, an innkeeper, a moneychanger (*agent de change*), two lawyers, and a government official (*substitut du procureur-syndic*). On the surface at least one could hardly imagine men more different from the *seigneurs* of the old families who frequented La Candeur, which nevertheless, after its founding in 1763, reluctantly had to acknowledge St. Geneviève as its "mother lodge."[31]

But lists of occupations and names can be deceptive. The ceremonies of St. Geneviève, however nonnoble its clientele, were among the most lavish that masonic records from any part of western Europe document.[32] The following description, recording an important ceremony held in 1779, is worth quoting at length for what it tells us about the secular and the sacred within the temple of a lodge that was exquisitely luxurious and almost entirely bourgeois. The occasion is the reinstallation of this Strasbourg lodge's affiliation with the Grand Lodge in Paris. We must try if we can to imagine the following:

> *Ordinary Decoration of the Lodge:* The lodge in the form of a long square is decorated by a hanging of sky-blue serge; adorned in the upper part by a double braid of gold; the garlands and flowers of the same metal are artfully attached at equal distances by knotted ribbons of gold. At the entrance to the Sanctuary, which is elevated by the mysterious degrees of the first grade, are placed the two columns

symbolizing the order, set on their bases and surmounted by their Corinthian capitals of gold.

The Throne [of the master] is covered by a blue canopy of the same material, enriched by braids and fringes of gold, the back is of a rich material and of a great brilliance. On the altar have been placed three silver candlesticks, the book of statutes and rules of the lodge, the book of the gospel, a sword, a compass, a mallet and the jewel of the Master. Above the canopy has been placed a blazing star, and in the circle of the Sanctuary are represented the sun and the moon, these three stars are done in a superior fashion. The three great stars are placed in the order that they are currently found sculptured and adorning the painting of the lodge. . . .

The officers of the lodge have before them tables covered by cloth tapestry adorned by braids of gold, on these tables are silver candelabra. . . . The orator has been placed on a chair decorated with the same ornaments. . . . Finally each dignitary is decorated with the jewels that are proper to him.

To the west behind the Surveillant are the arms of France, those of the Grand Master and the mark of the lodge on a golden scroll; in the middle of the lodge is a list of all the brothers who compose it, and in the sanctuary to the right of the Venerable [master] the reconstitutions of the Grand Orient of France, and to the left the particular statutes and rules of this lodge composed of forty articles; these three items are placed in decorated and carved boxes. [At the ceremony of installation] in the Sanctury on a base of marble an altar of antique gold and sculptured; a cloth of red serge enriched by braids and fringes of gold covers the altar. . . .

There reposes, displayed, the new Constitutions from the Grand Orient of France.[33]

Gold, blue serge, silver candelabra, classical columns, a Sanctuary, an altar—this is truly a temple, but of an unprecedented kind. At its center, on its altar created by brothers of essentially Catholic background, rests not a tabernacle, not a chalice and Host, but a document, in fact several documents: constitutions, rules, lists of members, and not to be left out, a copy of the gospels. This is a temple made by men to enshrine the constitutional legality of their assembly, to formalize and negotiate their imagined equality within which they may rise by degrees to a more perfect wisdom, within which they may display the opulence and luxury their collective contributions permit them to have. In this lodge of merchants no effect has been spared to enhance its grandeur. They too could have swords and coats of arms. The decorations are in fact more lavish than anything the records of its sister lodge, the aristocratic La Candeur, reveal.

In this closed temple the orator seeks to describe the joy that "has penetrated our heart on this occasion." He speaks of "the happiness, very illustrious and very dear brothers, of being reunited with the regular lodges of the Kingdom." On this occasion the officers "have reentered the class of simple workers in order to contribute . . . by their votes to the establishment of a new lodge and to the creation of three lights which must enlighten the stars which were extinguished."[34] These lights announce allegorically the happy changes and forthcoming regeneration of the lodge. The new master came forward from "the other workers and presented himself in the west in order to thank his brothers for his election . . . the brother in charge [of the ceremony] . . . placed one of the great lights to the east of the tableau [membership list] of the lodge, and the three stars at the altar are for marking the creation of the Venerable [master]; the master of ceremonies produced for this brother the jewels of his dignity . . . and conducted the master to the altar in order that he might repossess his place and open the lodge with the required formalities." Inspired by "this majestic and touching spectacle," the orator proclaims that he has "the sweet satisfaction of seeing men equally distinguished by their birth and their rank who have elevated altars of virtue and who are always faithful to its cult." The orator can barely contain the happiness that is provoked by "this respectable assembly." Could anything, we wonder, mar such a splendid occasion?

The world is not far from this Sanctuary even—or perhaps especially—on this occasion. Such happiness, we are told, is not often found in "the turbulence of the world." Pride pitilessly erases the lot of a considerable and precious part of the human race, "while putting between individuals an immense distance . . . perfidious interest desolates societies, bringing ruin and desolation to families and devouring the successful labors of the poor." By contrast, "good nature reigns in this lodge, a pure joy always animates the workers and vivifies their work."[35] Masons are men who do not sacrifice to the idol of fortune, who work for their riches by honest means, who pay their quota to the country, who do their duties as citizens, and who give their surplus to the indigent. The orator goes on to identify with "the war that rages in two hemispheres," that is, the American Revolution, and with "the brave military men who are ready to shed their blood for their country." The only happy societies are those which, like a prudent mother, follow the lessons taught by virtue; "mortals elevated in its bosom appear to be privileged beings, they are exempt from all the notions that degrade other men." Even the great legislators of history, the Solons and Lycurguses, have not been able to put their political institutions on a base untouchable by the revolutions of the times. Only the grand art, the masonic code, can provide that kind of certainty.[36]

The circumstance of this splendid ceremony, and this troubled oration, was the reinstallation of the lodge in 1779 into the bosom of the masonic family. A few years earlier, in 1773, the new Grand Lodge of Paris had unceremoniously expelled it for reasons of class and honor; St. Geneviève permitted too many actors, men of low social standing, to partake in its temple.[37] Indeed, from its earliest history up to the 1770s the lodge was composed entirely of men from the third estate, eventually almost all merchants along with a few prosperous craftsmen. In its early years, artists, actors, and musicians were more commonplace. The expulsion of the lodge meant that it became, in masonic terminology, "irregular," or "clandestine," or worse still in the domestic metaphors so cherished by the lodges, a "bastard."

The gradual upgrading of the social standing of its brothers may very well have been in response to the pressure created by the expulsion. The legality of the lodge depended upon the recognition of the Grand Lodge; that was the point of the ceremony just related. It was preceded by a lengthy correspondence with the Grand Lodge assuring it that the merchants in St. Geneviève were of the "best reputation," and in "secret" communication the lodge must also plead for the "good life and mores, the talent" of its orator, a young actor, Joseph St. Val.

The search for legitimacy and hence respectability did not, however, mute the anger of these bourgeois brothers.[38] The orator, who could have been the very actor whose station and rank had been so bluntly questioned, is almost menacing in his condemnation of pride, self-interest, and, indirectly, the failure to pay one's fair share of the tax burden, as well as the condition of the poor. The equality being proclaimed is among men of substance as witnessed by the lavishness of their temple, yet in order to proclaim it they must be designated "simple workers." From other records we know that they condemned the "hauteur" of the aristocrats in La Candeur, which had its own, earlier, dispute going on with the Grand Lodge. The virtue embodied in the masonic code, as understood in St. Geneviève, permitted a rhetorical identification with "the people."[39] In the face of the haughtiness first of La Candeur and then of the Grand Lodge, what other identification was possible?

In the very next year the orator reminds the lodge that the freemason "does not let himself be dazzled by the display of grandeur, nor by the pomp of Courts; he often notices behind these imposing externalities . . . the impertinent efforts of pride at hiding weaknesses and even sometimes the crimes of men who only occupy high ranks thanks to the accident of birth, or by intrigue, or by flattery, or perhaps by means even more infamous. . . . By contrast the true freemason respects the living image of the Grand Architect of the Universe . . . he is at all times a faithful subject, a zealous citizen, a tender father, a loyal spouse, a sincere friend." The refusal to identify with the mores of the somewhat caricatured aristocracy implies no rejection of "the duties attached to the State."[40] On other occasions orators of the lodge gloried in the fact that there have been monarchs "who have been honored by calling themselves brothers to the poorest artisans."[41]

Similarly, the orators maintained that while the degrees and grades awarded within the masonic hierarchy are valued, in this lodge it is clear that "we do not only accord our esteem to marks externally honorable; these all too often carry false merit." At the death of a brother who had not participated in the higher degrees of the order, his internal virtues and merit are extolled and self-consciously contrasted to the external symbols of status.[42] His "civil and masonic merits" are what must be remembered. The eulogizer is then quick to point out that freemasons "reject all materialism," the credo of *esprits forts*. The glorification of achievements in this world, regardless of birth, implied a metaphysic associated with the most virulent of Enlightenment heresies, with freethinking and materialism. The orator was intent upon distancing his brothers from anything so heretical and controversial.

Like many lodges, St. Geneviève was involved in the establishment of new lodges. A lodge's legality depended upon the recognition of other legally constituted lodges. In 1782 a lodge of doctors, surgeons, and students of medicine was established with the assistance of St. Geneviève, which represented the Grand Orient of France. Although of many national backgrounds, these young and largely Catholic medical men were united by their occupations and in most cases their military service. Completing the lodge were military officers and a few lawyers.[43] At the ceremony which created Les Beaux Arts, the master of St. Geneviève explained that "I hold with dignity the commission with which I have been charged" by the masonic central administration in Paris. It sought to ensure the "regularity" of the work of all lodges "in its regime."[44] The master also had another purpose. It was to instruct the new lodge in the *morale des grades*. The symbolic grades were meant to enhance the purity of the brothers' lives; "it is essential that you have a perfect knowledge of the qualities of spirit and the heart of a candidate."

Whatever quarrels St. Geneviève may have had with the Grand Lodge in the past are forgotten in its ardor to see that the new lodge give to it "a submission without limits, an inviolable attachment, the prompt execution of decrees." With that statement the master presented the new lodge with "lettres patentes de Constitution." Les Beaux Arts, he explained, should have an "immense happiness at being members of a society of virtuous men, in the sweetness of an intimate union that brings you together with a multitude of persons of all ages and all ranks, including some of the highest ranks, under the protection of illustrious leaders who preside over the order, in the satisfaction of finding everywhere a people of brothers eager to serve you and to give in turn their most tender affection to you."[45]

The vision presented to the new lodge was almost utopian, also almost feudal, as well as familial, in its sense of unity, order, hierarchy, loyalty, and obedience. Yet the language is cosmopolitan—"persons of all ages and all ranks." In reality the lodge was composed entirely of men of the third estate. Immediately the new lodge was told of the "great Prince to whom French masons owe their happiness."[46] The leaders of St. Geneviève, as we have seen, had no love lost for the local aristocracy. Yet they were monarchists, believing in the early 1780s, as did many French freemasons, that Louis XVI would effect genuine reforms. He is compared to only one other French king, Henry IV (d. 1610), who granted French Protestants a limited toleration. They were unstinting in their praise of Louis: "To be protected by a prince . . . the love of an entire nation, the benefactor of the universe and the terror of his enemies . . . [he] holds first place among us." Masonry has triumphed in this time of reason and philosophy, the orator continues, "I intend the art [of masonry] to create the wellbeing of all men and to regard them all as brothers."[47]

Incapable of enthusiasm for all men are "the inhuman egoists devoured by the ambition to cover their birth by the brilliance of titles and the gifts of fortune." In contrast to the egoism of the titled and wellborn stand those who shed their blood in defense of their country.[48] The "reputable Bourgeois of all ranks," as the orator describes the new brothers, "in the career of the sciences," have used the occasion to express their social and political antagonisms and loyalties.[49] They have assembled out of the hearing of the other estates, toward the end of the American War of Independence, and hence away from the aristocracy. It is clear that these merchants, and presumably the medical men who listened intently to their orations, deeply disliked men of title and fortune. Masonic values could easily be seen to reinforce the bias against birth and toward virtue and merit. Historians know that in the eighteenth century the vertical bonds uniting seigneurial society in France weakened as the horizontal bonds of class and profession strengthened.[50] The lodge of St. Geneviève offers further evidence for both phenomena. And while reference is made to "the people" in the discourses of St. Geneviève as it addressed Les Beaux Arts (composed largely of brothers lower than themselves in the third estate), these merchant brothers save their ardor for attacking the pretensions of the aristocracy. The people, although to be pitied, are remote from these proceedings. Not least, the

FIG. 9. A collection of various masonic symbols commonly used throughout the late eighteenth century.

lodge could be quite dilatory in paying its "brother servants," one of whom had to dun it for money.[51]

What is unique about these Strasbourg lodges is their social segregation. Behind the closed doors of the lodge ideology and rank are fitted together neatly, in ways that would not have been possible if the lodge had mixed the titled and the untitled. In each of the three lodges at which we are looking the social content of the discussion is markedly different. Almost certainly we are seeing a longstanding class antagonism, dating back to the time when La Candeur had objected to the social composition, and hence to the regularity, of St. Geneviève. Writing in 1765 a brother put it thus: "If the brothers of La Candeur had treated with less haughtiness all those whom they believe are not their equals in the civil estate, there would certainly be fewer irregular lodges." And in obvious irritation, "La Candeur never forgets to say that [St. Geneviève] is composed only of merchants; you will see that except for five, all who compose it are bourgeois."[52] It remains to be seen shortly how La Candeur expressed its social identity.

None of the values expressed or the orations given at the creation of the new lodge would have been complete without rituals. After having had brought to "the altar of the Venerable [Master] a silver warming dish filled with hot coals," the master places another one on it, thus signifying the purification of the new lodge. He then prays to "the Grand Architect of the Universe, You! who guides our writings, you who knows the plans that we have traced for the construction of your august temple." Each brother of the new lodge approaches the altar and gives his allegiance to the Grand Lodge by placing a hand on the book of the Constitution. "In the name of the Grand Orient of France . . . the lodge des Beaux Arts is installed." After much applause the master places the "*lettres de patentes de Constitution* in the sanctuary to the right of the throne in a frame prepared for that purpose."[53] In this ritual the constitutional has become the sacred.

Amid such displays of secular piety and harmony it is difficult to grasp the tensions and hostilities that lay just beneath the surface. We heard the class tensions in the orations, but the records of these lodges show numerous disputes within and between lodges.[54] Indeed, more than one historian has seen this disputing as unique to the lodges, as distinct from the other philosophical societies. The routine minutes of scientific societies or literary and philosophical societies do not display the level of social antagonism frequently visible in certain Continental lodges. Although not mentioning the masonic lodges, de Tocqueville once again sums up the phenomenon we consistently encounter: "Each group was differentiated from the rest by its right to petty privileges . . . even the least of which was regarded as a token of its exalted status." We now want to know why this kind of rivalry was particularly commonplace within the lodges.

The lodges were microcosmic civil societies where men and some women might take their social and political idealism. Any betrayal of the lodge seemed like a betrayal of one's cherished ideals of how a polity should operate. The point can be illustrated from the records of Les Beaux Arts and St. Geneviève. The former got into financial difficulties within two years of its founding by St. Geneviève. Plagued by creditors, some of the officers of Les Beaux Arts disposed of the lodge's furnishings, constitutions, stamps, jewels, and papers, apparently without consulting the other brothers, or so it was said in an angry report on their actions sent to St. Geneviève. What strikes the observer from this less emotional distance is the language employed in the denunciation of these actions: The offending brothers were accused of instigating a "despotism entirely opposed to the masonic laws . . . a hidden cabal . . . [of] advancing an imposture that does not merit the least confidence . . . the three brothers who are guilty [are condemned] to a perpetual exclusion."[55] Not least, and the teller of the tale is now enraged, "we have now arrived, my dear brothers, at the era of the most monstrous conspiracy that has ever appeared in the east [i.e., in freemasonry], conspiracy so reprehensible to the civil life [*au civil*] that it is worthy only of our reproof." These "false brothers . . . by a most unworthy conspiracy have employed force and treason for their rule and master."[56] With indignation the brothers in St. Geneviève, who have been asked to intercede by the Grand Lodge, were told about how the masonic sanctuary had been violated and they were asked for "assistance against their violences." This cabal stands in stark contrast to the peace and harmony that should reign in the masonic temple. Dramatically and indignantly the reporters of the crime ask their listeners "to contemplate in cold blood the scene prepared by the cowardice, the egoism, the ambition and the vengeance" of this cabal.[57] The temple has been profaned.

What is striking about the language used to describe this breach of the civil order is its own violence, the sense it gives that once the deed was done all brotherhood has vanished and men are stripped back to an original ruthlessness, to egoism and ambition. They have reverted back to being the profane who have been so carefully excluded. This sort of quarreling can be found in various western European masonic records of the eighteenth century. In 1786 a lodge in the southern Dutch city of Maastricht referred to itself as a "bourgeois lodge" composed of honest citizens who are not of the class distinguished by its opulence. They are in dispute with the Grand Lodge in Liège, this time over constitutional recognition. Liège is claiming authority over them; in response, the brothers in Maastricht are saying that they are not "slaves," that they will have none of this "despotism."[58] What is being done, they say, in language that is Rousseauian, is against "the spirit of Liberty and of the *franchise* which comes with the name Francs et Libre Maçons. Yes, the voice of . . . liberty is engraved in the heart of all men, but in a freemason it is particularly living."[59]

Although present during the 1780s in other parts of western Europe, the discontent we find in masonic lodges with which I am familiar in the Dutch Republic or the Austrian Netherlands, for instance, never employs language quite so stark and extreme as what the Strasbourg records contain. And they are consistent in their absolutism, their angry either–or quality, with the kind of language these same brothers used to describe in general terms the egoism of the titled and wellborn. We can conclude only that this is a social universe where trust is very fragile, where if fraternal bonding breaks down, there is little else to mitigate the personal hostility of men even from the same profession or class. From such anger and distrust might spring deeply radical postures. It seems appropriate to note that the founder of Les Beaux Arts went on during the revolution to become a supporter of the regicide.

The aristocratic brothers in La Candeur were for the most part hostile to the French Revolution. Decades earlier La Candeur had veered toward the more mystical and Germanic forms of freemasonry. The lodge was also self-conscious in its memory of the persecution to which the Strasbourg lodges had been subjected. From its minutes of 1763 we get the valuable evidence that it was the accusations about sexuality in the 1740s that led the French masons to gradually admit women, to create lodges of adoption. La Candeur created just such a lodge during the first year of its existence (1763), and generally the records of La Candeur show a high degree of integration between brother and sister masons. As we have seen, such patterns were much more common in aristocratic French masonry than in lodges composed largely or entirely of the third estate. In La Candeur a brother had the option of joining the women's lodge, and he paid 36 livres to do so.[60] Only in 1785 did the bourgeois membership of La Candeur become visible and the character of the lodge begin to change.

It is the earlier, less censored class discourse of the aristocratic brothers in La Candeur that commands our attention. Within this temple we can find some of the few masonic orations where the philosophes of the Enlightenment were actually attacked, in this instance for persecuting religion, for "preferring their reputation to the good order of their country and of God himself."[61] And in La Candeur commonplace masonic talk about the dangers of egoism could also be turned against the Enlightenment; "the egoism became so general in this century, aggravating . . . even and spreading its poison until the unions of the most sacred blood [*du sang*] are dissolved, making all too often the closest relatives into irreconcilable enemies."[62] Similarly, in La Candeur brothers used traditional religious language to refer to "the

Being of Beings, the God of Gods" rather than to the Grand Architect.[63] Yet clearly the two are meant to be interchangeable. In this aristocratic lodge the religiosity being expressed by laymen is closer to that of the seventeenth century than it is to the commonplace theism, even deism, of the late eighteenth century. Indeed, the search for "an intimate union" with God, in the mind of the brothers chosen to speak before La Candeur, distinguished the freemason from "*le vulgaire.*" In distinctively Catholic terms they talked about submission to the will of God and repentance, of listening to the inner voice that makes known His will.[64]

Yet there was also a distinctive social message in the religiosity expressed within La Candeur. Hereditary nobility had always sought to justify its existence by identifying nobility with virtue.[65] In the rhetoric of the aristocratic masons of Strasbourg, a man's inner virtue is what distinguishes him, not his sashes or jewels, not even his masonic degrees. "Nothing is more beautiful in Nature than a soul full of candor, who senses his own integrity."[66] The true freemason judges not by appearances, by "the exterior. He knows that man is governed by an intelligent spirit, and that the valor of his actions does not depend upon what is perceived. He places all his attention on the intention." The message here was double-edged. On the one hand it contained a subtle rejection of opulence; on the other it said to look beyond the luxury which is just there into the heart of a man. Such sentiments could have an egalitarian impact; they could also be used to elevate and exclude: "It is this elevation, this grandeur of spirit that makes the true mason preferable to all other men. . . . With his feet he touches the earth, but his head is in Heaven. Intimately persuaded of his high calling, he keeps always before his eyes the more grand examples, and works without pause for his perfection, and to advance the happiness of men like himself."[67] In this instance masonic religiosity is being used to redefine exclusivity without for an instant challenging its inherent right to exist and its usefulness.[68] The brothers in La Candeur believed themselves to be reformers who refused to recognize other lodges that "confer all the grades for the price of money, while we have suppressed this mercenary custom."[69] Buying degrees and offices was something only monied men had to do initially. These aristocratic reformers could also describe themselves as "simple workers," and their officers signed the minutes with a perfunctory bow toward the Enlightenment, that is, executed by *par les lumieres et officiers de la loge.*

Coupled with the claim to virtue could also be the claim that the freemason was the rationalist, in effect the Cartesian man. Thus although avowedly Christian, La Candeur could also champion rationalism as that which distinguished the freemason from the profane.[70] Once again, as was standard in masonic rhetoric, the profane are watching the lodge, or so the orator in La Candeur tells us. Indeed, he continues, in the time of Lord Derwentwater (Grand Master in the 1740s) it was said that "our assemblies proclaimed an estrangement from women." In the face of these charges freemasons adopted aristocratic women as their patrons. Incensed by the slanders of the profane, the orator paints the portrait of its new patroness: "The charms which a sweet nature has embellished . . . by a cultivated spirit, [such is] the nobility of sentiments, the goodness of the soul, the righteousness of heart, the equality of character, the charm of her society, the sweetness of mores."[71] Cultivated virtue, a nobility of the soul, these were the values praised by the orator. Then effortlessly he proclaims that these virtues reside in the new patron of La Candeur, the Baroness de Flachslande, whose husband is a member of the lodge. She is addressed as a sister, her "protection" is sought, and thus begins the lodge of adoption that ran parallel to La Candeur. She is offered "homage" and the ambience of the moment conjures up the remnants of chivalry as much as it does the patronage of saints. If true nobility could now also be symbolically feminized, access to the equality of all brothers nevertheless remains limited. In her response the baroness graciously accepts, and she identifies with "the virtues that you practice, despite the impenetrable veil that hides you from my sex."[72] The implication is that some mysteries will continue to be hidden despite the virtues of the baroness.

The religiosity of the lodge, complete with its Catholic overtones, should not be interpreted as necessarily proclerical. There were clerics in it and other Strasbourg lodges, abbés, priests, Lutheran pastors, candidates for theological degrees, all appear in the records.[73] Yet La Candeur is also the lodge we met earlier, when it displayed deep suspicions about a priest who wanted to know its mysteries but then did not want to join. Clearly the brothers feared that his intention had been to spy, possibly to report back to the authorities. Brothers who assisted him were roundly castigated, among them most especially the abbé de Klingen. In his other life as an ecclesiastic Klingen was active in defending the local clergy against the imposition of new taxes in 1771–72.[74] As a man of the first estate, relations with laymen, even with the nobility, could be fraught with distrust, in this instance despite the restraint provided by masonic etiquette and decorum.[75]

The social tensions that marred La Candeur's relations with the Grand Orient in Paris, or with lodges that it regarded as too bourgeois, could also affect relations between brothers where suspicion and distrust at moments appear to lie barely beneath the surface. The "affaire Klingen" dragged on for months, until finally a vote was taken on whether to expel him. At the actual meeting one brother found that he could not deposit his ballot (*son jeton*) in the box indicating support for Klingen, it being sealed by wax. He then reached into the anti-Klingen box, removed his ballot (and possibly a few others), and managed to get it into Klingen's box. A furor ensued, with the master accusing him of having taken out more ballots than simply his own—in other words, of having attempted to tamper with the election. "With the atrocity of this action" and his refusal to obey, the master ordered the master of ceremonies to "conduct this rebel" out of the meeting. His name is then stricken from its *tableau,* its list of members.[76] The abbé de Klingen in his turn wrote a letter of apology, which asserted that he was "a zealous member of this lodge." In time the storm passed.

This tempest in the Strasbourg temple cannot be understood separately from the deep divisions that in fact separated brother from brother. In France the Enlightenment offered an ideology of reason and merit which was embraced by the masonic lodges; indeed, they were partly responsible for its spread far and wide. All eighteenth-century European societies possessed deep divisions based upon every conceivable way of delineating inferiority and superiority, birth, wealth, manner, dress, education, accent, and so on. Of the western European societies examined in this book, France was by far the most encoded with the symbols and reality, legally enforced, of social rank and place.

We should be clear that people could be just as poor, or short-lived, or rich, or wellborn anywhere in the zone delineated by London, Edinburgh, Amsterdam, Brussels, and Paris. Everywhere in western Europe the ideology of the Enlightenment stood in contrast with vast and institutionalized differences of birth and status, only more so in France. Everywhere the contrast was as palpable as the tension created in modern democratic societies between our ideology and the reality of race, class, and gender differences. Yet in the eighteenth century, unlike the post-1945 Western value systems, perfectly respectable ideologies existed to justify and reinforce the inequities of birth and rank, to render what we would call intolerance acceptable. Eighteenth-century men and women could judge and discriminate against one another openly, not necessarily covertly through institutions or silent judgments. Only the norms and conventions set by social expectations, by the conventions of politeness, restrained the eighteenth-century discriminator of status and birth. To believe in one's inherent superiority, or to disdain the mores or values of those deemed inferior, or for that matter superior, was simply a part of the individual's mental universe.

Quarreling was so endemic to the French lodges precisely because they were in the front line, as it were, of mediating two mental universes. The first and older one endorsed deference, birth, and inherited status. The second, which was newer and more democratic in its implications, argued for men, generally not women, as creatures equally capable of reason, and hence best judged by their merits. The lodges brought together men who would otherwise have had little or no occasion to break bread together. However much the Enlightenment's endorsement of human equality was tied inexorably to literate and polite culture and deeply distrustful of "the people," it was palpably different from the rationale that justified separate and privileged estates. As de Tocqueville puts it, "Education and a similar style of living had already obliterated many of the distinctions between the two classes. The bourgeois was as cultivated as the nobleman and his enlightenment came from the same source."[77]

The dilemma of the Enlightenment (and thus of the modern world)—democratic ideology versus the social reality of inequality—is already present in the civil society created by the masonic lodges of the late eighteenth century. In France this provoked tension and quarreling so intense that it indicated not just bad feelings, but also genuine hostility. We cannot ignore the violent tone that characterized the Strasbourg quarrels we have just witnessed. The Enlightenment may be said to have caused the democratic revolutions of the late eighteenth century in two senses: Its maxims, however hypocritically they may have been embraced, argued for equality and thus exacerbated the differences among and between men (as well as it fostered the search for gender equality).[78] Concomitantly the Enlightenment created an unbreachable cleavage between the culture of the literate, urban, and comfortable, and the many less than literate, often rural, and certainly uncomfortable masses. Not least, enlightened culture questioned the necessity for an entrenched clergy, indeed for any clergy. Thus could men caught in the old order but attracted to the Enlightenment quarrel interminably. No sooner had the "affaire Klingen" ended when La Candeur replaced it with consternation toward the Grand Lodge in Paris because of the inferior social standing of its representative.[79]

Part of the reforming zeal of La Candeur found a more positive, less cantankerous, expression in the societies associated with it and open to nonmasons.[80] The *Société harmonique des amis réunis* (to be distinguished from the Paris lodge Amis Réunis) was specifically mesmerist and among its most visible membership were doctors, surgeons, and women. In late eighteenth-century France medical reformers were among those most active in attacking the social conditions of the poor and were frequently influenced by enlightened prescriptions. No radical social message about the poor appears overtly in the records of the Société, but the compassionate and empathic message of the medical reformers is very much in evidence. "Medicines are rare . . . men have by consequence very great need for a unified, simple and efficacious medicine, such as animal Magnetism."[81] These altruistic sentiments recur in the society's minutes and correspondence as well as in the claims made by Mesmer and his followers.

As Robert Darnton has shown, mesmerism was the vogue of the 1780s. Mesmer began with Newtonian science and the latest research on electricity and wound up in a kind of medical mysticism. Using electricity to attempt cures for everything from lumbago to gout had been widespread in Britain at midcentury, and the Continental practitioners like Mesmer were on one level being perfectly scientific according to the practices of the day. On another, Mesmer specifically appealed to high society and offered animal magnetism as the cure-all for every imaginable physical and psychological ailment. He adopted the posture of the scientist as magician, claiming the unique power to channel the forces of nature in the service of human need. To join his society in Strasbourg, which was led by one of the most prominent of the town's officials, entailed an initiation fee of 100 louis (600 livres), an immense sum. Part of the reason for paying it may have been the promise of power over nature, not least, over illness and disease, that mesmerism offered. Being a mesmerist adept could heighten one's sense of power and control in the world.

Despite the overt appeal to the elite, some of mesmerism's followers took its doctrines in radical directions and used its goals of health and well-being to attack the ills of society and to argue for the need for some kind of revolution. The official academies of science took a dim view of all this toying with magnets and fluids, condemned mesmerism, and put its followers in the position of appealing to the general public for support.[82] Thus mesmerism, although promising power to its elite initiates, could also inspire both by its doctrines and by its antiestablishment posture, a radical critique of the established order endorsed by the traditional academies and their leaders.

Among the most ardent of Mesmer's supporters, particularly in Strasbourg, one of the provincial centers of the animal magnetism movement, were women. "Reassured! that the weakness of my sex does not place an obstacle in the way of participation in the sublime discovery of M. Mesmer . . . I dare, in keeping with the great faith which is imprinted upon me and affirms the particular progress I have made on my own health . . . [and] ask as a mother of a family to be initiated as a disciple."[83] Thus began a woman's application for membership, which was in turn brought before the "national assembly" of the society. As we shall see in the pages ahead, there were many national assemblies meeting in France after 1773, all under masonic auspices or inspiration. Men and women wrote to the mesmerist society from all over France and Germany requesting membership and convinced of the existence of a powerful Agent, named by the society "the magnetic fluid . . . [which] is able to produce a great revolution . . . for honest and sensitive souls."[84]

The mesmerist movement was too widespread and complex to be explained or subsumed entirely under the rubric of an extended freemasonry. Yet the significant masonic participation in it, the support given Mesmer by lodges both in his native Vienna and in France, provided him with ease of access throughout central and western Europe. Not least the metaphysics of mesmerism—if I may use the phrase—resonated with the great philosophical literature of the Enlightenment, with its most virulent heresy, namely, with materialism. We remember the Dutch freemasons back in the 1750s being accused of following the freethinkers Radicati and Tindal (pp. 82–83); we know that the French materialist Helvetius (and his wife) were deeply involved in freemasonry; that Rousset de Missy, the head of Amsterdam freemasonry, was a pantheist; that Jean Paul Marat was both freemason and materialist; and that the abbé Yvon, Diderot's associate, was in his materialist phase just at the time he was lecturing to his brothers in Amsterdam. Just as important, we know that whenever they could, freemasons denied the charge of being materialists. Yet in their secularism they were very much the unwitting stepchildren of freethinking and materialism, of what I have described as the Radical Enlightenment. Most brothers, of course, would not truck with anything so dangerously antireligious, so notorious in the minds of clergy and censors.

Now, late in the century, we have materialism coming back, revived and sanitized, in the form of mesmerism. It simply asserted God's control over the apparently self-moved perturbations and movements of nature. Most important, unlike the determinist tendency in most materialist postures, mesmerism asserted the human ability to control the forces of nature and thereby to establish a bodily equilibrium which cannot be disturbed by the acceleration and diminution of the movements within nature.[85] In this one claim it departed from the social message most commonly found in the materialist tradition, the belief that there were forces at work in nature and in society which were so powerful that they simply required a free expression. Materialism classically conceived was also anticlerical, but mesmerists sought to be received not only by the rich and wellborn but also by the clergy.

The remarkable thing about the mesmerist movement of the 1780s is how fashionable, even respectable, it became given its metaphysics. At the heart of European materialism from Toland to d'Holbach lay the assertion, based upon one reading of Newtonian physics, that motion is inherent in matter, that all of nature is alive, that soul and body are one, all material, all entirely of this world. The Christian, or even deistic, opponents of materialism from Newton (d. 1727) and Voltaire on, had always denied the truth of materialism's most basic premise, that nature could in effect operate entirely on its own initiative. Although pious to the core, mesmerism quite remarkably picked up on the turbulent metaphysics of the materialist tradition: "Movement exists in all parts of the universe . . . the decomposition of different parts of matter disseminated in space . . . by reason of this primitive law the molecules are analogous and all of nature is only a vast laboratory where all the operations go on continuously." So stated a member of the Strasbourg society in a treatise on "The Universal Magnetism" that was similar to what other mesmerists of the time were saying in their metaphysical statements.[86]

Much to the worry of even its pious supporters, mesmerism took up materialist metaphysics and then simply asserted that God exists and oversees the turbulence, activity, and self-regulation of Nature. Human beings are often caught in this turbulence; indeed, small particles as well as large bodies are governed by these perpetual motions. Once immersed in the mesmerist tub an object was attended to by the magnetist, who held an iron rod; "in this state the tub, being perpetually maintained by the current of gravitation determined by the magnetic rod placed over the plant, can be compared to a lake of movement each of whose iron branches reaching to the circumference will be so many rivers of repairing action which . . . I have observed." So explained a Strasbourgian mesmerist. When applied to the sick, the magnetic fluid could be passed from the healthy person to the sick: "Of all of these repairing movements of a man in a state of illness none of them seem to be more appropriate than that which he receives from his equal [*son semblable*] in a state of health." This social experience, "the action of man," of individual to individual, is also capable of making men happy.[87] "Man seen in his purely physical state, as all the other parts of matter, & the proper movement of his organization being subordinated to the general movements . . . the length of his existence is dependent on the harmony of these parts."[88] Particles of iron are especially able to affect these movements, having been endowed with that power by "the grand artist of the world." And thus a portion of the treatise by our Strasbourg mesmerist ends: "Movement is the principle of the permanent existence of the universe."

Many of the followers of mysticism and theosophy, to which mesmerism is deeply indebted, became after 1789 counterrevolutionaries, retreating into the mystical writers of the seventeenth century and earlier.[89] It was possible to ignore or to despise the actual turbulence of the world even, or perhaps particularly, in 1793. Yet the human order that mesmerist metaphysics endorsed, regardless of the elite status of most of its practitioners, was in fact implicitly democratic and inherently reformist. Particles of matter moving of their own volition, governed by material forces and laws, had been a metaphysic of radicals on both sides of the Channel since the mid-seventeenth century. Levellers and Diggers in England, libertines like Cyrano de Bergerac in France, spinozists in the Dutch Republic—however much they differed on all sorts of political principles—had since then proclaimed matter as the universal locus of energy in the world. Now in the 1780s in France these doctrines returned, not just among the salon materialists but in the vastly publicized and popular form of mesmerism. Freemasonry assisted in the propagation of mesmerist materialism, and thus unwittingly helped to lay the metaphysical foundations of democratic thought. When combined with the practice of representative and constitutional government offered by the lodges, the mystical elements offered by mesmerism could fuse both into an emotionally powerful mixture.

The very earliest accusations against freemasonry as one of the causes of the French Revolution picked up precisely on the mystical and theosophical elements found in the lodges of the 1780s. The attackers equated magnetism and theosophy with fanaticism and sectarianism.[90] They related both to the Illuminati, a secret political society founded in Germany in 1776 and modeled on the structure of the lodges. They argued, not always very coherently, that the liberty practiced by the lodges encouraged men to stop thinking and also to take a posture in the world where they are without country, without parents, without citizenship, broken away from the ties that attach men to society.[91] Nothing we have seen so far in the many lodges we have visited suggests such a nihilism. Yet there was some way in which the lodges of the old regime were unceasingly restless. They had found a kind of liberty and equality that irritated as much as it placated; by 1793 some brothers will have given up on the lodges as places where social change might be effected. In the Parisian club known as the Cercle Social, where much of the leadership had once been freemasons, it was believed that the lodges had been necessary only "in a despotic society."[92] They equated the old order in France with despotism and saw the lodges as far too bound up in its contradictions. As we have just seen, there was a half-truth in the assessment.

9

Le Régime Ancien et Maçonnique: The Paris Grand Lodge and the Reform of National Government

At a time when no one could have foreseen our revolution, I attached myself to freemasonry, which offered a kind of image of equality, just as I attached myself to the parlements, which offered a kind of image of liberty. I have since given up the phantom for the reality.

"Voici mon histoire maçonnique" a manuscript written in self-defense by LOUIS PHILIPPE JOSEPH D'ORLÉANS, *also known as* PHILIPPE D'EGALITÉ.[1]

Philippe d'Egalité, as the duc d'Orléans chose to call himself after 1789, had been a Grand Master. In 1793 during the Reign of Terror he wrote the preceding statement as the opening of his self-justification to explain why he had once been an active freemason. It sits to this day as a manuscript amid his papers, written in minuscule, beautifully crafted penmanship. As one of the nearest blood relatives to the recently guillotined king, Philippe d'Egalité was the object of deep suspicion; indeed, in 1793 he would meet the fate of his cousin. What is remarkable about his claim to have found in freemasonry a kind of equality, which he in turn gave up for the real thing, was that he had to make it at all. He has been attacked not by antirevolutionaries but by the Revolution's supporters for having been a freemason.

By 1793 freemasonry was suspect to both the French left and the French right. The Revolution had created a new and distinct political culture that was rapidly involved in repudiating its past. To that extent the fate of the lodges during the Revolution does not necessarily help us to unravel their character and role prior to it. But there is enough evidence from the 1780s that helps us to understand what the duc d'Orléans may have meant when he said that the prerevolutionary lodges offered a kind of equality. In the new civil society of the eighteenth century, the lodges, like the parlements and estates general of ancien régime Europe, had offered a distinct political experience. In its time the experience had been Janus-faced: It looked toward a new form of political culture, constitutional and representative, and hence toward new definitions of liberty and equality; yet it was also old, for in this new public arena the traditional symbols of status were retained, hierarchy and degrees, deeply formal civility, the mystical and the religious—all were imitated and to that extent preserved. Both tendencies, the new and the old, are visible within French freemasonry during the late eighteenth century. Similar tendencies have also been noted within German freemasonry in precisely the same period.[2]

Strasbourg afforded us a rare glimpse into a variety of lodges and quasi-masonic associations. In the previous chapter we witnessed the Strasbourg lodges' quarrel for reasons of social class and estate, but also about alternative visions of how to reconcile the claims of merit with the realities of birth and wealth. From very different postures, the lodge of aristocrats and the one for merchants offered formulas for reform and renewal. In this babel certain phrases stood out: reform and decay, the corruption of society, the light of nature, the contract between brothers, primitive virtue, the return to nature.

The phrases and prescriptions offered in Strasbourg were remarkably similar to what was being said in lodges all over France, and it seems reasonable to lump the strident rhetoric of the 1770s and 1780s in the same category, Rousseauian. As noted in chapter 6, Rousseau's analysis of societal decay and his antidotes actually fitted with remarkable ease into general, originally British, masonic discourse with its utopian impulses. It also fitted with a vocabulary that concerned freedom and natural rights and can be found throughout the century among French artisans as well as aristocrats.[3] Talk of natural rights also owed much to the tradition of classical republicanism transmitted by the ancients, by Machiavelli, and not least by French translations of the seventeenth-century English commonwealthmen. As adopted to a masonic context in the 1770s, the equality of all brothers, a standard phrase derived from the guild tradition, became the "primitive equality" of all brothers.

One Strasbourg orator expressed the Rousseauian impulse by designating the lodge as a retreat from the tumult of the world. In it nature can be studied and contemplated in silence. The masonic edifice is a hospice for honest men; "they have built a Temple to wisdom, to renew there with all free and loving souls, the contract of the primitive fraternity." Refreshed by this experience, the mason can return to society.[4] Given the sublime and pure nature of the temple he has just left, at least in his dreams, society might leave much to be desired. Certainly masonic quarreling of the period suggests that it did.

However fractious the life of the lodges, no version of European freemasonry has been more heavily contested and more documented than late eighteenth-century French masonry. Probably every freemason at the time has now been unearthed. Even the words most frequently used in French masonic songs and poems, or given as names of lodges, have been counted and analyzed. Predictably fraternity, equality, and harmony figured high in the count. Of course, most masonic literature written in French could have been published anywhere French-language presses operated, and only the most ethnocentric view would imagine that it was intended solely or entirely for the French market. As we have seen, French was the lingua franca of freemasons all over Europe. Especially in the period prior to the 1760s when the lodges were less commonplace outside of Paris and a few northern and coastal towns and cities, French-language tracts, almanacs, and other publications, attracted an international body of consumers. Thus what we can learn from the published literature of the French lodges might have been known to many other Europeans.

By the 1780s freemasonry in France was so widespread as to be commonplace. There were 62 lodges in France prior to 1759, another 70 were created between 1750 and 1759; in the next decade alone there were 182 new foundings. Freemasonry's popularity can be measured by how the costs of initiation kept up with inflation. In one lodge in 1778 initiation cost 36 livres; by 1781 it had gone up to 60.[5]

However popular, by the 1770s and 1780s French freemasonry, as we witnessed in Strasbourg, was also deeply troubled. The great French historian of the intellectual origins of the French Revolution, Daniel Mornet, noted back in the 1930s how the climate of discussion in France during the 1770s became particularly heated, the cadence of discourse became shrill and impatient. More recently the monumental work of Daniel Roche on French sociability noted in passing the tensions and dissensions within the lodges, but his interests did not lie in trying to explain the reasons for the quarreling.[6] As we shall see as we now examine discussions within the Grand Lodge of France, renewed and reformed in 1773, Mornet had been very close to the mark. The purity of the temple, not simply locally but also nationally, was indeed being compromised by social hatreds and antagonisms. In the masonic temples where scarcely an artisan could be found, the anger being expressed was not about work and wages but about privileges and place, about deference and respect.[7]

Most lodges also liked their social exclusivity. Addressing superiors and inferiors as "brother" fostered a sense of being accepted and accepting. Brothers identified with social harmony and hierarchy, with the status quo, and they could not understand why the lodges, having freed individuals to speak their mind and to act as if they had real power, were in turn also the loci of angry recriminations, jealousies, and hatreds. In the case of the Grand Lodge in Paris it sought to institute reforms while strengthening and preserving aristocratic leadership. The major reform of 1773 established the national Grand Lodge as "the legislator of the order in France." The purpose of giving the Grand Lodge more power through a nationally representative general assembly was "to set up the Grand Orient National which would not be subject to the revolutions and vicissitudes of the time."[8] By the end of this chapter we should better understand why by 1793 Philippe d'Egalité's dedication to freemasonry had become so suspect. Yet the troubles we are about to analyze were not confined entirely to ancien régime France. The disputes within the French lodges remind us of the quarrels between the Amsterdam lodge and The Hague in the 1750s discussed in chapter 4.

As we saw in the introduction, the French lodges at their origin were infinitely more commercial than they were aristocratic. Yet they had sought and received, as early as the 1740s, aristocratic patronage. Complicating the early history of such patronage was the presence of originally British and then, through naturalization, French aristocrats of Jacobite and Catholic sympathies (p. 24). The earliest French

Grand Master was Charles Radcliffe, the self-styled Earl of Derwentwater, who was executed upon his return to Scotland in the rebellion of 1745. The most famous and intellectual of all the early masters was the Chevalier Ramsay, a Jacobite Scot, a Catholic, and a gifted masonic orator. These early Jacobite associations require attention if we are to understand the various postures and cultural tendencies within the French lodges.

Generally historians have not known quite what to do with the stalwart but exiled Jacobites except to see them as romantic patrons of an essentially lost, and backward-looking, cause. When their cause merges with a commitment to freemasonry, defined as progressive and modern in its aspirations and outlook, the historian is confounded by an ostensible paradox. One solution has been to see the Jacobite influence as confined largely to the period prior to 1740 and thus divorce it from the last decades of eighteenth-century French masonic history with its complex, but real, tendencies toward reform, if not republicanism.[9] The other, and more satisfying, solution seems to lie in acknowledging that eighteenth-century French aristocratic culture from Montesquieu to the *parlementaire* opposition of the 1770s could be deeply traditional in relation to the political role of the aristocracy in the state and still be openly reformist and sympathetic to the culture of Enlightenment, indeed could be a focus for it.

Freemasonry provided a perfect outlet for these reformist impulses from Montesquieu, who was initiated in London in 1730, to many of the *parlementaire* opponents of monarchical and ministerial centralism who found a place in the lodges of the 1770s. The Grand Master named in the police reports of the 1740s, the Count of Clermont (pp. 6–7), toward the end of his life (d. 1771) opposed Louis XV's attempt to strip the *parlements* (i.e., judicial and aristocratic courts) of their prerogatives. The attempt is known as the Maupeou affair and it enflamed both aristocratic and enlightened opinion in the early 1770s. Not accidentally those years saw the revival of masonic central government, that is, the creation of the Grand Orient in Paris, and with it the aggressive advocacy of constitutionalism, the rights of representatives, and especially the creation in 1773 of the masonic National Assembly.[10]

Within a French context, Jacobitism could fit well enough into the aristocratic mind bent upon reform. Bearing in mind that many French aristocrats of reforming persuasion would have had little time for Jacobite sentiments—like Montesquieu,whose English friends all were Whigs—nevertheless, we should keep in mind that Jacobitism could be progressive on some issues, however reactionary its Stuart origins may appear. Loyalty to the Stuarts could be imagined to combine dedication to the hereditary succession of kings with some sort of representative government. It should be recalled that after 1685 the Stuarts claimed to favor religious toleration for English Protestant minorities. Such a posture in France was radically reformist, opposed to the harsh revocation of Protestant rights undertaken by Louis XIV in precisely 1685. And not least, Jacobitism was steeped in legend and antiquity. After the accession (and subsequent defeat) of James II (1685–88), Jacobitism was, right up to 1745 and beyond, deeply Catholic. In the 1740s being a French Jacobite could also mean loyalty to French interests against those of Britain and its Whig court.[11] Nor should we forget that even in Britain being a Jacobite in the period after 1715 did not preclude a willingness to engage in popular politics (as well as conspiracy). In a certain sense Jacobitism could be the posture of "the country," that is, disgruntled gentry or small yeomen, against an overbearing and corrupt "court." The Jacobite was part of the spectrum of British political culture, however extremist his loyalty to the Stuarts may have appeared.

Something of the British yet Jacobite origins of French freemasonry survived in the conservative wing of aristocratic freemasonry right into the 1760s. With remarkable historical memory conservative freemasons attacked Cromwell as if he were alive and well. They denounced the "cromwellists" as fanatics.[12] Yet in the late 1730s and early 1740s exiled British Jacobites and their French sympathizers could long, and even plot, for a popular uprising across the Channel, an uprising that would restore the Stuart dynasty but presumably retain parliament.

We cannot imagine Jacobitism as the driving impulse in French aristocratic freemasonry by midcentury. Rather it was one of its roots, and those origins may help to account for the simultaneously enlightened, baroque, and occult—even pious—freemasonry that we found so prominent in the Strasbourg lodges of the 1770s and 1780s, among others. Certainly in Toulouse, where one of the oldest French lodges was founded (c. 1741) by a minor Irish nobleman, a Jacobite and Catholic who was naturalized by Louis XV, most of the lodges there remained committed to Church and King right up to 1789.[13] Their most recent and excellent historian sees the conservative lodges of Toulouse as almost completely untouched by the science and rationalism we traditionally associate with the Enlightenment. In the lodges which share a similarly pious ambience I have interpreted their "conservatism" somewhat differently and emphasized the reformist elements which they reveal. Only a small number of masonic lodges in eighteenth-century Europe were hotbeds of enlightened and radical idealism. What does seem to be universal in the lodges, whether bourgeois or aristocrat, and however socially restricted, was the impulse to reform and renew, to perfect the civil polity enveloped in the sociability of the lodge.

In general, however, it remains true that the overview of French freemasonry as a national phenomenon in this chapter reveals a movement dominated by aristocrats more in touch with the Enlightenment than with Jacobitism or mysticism. They were liberal and reformist in matters of governance and social welfare as well as in the language they employed, yet they sought to ensure a "proper" social mix in the local lodges. The French aristocracy had more privileges to protect, more at stake in any reformist vision of a new social order than almost any other elite in western Europe. De Tocqueville put it rather harshly: "These odious prerogatives inspired their possessors with a pride as inordinate as it was shortsighted."[14] We should hardly be surprised to find masonic lodges, including the Grand Lodge in Paris, reflecting aristocratic interests and preoccupations. What is important in this phenomenon is the way in which it conforms to the model we have found in freemasonry from Dundee to London, Paris, Amsterdam, Nijmegen, Brussels, and Berlin: The closed temple mirrored political values, the microcosm of the lodge was political, however disparate the interests represented from lodge to lodge, the social and the civilizing were inevitably civic.

But we do not want to be too schematic and rationalist about the lodges. There is another aspect of French freemasonry that is beyond the scope of this chapter, and indeed this book. The symbolic universe of the freemason is yet to find its historian or perhaps its historical anthropologist. As already noted, French and oftentimes Catholic freemasonry was especially lavish in its use of degrees, symbols, and ceremonies. All masonic religiosity used plateaus and levels; the French just did more of it and early on described their symbolic form of freemasonry as "Scottish." Although almost certainly not from Scotland, this baroque freemasonry, so popular on the Continent, especially among the aristocracy and high bourgeoisie, may owe something to the Jacobite influences at work in the early decades. It also, of course, could reinforce a sense of hierarchy; in addition, its ceremonial side fitted more comfortably with men and women long used to Catholic rituals. We should never underestimate the emotional pull of masonic rituals, the intensity of the loyalty they could inspire. Sometimes sociability is about a wider range of human needs than we are able to re-create in this or any other book.

The rituals may also be related to another factor present within French aristocratic culture by midcentury. The pattern of ennoblements instituted by the crown had created a new ideology of moral valor and professional capacity, as distinct simply from birth or military prowess, as the new criterion for nobility. The mysticism of the masonic degrees combined the mystique and magic of ultimate social ascendancy and the dedication to order, hierarchy, and perfectibility with the newer masonic ideology of merit. Paradoxically, a man rose to higher and more ornate and mystical status within a lodge because of practical virtue and obvious merit. At least that was the claim. Yet he was not expected to give up his larger social and political interests. In 1789 the first grade in a new masonic order taken in Strasbourg had the brother swear that "I would not hesitate to oppose myself to the enemies of my Sovereign, my Country and my Religion."[15] Not surprisingly, freemasons of the 1790s were just as likely to be royalist exiles as Jacobins.[16]

But a goodly number of French freemasons became Jacobins. After their exile, a masonic Jacobin from Reims who spent much of his idle time writing the history of freemasonry made some interesting observations on the lodges prior to the Revolution. He believed that the prerevolutionary Grand Lodge had dragged its feet in adopting the true "*ecossisme,*" that is, the Scottish rite, only in 1786. It did so, he believed, because its aristocratic leadership did not want to open the degrees practiced in certain lodges to the entire fraternity. Thus, and perhaps not surprisingly, Scottish freemasonry, in spite of, or perhaps because of its mystical tendencies, could fall on what became the left, as well as what was clearly on the right, of the revolutionary spectrum. We can now begin to see that the Paris Grand Lodge was of the old order even as it sought innovations that would ultimately be incompatible with it.

According to our exile, when more middling men were admitted to all the Scottish degrees and ceremonies they believed that it brought them closer to the true masonry, which had begun in England during the 1640s.[17] An early nineteenth-century masonic handbook made much the same point: "The mores of the English and the spirit of liberty they uphold in their laws, that was the principle cause of the establishment and popularity of freemasonry in England."[18] While almost certainly Jacobite in its origins—and if not, then baroque and Catholic in its initial stance—

the French version of Scottish rite masonry, so popular in the 1770s and 1780s, could also express the aspirations of bourgeois men for status and the recognition of their merits. Degrees invented for the aristocracy could be coveted by their inferiors. The complexity of French freemasonry, both as to the types of lodges and the variety of ideological postures they could assume by the 1770s if not before, should not obscure the fact that these were places where all the impulses to reorder and reshape the world in one's own image could find expression. Even before French freemasonry largely expressed Enlightenment ideals, it expressed a new public space, a new form of civil society.

Inevitably private sociability imitated the highly stratified social order around it. Add to that porosity the aspirations of the Enlightenment and we find brothers who believed themselves when "fraternally assembled under the geometric point [to be] known as the only men enlightened by the true light." In such a lodge a man's inner enlightenment could be so finely calibrated as to take him through twelve grades, or degrees, from apprentice to "Chevalier de l'Orient, Rose-Croix, Chevalier du Temple, Philosophe-Inconnu, Sublime-Philosophe," ending up with "Maître à tous Grades."[19] Whatever its intention, the system of grades or degrees was inherently costly. Every grade called for a donation to the lodge, entailed its own wardrobe and jewelry, and required the inevitable banquet that went along with joyous events. Within this system some brothers achieved a more perfect masonic experience as well as greater status and honor amid their imagined equality.

Given the hierarchical nature of the French lodges, we should take up the issue of their specifically democratic tendencies. In that respect and on the national level, masonic practices of the 1770s and 1780s reveal contradictory impulses. The new Grand Lodge demonstrates the reforming agenda that many private societies throughout western Europe adopted late in the century. Immensely energetic and led by a corps of officers, most of them from the aristocratic second estate, it set about the work of reform and renewal. After months of discussion the "Corps Maçonnique de France" established the "General Assembly composed of deputies from the provinces as well as Paris truly representing the Masonic body of France . . . its first object to decide the statutes, and to give to the regime of the Order a form capable of erasing the abuses which one believes to find the source in the former administration."[20] The assembly elected the new officers of the Grand Lodge, and it was composed of seventy-seven members divided into three chambers, one for general administration, one solely for the affairs of the Paris lodges, and one for the provinces. Regular meetings were to be held, records kept, order and harmony maintained, dues collected, stamps and seals maintained—all on a national level. The purpose was to create an active and explicitly reforming national government for French freemasonry. Even the orator for the new national Grand Lodge was to be used as the agent for communicating the decisions made by the secretaries of the Lodge.[21] And a monthly circular went out from the Grand Lodge to every lodge in the country; this was an invaluable record from which we can reconstruct the plans and activities of the new central government of French freemasonry.

The effect of the renewed centralization undertaken by the Grand Lodge was to create opponents in some quarters. One even wrote a tract which the Grand Lodge sought, quite successfully, to suppress. In it a Parisian brother, frère de La Chaussée, appeals to his frères against the attempts to expel him. He accuses his opponents of "attacking my civil reputation." He argues for the way things once were in the lodges, for a time when "the principles of equality were not undermined by the accident of birth or rank."[22] La Chaussée acknowledges that anarchy had reigned at moments in the past, that "bourgeois of the lowest *étage,* to artisans, workers, menial workers, even domestics had defiled our mysteries."[23] But he deeply resents the authority embraced by the new Grand Lodge, its "administrative authority becoming an imperial despotism, and the voluntary submission of masons, a slavery."[25] We need not accept the whole of La Chaussée's negative assessment to see that the introduction of greater legislative powers for elected representatives was not necessarily combined with the desire to democratize the social mix of the lodges. The inspiration behind the setting up of the Grand Lodge came from enlightened aristocrats who sought order and control through the use of representative institutions.

The effort to impose order and discipline led to open quarrels with lodges that did not conform. Under the rubric of trying to establish "a grand Republic . . . [with] virtue at its base, " the Grand Lodge waged bitter disputes with "rebels" who sought to set up unauthorized lodges or who admitted undesirable men or women, actresses, for example, into the lodges.[25] The orators of the Grand Orient were also openly flattering of both aristocracy and monarchy. They were concerned that servants in the lodges not be given the passwords. Yet they were also deeply critical of contemporary society.[26] Perhaps the critical posture was partly responsible for a massive effort undertaken in the 1780s to make charity available in a variety of forms to all brothers and their families in need. The Grand Lodge appealed to all "sensitive and virtuous souls" to help it establish a home for veterans, and especially for their orphaned children.

The critical posture of the Lodge's leadership continued through the early stages of the French Revolution. In the circular sent to all lodges in late 1789 the tone is cautious but optimistic: "Never has freemasonry had a field more vast . . . today, my very dear brothers, our duties have multiplied . . . as citizens, the country must be pleased with our services . . . [but] you remember with regret the times of anarchy when disorder took the place of discipline." By contrast, the government of the lodges is extolled as a model of order, in particular the "Assembly of Representatives . . . has become their proper Legislators." Even in the early years of the Revolution when many lodges simply ceased to meet, the Grand Lodge imagined that it could offer direction to the nation: "Although France has adopted equality as the basis of its regime, she is nevertheless populated by men subject to passions and errors: it is therefore up to those imbued with true principles to give the example." From this lofty stance the Grand Lodge of 1791 urged "fraternal charity," however "scattered and divided" brothers had become.[27] It also sought to reorganize the masonic system of national government, to find "a new mode of existence for the Grand Orient." By 1793, as the fate of Philippe d'Egalité unfolded, the Grand Lodge must have realized that no amount of restructuring would save some of its aristocratic leaders from suspicion. Their calls for patriotism made in circular after circular from 1789 were not sufficient to deter their detractors or to avoid having the issue of aristocratic leadership raised and its validity ultimately denied. By 1793 the

Grand Lodge and countless other lodges had effectively ceased to operate. But in the 1770s and 1780s they had been, to use a favorite masonic symbol, beehives of activity.

By 1780 the Grand Lodge was supporting a home for over fifty orphans, a dozen of whom, presumably the orphans of army officers, were of "noble extraction." "All the classes" were to receive education in reading and writing, but the study of languages and mathematics was to be reserved for the children of the nobility and the sons of officers.[28] In the same year the Grand Orient acquired a chateau on the Rhine intended for widows and orphans, and plans were put in place to establish a bank for the use of brothers, which would offer loans at favorable rates.[29] The largely aristocratic Grand Lodge was actively involved in dispensing charity to brothers who wrote to its committee from all over the country. It did have a fund where small sums, a few livres per month, were given out on a regular, annual basis to deserving brothers.

Men and women freemasons, as well as widows of brothers, wrote to the Grand Lodge and appealed for its "generosity" to relieve them in their miserable state.[30] Repeatedly they refer to the fraternity as a family of which they are legitimate sons. Invariably, they explain, they or their natural families have been stricken with misfortune, disease, accidents at sea, sudden paralysis, limbs lost at war—in short, disasters unforeseen for which they are in no way responsible. We sense in the letters that the supplicant has literally nowhere else to turn. "I have two small children. We are without bread, without money." Sometimes the writer is a brother servant who is begging the lodge for work. A few letters are addressed directly to the Grand Master; in 1787 that was the Duc d'Orléans himself.

Most letters invariably make clear that when good fortune had reigned the writer had been a faithful brother, had risen through many degrees, and always had been a man of merit. Once meritorious and hence, through virtuous conduct, successful, somewhat ironically, only fate and bad luck can be invoked to explain a brother's demise. Many of the correspondents tell that they are far from their place of birth either in France or abroad. These are travelers whose profession, trade, or engagement in war has taken them from their places of birth, from Ireland, Denmark, Portugal; now they are without support. The arguments they give as to why they should be helped vacillate between a plea for generosity, beneficence,—in short, voluntary charity,—and the reminder of "the solemn engagement that our contract obliges us to our brothers."[31] The supplicants are humble and woeful but they are not shy in reminding their brothers of the obligations that come with virtue and fraternity. These indigent brothers of the 1780s tell us that they are caught between two worlds: the one essentially paternalistic, where personal loyalty and charity of rich to poor supposedly prevent the unfortunate from starving; the other where men and women of merit, citizens of a commercial and international order, believe they are entitled by their social contract within their private enclaves to a modicum of care when in desperate need. From the letters it would seem that no other agency of church or state was able to provide a sufficient net for men and women who, for whatever reason, were in danger of falling through, literally, as they tell us, of starving.

In the 1780s the Grand Lodge began to make explicit the analogy between the masonic order and the political order, between the lodges as centers of social virtue and enlightenment and what was supposedly needed in the larger civil polity: "In the physical order and in the political order, the place that French Masonry should occupy in the common center has already been fixed. . . . If there must be a center for illumination [*de lumières*] in the Masonic Order, it is no less necessary in the political order . . . the Masons, submissive to the Sovereign, or as Citizens and as Subjects, have an even stricter duty than the rest of mankind to respect the law . . . to work in common for the general good of humanity." Given their special obligations and interests, the Grand Lodge assured the other lodges of the necessity of having a strong masonic presence in Paris. There the government could "observe their actions."[32] However elevated in social estate or place individual masons may have been, as late as the 1780s French freemasons worried about the suspicions of the profane, especially the profane with governmental authority.

"The French Masonic regime" is "a free association" in which each man has a role in creating the law, in which "all masons" have a vote and can choose their deputies.[33] Meeting in their respective three chambers where each deputy has a vote, and then meeting as a whole, brothers voted upon and levied dues by plurality. Representatives to the general assembly cast their vote individually, never by chamber. In a circular of 1781 the Grand Lodge described this system of representation in precise detail. Amid attention to the mechanisms of representative government, the Grand Orient also adopted a posture of great empathy for the poor and the orphaned: "The population is the greatest riches of a State." It exhorted member lodges to contribute generously to its charitable projects.[34] Such projects, it was argued, were for the good of the nation; masonic *bienfaisance* was compared to the tender regard that the monarch has for his people. After levying an annual fee of 3 livres on each brother, the general assembly of the Grand Orient proceeded to publish in the monthly circular the debate held by the deputies on the subject of the tax and the equality of all brothers. Should the tax be proportional, or should all brothers pay the same because they share equally in the benefits that will come from this tax for charity? This was a complex subject intelligently discussed. Elaborate thought processes were not necessary to see the analogy between this discussion of who in the masonic nation should pay taxes and under what circumstances and the larger question of tax exemptions for the first and second estates, for the historically privileged clergy and the aristocracy. The decision of the general assembly was that no brother, except the indigent, should be exempt from the tax; however minor, it should be binding on the entire masonic community.[35]

When economic conditions took a bad turn in 1787 the aristocratic leadership of the Grand Orient assured brothers that by the charity they had put in place earlier they were assisting the "paternal" purposes of the national government.[36] The committee in charge of dispensing charity dealt with increasingly large numbers of "children," who often wrote out of desperate need. But there were other kinds of children who had begun to make their appearance within the lodges. In the late 1780s acrimony was everywhere apparent. The Grand Lodge issued a special circular that reprinted the statutes of the national order. The reprint was accompanied by a deeply troubled attack on "the children of Enthusiasm," who have appeared in some lodges. The self-defense continued: "Respectable lodges are persuaded without doubt that [the Grand Lodge] has acted with solicitude and with activities in every way maternal."[37] Yet no amount of language, we are led to believe, would assuage the brothers hostile to the Grand Lodge. The term "enthusiasm"—in whatever European language—conjured up ancient fears of religious sectaries and civil war. Ironically it will be exactly the word used against the freemasons by the earliest opponents of the Revolution. Yet in 1787 the Grand Lodge is not worried about revivals of old sectarianisms; it is concerned about those who "attempt to propagate dangerous innovations."[38]

Among the issues that are being contested was the control exercised by the Grand Lodge over the awarding of the masonic higher degrees. The innovators accused "the Grand Orient, contrary to all truths, [of] attempting to limit the symbolic regime." The Grand Lodge responded by saying that it was only attempting to protect the regularity of the degrees. In fact we now know that pressure had forced the Grand Lodge to loosen the requirements, financial and otherwise, around the so-called Scottish rite.[39] More brothers wanted the honor and status that came with those degrees than the aristocratic Grand Lodge was willing to grant left to its own inclinations. Descriptions written by one of the Strasbourg brothers in St. Geneviève who was a delegate to the Paris meetings of the Grand Lodge speak of the envy and suspicion that greeted any new "chapter of the high grades." The opponents "wrapped themselves in the mantle of the general good," in short, general principles of what constitutes proper order and the good of society are being brought to the discussion about who should be deemed meritorious, for that was what the degrees were supposed to symbolize.[40] All who sought these degrees, not surprisingly, believed themselves to be entitled to them.

In the 1780s within the confines of their lodges some brothers argued for greater equality. Still others as deputies to the masonic national assembly debated the relationship between taxation and benefits, and they prescribed their system of governance by elections and representation as a model for the nation, for "*l'état politique*." By 1792 the enemies of freemasonry and the French Revolution found these debaters to have been nothing other than conspirators. That they were not. But they were participating in a system of governance inherited from another revolution, dimly remembered. Its meaning was known in part because some brothers believed that the version of the civil polity they created in their private sociability had first taken shape in revolutionary England. In that belief, as we can now understand it, they were more right than even they could have imagined.

One of the institutions that transmitted English constitutionalism onto the Continent was freemasonry. However many innovations, degrees, rituals, and feasts Continental masons invented, and however much they closed the lodges to particular classes or social groups, they never altered the ideology of work and merit, and of all brothers meeting upon the level, that came from Anderson's *Constitutions* (London, 1723) as well as the many "exposures" that made their way across the Channel or were invented there. Thus with the constitutionalism came a heavy dose of republican language undoubtedly derived from a multitude of sources. At least one French historian views the masonic phenomenon as inherently and simply democratic,[41] and of course such an interpretation is compatible with then seeing the lodges as breeding grounds for Jacobinism, for the imaged horrors of democracy unleashed by the French Revolution. This book sees little merit in that historiographic tradition.

The point about the Enlightenment in France was that it helped to create a secular culture wherein civil society could take shape. In the lodges, and later the philosophical societies, impulses profoundly political could be formulated, discussed, and preached. As a result of the French Revolution bourgeois brothers and their values make more sense to us than do the aristocratic leadership of the Grand Lodge. Both were present in the 1780s and before, both were being political as they spoke about virtue and nobility, both permit us to delineate the Enlightenment as it was lived in the most important ancien régime of the century. We can relate freemasonry to the French Revolution because in the lodges of the 1770s and 1780s some of its eventual promoters and opponents can be heard discussing how society and government should be, before each would be simultaneously changed forever.

Conclusion
The Enlightenment Redefined

Historians once understood the Enlightenment as the work of about twenty men, the great philosophes and their followers. The study of Voltaire, Diderot, Hume, Franklin, and the rest remains a thriving industry, particularly in English-language scholarship. It may be described as analogous to the historiographic emphasis that was once placed upon the great magisterial leaders and theologians of the sixteenth-century Protestant Reformation, Luther, Calvin, Zwingli, and so on. But in contemporary scholarship, the Reformation is now seen as a vast cultural upheaval, a social and popular movement, textured and rich because of its diversity. So too we must now begin to understand the Enlightenment.[1]

The call for a textured social and political history of the Enlightenment was first made many years ago by Franco Venturi speaking at the Trevelyan Lectures.[2] Historians working in the French Enlightenment, and especially in the Dutch, and occasionally in the Scottish Enlightenment, have gone part of the way toward answering his call (as has Venturi himself) and have done so by arriving at a more social and cultural understanding of the historical era where modern thought begins.[3] We now know a great deal about the new enclaves of enlightened sociability, about the reading societies, salons, scientific academies, and philosophical societies; so too do we know a great deal more about the disseminators and even the buyers of books which they, and we, would classify as enlightened.

Yet even more knowledge is required before Venturi's call can be satisfactorily answered. To date, and quite recently, historians of political culture in England, The Netherlands, and Germany display the greatest vitality in the project of texturing the Enlightenment. This has required innovation in both theory and research.[4] We have now begun to see eighteenth-century political culture, despite its ancien régime qualities, as being capable of revealing the sources of modernity. We have focused upon nonparliamentary, ostensibly civic forms of behavior, and discerned in them a nascent political consciousness. Most remarkably, historians of culture find in the new zone of voluntary associations the makings of civil society. We find this nascent process in radically different sets of national circumstances. Some historians detect a noticeably modern civic consciousness in voluntary associations in midcentury Britain, in clubs to promote the "useful" in the Dutch Republic, and similarly in secret societies (of both left and right) in the absolutist German states. These insights depend upon a more subtle understanding of politics than is normally found in traditional political history with its emphasis on the formal institutions of government.

Very slowly we are beginning to assess the civic meaning of the new secular culture found throughout western Europe. By searching amid the enclaves of masonic fraternizing in a variety of national histories, this book has sought to enhance the social and political tendency within Enlightenment scholarship. It has sought to demonstrate, at least in western Europe, the universal character of the Enlightenment's concern for the civic and the ideological, for contemporary issues of power, for expanding the definition of the public, both its space and who shall have access to it.

In each national setting western European elites of the eighteenth century, from minor aristocrats to merchants and literate professionals, created new forms of political consciousness that looked away from the passivity of the subject, toward the activity of the citizen, away from absolutism and oligarchy, toward more representative forms of government. The vehicle for that transition can be found in the zone of civil society created not simply in the theories of the philosophes but also in social practices, and in almost every European country from the early 1700s onward. Freemasonry, as I have attempted to show, was only the most overtly civic of the many new voluntary societies, and all the more important as a result. Its importance, especially in western Europe, was nowhere greater than in the French Enlightenment.

Two trends are observable in the recent historiography of the French Enlightenment. The first trend, and it is not unique to French history, is the turn toward the linguistic; the second, largely confined to French historiography, is known as the work of the Annales school. We shall return to its efforts to quantify the Enlightenment and to locate its adherents and promoters—the readers and publishers of enlightened books. It seems important to say something first about the turn toward the linguistic, in part because it is more recent and hence innovative, and more problematic. The search for the languages of the past, for discourse, or discourses embedded in texts—now seen by some historians as the essence of the historical experience (as best it can be reconstituted)—has many intelligent advocates and practitioners.[5] Clearly language has a great deal to do with the enterprise of the cultural historian, or for that matter any historian.[6] Language, however, is spoken by people, and therefore its meaning is socially negotiated.[7] The problem presented but not resolved by the turn toward language lies in our being able to distinguish among and between languages. If all is language, then the importance of language assumes the importance of any other absolute, for instance, the material interests postulated by Marxist historians. The determination of which language, or which material interest, achieved dominance cannot be brought any closer to understanding simply by postulating the one, or the other, as supremely important, as the medium through which, and because of which, human beings practice and negotiate power and authority.

Perhaps we need to acknowledge that all aspects of the human condition to which we give importance receive the assignment as the result of a social negotiation. This negotiation occurs over physical objects, for instance, over land and food; it also occurs over words. If the meaning of a word becomes the determinant of human action and motivation, then we must recognize that the agreement to make any set of words important is a social negotiation, that is, not a magical process and hence ultimately unknowable, but rather a process to which human speakers of language bring all that they value. Even the agreement to designate paper cut in uniform sizes and sewn together with black letters on its "pages" as a book requires a social process that engages the whole human being, as speaker, crafter, thinker, buyer, and seller.

Once so designated, of course, the book becomes a "text" by a similar, yet even more complex, process of negotiation. Once it has occurred, linguistically inclined historians get awfully interested. Texts, they intelligently argue, have a life of their own. Recently historians of the Enlightenment such as Dena Goodman have laid emphasis upon the texts of the great philosophes as dynamic entities: "I would like to know how writers might change the world through the writing of texts," she writes.[8] The political texts she analyzes are treated as actors in themselves, with both a form and content intended to transform the reader. Her analysis rightly presumes that people changed their thinking on fundamental issues in the course of the eighteenth century: "The citizens of the eighteenth century Republic of Letters were the first to see themselves in both the literary and political terms that the name of their community implies."[9] Clearly the texts of the great philosophes played a fundamental role in creating the new citizens.

Yet in placing emphasis on the enlightened text as dynamic in and of itself, how different is this from Cassirer's approach to the Enlightenment first published in 1932? In a classic work he explicated the Enlightenment's definition of reason as empirically grounded and inherently critical of orthodoxy, and he embraced it as the metaphysical reality of reason. As a true believer, Cassirer defined reason as dynamic in relation to the historical process, as "the original intellectual force which guides the discovery and determination of truth." He then analyzed the power of reason "to bind and to dissolve" in the Enlightenment.[10] For Cassirer reason became in the eighteenth century "a kind of energy, a force . . . [that] dissolves everything believed on the evidence of revelation, tradition and authority." We may wish texts to possess a similar and independent ontological existence—just what Cassirer wanted for the rationality he saw embodied in them and proclaimed by the Enlightenment. We may want the text to exist as a historical force explanatory in itself. But do texts in fact possess such an ontological standing?

Texts can be regarded as entities only if they are simultaneously understood as speech acts. Senders and receivers of speech acts (i.e., people) are not indifferent; rather, the message they give and receive "derives from its use in a determinate situation and, more precisely, in a socially structured interaction."[11] What we are doing for the Enlightenment by returning to the enclaves of sociability is attempting to recreate one of the situations of its texts, in this instance the speech acts of hundreds of fraternal speakers and listeners. But the critic may say that there are so few "great" texts being sent out or received in the lodges that we cannot any longer locate Cassirer's Enlightenment. Indeed, the critic may wish to pretend that speech acts bear no relation to texts crafted in the isolation of the study, that writing has little if anything to do with any community of sociability. This seems a facile distinction, without merit in relation to how and when people think, and how seamless a process thinking, speaking, and writing appear to be. The discourse of an age consists in countless speech acts delivered with greater or lesser formality or spontaneity, imbued with greater or lesser originality, or none at all, but at the actual moment of speaking or writing no more or less privileged. The status of the act, as well as the longevity of its impact, is the result both of the intention of its originator and of how and by whom it is received.

Clearly the many and varied voices found in the zone of the new civil society are only part of the story of the Enlightenment, one locus of enlightened acts of speech. Introducing them into the historiographic discussion, however, has the effect of enriching it. We move the discussion beyond the idealism of Cassirer, as well as beyond the proclivity toward static objectivism present in modern language theory.

The great strength of Cassirer's approach to the Enlightenment (and by analogy the methods of the historian of language) is also its weakness. The map he gave us is still useful, but it floats above the terrain, pinpointing only the tallest buildings, all the texts of the major philosophes, ignoring the many architects, master builders, and artisans who helped to create them as texts and then in new social enclaves gave them various and distinctive meanings. In Cassirer's hands the Enlightenment became reified, its texts scriptural. Asserting the independence of the text for reasons drawn from language theory may be done with the intention of avoiding the platonizing of Cassirer, but it also inhibits the creation of the master narrative that moves from text to text. This was the major strength of Cassirer's approach. Since language has its own rules, or so the most extreme exposition of the theory goes, it no longer becomes interesting to recapture the dialogue among and between texts. Cassirer, and many of the historians from the 1930s to the 1960s who wrote so convincingly about the Enlightenment, at least managed to map out its overall development, the influence of text upon text, of science upon social thought, and so forth. By contrast it is not clear what in the end binds the linguistically self-contained texts currently being postulated to a coherent and dynamic cultural movement.

In the 1960s Peter Gay gave us a magisterial synthesis of the thought of the magistrates of the Enlightenment, those twenty or so philosophes. It may prove to have been the last and best example of a genre of historical writing that is closer to Cassirer than it is to Venturi.[12] From the historiographic tradition represented by Cassirer and later and more subtly by Gay, we get the best litmus test yet devised for assessing participation in the European Enlightenment, whether conservative, moderate, or radical, namely, the willingness to accept the new science, particularly in its Newtonian form. Not least, out of the genre of what I shall call the magisterial historiography of the Enlightenment, came the sense of the philosophe as embattled, as being what Gay calls the "party of humanity."

If the texts of the great philosophes were forces hurled into space, the ultimate gravitational force that gave them a trajectory and brought them back to earth lay in the combined energy of some men and a few women brought together in the new enclaves of sociability. In the philosophical societies, the scientific academies, the salons, and, as I have argued here, most especially in the masonic lodges, the context for the text was created, discussed, and reformed, just as members were simultaneously molded, instructed, disciplined, censured, and complimented as the result of their interaction. The shared sense of the importance of their activity, reinforced by dues, ceremonies, ornaments, and decorations, as well as by libraries purchased and lectures attended, or, in the scientific academies, by nature observed and thus engaged in ways that promised control—this made some men and a few women different.

Because brought together by their cultural interests, and not by their religion or occupation or social status, sociable people were forced to negotiate as individuals. But rather than imagining them as atoms in a void, we need instead to imagine a plenum filled with atoms disguised by size, shape, color—in other words by beliefs, values, affectations, virtues, vices, and most especially by elaborately encoded marks of social and economic status. The negotiations into which sociable participants had forced themselves by virtue of their interest in finding fraternity, or conviviality, or knowledge, required rather considerable self-restraint and discipline, not to mention in the masonic case an elaborate ideology that incessantly repeated certain words: brotherhood, equality, virtue, and so on. But the words dealt with, or perhaps sought to reconcile, other social negotiations. As we have seen in past chapters many brothers did not like other brothers for reasons that were more than characterological, that had to do with power and interests, with the deep social and economic divisions of the European anciens régimes.

Once we enter into the realm of powers and interests we are face to face with the political. Thus in all the new social spaces of the eighteenth century, even in the officially sponsored French academies, historians have looked and found political language.[13] The societies, lodges, and academies inevitably created their own internal politics. They were also places where political values and ideologies from the larger society could be negotiated, discussed, and refined. In the examples we have seen from the masonic lodges the membrane between private politics and public politics could be remarkably porous. In the lodges the attentions of men were focused self-consciously on constitutions, on governance, legality, legitimacy, social order, self-improvement, and harmony. I have argued here that focusing on the civic in private and in ways that were empowering made more likely its being focused upon in the public realm.

The constitutional practices employed by the freemasons were derived from seventeenth-century England. English Whigs (as well as a few Jacobites) transmitted those practices onto the Continent. The lodges thus became one link in the chain that connects English political culture, and in particular its revolutions, to the late eighteenth-century democratic revolutions on the Continent. In the lodges from Amsterdam, Nijmegen, Liège, Paris, or Strasbourg, the old order was acutely mirrored while it was being transformed. Everything men knew about society and government through their life experiences was brought to the "work" of the lodge. Some of what they knew came from sources very old, from humanistic and classical education, but some of their knowledge also came from the philosophes. Into the mental universe of the lodge also came debates about the constitution or about despotism or about privilege, the terms of which varied from country to country and employed a multiplicity of languages. In England political discourse could be court or country, in France it could be parlementaire or monarchist, Jansenist or Rousseauian, in The Netherlands it could be patriot or Orangist. In all places in western Europe it could be republican with a strong indebtedness to the English Commonwealth tradition. Indeed, so many political vocabularies could be spoken in eighteenth-century culture that one historian has wittily labeled the process "ideo-linguistic promiscuity."[14] The lodges, like some of the other philosophical societies, brought legitimacy to these many conversations.

In addition, the greater or lesser exclusivity of all the new societies when combined with their search for wisdom or knowledge allowed their members to imagine themselves as enlightened, as completely modern, up on the latest learning or just news.[15] The experience of private sociability acted as a counterweight, even a rival, to the experience of the court, the church or corporation, guild or confraternity. But those experiences were also important in the political culture that took shape in the eighteenth century. For one thing the older forms of socializing made the new secular sociability of the eighteenth century happen more easily. We can see this most clearly in England, where Protestants long schooled in the discipline of sermon attending helped to create the audience for the scientific lecture, one so large that by midcentury dozens of lecturers were able to make a living doing nothing else.[16] Under certain circumstances traditionally religious communities could also possess political postures and articulate opposition to authoritarian or established governments or elites. Methodists and Unitarians in Britain, Mennonites in the Dutch Republic, and especially Jansenists in France could and did speak politically.[17]

Yet sometimes the older forms of fraternizing and community were hostile to the new rivals, which by the 1770s would replace them as the locus for discontent and dynamic change. Science was suspect in many religious quarters throughout much of the seventeenth and even into the eighteenth century. Whereas Unitarians and Mennonites fostered the new science, Methodists were known to attack Newton as a symbol of a social order they distrusted. Eighteenth-century Jansenists showed no particular interest in promoting the new science. Yet they were better about it than the Jesuits, their great and bitter rivals. The French Jesuits, who attacked freemasonry in their schools, never taught Newtonian science until the 1750s.[18] By then the fathers of the young men in their charge could have been meeting under the auspices of the Grand Architect of the Universe, the new version of the deity invoked by the lodges and made possible by science.

In one sense enlightened sociability should be seen as an inevitable response to the economic and commercial development of the West. Western European towns and cities were oftentimes much bigger by the middle of the eighteenth century, and more prosperous. European mastery of the world through trade, colonization, and enslavement had an impact upon the cities, and hence their cultural lives. Sociability was a refuge from the anonymous; the lodges were familiar places for merchant travelers far from home. They were also signs of surplus money, of consumption and prosperity among the upper layers of European society. The printed word in all its forms had also vastly expanded by the middle of the century, and it brought news of distant worlds with peoples of vastly differrent beliefs and values. At least one historian believes that the origin of atheism as a systematic way of thinking has to be understood in relation to the jolt international trade inflicted upon Western theology and its self-perpetuating insistence that everyone by nature believed in God.[19] Any early eighteenth-century reader of travel literature about exotic people could tell that the claim was nonsense.

The printing press and the literature it spawned far and wide cannot be separated from sociability; indeed, the first literary and philosophical societies in Britain met around gatherings of readers of *The Spectator,* a witty journal filled with the latest news from London. By the middle of the century, again, just about any heresy or critique of established authority could be printed in one of the main western European languages (French, English, and Dutch), especially if printer or author or both were prepared to be anonymous or clandestine. If worse came to worse, they circulated manuscript copies from hand to hand, often to be discussed in the Parisian salons run by women.[20] A manuscript put into circulation around 1719 (and printed then in a very limited edition) said that Jesus, Moses, and Mohammed were the three great impostors. Our masonic master Rousset de Missy concocted the edition from a variety of sources, not least Spinoza and his own imagination, and now almost every major European library has a copy of it. The manuscript had been copied over and over and circulated in every country. Eventually it was reprinted during the French Revolution complete with a new treatise showing how corrupted the old religions had been, prior to the establishment of the republic and its cult of the Supreme Being.[21]

We now know more about the printed word, its physical production, its cost, its circulation, the backgrounds of its authors and readers than did the generation of historians who wrote about the Enlightenment up until the mid-1970s. Again the most innovative work has been done by students of the French Enlightenment, for example, Robert Darnton and Daniel Roche, although some of the methods of the Annales school were anticipated by Daniel Mornet in his classic *Origines intellectuelles de la Révolution française* (Paris, 1933).[22] *Living the Enlightenment* would have been easier to write for an English-speaking audience if Mornet's book had ever been translated. All would then be familiar with the importance that he attached to the masonic lodges and the care with which he handled the subject of their role in the French Revolution. Most important he actually read the masonic records available to him; he saw the importance of the text. He did that in the early 1930s at a time when paranoia about the Jewish–Masonic conspiracy was rife in Europe, and would in the end engulf large portions of it.

Sometime between 1945 and now, freemasonry largely dropped out of serious scholarship, with some important exceptions.[23] Those I have addressed in the introduction where there is a discussion of the interpretations given to freemasonry by Furet and Koselleck, and, by extension, Halévi. The reasons for the subject's neglect in English-language scholarship are complex: the topic has been dominated by devotees and opponents, none of them very careful in their use of evidence;

secrecy has been seen to be irrational and hence freemasonry can be lumped by some with the "lunatic fringe." Not least, the lodges have ceased, at least in the United States and Britain, to be enclaves of the liberal and progressive as they were in nineteenth-century Europe. As a result, the quantitative scholarship of what is called the Annales school of Enlightenment studies has focused on the lodges in quantitative ways—in that Halévi's work is superb—but paid little attention to the content of masonic discourse or to the meaning of masonic practices. In not addressing the masonic text historians of the Enlightenment have missed the one movement of the century that embraced its progressive aspects, was quantitatively much larger in membership than the academies, and provided one of the few forums where philosophes and their followers met with men of commerce, government, and the professions. However distant from the salons of Paris, brothers consistently imagined themselves as among "the enlightened."

As a result of the impact of Annales scholarship we are left at the moment with what Aram Vartanian has described as "two Enlightenments [which] evolved, side by side, in eighteenth-century France: the intellectual one that is the subject of common knowledge [i.e., the Enlightenment of the philosophes], and a popular, essentially non-intellectual analogue, about which as yet little is known."[24] The quantitative work of the Annales historians of the French Enlightenment—and we should not leave out Michel Vovelle, who documented the decline of traditional religiosity through the study of last wills and testaments—has cracked open the door to seeing the Enlightenment as a social movement with political implications. Here I have attempted to open it more. As Vartanian observed, having these two Enlightenments is not exactly the happiest historiographic place to be. For surely they must bear relation one to the other. He reckons that there were probably no more than fifty thousand individuals in France, "most of them probably coming from the middle and upper bourgeoisie, a sizeable number from the nobility," who had their secularized religiosity formed through exposure to the writings of the philosophes. I think the estimate is a bit low; there had been perhaps thirty-five thousand men, and possibly over a thousand women, in French lodges by the 1780s.[25] But how do we get at the thinking of even a few thousand of them; where do we find the bridge between these two Enlightenments, the Enlightenment of the philosophe and the popular Enlightenment?

The Annales school has suggested that we look at the French provincial academies with about twenty-five hundred academicians in any one year as one rather narrow bridge between the two Enlightenments. Clearly, as Vartanian notes, the academies display aspects of what I call civil society. They voted, discussed, and debated, and they regarded knowledge and rhetoric as important enough to be shared and as instruments of power. These participants in the new civil society were for the most part neither major philosophes (the Royal Society in London even denied Diderot membership because of his materialism; the Dutch academy of science in Haarlem went after Joseph Priestley for similar reasons) nor the purveyors of heresy and irreligion. They were, however, progressive in relation to the material order, wanting nature studied, in some places fostering engineering projects, and they embraced the ideology of reason, order, and harmony as essential to the natural and human order.

Yet particularly in France there was an official quality to the academies. They were closely linked to the state, so closely in fact that in the Revolution they were mercilessly purged. Although one historical sociologist has tried to see the Enlightenment as a state-sponsored phenomenon, the opinion does not meet the test of historical scholarship and would have been almost laughable to many a philosophe who did time in the Bastille for what he had written, fled from the censors, often to the Dutch Republic, or just chose to live near a border.[26] The sociologist based his argument partly on the findings of the Annales school and the attention it has rightly focused on the provincial academies. The lodges, by contrast, could not even be remotely described as state sponsored. However identified they could be with king or oligarch, they occupied a space between the official and the officially suspect. In the lodges local intellectuals—with publishers as remarkably front and center in the lodges often as their orators—mixed with merchants and professionals, and these are the groups where we can find wills being dechristianized, books bought, and official institutions castigated for their backwardness. Think of the brothers in Amsterdam listening to the exiled abbé Yvon, their orator, and imagining themselves in the very presence of Diderot and his circle. With such an image in mind the Enlightenment breaks out of the circles of the philosophes, out of the provincial academies, and enters a wide spectrum of literate male, and occasionally female, society.

It also crosses every national border. France was not the only locus of the new culture of Enlightenment. One of the great strengths of the older historiography about the philosophes (master practitioners being Peter Gay, earlier Ernst Cassirer, Carl Becker, Paul Hazard, and Daniel Mornet) was their knowledge of cultures other than France. They could traverse the Atlantic, as well as the Channel, not to mention the borders through the Low Countries and of course Germany. The international perspective they brought to the study of eighteenth-century culture was in turn built upon by R. R. Palmer, who gave us a model of the late eighteenth-century revolutions in the American colonies, the Low Countries, France, Germany, Ireland, and the Austrian lands.[27] We may grow impatient with the tidiness of the international model, with all that it leaves out, with its built-in assumption that Enlightenment and Revolution universally equal progress. But surely it is a more profound historiography that writes about the late eighteenth-century revolutions from a perspective both international and sympathetic rather than one of barely concealed dislike. At the moment a few historians who write about early modern revolutions do not much like revolutions. They argue that the principles articulated in 1789 led to the Terror.[28] Arguments such as these leave the historiography of the Enlightenment with basically two choices: Detach the Enlightenment from those revolutions, in particular the French Revolution, or adopt the posture of extremists (p. 14) and condemn the Enlightenment.

For better or for worse we are the children of both Enlightenment and Revolution. Many in the postwar generation who now write history would not have been so privileged had it not been for the democratic principles first articulated in the English Revolution, both in the 1640s and again in 1689, affirmed and vastly transformed by the late eighteenth-century revolutions. One of the extraordinary achievements of the early nineteenth century in western Europe was the vast expansion of educational opportunities deeper into society, intended for both girls and boys. That expansion which we can witness from Amsterdam to Paris cannot be understood apart from the legacy of enlightened political culture as it sought to create from the 1790s on, in each country, a universal national culture. In that endeavor are present elements of the utopianism that masonic discourse could so readily express. Before the utopian elements in enlightened discourse could be transformed into the thinkable, one great break with the past had to occur. It was the French Revolution that self-consciously broke away and in the process invented modern politics.[29] The eighteenth-century antecedents of our politics and of democratic discourse must be acknowledged, and these antecedents are more readily located in the lodges than in any other form of Continental sociability.

In the final analysis freemasonry, for all of its exclusivity, secrecy, and gender bias, transmitted and textured the Enlightenment, translated all the cultural vocabularies of its members into a shared and common experience that was civil and hence political. Rather than imagining the Enlightenment as represented by the politics of Voltaire, or Gibbon, or even Rousseau, or worse as being incapable of politics,[30] we might just as fruitfully look to the lodges for a nascent political modernity. In them discourses both civic and enlightened merged and old words like fraternity and equality took on new meanings, with which in 1789 the whole of the West became suddenly familiar. Perhaps we can now better understand why opponents of the French Revolution thought they knew which of their enemies, among their many enlightened foes, was most obviously to blame for what had happened.

Notes

Introduction

1. The following account is based on Bibliothèque de l'Arsenal MS 11455, dated 1740, and most extensively on MS 11556, ff. 277–352, 1743–46. The existence of these manuscripts and their relation to others in the possession of the Vatican are noted in Jose Antonio Ferrer Benimelli, *Los Archivos Secretos Vaticano y La Masoneria,* Caracas: Universidad Catolica, 1976, pp. 86–93.

2. MS Arsenal 11556, f. 300; interrogation of Nicolas Mornay, lapidary, Catholic, aged 29, received in the lodge at the Hotel de Soissons. The master of the lodge was a merchant of wine; lodge meetings also held in the apartment of Sr. Miloir: "le but de cette assemblée etoit d'elire un maitre de loge qui se choisiroit deux surveillants avec mention que le procès verbal d'Election seroit remis en mains du secretaire G. de l'ordre le quel est le Sieur Perret Notaire. A dit qu'oui."

3. Ibid.: "que le premier de ce mois il a signé avec plusieurs autres freymaçons un acte de Convocation pour s'assembler le trois du present mois . . . et que le but de cette assemblée etoit d'elire un maitre de Loge." The same questions, and the question about who wrote the act, are posed to the next prisoner, f. 302; and the next, f. 304; same questions are asked of Joseph Potel, 27, a Catholic, employed at "la volaille," f. 298.

4. B. N., FM 184, Joly de Fleury f.75, 4 May 1744: "Toute association, de quelque genre qu'elle soit est toujours dangereuse dans un Estate, et surtout quand on y met un Secret et un apparence de Religion, qui pourroit bien cacher beaucoup de libertinage."

5. MS Arsenal 11556, f. 347, the spy Dadvenel writing on 5 February 1746: "que c'est Danguy La vielle qui y a presidé comme Le venerable, ou le Maitre de Loge; charpentier, La mussette y etoit; il y avoit un Negre qui . . . [?] du Roy une trompette des Gardes du Roy; un Sergent du Regimen du Roy. . . ." This may have been a different lodge.

6. This information comes from a remarkable set of letters written to M. Bertin du Rocheret, wine merchant and Président de l'Election in Epernay, from his brothers largely in Paris; B.N., MS Fr. 15176, ff. 17–18, 25–26, on persecution; f. 29, about two men and Chr. du Roguemont, "mousquetaire noir qui ont estes recus dans notre société."

7. Ibid., f. 228, Calviere to Bertin, 5 April 1740: "Vous trouverée notre venerable ordre,

un peu changé a votre retour; le pouvoir legislatif a passé en autres mains, plus élevées a la verité mais moins accoutumées a manier la truelle; il est même a craindre quil ne s'y glisse quelque legere ceinture de despotisme; ce qui vois le savez mieux que moy, est le poison le plus dangereux pour toutte espece de société, et le présage quasi certain de la chutte des republiques les mieux fondées." And in the 1770s when the National Grand Lodge is formed in Paris, see B.N., FM 1.118, f. 125: "il sera législateur de l'ordre en France."

8. MS Arsenal 11556, f. 312; the women were "la demoiselle Essilie, la demoiselle Navarre, la demoiselle La Guereniere, et la Dlle. Sophie." In total 28 men and four women were present at this lodge meeting. Some, but not all of these details are recounted in David Garrioch, *Neighbourhood and Community in Paris, 1740–1790,* Cambridge: Cambridge University Press, 1986, pp. 177–79.

9. MS Arsenal 11556, ff. 344–46, 30 January 1746: "La maitresse de Cabaret ou c'est tenu la loge ignore ce qui y passe chez elle comme elle est veuve, elle a un Garçon de confiance qui est francmaçon." This is from the spy d'Advenel.

10. Ibid., f. 298, asks Joseph Potel how much he paid to join the lodge, how many meetings he went to, if he had written the act of Convocation. He responded that he paid 24 livres, went to three meetings in the apartments of S. Abilon, one in a cabaret on rue Gallande owned by a widow who has "un garçon de confiance qui est francmaçon et fait tenir la loge." The last comment about the widow is from the spy. See f. 331 for particular interest in the three religious who were in the lodge. The charge of sodomy was put forward against London freemasons as early as 1723; see [Anon.,] *The Free-Masons; an Hudibrastick Poem,* London: A. Moore, 1723. Clearly, as the Bertin letters reveal, freemasons in the 1730s in France had been accused of engaging in the illicit; B.N., MS Fr. 15176, ff. 25–29.

11. MS Arsenal 11556, f. 69.

12. Ibid., f. 328, an anonymous letter to M. DeMaraille, lieutenant general of police: "ce pontif des maçons quoique tres effrayé à reconnu le miracle que ses habits augustes et pontificaux et le poche brillante de la maçonnerie ont operé sur vous quoique dans sa poche renfermé; il faut qu'un rayon de le toille flamboyante quoique eclipsée vous aye aveuglé alors par sa penetration, le grand pontif maçonnel [sic] à été alors grand prêtre, et Alexandre, grand prêtre par le miracle, et Alexandre par Lefroy, il etoit a la suitte d'un bon prussien. . . ." I am presuming that "sa poche brillante" refers to the masonic tools always present during the ceremonies—compass, level, etc. Given this evidence it seems doubtful that the police regarded this group simply as an unofficial trade association, as suggested in Garrioch, op. cit., p. 179.

13. The sentence of the police is printed in Pierre Chevallier, *Les Ducs sous L'Acacia ou Les premiers pas de la Franc-Maçonnerie française 1725–43,* Paris: Vrin, 1964, pp. 122–31, 198–99.

14. Thomas Brennan, *Public Drinking and Popular Culture in Eighteenth Century Paris,* Princeton: Princeton University Press, 1988, p. 271, citing a police prohibition dated 1727. Cf. Bibliothèque historique de la ville de Paris, MS 665, containing masonic songs and poems from the 1730s which speak of persecution.

15. Brennan, op. cit., pp. 271–72, quoting a police code from midcentury.

16. [Anon.,] *Lettre ecrite par un maçon à un de ses amis en province,* n.p., dated 20 November 1744, pp. 6–7. B.N., call no: 758.

17. *Eloge de la Maçonnerie et des Maçons; prononcé par un Frère dans une Loge qui se tint à Paris le 25 Novembre 1744,* n.p., 1744, p. 11; this tract was bound with Hp. 758 cited in note 16.

18. [Anon.,] *Lettre de M.L'abbé DF*** à Madame La Marquise de ***. Contenant le véritable Secret des Francs-Maçons,* Anvers, 1744, pp. 7, 26: "Il est de l'essence de la société que cela soit ainsi; comme il seroit de l'essence d'une Société de Dames qu'il n'y eut

point d'hommes. . . . Est-il deshonorant pour le beau Sexe de n'être point assis sur les Fleurs-de-Lys?" This tract opens with mention of the Count of Clermont and its focus is on the French situation. Its place of publication is either false or safe. Its author has been identified as the abbé Pierre Desfontaines; see Jacques Lemaire, *Les Origines françaises de l'antimaçonnisme (1744–1797),* Brussels: Editions de l'Université de Bruxelles, 1985, pp. 39–43.

19. *Eloge . . . 1744,* p. 15: "qui pourra dissiper tous ces monstres, mettre une digue aux débordemens des passions, & rétablir l'ordre parmi les humains. Loix sacrées des Maçons, c'est à vous à qui cet ouvrage est reservé; c'est à vous à faire pâlir le crime, à frapper le criminel, à defendre l'innocence, à relever la faiblesse, & à forcer les hommes à être heureux. O honte de la nature! O confusion de l'humanité! faut-il que l'homme ne puisse être libre sans être criminel? Faut-il se rendre esclave pour être vertueux? Oui, mes chers Frères, telle est notre condition, nos passions veulent des loix, nos desirs injustes & téméraires ont besoin d'un frein; pour devenir sages, il faut nous enchainer nous-mêmes: car enfin que sont nos loix, sinon un joug qu'on s'est imposé, un reméde à des maux inévitables, une défense publique d'être injuste sous peine d'être puni; mais ce joug, ce reméde, cette défense suivie de la honte pour les vrais Maçons, des menaces & des châtimens pour les prophanes, ont assuré le repos à l'Univers, la crainte de la peine a resserré la cupidité humaine, les mortels sont devenus équitables, humains, bienfaisans, à la vûe du glaive vengeur de nos loix."

20. Ibid., p. 17: "En sa présence tout change, tout se renouvelle, tout se réforme dans l'univers, l'ordre s'etablit, la régle & la mesure se font connoître, le devoir est suivi, la raison écoutée, la sagesse connue, les mortels, sans changer de nature, paroissent des hommes nouveaux."

21. Ibid., p. 18: "Quand je considere, mes Frères, pourquoi dans le monde certains états, certaines professions, n'attirent à ceux qui y sont engagés, ni honneur ni gloire, je trouve que c'est à cause du peu d'avantage que la République retire de ces mêmes états, les hommes n'attachant l'idée de grandeur qu'à ce qui leur est utile, ne donnant leur estime & leur respect qu'à ce qui contribue à leur bonheur."

22. [Anon.,] *La Muse Maçonne, ou recueil de poésies diverses, odes, cantates et discours . . . par le Fr. D*B***,* The Hague: van Laak, 1773, containing *Discours prononcé par le Grand Maitre des Francs-Maçons de France dans la Grand Lodge assemblée solemnellement à Paris. . . . 5740 [1740],* pp. 113–14. Probably delivered by the Chevalier Ramsay.

23. A 1742 painting by Cornelis Troost of Stadtholder William IV inspecting the cavalry features a Negro drummer astride a strutting black stallion at the very head of the procession. The painting is in the Rijksmuseum, Amsterdam, and I owe this information to Allison Blakely.

24. I owe the point to Garrioch, op. cit., pp. 177–78.

25. For example, see the statistics recorded by Maurice Agulhon, *Pénitents et Francs-Maçons de l'ancienne Provence,* Paris: Fayard, 1968, pp. 174–75. We can find membership lists from all over Europe that are remarkably similar to the mix that Agulhon found. For example, B.N., FM MS 552, f. 3, list for a lodge in Brussels, 1773: various officials of the Prince de Whareemberg and the Duke of Aremberg (sic), merchants (negociant), a manufacturer (fabriquant), officials of the lottery and the tottine; a lawyer. See also Hugo de Schampheleire, "L'égalitarisme maçonnique et la hiérarchie sociale dans les Pays-Bas Autrichiens," in Hervé Hasquin, ed., *Visages de la Franc-maçonnerie belge du XVIIIe au XXe siècle,* Brussels: Éditions de l'Université de Bruxelles, 1985, pp. 21–81. These statistics show the lodges admitting more men of the "middle bourgeoisie," i.e., the liberal professions, small merchants, higher level public officials, army officers, by the late 1770s in Belgium. Even in the 1780s lodges were 31 percent aristocracy.

26. B.N., MS Fr 15176, f. 43, from the late 1730s: "elles seront les premiers a blamer l'indiscretion d'un homme qui a communiqué au commun peuple qui n'estoit reservé que l'homme de merite."

27. Here I mean to disagree with Ran Halévi, *Les Loges maçonniques dans la France d'Ancien Régime aux origines de la sociabilité démocratique,* Paris: Armand Colin, 1984. See also Gary Kates, *The Cercle Social, the Girondins, and the French Revolution,* Princeton, N.J.: Princeton University Press, 1985, pp. 89–92. See also the useful comments by Marcel David, *Fraternité et Révolution Française,* Paris: Aubier, 1987, pp. 36–38.

28. On the ideology of merit and republicanism see Jonathan Scott, *Algernon Sidney and the English Republic, 1623–1677,* Cambridge: Cambridge University Press, 1988, p. 104.

29. The earliest attack I can find is in [Anon.,] *Essai sur la secte des illuminés,* Paris, 1789. The only copy I have located is in the Bibliothèque historique de la ville de Paris.

30. Ibid., p. 41: "quels que soient les travaux des Maçons, ils donnent lieu à une association; cette association entraine des assemblées; ces assemblées sont remplis par des discours éloquens; de l'éloquence religieuse au fanatisme il n'y a pas loin; ces discourse excitent le desir de connaitre." This text is repeated almost verbatim in [Anon.,] *La Loge rouge devoilée à toutes les têtes couronnées,* nouvelle edition, July 1790, p. 8.

31. *La Loge rouge,* pp. 16–17.

32. These quotations come from [Abbé Lefranc,] *Le Voile Levé pour les curieux, ou le secret de la Révolution révélé a l'aide de la Franc-maçonnerie. Ouvrage revu par l'auteur de la Conjuration contre la Religion catholique & les Souverains;* 2nd ed., Paris, 1792, pp. 6–7, 20–33, 60. For a discussion of this tract see William James Murray, *The Right-Wing Press in the French Revolution: 1789–92,* Woodbridge, Suffolk: Royal Historical Society, Boydell Press, 1986, pp. 253–56.

33. Henry More, *An Antidote against Atheism, or, An Appeal to the Natural Faculties of the Mind of Man, whether there be not a God.* The second edition corrected and enlarged . . . London, 1655, first sentence of the preface.

34. *Le Voile,* p. 62. This tract can be found at the Library of the Grand Orient, Paris, shelf no. 5161.

35. B.N., FM 1.13, f. 393, the lodge *L'Ecole des Moeurs* in Morlaix: "Dans l'ordre civil, les deputes d'une Province la representent aux assemblées générales de la Nation; il en est de même des LL." Undated, the letter is in a collection from the 1780s and could be as late as 1789. In a letter of 21 December 1789 from the lodge in Le Havre, same folder, f. 263, the parallelism is also made explicit with the lodge referring to the "national assembly" of the freemasons.

36. "Rise of the Russian New Right," *International Herald Tribune,* 1 August 1989, p. 2.

37. Abbé de Barruel, *Memoires pour servir à l'Histoire du Jacobinisme,* vol. 2, London, 1797, p. 262. For the influence of the book see Emily Lorraine de Montluzin, *The Anti-Jacobins, 1798–1800,* New York: St. Martin's Press, 1988. See also Michel Taillefer, *La Franc-Maçonnerie toulousaine: 1741–1799,* Paris: E.N.S.B.-C.T.H.S., 1984, pp. 215–22; this is probably the best French monograph on freemasonry.

38. Barruel, *Memoires,* pp. 429–31.

39. Abbé de Barruel, *Les Éclipses, Poeme en six chants, dedié à sa Majesté, Traduit en Français,* Paris, 1779, pp. ix–xii. The translation from the Latin and the preface are by Barruel. The poem is by the abbé Boscovich, who in the hyperbole of Barruel, is "a Newton in the mouth of Virgil." For his attack on materialism, [Barruel,] *Les Helviennes ou Lettres provinciales philosophiques,* Amsterdam and Paris, 1781.

40. A major exception writing in English is R. R. Palmer, *The Age of the Democratic Revolution. A Political History of Europe and America, 1760–1800,* Princeton, N.J.: Princeton University Press, 1959.

41. Abbé Barruel, *Mémoires,* vol. 2, p. 278.

42. Ibid., p. 282.

43. Ibid., p. 284.

44. Ibid., p. 278–79.

45. Michael Roberts, "Liberté, Egalité, Fraternité: Sources and development of a slogan," *Tijdschrift voor de Studie van de Verlichting* 4, no. 3–4 (1976): 329–69.

46. Palmer, op. cit., vol. 2, p. 180.

47. Clarence Crane Brinton, *The Jacobins. An Essay in the New History,* New York: Russell and Russell, 1961, p. 14.

48. Kates, op. cit., pp. 91–92.

49. François Furet, *Interpreting the French Revolution.* Translated by E. Forster, New York: Cambridge University Press, 1981, p. 179.

50. Ibid., p. 179. Furet refers here to the type of political man who would be needed, and who was found among the Jacobins, to actualize the transition from philosophical power to political power.

51. See Halévi, op. cit.

52. Daniel Roche, *Le siècle des lumières en province. Académies et académiciens provinciaux, 1680–1789,* vol. 1, Paris: Mouton, 1978, p. 264.

53. Lucien Jaume, *Le discours jacobin et la démocratie,* Paris: Fayard, 1989, p. 40, citing Cochin.

54. Introduction by Pierre Chaunu, in André Delaporte, *L'Idée d'Égalité en France au XVIIIe siècle,* Paris: Presses Universitaires de France, 1987, p. xi.

55. Ibid., p. 50. For a postwar example of right-wing conspiracy theory and the freemasons see Pierre Saint-Charles, *La F.M. au Parlement,* Paris: La Librairie Française, n.d. but from the citations the late 1950s.

56. Reinhart Koselleck, *Critique and Crisis. Enlightenment and the Pathogenesis of Modern Society,* Cambridge: MIT Press, 1988, p. 80. (Originally published in German in 1959.)

57. Ibid., pp. 81, 85.

58. Ibid., p. 91.

59. Ibid., p. 132.

60. Ibid., p. 133.

61. Ibid., p. 165.

62. Ibid., p. 166.

63. Ibid., pp. 184–85.

64. B.N., MS FM 1.94, ff. 22–58. The manuscript is dated 1735. We find, for example, f. 26: "La pluralité des membres de chaque loge assemblée auront le privilege de donner des instructions à leurs maitres et surveillans avant l'assemblée du chapitre ou loge generale . . . et aussi avant l'assembée annuelle, et de la grande loge, parce que leurs maitres et surveillants sont leurs representants et doivent annonces leurs sentimens . . . toutes choses doivent être faits, et determines dans la grande loge a la pluralité de voix, chaque membre en ayant une, et le Grand Maitre deux"; f. 34: "l'election"; f. 58: "le gouvernement de G.M. Philipe Duc de Wharton."

65. See, for example, *Discours prononcé le jour de S. Joseph devant une assemblée de Maçons civils et militaires . . . Par le Fr.,* Liège, 1785.

66. A similar point is made in David, op. cit., pp. 36–40.

67. Scholarship on such lodges has been available since the 1960s. See Régine Robin-Aizertin, "Franc-maçonnerie et Lumières à Semur-en-Auxois en 1789," *Revue d'histoire économique et sociale* 43 (1965): 234–41. Cf B.N., FM MS 1.14, f. 351, 10 May 1790, with the Grand Orient presenting f. 1371 to the National Assembly.

68. Quoted from Michael L. Kennedy, *The Jacobin Clubs in the French Revolution. The*

First Years, Princeton, N.J.: Princeton University Press, 1982, p. 300–301. My italics. On civil society as a concept see Charles Taylor, "Modes of Civil Society," *Public Culture,* 3 (1990): 95–118.

69. Furet, op. cit., p. 176.

70. *Commission pour la bicentenaire de la Revolution Française. L'Image de la Revolution Française. Programme. Sorbonne 6–12 Juillet 1989.*

71. Bibliothèque Municipale, Reims, manuscripts of Pierre Prieur, MS 1940, no. 58, a discourse spoken before a lodge of exiles in Belgium, 1818; and no. 72, where this new direction freemasonry took is given the precise date of 1646. On Prieur in the Revolution, see Pierre Lamarque, *Les Francs Maçons aux États Généraux de 1789 et à l'Assemblée Nationale,* Paris: EDIMAT, 1981.

72. Furet, op. cit., p. 198.

73. Ibid., p. 187.

74. Johel Coutura, "L'Activité d'une loge de Bordeaux entre 1780 et 1782," *Dix-Huitième siècle,* no. 21 (1989): 267. Evidence found in a manuscript recently discovered and available at the Library of the Grand Orient, Paris.

75. H. Rodermond, *De Vrijmetselaarsloge La Bien Aimée, Amsterdam, 1745–1985,* The Hague: Maçonnieke Stichting Ritus en Tempelbouw, 1985, p. 38; Photograph of the Visitors Book for that year, which does indeed show the signature of Marat.

76. Jürgen Habermas, *The Structural Transformation of the Public Sphere. An Inquiry into a Category of Bourgeois Society,* Cambridge: MIT Press, 1989, pp. 50–52. (German edition first appeared in 1962.)

77. Ibid., p. 35. Cf. Benjamin Nathans, "Habermas's 'Public Sphere' in the Era of the French Revolution," *French Historical Review* 16 (1990): 620–44.

78. On this point see Joan B. Landes, *Women and the Public Sphere in the Age of Englightenment,* Ithaca, N.Y.: Cornell University Press, 1988, pp. 17–65.

Chapter 1

1. [Anon.,] *La Franc-Maçonne ou Revelation des Mysteres des Francs-Maçons par Madame***,* Brussels, 1744, pp. 18–19. Note the interesting, although doubtful, claim that this tract is by a woman. On p. 68 it is mentioned that a Jew is turned down for membership. Cf. [Anon.,] *L'Ordre les Francs-Maçons Trahi,* Amsterdam, 1747 (1st ed., 1745); this tract also raises the specter of Cromwell, and it was widely reprinted and translated into Dutch and German; see University Library, Leiden, Marchand MSS 44:2, f. 64, for a discussion of it and Rousset de Missy's answer to it. For a general discussion of this early antimasonry and some of its authors, see Jacques Lemaire, *Les Origines françaises de l'antimaçonnisme (1744–1797),* Brussels: Editions de l'Université de Bruxelles, 1985.

2. See Harry Carr, ed., *The Early French Exposures,* London: Quatuor Coronati Lodge, 1971, pp. 282, 291. The text is [Anon.,] *Les Francs-Maçons ecrasés,* Amsterdam, 1747. This was an elaborate account that went into great detail as to the supposed link between Cromwell and the freemasons. Its preface is clearly directed against Rousset de Missy. The tract made an impact later in the century among those who saw the freemasons as responsible for the Continental revolutions. See the notes taken by a freemason concerned with the upheavels in German freemasonry late in the century; Gemeente Archief, Amsterdam, Backer MSS, P.A. 172.765.

3. [Anon.,] *Le mal epidémique des Francs-Maçons* [, 1748]; copy to be found in Margaret C. Jacob, ed., *Freemasonry. Early Sources on Microfiche, 1717–1870. From the*

Grand Lodge Library in The Hague, Leiden: Interdocumentation, FVR-3.8/1. This is an extremely rare pamphlet which turned up in a Dutch collection. The original is in The Hague.

4. [Anon.,] *Le Voile Levé pour les curieux, ou le secret de la Révolution révélé à l'aide de la Franc-Maçonnerie,* 2d ed., Paris, 1792, pp. 7–8. The first edition is from 1791.

5. *Les vrais jugemens sur la Société des Francs-Maçons . . . ,* Brussels, 1752, p. 2; this tract prints in French the Bull of 1738. It can be found readily in Jacob, op. cit., FVR-3.16/1. On the lack of knowledge of the bull, or interest in it when known in Belgium and France during the eighteenth century, see Pierre Cockshaw, "Observations sur les deux premières bulles de condamnation des Francs-Maçons (1738 et 1751) et leur réception dans nos régions," in H. Hasquin, ed. *Visages de la franc-maçonnerie belge du xviiie au xxe siècle,* Brussels: Editions de l'Université de Bruxelles, 1985, pp. 73–87. For copies of the 1738 and 1751 encyclicals see Georges Virebeau, *Les Papes et la Franc-Maçonnerie,* Paris: Documents et Témoignages, 1977, pp. 15–20.

6. Kloss MSS 240.E.95, unfoliated: "quelques enthousiasts ont voulu ajouter une d? epoque, contenant l'histoire de la révolution faite en Angleterre [?] ai Olivier Cromwel, parcequil avoit relevé l'ordre. Mais quel rapport la malheureuse catastrophe de Charles I a-t-elle avec le temple et ses deffenseurs? Ce feroit faire de notre ordre l'intendant de la rebellion!" Cromwell is said to have revived the freemasons in another manuscript history, Depôt complet des Connaissances de la Franche-Maçonnerie, 1776, f. 1. (over 500 folios). This manuscript also has the story about the Jesuits and the effort to associate freemasonry with rebellion. See also chapter 6.

7. [Anon.,] *Considérations filosofiques sur la Franc-Maçonnerie. Dédie à tous les Oriens en France, par un Député de Jérusalem,* Hambourg, 1776 [clearly Paris]. It is just conceivable that this is an antimasonic work as the tone is ambiguous. The Cromwell story appears among the papers of a Dutch freemason of the 1780s; see Gemeente Archief, Amsterdam, Backer MSS, P.A. 172, p. 87, and P. A. 172.765.

8. Johel Coutura, "L'Activité d'une loge de Bordeaux entre 1780 et 1782," *Dix-Huitième siècle,* no. 21 (1989): 273.

9. *Etat du G.O. De France,* vol. 1, second part, 1777, pp. 92–94.

10. [Anon.,] *Premièrs discours prononcé dans la cent vingt-unième assemblée . . . de la R.L. des Amis-réunis, au nom des Membres à tous Grades . . . 22 Fev. 1778,* pp. 29–30 (*Discours prononcé . . . .* 1780). Written in praise of the masonry advocated by Count Zinnendorf.

11. Bibliothèque Municipale, Dijon, MS 1279, "Recueil de pièces concernant la Franc-Maçonnerie," Fonds Baudot, ff. 63–65, "Discours 10 9bre 1765": "Les Roix les princes les seigneurs en revenant de la palestine dans leur pays y etablirent des loges on voit de la plusieurs loges erigées en Allemagne en Italie en Espagne en France en Angleterre et en Ecosse. Jacques lord Stuard fut grand Maitre d'une loge etabli à Kevenuller ou Kilwinning. . . ." This is copied from Ramsay's discourse published in 1738; for a facsimile copy see G. van Veen, "Andrew Michael Ramsay," *Thoth* 28, no. 2 (1977): 27–57. There is a manuscript translation of Ramsey's discourse in Dutch; Library of the Grand Lodge, The Hague, MS 123.B.4.

12. E. F. Bazot, *Manuel du Franc-Maçon,* 3d ed., Paris, 1817, p. 95; and for the Druids, p. 89.

13. Library of the Grand Lodge, The Hague, MS 122.C.10, unfoliated.

14. *Rede so ben der Aufnahme Zweener Candidaten in den Freymaurerorden gehalten worden,* 1784, n.p., p. 4; while at the same time proclaiming the peace and quiet of the state.

15. F. C. Heitz, *Les Sociétés politiques de Strasbourg pendant les années 1790 à 1795. Extraits de leurs procés-verbaux,* Strasbourg, 1863, p. 2.

16. For the 1740 discourse of Chevalier Ramsay that sets forth this history from the time

of the Crusades see [Anon.,] *La Muse Maçonne, ou Recueil de poésies diverse, odes, cantates et discourse, par le Fr. D* B****, The Hague: Van Laak, 1773, pp. 113–19. This is the same oration that calls for "a vast work" to bring together all the world's learning. Copies turn up in Reims, The Hague, and Dijon.

17. Library of the Grand Lodge, The Hague, MS 122.C.42, f. 6, dated 1781: "Ce nom même dans un siecle plus prochain a produit une plus grande erreur. Des revolutions ayant dispercees pour quelques lustres la société maçonne, les bijoux s'etant egarés ils n'ont pas avoir l'intelligence d'en faire la recherche dans d'autres loges plus eloignees qui n'avoient point essuiés des semblables évenements." This ceremony is from Maastricht.

18. Gunnar von Proschwitz, "Constitutionel. Anglicisme ou mot français?," in *Idées et Mots au siècle des lumières. Mélanges,* Paris: Jean Touzot, 1988, p. 73. The first quotation is from *The Craftsman,* the second from the *London Journal,* both from 1734.

19. See Margaret C. Jacob, *The Radical Enlightenment: Pantheists, Freemasons, and Republicans,* London: George Allen and Unwin, 1981, pp. 110–11.

20. W. McLeod, "More Light on John Coustos," *Ars Quatuor Coronatorum,* 95 (1982): 117–19; cf. *Procedures curieuses de l'Inquisition de Portugal . . . revues & publiees par L.T.V.I.L.R.D.M.*, MMDCCCIII (probably 1744, and R.D.M. may be Rousset de Missy).

21. See the Waldegrave MSS, Chewton Mendip, Somerset; cited by the kind permission of Lord and Lady Waldegrave.

22. See the comments of Linda Colley, *American Historical Review,* June 1990, p. 818. Cf. Paul K. Monod, *Jacobitism and the English People, 1688–1788,* Cambridge, UK: Cambridge University Press, 1989.

23. See Ran Halévi, "L'idée et l'événement. Sur les origines intellectuelles de la Révolution française," *Le Débat,* no. 38 (January/March 1986): 145–63.

24. [Anon.,] *La Reception mysterieuse. Des Membres de la celebre Société des Francs-Maçons contenant une Relation generale & sincere de leurs ceremonies. Par Samuel Prichard . . . suivie de Quelques autres Pièces curieuses, relative à la Grande Bretagne, avec des Observations historiques & Geographiques . . . ,* London: Par la Compagnie des Libraires, 1738, pp. 52–54. The additions to Prichard begin at the end of page 50 and go on for over 100 pages. For convenient access to the original Prichard text see Harry Carr, ed., *Samuel Prichard's Masonry Dissected, 1730. An Analysis and Commentary,* vol. 8, Bloomington, Ill.: Masonic Book Club, 1977. Rousset de Missy is not an impossible candidate for authorship of this French tract. The dates and place are right, and he was one of the few freemasons who had that kind of grasp on seventeenth-century history.

25. *La Reception mysterieuse,* pp. 56–57: "A prendre dans un sens politique ces deux mots joints ensemble, ils souffrent tout autre explication. La Société qui en a choisi les qualités, attachées separement à chaque partie de ce composé, se pique d'une grande liberté, d'une franchise en leurs manieres."

26. Ibid., p. 23. The publisher listed in the back of this tract, Jacques Jacob, did operate in Liège at this time; see Chev. De Theux De Montjardin, ed., *Bibliographie Liègeoise,* Nieuwkoop: De Graff, 1973, listed for 1738. Reprint of the 1885 edition of this bibliography.

27. *La Reception mysterieuse,* pp. 46–47.

28. Souverain Chapitre Charles Magnette de la Parfaite Intelligence et l'Etoile Reunies, *Liège. Loges et chapitres du xviiie au xxe siècle,* Liège, 1985, pp. 9–18. (Privately printed.) A merchant from Liège was identified by the Inquisition in Portugal as a freemason in the early 1740s. It remained a safe haven for some decades to come, although in 1781 the French authorities actually violated its border in order to confiscate dangerous books; see Jeremy Popkin, "Pamphlet Journalism at the End of the Old Regime," *Eighteenth Century Studies* 22 (1989): 363.

29. See *Recit historique,* esp. pp. 25–27, bound with *La Reception mysterieuse,* London,

1738. Note the emphasis on Namur and its role as a barrier fortress; in this period the Duc d'Ursel was head of its Estates General and, according to a letter by Rousset de Missy, also head of a lodge.

30. [Anon.,] *Apologie Pour l'Ordre des Francs-Maçons*. Par Mr. N. . . , The Hague: Pierre Gosse, 1742, pp. 27–28.

31. For an examination of the link between the impulse toward secretive fraternizing and the desire for revolution, see James H. Billington, *Fire in the Minds of Men. Origins of the Revolutionary Faith,* New York: Basic Books, 1980.

32. Coutura, op. cit., pp. 266–67; based upon the recently discovered records of a lodge in Bordeaux, 1780–82.

33. See Thomas Devine, "The Merchant Class of the Larger Scottish Towns in the Later Seventeenth and Early Eighteenth Centuries," in G. Gordon and B. Dicks, eds., *Scottish Urban History,* Aberdeen: Aberdeen University Press, 1983, pp. 93–97.

34. Ministère des affaires étrangéres, Paris, Archives des affaires étrangères, Angleterre. Mémoires et Documens, vol. 8, ff. 187–97, "Etat de la Religion en Angleterre. Par raport à la Doctrine & à la politique"; contains descriptions of deists, atheists, etc.

35. *The Constitutions of the Free-Masons. Containing the History, Charges, Regulations, &c. of that most Ancient and Right Worshipful Fraternity. For the Use of the Lodges,* London: Printed by William Hunter, for John Senex . . . , London, in the Year of Masonry, 5723; Anno Domini, 1723, p. 68.

36. Ibid., p. 33. Note this early usage of "politics" by a Jacobite pamphleteer: [John Ferguson,] A.B. *A Letter to Mr Secretary Trenchard, discovering a conspiracy against the Laws and Ancient Constitution,* London, 1694, p. 10: "a man may be treated as a traytor against King William . . . for maybe a piece of Banter upon the Green-Ribbon Secretary, or a Lampoon upon the mighty statesman, perfect in the Politicks by the Degrees he took at the Rose-Club [a Whig society]."

37. [Anon.,] *The Constitutions of the Free-Masons. Containing the History, Charges, Regulations, &c. of that most Ancient and Right Worshipful Fraternity. For the Use of the Lodges,* London, 1723, preface, passim. The compilation of the text and preface is universally attributed to James Anderson. There were other secret fraternities in the period that laid claim to no such elaborate history. See, for example, University Library, Cambridge, MSS ADD 5340 for the records of the Zodiac Club, 1725–42, which existed to help its members gain preferment in the church.

38. [Anon.,] *The Constitutions of the Ancient and Honourable Fraternity of Free and Accepted Masons* . . . , Worcester, 1792, pp. 49, 137.

39. We can watch this evolution in [Anon.,] *La Reception mysterieuse* . . . , London, 1738, p. 60, where "étranger" is explicated in a footnote as "les profanes," and p. 37, where "cowan," used in the Prichard text, is translated "étranger." The term may come from the old masonic catechisms where brothers are shocked "to see any of their Brethren profane or break through the sacred Rules of the Order." See Douglas Knoop, G. P. Jones, and Douglas Hamer, eds., *The Early Masonic Catechisms,* Manchester: Manchester University Press, 1963, p. 24.

40. David Stevenson, *The First Freemasons. Scotland's Early Lodges and Their Members,* Aberdeen: Aberdeen University Press, 1988; and Stevenson, *The Origins of Freemasonry. Scotland's Century, 1590–1710,* Cambridge: Cambridge University Press, 1988; both books arrived after this chapter had been written but in sufficient time to permit their conclusions to be evaluated.

41. Stevenson, *The Origins of Freemasonry,* pp. 94–96.

42. Frances Yates, *Giordano Bruno and the Hermetic Tradition,* London: Routledge & Kegan Paul, 1964; and her *The Rosicrucian Enlightenment,* London: Paladin, 1975.

43. The quotation is from [Anon.,] *The Secret History of the Free-Masons. Being an Accidental Discovery, of the ceremonies Made Use of in the several Lodges . . .* , 2d ed., London, 1725, p. iii; this tract prints a portion or version of the Old Changes with the references to Hermes. For papal polemics see [Anon.,] *Les vrais jugemens sur la société des Francs-Maçons,* Brussels, 1752.

44. *The Book Of the Antient Constitutions of The Free & Accepted Masons,* London, 1726, pp. 6–7. Reprinted in John E. Cox, ed., *The Old Constitutions,* London: Richard Spencer, 1871.

45. [Anon.,] *The Objections of the Non-subscribing London Clergy against the Address from the Bishop of London,* London: A. Baldwin, 1710, p. 3; the remark is made in passing. I owe this reference to John Hammond.

46. See Alexander Skene, *Memorials For the Government of the Royall-Burghs in Scotland,* Aberdeen, 1685, pp. 66–69. I owe the reference to Gordon DesBrisay.

47. L. R. S. Shelby, "The Role of the Master Mason in Medieval English Building," *Speculum* 39 (1964): 387–403; and Shelby, "The Education of Medieval English Master Masons," *Mediaeval Studies* 32 (1970): 1–26.

48. Stevenson, *The First Freemasons,* p. 30. Cf. Harry Carr, *Lodge Mother Kilwinning. No. O. A Study of the Earliest Minute Books,* London: Quator Coronati Lodge, 1961, which documents the same process at work in Kilwinning, even earlier than in Dundee.

49. B.L., MSS ADD 3848, ff. 179–85, "History of Masonry," 1646, by Edward Shankey, where all these points are made and elaborated upon.

50. Elias Ashmole, *Memoirs of the Life of that Learned Antiquary . . . Published by Charles Burman, Esq.,* London, 1717, p. 15. Ashmole was in turn close to the Oxford antiquarian of the next generation, John Aubrey, who discussed with the freethinker John Toland the meaning of the Druids and Stonehenge; cf. Michael Hunter, *John Aubrey and the Realm of Learning,* London: Duckworth, 1975, pp. 59, 205n. Note also Randle Holme's claim that he is a mason; Randle Holme, *The Academy of Armory, or A Storehouse of Armory and Blazon. Containing the several variety of Created Beings, and how born in Coats of Arms,* vol. 3, Chester, 1688, p. 393.

51. David Stevenson, "Masonry, Symbolism and Ethics in the Life of Sir Robert Moray, FRS," *Proceedings of the Society of Antiquaries of Scotland* 114 (1984): 407–8.

52. Ibid., pp. 419–25.

53. Alex. J. Warden, ed., *Burgh Laws of Dundee with the History, Statutes and Proceedings of the Guild of Merchants and Fraternities of Craftsmen,* London, 1872, p. 167, for 1697–99.

54. Ibid., p. 186.

55. Ibid., p. 177.

56. Ibid., pp. 193–94.

57. Anthony Black, *Guilds and Civil Society in European Political Thought from the Twelfth Century to the Present,* Ithaca, N.Y.: Cornell University Press, 1984, p. 43. See also the comments of Daniel Mornet on the way in which freemasonry was embedded in the French ancien régime: Daniel Mornet, *Les Origines intellectuelles de la Révolution française (1715–1787),* Paris: Armand Colin, 1933, pp. 375–87.

58. Archives and Record Center, Dundee, Scotland, MS Dundee Mason Trade, Lockit Book, 1659–1960, unfoliated, here cited by date. I am indebted to Roger Emerson for bringing the existence of this archive to my attention. On this process in other places in Scotland see "Our Predecessors—Scottish Masons of about 1660," by A. C. F. Jackson, in *Yearbook of the Grand Lodge of Antient Free and Accepted Masons of Scotland,* Edinburgh, published by the Grand Lodge of Scotland, 1980. In Warden, op. cit., this passage is curiously interpreted to apply only to payment of money instead of dinner. But more is stated in the text as quoted; see Warden, p. 580.

59. The term craft guilds is more correctly English than Scottish. The Scots would say "craft" or "trade." I owe this point to Gordon DesBrisay.

60. Warden, op. cit., pp. 262–63.

61. Archives and Record Centre, Dundee, MS GD/GRW/M 2/1, entry dated 3 May 1711, "from James Cox in part of his freedom, 16:13:4." Total income for that year appears to have been 49 pounds. Pounds Scots should be divided by 12 for the equivalent pounds sterling. In the late seventeenth century skilled masons could be paid 3.5 to 5 pounds Scots per week. For a description of the Dundee lodge, see Stevenson, *The First Freemasons,* pp. 94–97. I am grateful to Gordon DesBrisay for assistance with this paragraph.

62. William Mackay Mackenzie, *The Scottish Burghs,* Edinburgh: Oliver and Boyd, 1949, p. 69, citing a charter of 1364. Occasionally "freedom" and "liberty" were used interchangeably in the sixteenth century, p. 135. Note that women were occasionally admitted as burgesses, p. 140.

63. Stevenson, *The First Freemasons,* p. 97. One version of the *Constitutions,* now extremely rare, *The Old Constitutions Belonging to the Ancient and Honourable Society of Free and Accepted Masons,* London: J. Roberts, 1722, pp. 16–17, encouraged workers to protect their wages and labor and absolutely forbade a mason from taking over the work of another.

64. Bodleian Library, Oxford, MS Rylands, d. 9, pp. 119 et seq., giving names and occupations.

65. Mackenzie, *The Scottish Burghs,* pp. 186, 189–90, noted in 1721 and 1735.

66. On this process see Eric Wehrli, Jr., "Scottish Politics in the Age of Walpole," Ph.D. diss., University of Chicago, 1983, pp. 10–11.

67. Dundee, *Charter, Writs and Public Documents of the Royal Burgh of Dundee . . .* 1292–1880, Dundee, 1880, pp. 147–49. For the workhouse, see Warden, p. 190, and p. 191 on famine in the vicinity.

68. James Thomson, *The History of Dundee,* Dundee: Durham and Son, 1874, p. 134.

69. Warden, op. cit., pp. 191–92.

70. Thomson, op. cit., p. 119. There is little correlation between the names of known Jacobites in 1745 and the membership lists of the freemasons, yet note that the name of one Thomas Blair, merchant, can be found in both.

71. David Allen, "Political Clubs in Restoration London," *Historical Journal* 19 (1976): 561–80. The association of freemasonry with Whiggery was continued by the Tories; see Simon Robertson Vasey, "The Craftsman, 1726–1752, An Historical and Critical Account," Ph.D. diss., University of Cambridge, 1976, pp. 58, 184ff. Cf. Linda J. Colley, "The Loyal Brotherhood and the Cocoa Tree: The London Organization of the Tory Party, 1727–1760," *Historical Journal* 20 (1977): 77–95.

72. Clerk to the Mason Trade, Dundee Mason Trade, Lockit Book, 1659–1960, unfoliated, but dated nearly annually from 1659. For similar language see Carr, *Lodge Mother Kilwinning,* pp. 27–28; yet see also pp. 34 and 186, where the term "elected" is used in 1645 and henceforth appears intermittently and is synonymous with "chosen." Its usage begins to take on the modern meaning in the 1670s as gentry began to take office in the lodge.

73. Dundee Mason Trade, Register of entries of Masters and Journeymen, 1659–1779, MS GD/GRW/M3/1, 28 December 1667. For the right to confer those privileges see the records of the Register of Deeds of the Burgh of Dundee, vol. 26, pp. 903–5, dated 1659, printed in *Ars Quatuor Coronatorum* 99 (1986): 194–95.

74. Thomson, op. cit., p. 255. Guildsmen could also refer to their "libertys," a term interchangeable with "freedom"; see Warden, op. cit., pp. 584 et seq. on the wrights.

75. Dundee Mason Trade, Lockit Book, entry for 27 December 1708.

76. I owe the point about local government to Gordon DesBrisay. See his "Authority and Discipline in Aberdeen: 1650–1700," Ph.D. diss., St. Andrews University, 1989.

77. Dundee Mason Trade, Lockit Book, 27 December 1734: a doctor, a merchant, and two men of "honourable" rank.

78. Ibid., p. 125. He introduced potatoes for sale in 1753.

79. Lockit Book, 27 December 1734.

80. Ibid., 3 January 1735.

81. Carr, *Kilwinning,* pp. 193–95.

82. Ibid., pp. 228–29.

83. B.A. MS 6, f. 11, from Rousset de Missy, 11 April 1756, "La lettre de notre institution etoit du Venerable Linslager, maistre de la loge de Leuwarde, qui en avoit reçu la permission d'Ecosse."

84. Sederunt Book, 1736–1807, 27 December 1737.

85. Ibid., 5 November 1761.

86. Register of entries of Masters and Journeymen, 1659–1779, entry for 27 November 1659.

87. Dundee Lockit book, 1659–1960, f. 1; cited by Stevenson, *The First Freemasons,* p. 197, as Inventory 13.1.

88. On the older, less formal procedure of the "essay and sufficient tryall," see Carr, op. cit., p. 24.

89. B. P. Lenman, "The Industrial History of the Dundee Region from the Eighteenth to the Early Twentieth Century," in S. J. Jones, ed., *Dundee and District,* Dundee: British Association for the Advancement of Science, 1968, p. 163.

90. David Rollinson, "Property, Ideology and Popular Culture in a Gloucestershire Village, 1660–1740," *Past and Present,* no. 93 (1981): 70–79. Cf. Peter Burke, *Popular Culture in Early Modern Europe,* New York: New York University Press, 1978.

91. On the rhetoric of liberalism, see William M. Reddy, *Money and Liberty in Modern Europe,* New York: Cambridge University Press, 1987, pp. 76–78.

92. Warden, op. cit., p. 582, citing the manuscript sources of the Dundee masons for 1684 and the admission of one Captain Andrew Smyton, one of the earliest nonmasons to be admitted.

93. See Mary Ann Clawson, *Constructing Brotherhood. Class, Gender, and Fraternalism,* Princeton, N.J.: Princeton University Press, 1989, p. 14. This book, which arrived after most of my book was written, comes to many of the same generalizations.

94. See Jacob, *The Radical Enlightenment,* pp. 130–31. On the early masonic usage of the term "constitutions" see B.L., MS Sloane, 3329, f. 142, "A Narrative of the Freemasons words and signs," here referring to "Charges in ye Constitution" clearly written in a guild context, but in a hand dating from midcentury. It may be related to MS Register Book (C), IX, ff. 240–52, Royal Society of London.

95. For a copy of the major portion of Anderson's text, see Jacob, *The Radical Enlightenment,* pp. 279–87.

96. Bristol Record Office, Bristol, U.K., MS 20535(291). Warrant dated 1738 from the Grand Lodge in London to permit the establishment of a lodge in Tewkesbury; reply from Edward Popham accepting these conditions, same date. For mention of this lodge, see T. O. Haunch, "The Formation, 1717–51," in United Grand Lodge of England, *Grand Lodge, 1717–1967,* Oxford: Oxford University Press, 1967, p. 85.

97. Bristol Record Office, MS 20535(291), unfoliated.

98. Ibid. The discussion of secrets, virtues, and the duties of subjects and fathers is from a charge given for the year 1739 at the election of officers for 1740. The speaker is the master, one E. Popham, of the lodge in Tewkesbury.

99. Ibid., "A Charge by the Master for the Year 1740 at the Election of Officers for the Year 1741," f. 13.

100. Ibid., f. 4: five shillings to be paid by each member, each quarter; two guineas plus a sum "for clothing," i.e., gloves and other items of regalia, upon admission.

101. Jacob, *The Radical Enlightenment,* pp. 130–37.

102. Black, op. cit., p. 43. See also the comments of Daniel Mornet, op. cit., pp. 375–87, on the way in which freemasonry was embedded in the French ancien régime.

103. Heather Swanson, "The Illusion of Economic Structure: Craft Guilds in Late Medieval English Towns," *Past and Present,* no. 121 (November 1988): 39.

104. Ibid., p. 26.

105. D. Knoop, G. P. Jones, and D. Hamer, eds., *The Wilkinson Manuscript,* privately printed, 1946, p. 33, quoting from a masonic catechism of the 1720s, but possibly from an earlier date.

106. Black, op. cit., p. 153.

107. *Constitutions,* London, 1723, pp. 35–36.

108. Black, op. cit., part 3.

109. John Money, "Freemasonry and the Fabric of Loyalism in Hanoverian England," in Eckhart Hellmuth, ed., *The Transformation of Political Culture. England and Germany in the Late Eighteenth Century,* The German Historical Institute, London: Oxford University Press, 1990. I have been helped in thinking about this chapter by Mary Douglas, *How Institutions Think,* Syracuse, N.Y.: Syracuse University Press, 1986, esp. pp. 46–47.

110. Philip Jenkins, "Jacobites and Freemasons in Eighteenth Century Wales," *Welsh Historical Review* 9 (1979): 391–406.

Chapter 2

1. Rev. William Martin Leake, *A Sermon preached at St. Peter's Church in Colchester on Tuesday, June 24, 1777 . . .* Colchester, 1778, pp. 14–15. For an account of operative masonry in London as late as 1708, see [Anon.,] *A New View of London; or an Ample account of that city . . . ,* London, 1708, p. 611.

2. See Peter Borsay and Angus McInnes, "Debate: The Emergence of a Leisure Town: Or an Urban Renaissance?," *Past and Present,* no. 126 (1990): 189–202: "The fact that two historians have found evidence of vitality and major movement within the urban sector is the overriding issue."

3. Mona Ozouf, *L'École de la France. Essais sur la Révolution, l'utopie et l'enseignement,* Paris: Gallimard, 1984, pp. 268–70.

4. See Reed Browning, *Political and Constitutional Ideas of the Court Whigs,* Baton Rouge: Louisiana State University Press, 1982, chapter 7.

5. Paul K. Monod, *Jacobitism and the English people, 1688–1788:* Cambridge, Cambridge University Press, 1989, pp. 300–305.

6. Leake, op. cit., p. 19.

7. See Margaret C. Jacob, *The Radical Enlightenment: Pantheists, Freemasons, and Republicans,* London: George Allen and Unwin, 1981, p. 280, for the text of Anderson's *Constitutions* (1723).

8. Gregory F. Scholtz, "Anglicanism in the Age of Johnson: The Doctrine of Conditional Salvation," *Eighteenth Century Studies* 22 (1988–89): 191–93.

9. [Anon.,] *Select Orations on Various Subjects; viz. The Divinity and Sublime of Masonry, as display'd in the Sacred Oracles,* London, printed for John Tillotson, 1737, p. 8. The copy in the Library of the Grand Lodge, London, has the tract ascribed to Orator Henley.

10. For this sort of patriotic sentiment, see a typical annual almanac, *The Freemasons' Calendar or an Almanac, for the Year of Christ 1776,* London, 1776, pp. 45–46.

11. A similar point is made in Kathleen Wilson, "Inventing Revolution: 1688 and Eighteenth-Century Popular Politics," *Journal of British Studies* 28 (1989): 353–54.

12. One of the more convenient places to get at this literature is in Rev. G. Oliver, *The Golden Remains of the Early Masonic Writers,* 4 vols., London, 1847. For songs, see C. Brockwell, *A Collection of Freemasons' Songs. To Which Is Prefixed A General Charge to Masons,* London, 1904.

13. Rev. Brother James Smith, *A Sermon preached at the Chapel in Deal . . . 1779 before the Provincial Grand Lodge of Kent,* Canterbury, 1779, p. 5.

14. Oliver, op. cit., vol. 1, p. 267; see also Rev. Thomas Davenport, *Love to God and Man Inseparable. A Sermon preached before . . . the Society of Free and Accepted Masons . . . 1764,* Birmingham, 1765.

15. W. Smith, *The Free-Mason's Pocket Companion,* 2d ed., London, 1738, pp. 6–11; cf. a German translation, *Freundliche Nachricht von den Frey-Maurern,* Frankfurt am Main, 1740; and *Histoire des Francs-Maçons contenant Les Obligations et Status . . . ,* 1747, introduction signed by le Frère de la Tierce.

16. [Anon.,] *Masonry: A Poem. To which are added several Songs,* Edinburgh, 1739. Cf. Edward Oakley, *A Speech Deliver'd to the Worshipful Society of Freemasons* 1728, and bound with *Cole's Constitutions,* ed. William J. Hughan, Leeds, 1897; almost the entire speech on the Palladian.

17. "On the Rise and Progress of Freemasonry," in Oliver, op. cit., vol. 1, pp. 32–34. For attacks on Hobbes coming from later in the century, see Wellins Calcott, "On the Advantage of Society," in the same collection, vol. 2, p. 34; and on p. 205.

18. Ibid., vol. 1, pp. 44–45.

19. Ibid., p. 45.

20. Ibid., p. 49, from "A defence of Masonry, occasioned by a pamphlet called *Masonry dissected* . . . A.D. 1730," by Dr. Anderson, presumably James Anderson.

21. "On the Masonic Duties," in G. Oliver, ed., *Masonic Institutes by Various Authors,* bound with *The History of Masonic Persecutions,* New York, 1867, p. 389.

22. Ibid., p. 390.

23. *The Pocket Companion* . . . , London, 1759, p. 330, written by Isaac Head, a prominent masonic writer of the period.

24. Wellins Calcott, *A Candid Disquisition of the Principles and Practices . . . of Free and Accepted Masons,* London, 1769, p. 36; and in many subsequent editions.

25. See Donna T. Andrew, *Philanthrophy and Police. London Charity in the Eighteenth Century,* Princeton, N.J.: Princeton University Press, 1989, pp. 94–97.

26. I owe this point to Steven Conrad Bullock, "The Ancient and Honorable Society of Freemasonry in America, 1730–1830," Ph.D. diss., Brown University, 1986.

27. *Ahiman Rezon: or A Help to a Brother; Shewing the Excellency of Secrecy . . . ,* London, 1756, p. x.

28. Ibid., p. 28.

29. Ibid., p. 16.

30. Ibid., p. 15.

31. Ibid., pp. 4–5, 14, 27.

32. *The Ancient Consitutions and Charges of the Free-Masons with a True Representation of the Noble Art in several Lectures or Speeches,* London, printed and sold by Brother Benjamin Cole, 1751, pp. 3, 5, 9, 63.

33. Margaret C. Jacob, "The Knights of Jubilation: Masonic and Libertine," *Quaerendo,* 1984, pp. 62–75.

34. The 1759 *Pocket Companion* reprints a sermon by Isaac Head, *A Charge deliver'd to a constituted Lodge . . . Histon, Cornwall . . .* , 21 April 1752, pp. 329–30.

35. Wayne A. Huss, *The Master Builders. A History of the Grand Lodge of Free and Accepted Masons of Pennsylvania,* Philadelphia: Grand Lodge of Pennsylvania, 1986, pp. 48–54.

36. James Fordyce, *The Temple of Virtue. A Dream,* London, 1759, pp. 23–25. The book was seen into print by Fordyce's brother and hence turns up in card catalogues under his name.

37. Ibid., p. 47.

38. Ibid., p. 63–64.

39. Ibid., p. 71. In case the reader is in any doubt as to who is intended, an anonymous and contemporary hand has written "Pitt" on the British Library copy.

40. See Jacob, *The Radical Enlightenment,* pp. 175, 263.

41. Thomas Edmondes, Esq., G.W., *An address delivered at the Stewards Lodge, held at the Horn Tavern, Fleet Street, London, November 16, 1763,* p. 17.

42. Oliver, *The Golden Remains,* vol. 1, pp. 178–79 and 193, from "On the Government of the Lodge. Delivered before the brethen of St. George's Lodge, No. 315, Taunton," 1765.

43. Richard Wallis, *Decency & Order the Cement of Society: Being a Discourse delivered before the Society of Free and Accepted Masons . . . 1769,* Newcastle, 1769, p. 16.

44. *A Charge delivered at the Constitution of Lodge No CXXX at the Swan In Wolverhampton . . . October, 1764. By the . . . Grand Master,* Birmingham, 1765, pp. 6, 9.

45. Davenport, op. cit., pp. 15–16. On freemasons and radicals, see John Money, *Experience and Identity: Birmingham and the West Midland, 1760–1800,* Montreal: McGill University Press, 1977, pp. 137–40.

46. Davenport, op. cit.

47. Rev. J. C., a Brother, *A Sermon preached at Bury St. Edmund's . . . , Bury,* printed and sold by Brother W. Green, 1773, pp. 11–12.

48. William Hutchinson, *The Spirit of Masonry in Moral and Elucidatory Lectures,* London, 1775, p. 153.

49. Ibid., p. 211; and see appendix, which reprinted a letter supposedly by Locke. Also reprinted in W. Meeson, *An Introduction to Free-Masonry,* Birmingham, 1775, pp. 138–39, and see p. 169. On the revival of Locke among radicals of the 1780s see Wilson, op. cit., p. 360.

50. William Preston, *Illustrations of Masonry, A New Edition,* London, 1778, pp. 138–39, 169. Here Preston reprints a letter supposedly by Locke dated 6 May 1696 to the Earl of Pembroke wherein Locke claims that Anthony Collins gave him a manuscript about freemasonry and that he was sufficiently impressed by it to join the fraternity.

51. [Anon.,] *The Consitutions of the Ancient and Honourable Fraternity of Free and Accepted Masons . . .* , Worcester, Mass.: Isaiah Thomas, printer, 1792, pp. 36, 49, 137–39. Copy to be found at the Library Company, Locust Street, Philadelphia.

52. *On the design of Masonry. Delivered in the Union Lodge,* Exeter, No. 370 . . . 1770, in Oliver, *Golden Remains,* vol. 1, pp. 197–99.

53. Ibid., pp. 208–9.

54. Rev. Brother James Smith, *A Sermon preached . . . in Deal,* pp. 8–9.

55. Ibid., p. 10.

56. *Relation apologique et historique de la société des Franc-Maçons par J.G.D.M.F.M.*, Dublin: Patrice Odonoko, Libraire et Imprimeur, 1738. This is almost certainly a false imprint. In G. Oliver, *The Relevations of a Square,* London, 1855, pp. 61–62, it is claimed that Martin Clare is responsible for this tract.

57. *Relation,* pp. 10–17, 28.

58. Ibid., pp. 32–33.

59. Ibid., p. 62. But anti-Semitic comments do occasionally occur in masonic literature, e.g., Rev. John Hodgets, "On Brother Love. Delivered at the Constitution of the Harmonic Lodge, Dudley, 1784," in Oliver, *Golden Remains,* vol. 1, p. 243.

60. [Anon.,] *Shibboleth: or, Every Man a Free-Mason. Containing a History of the Rise, Progress, and Present State of that . . . Order. By a Pass'd Master,* London, 1765, p. 44.

61. John Toland, *Reasons for Naturalizing the Jews in Great Britain and Ireland,* London, 1714, in *Occasional Papers. English Series No. 3. Pamphlets relating to the Jews in England . . .* , San Francisco: California State Library, 1939, p. 64.

62. Christopher Hill, "Till the Conversion of the Jews," in Richard H. Popkin, ed., *Millenarianism and Messianism in English Literature and Thought, 1650–1800. Clark Library Lectures, 1981–82,* New York: Brill, 1988, pp. 12–36.

63. John Toland, *Pantheisticon: or the Form of Celebrating the Socratic Society,* London, 1751, pp. 57, 100.

64. Ibid., p. 65.

65. Kloss MSS 191.E2, a collection of manuscript tracts made by Kloss and labeled by him "de Morçeaux d'Architecture composés par differens frères pour differentes Loges en France, etc., 1780–1820." The piece to which I refer begins with a discourse on masonic religion and its relationship to the ancient religions. It proceeds to a tract on the Druids, both male and female priests, and then "Seconde partie. L'objet de cette seconde partie est de demontre l'analogie qui existe, entre la moral, les ceremonies, et les coutumes celtiques; et la morale les ceremonies et les coutumes maçoniques. . . . Relativement au gouvernement maçonique, même analogie; les druides vivaient en commun, elisaient leurs chefs; ils presidaient aux assemblées Generales; etant les plus intruits, ils elisaient les maitres des deliberations dates les assemblées." Mention of the Grand Orient dates this text from after 1773, but almost certainly before 1789.

66. John Shaftesley, "Jews in English Freemasonry in the 18th and 19th Centuries," *Ars Quatuor Coronatorum* 92 (1979): 34–38. Grand Lodge of The Netherlands, MS "Kronick Annales," where Salomon Noch is listed among the original founders of the first Dutch lodge, 8/19 November 1734; cf. Jacob Katz, *Jews and Freemasons in Europe, 1723–1939,* Cambridge, Mass.: Harvard University Press, 1970, pp. 8–22.

67. For a good example see *The Ancient Constitutions and Charges of the Free-Masons,* London, printed and sold by Brother Benjamin Cole, pp. 25, 37.

68. [Anon.,] *Masonry: A Poem. To which are added several Songs,* Edinburgh, 1739, p. 23.

69. *Relation apologique,* p. 57. For an attack on masonic drunkenness see Peter Farmer, *A New Model for the Rebuilding of Masonry on a Stronger Basis than the Former; with a Sound Constitution . . . dedicated to Mr. Orator Henley,* London, 1730, p. 14, and on sodomy, p. 22. Orator Henley was an outspoken street preacher who inveighed against the government during this period.

70. [Anon.,] *Shibboleth: or, Every Man a Free-Mason. Containing a History of the Rise, Progress, and Present State of that . . . Order. By a Pass'd Master,* London, 1765, p. 44.

71. Harry William Pedicord, "While Gloves at Five: Fraternal Patronage of London Theatres in the Eighteenth Century," *Philological Quarterly* 45 (1966): 277. For an early discussion of manner, see Martin Clare, *An Address to the Body of Free and Accepted Masons . . . December 11, 1735.*

72. Rev. Arnold W. Oxford, *No. 4. An Introduction to the History of The Royal Somerset House and Inverness Lodge,* London, 1928, p. 16.

73. Thomas Hale, *Social Harmony. Consisting of a Collection of Songs and Catches,* [London,] 1763, pp. 13–14.

74. Linda J. Colley, "The Loyal Brotherhood and the Cocoa Tree. The London Organization of the Tory Party, 1727–1760," *Historical Journal* 20 (1977): 77–95, esp. p. 80, commenting that the Tories possessed no effective counterpart to the Kit-Kat Club, and that the Loyal Brotherhood borrowed "some of the more decorative elements of freemasonry." See its manuscripts, B.L., MSS ADD 49360.

75. Magdalen College, Cambridge, Pepys Library, MS Misc. 7, f. 484. Supplied through the kindness of J. R. Jacob. For Kit-Cat, see B.L., MSS ADD 40060, ff. 1–2. The text continues: "What faith the priests of all Religions hold / What old Socinus and Molinus teach / And what the modern Philadelphians preach." For a general discussion of the club, see Kathleen M. Lynch, *Jacob Tonson. Kit-Cat Publisher,* Nashville: University of Tennessee Press, 1971, pp. 41–46.

76. B.L., MSS ADD 49360, Board of Loyal Brotherhood, 1709–1713/14, f. 10; and f. 35 on drinking in moderation and only to Church and Queen.

77. A. S. Frere, *Grand Lodge, 1717–1967,* Oxford: Oxford University Press, 1967, pp. 31–32, Anderson's 1738 history was attached to a new edition of the *Constitutions;* Frere mentions that this lodge is treated with some suspicion. For more on Clayton, see Henry Horwitz, "The Mess of the Middle Class Revisited: The Case of the 'Big Bourgeoisie' of Augustan London," *Continuity and Change* 2, no. 2 (1987): 263–96. Clayton was reportedly the son of a poor carpenter, p. 270.

78. [J. Scott,] *The Free-Masons Pocket Companion,* Glasgow, 1765, p. 66.

79. Lambeth Palace Library, London, MS 933, f. 55.

80. Guildhall Library, London, MS 5992, dated 20 October 1677.

81. D. Knoop, G. P. Jones, and D. Hamer, eds., *Early Masonic Pamphlets,* Manchester: Manchester University Press, 1945, pp. 34–35. And see pp. 68–69 for class antagonism against the newly risen.

82. *The Craftsman,* 16 April 1737, no. 563. See also B. L. 164.1.25, *The Freemasons,* 1723, an obscene poem.

83. Farmer, op. cit., esp. p. 9 for accusations of place seeking; p. 14 for drinking; pp. 22, 23–25 for accusations of sodomy and libertinism.

84. For the social composition of one lodge, see Bodleian Library, Oxford, MS Rylands, d. 9, lodge at St. Paul's Head, Ludgate Street, 1730, which had 107 members. This manuscript also gives their occupations. It was overwhelmingly mercantile with wine merchants, apothecaries, bankers, carpenters, jewelers, tailors, three attorneys-at-law, and a few men listed simply as "Gent." or Esq.

85. *Resolutions of the Society associated for the purpose of obtaining a parliamentary Reform, Freemasons Tavern, 26 April 1792;* and B.L. E.20.18(6), *Observations on an Address to the Freeholders of Middlesex assembled at Freemason's Tavern; delivered to the Chairmen, and read to the Assembly, Dec. 20, 1779.*

86. See John Money, "Freemasonry and the Fabric of Loyalism in Hanoverian England," in Eckhart Hellmuth, ed., *The Transformation of Political Culture. England and Germany in the Late Eighteenth Century,* The German Historical Institute, London: Oxford University Press, 1990, pp. 235–70, with invaluable statistical work on lodges and membership in the century.

87. On that religiosity see Neal C. Gillespie, "Natural History, Natural Theology, and Social Order: John Ray and the 'Newtonian Ideology,' " *Journal of the History of Biology* 20, no. 1 (1987): 1–49. On the training ground for liberal Protestantism, see John Gascoigne, *Cambridge in the Age of Enlightenment,* Cambridge: Cambridge University Press, 1989.

Chapter 3

1. The subject of the Continental establishment of freemasonry is not entirely settled. The nineteenth-century German masonic historian George Kloss compiled a list of Continental lodges from the records available to him. It began with a lodge in Madrid in 1728 established by Lord Colerane; then one in Gibraltar; then Paris, Lower Saxony, and finally The Hague in 1734. Kloss knew his subject well, but the sources for his information now appear to be lost. For his list see Kloss MSS 89; available on microfiche in Margaret C. Jacob, ed., *Freemasonry. Early Sources on Microfiche, 1717–1780. From the Grand Lodge Library, The Hague,* Leiden: Interdocumentation, FVR-15.37/1.

2. On these various persecutions as recounted by the masons themselves, see [Anon.,] *Le Franc-Maçon dans la Republique ou Reflexions apologiques sur les persecutions des Francs-Maçons par un Membre de l'Ordre . . . ,* Frankfurt and Leipzig, 1746. Rousset de Missy said that the duc d'Ursel had established a lodge. He was governor of the province from 1732 to 1738 and represented the Austrian empire. See Th. Pisvin, *La Vie intellectuelle à Namur sous le Régime autrichien,* Louvain: Publications Universitaires de Louvain, 1963, p. 2. Namur was a town in the line of defense against France and had a barrier fortress. For the establishment of a lodge in Ghent in 1763, see Library of the Grand Lodge, The Hague, MS 41:48(2), 18 December 1763; minutes from the Grand Lodge in The Hague.

3. Archives Départementales, Côte d'Or, MS 1F 297, "Livre des Constitutions et Reglemens Generaux des Francs et Reçus Maçons en particulier pour La Loge de Lausanne Aprouvée par tous les Frères le 30 Decembre, 1741."

4. See *Acta Historico-Ecclesiastica,* Weimar, 1736, pp. 105ff; 1738, vol. 12, pp. 1050.

5. [Anon.,] *Gedenkteeken, by eene plegtige Gelegenheid opgerecht;* printed oration intended only for the brothers dated 10 March 1773, probably by C. van der Lijn.

6. On freemasonry in Catholic countries, see, in particular, Jose Antonio Ferrer Benimeli, *Masoneria, Iglesia e Ilustracion. Un conflicto ideologico-religioso,* 4 vols., Madrid: Fundacion Universitaria Espanola, 1976.

7. Bertrand Diringer, *Franc-Maçonnerie et Société à Strasbourg au XVIIIeme siècle,* Strasbourg: Université des sciences humaines, Mémoire de Maîtrise, 1980, p. 27.

8. See his comments in Grand Orient de France, *Franc-Maçonnerie et lumières au seuil de la Revolution francaise, Colloque, 1984,* Introduction by M. Vovelle, published by the lodge, Paris, 1964, p. 88.

9. For one such visitors' book, see B.A. MS 41.89, *Teeken Boek der Br. Visiteurs,* for the years 1765–82.

10. There are exceptions. For example, see [Anon.,] *Masonry. The Way to Hell, A Sermon: Wherein is clearly proved, Both from Reason and Scripture, That all who profess these Mysteries are in a State of Damnation,* London: printed for Robinson and Roberts . . . , 1768, where the emphasis is on debauchery. On antimasonic satire in the American colonies, see J. A. Leo Lemay, ed., *Deism, Masonry, and the Enlightenment. Essays Honoring Alfred Owen Aldridge,* Newark: University of Delaware Press, 1987.

11. H. Gerlach, "De Grondvesting van de Nederlandse vrijmetselarij te 's Gravenhage," *Thoth* 32 (1981). *Thoth* is an official publication of the present Grand Lodge of The Netherlands and contains many valuable articles on the history of the order. Note mention in this article of contact with the Franse Comedie in The Hague; see chapter 5.

12. See Hugo de Schampheleire, "Une loge maçonnique à Rotterdam, fondée avant 1721/22", *Lias* 8 (1981): 79–85; and Johan A. van Reijn, "Een Rotterdamse Loge omstreeks 1721," *Thoth* 33, no. 5 (1982): 237–44. On the organization in The Hague, see this chapter. On Rotterdam, see P. W. Klein, "'Little London': British Merchants in Rotterdam During the Seventeenth and Eighteenth Centuries," in D. C. Coleman and Peter Mathias, eds.,

Enterprise History. Essays in Honour of Charles Wilson, Cambridge: Cambridge University Press, 1984.

13. For a copy of that decree, see *Het Kapittel, "La Bien Aimée", Amsterdam 1755–1980,* published by the lodge, Amsterdam, 1980, p. 10.

14. Letter quoted in Dr. P. J. van Loo, *Geschiedenis van de Orde van Vrijmetselaren onder het Grootoosten der Nederlanden,* The Hague: Maçonnieke Stichting, 1967, p. 3; written in English, The Hague, 30 December 1735, signed C. J. Philorangien (clearly a pseudonym).

15. Ibid., p. 2, quoting the London *Daily Advertiser* for December 1735.

16. For a good discussion of this lodge and the controversy we are examining, see R. J. H. van Lith, "Duyvelskaarten en Godtloozen. Anti-maçonniek geschrijf in de geschiedenis van de Nijmeegse vrijmetselarij 1752/53," Doctoraalscriptie, University of Nijmegen, Faculty of Modern History, 1988. My thanks to the author for making this text available.

17. A. W. F. M. van de Sande, "Vrijmetselarij in Nijmegen in de achttiende en negentiende eeuw. Een socio-culturele schets," *Numaga* 32–33 (1985/86): 55–64. Cf. Hubert P. H. Nusteling, *Binnen de Vesting Nijmegen. Confessionele en demografische verhoudingen ten tijde van de Republiek,* Zutphen: De Walburg Pers, 1979.

18. Dr. Williams's Library, London, MS 24.157(41), dated 6 August 1760, Utrecht, from Samuel Kenrick to James Wodrow.

19. John Stuart Shaw, *The Management of Scottish Society, 1707–1764,* Edinburgh: J. Donald, 1983, pp. 27, 32.

20. The controversy is reported in *Leydse Maandagsche Courant,* 12 June 1752.

21. On the background of these men, see Van Lith, op. cit., pp. 26–28.

22. G.L., *Brief van een Vry-Metselaer van de St. Lodewyks Loge te Nymegen, aan . . . Everhard Haverkamp,* n.p., n.d.; clearly published in 1752 and catalogued under B.no.68, manuscript letter attached to the back is dated 10 June 1752, Arnhem, 11 ff. The original reads: "ik zeg, en ik blijff er beij, wat hebjes mee te doen, om zoo een leven te [maken?] het heele land is er vol van. Gisteren war ik in de [?] winkel naast ons. Och! het war vrymetselaar voor, vrymetselaar nae. Jae, zey Caatje, dat oude Mensch dat daar in de winkel zit, daar word niet anders gesproken." The writer of this letter ends it with family greetings "groet uw vader, kust uw zusters, en koomt te saamen op der kermis." It is signed: "Lieve Neeve U Ed. dienstwillig Nichte. P.S. Zie neeven ik zouw er myn naem wel ondersetten maar je weet, de wereld is Zoo wonder." This is from a "niece" to a "nephew," that is, in Dutch kinship, from a first cousin and a woman.

23. Ibid.: "ik heb er van te vooren nooijt van gehoort, en Zulke godloose dingen! Foeij! En dat gij uw aanlegt tegens Dominus Broen. Zoo een Man! en die is U lui veel te snooij aff; en hy heeft gelt als water." And later: "Ziet Domine Broen eens die heeft wel 100 duijsent gulden, en leeft als een Bisschop."

24. Ibid.: "all die Franse kost en ragouts en bruijne soup is een bederf voor de beurs, en voor de Maag op zijn oud gelders, daar heeft men . . . se van."

25. Diringer, op. cit., p. 11; in 1747 a fiancée in Strasbourg demanded that her betrothed renounce his membership in the local lodge.

26. Ibid.: "Want te Nieuwkerk is een man geweest, die zoo sterk wierd gedreven door den Geest dat hij tusschen Hemel en Aarde hing: En dat heeft Domine Kuijper selfs gesien."

27. Ibid.: "Want als de Dominees beginnen dan hebbense niet gedaan. Zij zijn Vuijl, en Ze zullen uw luij bederven, let er op, en ze zullen maaken, dat gij geen advocaat sult krijgen om ijets voor uw te schrijven, die zullen se ook al aan vliegen. wat dan gedaan! en gaat al nae de Heeren. Jae! Knapkoek! geen Mensch will ze bijten: zij hieten Leeuwken."

28. Ibid.: "Zoo waar ik zit en schryff, ik wouw het ook wel eens weesen. Maar als het quaadt was ik wouw er weer uytschyden. Dogh de vrouwen komen er niet in. En als ik het

weer wel bedenke, zoo zouw het niet goed weesen, dat dit een ander hoorde, ik kreeg seker den Dominee bij mij, dan kreeg ik de Dood op mijn lijff."

29. B.A. MS 41:6, f. 91, for 1756.

30. On neighborhood insults in this period in Paris, and the almost total absence of charges of blasphemy and irreligion, see David Garrioch, "Verbal Insults in Eighteenth-Century Paris," in Peter Burke and Roy Porter, eds., *The Social History of Language,* Cambridge: Cambridge University Press, 1987, p. 113. The population of Amsterdam would have been near 200,000 in this period.

31. For evidence, citing a 1922 biography of Moray by A. Robertson, see David Stevenson, "Masonry, Symbolism and Ethics in the Life of Sir Robert Moray, FRS," *Proceedings of the Society of Antiquaries of Scotland* 114 (1984): 419.

32. On that history, see the opening remarks of John Michael Montias, *Vermeer and His Milieu. A Web of Social History,* Princeton, N.J.: Princeton University Press, 1989, pp. 4–7.

33. G.L. MS 41:42b, 146a, 7 January 1761, letter of C. B. de Boetzelaer to J. Schreuder.

34. [Anon.,] *Lettre d'un Franc-maçon de la loge de S. Louis de Nimegue au venerable, pieux et savant Everhard Haverkamp . . . traduite du Hollandois,* Nijmegen, 1752, pp. 30–32.

35. [Anon.,] *Requetes de Messieurs . . . Merkes,* n.p., n.d., pp. 114–15. The copy at the G.L. is sign A.No.14.

36. Ibid., p. 113. The whole passage is interesting: "Ces prétendus zélés pourroient de meme refuser d'admettre a la Ste.Table les Participans des Compagnies des Indes Orientales & Occidentales, par raport au Négoce des Esclaves, les Fermiers des Impots publics, les Bateliers du Rhin, les Vassaux, les membres des Ordres de Chevalerie." It should be noted that lodges in nineteenth-century America could hold slaves; see Steven C. Bullock, "The Ancient and Honorable Society of Freemasonry in America, 1730–1830," Ph.D. diss., Brown University, 1986, p. 209.

37. *Het Schadelyke van de Societeit der Vry-metselaars voor kerk en borger-staat . . . Gedrukt buyten de Loge der Vry-metselaars . . . ,* n.p., n.d. [but clearly 1752], pp. 39–40: "Dat dit warrachtig is, hebben die selve Revolutien in Engeland, waar van den Schryver gesproken heeft, meer dan eens getoond." The tone of this tract suggests that it is by a critic of the masons, but this is not clear. For our purposes it could be from either side; the point is the dialectic that emerges in the discussion.

38. *Brief van een Vry-Metselaer . . . Over den gedeelte der Toepassing van zyne leer-rede . . . den 22. Maart 1752. in de Groote Kerk te Nymegen . . . ,* p. 47.

39. Ibid., p. 46.

40. University Library, Leiden, Marchand MSS 2, ff. 46, 64, Rousset to Marchand.

41. H. Rodermond, *De vrijmetselaarsloge "La Bien Aimeé" Amsterdam, 1735–1985,* The Hague: Maçonnieke Stichting, 1985, p. 20. From the manuscript correspondence of the lodge with another (spelling modernized by the author): "Het jaar 1747 en een gedeelte van 1748 is, mag men wel zeggen, schitterend geweest. Men durfde bijna in het openbaar te verschijnen. Alle angst was verdreven en de gevoelens waren behoorlijk veranderd. . . . De burgerlijke wanklanken van het jaar 1748 hadden invloed op onze Loge. Sommige van onze Broeders waren er vatbaar voor, anderen werden er door geraakt en de meesten waren er verontwaardigd over en het scheelde niet veel of er heerste ook verdeeldheid in de Loge zelf."

42. For an early attempt to associate the lodges with freethinking in the German-speaking lands, see [Anon.,] *Der Freidenker ausser der Loge. Eine feierliche Rede an einem hohen Fest-Tage in der . . . Loge derer Freidenker, gehalten vom B.R.,* London, n.d. The imprint is false, and the date, according to G. Kloss, may be 1744. G.L., sign 211.B.59.

43. [Anon.,] *Redevoering over het gedrag der Vry-Metselaaren, Jegens den Staat.*

Uytgesproken op St Jansdag in eene Wettig vergaderde Loge, Door een Lid derzelver Vergadering, Amsterdam, 1752, pp. 3–4. Found in University Library, Amsterdam, sign D.32.

44. Ibid., pp. 27–29.

45. Ibid., p. 5.

46. See Simon Schama, *The Embarrassment of Riches. An Interpretation of Dutch Culture in the Golden Age,* Berkeley: University of California Press, 1988, pp. 202–3, 152, and passim.

47. *Redevoering . . .* 1752, p. 6: "een sluypvergadering van een Party". "Zy beschouwen ons als schromelyke en met Staatszaken verwarde geesten." The charge of seditious conspiracy had been leveled in the 1740s as well; see [Anon.,] *Le Tonneau jette ou Reflexions sur la pretendu Decouverte des Misteres de l'Ordre des Franc-Maçons à S.A. Mgr le Prince W . . . par un Membre de l'Ordre,* The Hague, 1745, p. 15. Clearly the accusation of naturalism was being spread also in German-speaking freemasonry; see Bruder Redner, *Das Erhabene, wozu die Freymaureren ihre achten Schülerfuhren wurde in einer Rede an dem Johannis-Tage 1744 . . .* Halle, 1744, p. 11.

48. University Library, Leiden, Marchand MSS 44:2, f. 64. These are notes made by Marchand on the anonymous exposure, *L'Ordre des Francs-Maçons trahi,* Amsterdam, 1747: "Selon les uns, c'est une compagnie Philosophique, et même religieuse, qui ne tend qu'au Bien-étre du Genre Humain, et même qu'au Salut éternel, s'il étoit vrai qu'on y professât une plus grande Purété de Moeurs et de Doctrine, même un Déisme tout-à-fait épuré." These notes are undated and could therefore have been made at any time between 1747 and Marchand's death in 1756. One of earliest anthropological accounts of religion was done by the freemason and French refugee A. A. Bruzen de la Martinière, who along with J. F. Bernard worked on *Ceremonies et coutumes de toutes les peuples du monde,* Amsterdam, 1736; commonly listed under the name of Bernard Picart, who did the engravings. See John Landwehr, "De Vrijmetselarij op de korrel," *Thoth* 1 (1981): 35.

49. *Redevoering . . .* 1752, pp. 16–17. "Nimmer heeft een Vry-Metselaar zich vervoegt in de sluypwinkels der Schriftbespotters. Hy bindt zich niet aan Tindale."

50. University Library, Leiden, Marchand MS 43, over 500 folios. One post–World War II bibliography lists a Dutch translation of Tindal's text, with no place or date. No copy has been located. See Th. H. M. Verbeek, "Voorlopige bibliografie van 18e eeuwse vertalingen . . . ," *Documentatieblad Werkgroep Achttiende Eeuw,* no. 22 (1974): 28. On Marchand in general, see Christiane Berkvens-Stevelinck, *Propser Marchand. La Vie et l'Oeuvre (1678–1756),* Leiden: Brill, 1987.

51. R. H. Vermij, "Tolands eerste brief aan Serena. Een episode uit de geschiedenis van het deïsme in Nederland," *Documentatieblad Werkgroep Achttiende Eeuw,* 21, no. 1 (1989): 13–22.

52. Margaret C. Jacob, *The Radical Enlightenment: Pantheists, Freemasons, and Republicans,* London: George Allen and Unwin, 1981, pp. 172–73; cf. Franco Venturi, *Italy and the Enlightenment,* London: Longman, 1972, pp. 63–102.

53. Jacob, *The Radical Enlightenment,* p. 181, n. 74.

54. Ibid., p. 16.

55. *Redevoering over het gedrag der Vry-Metselaaren,* p. 18.

56. Ibid., pp. 29–30.

57. B.A., Brievenarchief, letter dated 25 October 1755, from the lodge La Charité.

58. G.L. MSS de Vignoles, "L'Art Royal de la Maçonnerie doit être bien analogue à cet esprit de douceur et de sagesse, qui fait la base du gouvernement des Etats-Generaux des Provinces Unies. . . ."

59. Kloss MSS 190.E.47, "Quant à l'indépendance que vous reclamez, jamais la société n'a admis d'esclavage, et le vouloir introduire, ce serait détruire son essence. Notre Gouver-

nement ne sera connu, qu'autant qu'on y verra l'heureux mélange, qui se trouve dans celui de Hollande. Les Etats Generaux composés des Députés de chaque Province forment le tribunal souverain de la Nation. [It should be noted that this was in fact an inaccurate rendering of the legal status of the States.] Ceux de chaque Province en Particulier, quoique subordinés, n'en sont ni moins souverains, ni moins indépendans; et la Jurisdiction des Villes jouit, sous ces derniers de toute souveraineté sur leurs territoires. Cette sage république avoit, j'ay osé le dire dans la G.L. de 1756, pris dans l'Administration de la société la forme, qu'elle a donné à la sienne. Jaloux de leur liberté, tous les Etats, qui devaient le composer, voulurent assurer leur indépendance, mais ils sentirent en même tems, que sous un point d'union, qui tint toutes les parties ensemble, le [word left out] qu'ils formaient de tant d'états divers, serait si peu ferme, qu'il romproit bientôt."

60. *Gedenkteeken by eene plegtige Gelegenheid opgerecht,* privately printed for use only of the brothers, 1773, p. 10.

61. G.L. MSS Vignoles, history, f. 3: "Tant de Loges, aiant uni dans leur sein les premiers de l'Etat, se crurent a l'abri de réveiller les inquiétudes de leur gouvernement; et songerent efficacement à donner une consistance solide à la sociéte, en mettant à sa tête un frère également cheri dans la société Maçonnique par son zele, et distingué dans la république par l'illustration de sa naissance et par le crédit que lui assuroient ses vertus."

62. Ibid. The original reads: "au nom du Marquis de Carnarvan G.M. les autorisa a former et établir a la Haye une G.L.N. pour les Etats généraux des Provinces Unies, généralité et Colonies Dépendantes."

63. Ibid.: "Apres avoir consulté des frères distingués par leur Zele et leurs connoissances tant des loix du pais que des points qui sont véritablement essentiels à la Maçonnerie, ce G.M.N. fit proposer a l'assemblée de Juin 1761, qu'aucune Loge n'eut qu'à la suite à faire preter d'engagement que sur la parole de l'honneur, ce qui devroit etre fait aiant la main sur un livre, qui renfermeroit ou les constitutions de la societé ou les principles du droit de la Nature." A hand, not in the same ink and apparently not contemporary, has added "qu'on substitueroit par consequent à la bible."

64. B.A. 46.

65. We know this from the language found in the masonic defenses: [C. van der Lijn,] *Vertoog dienende tot aantooning van de ongegrondheid der Lasteringen, de Orde der Vry-Metselaars . . . ,* 1764, preface, pp. 5–7, 11; [Anon.,] *Gedenkteeken by eene plegtige gelegenheid opgerecht,* p. 9, dated 1 March 1773. Also probably by the same.

66. Aubrey Rosenberg, *Tyssot de Patot and His Work, 1655–1738,* The Hague: Nijhoff, 1972, p. 93 and passim.

67. P. G. M. Dickson, *Finance and Government under Maria Theresa, 1740–1780,* Oxford: Clarendon Press, 1987, vol. 1, p. 60n.

68. See Margaret C. Jacob, *The Radical Enlightenment,* pp. 280ff, a reprint of the 1723 *Constitutions.* For a good place to begin with "official" masonic history consult any issue of *Ars Quatuor Coronatorum* published annually in London by the Grand Lodge. In the discussion that follows I am referring to the Royal Society, London, MS Register Book (C), IX, ff. 240–52.

69. See Graham Maddow, "Constitution," in Terence Ball, James Farr, Russell L. Hanson, eds., *Political Innovation and Conceptual Change,* Cambridge UK: Cambridge University Press, 1989, p. 59. The Royal Society manuscript also speaks of the original French king, Charles Martell, as being "elected." It is signed and dated, Thomas Martin, 1659.

70. Johan A. van Reijn, "John Theophilus Desaguliers, 1683–1983," *Thoth* 34 (1983): 165–203.

71. Their letter is printed in de Schampheleire, op. cit. pp. 79–85.

72. T. M. Devine, "The Scottish Merchant Community, 1680–1740," in R. H. Campbell

and Andrew S. Skinner, eds., *The Origins and Nature of the Scottish Enlightenment,* Edinburgh: J. Donald, 1982, p. 28.

73. On Belgian freemasonry see H. de Schampheleire, *Aperçu des principaux travaux recénts relatifs à l'histoire de la franc-maçonnerie belge, suivi d'un état des archives et des bibliothèques maçonniques. Rapport présenté au Symposium "Geheime Gesellschaften" organisé par "la Lessing-Akademie" (Wolfenbeutel) les 6–10 Avril 1976.* There is also a center for the study of the topic, Centrum voor de Studie van de Verlichting, Brussels. See also Bertrand van der Schelden, *La Franc-Maçonnerie Belge* sous le régime autrichen, Louvain, Librairie universitaire and Hugo de Schampheleire, *De Antwerpse Vrijmetselaars in de 18e eeuw,* Brussels, 1971. The evidence for freemasonry in Brussels from the 1740s and 1750s comes from the letters of Rousset de Missy to Prosper Marchand, University Library, Leiden.

74. B.A., Brievenarchief, Rousset's letter is dated 11 January 1756; also MS 41.6 Notulen 1754–57, ff. 109–11, contains the signatures of visitors in the year 1756, among them at least two members of lodges in Antwerp. Among the other signatories are men from France, Germany, England, Switzerland, and Surinam. For Liège see *Liège. Loges et Chapitres du XVIIIe au XXe Siècle,* Brussels: Souverain Chapitre Charles Magnette de la Parfaite Intelligence et L'Etoile Réunies, 1985, chapter 1.

75. On Ursel (b. 1665), see Rouhart-Chabot, "La réforme des Etats de Namur et les archives du duc d'Ursel," *Anciens pays et assemblées d'Etats, Etudes publiées par la Section Belge de la Commission Internationale pour l'histoire des assemblées d'états,* vol. 14, 1057, pp. 122–24; and G. Baurin, *Les Gouverneurs du Comté de Namur, 1430–1794,* Namur: Baurin, 1984.

76. On Catholic Europe, see Benimeli, op. cit. Volume 4 contains an extensive bibliography. For one of the earliest German lodges, see *Annalen der Loge zur Einigheit, der Englischen Provincial-Loge . . . zu Frankfurt-am-Main, 1742–1811,* Frankfurt, 1842. There is a very helpful survey of this early literature by Lisa Zemelman (UCLA), unpublished paper presented to the Max-Planck Institut für Geschichte, Göttingen, 1984.

77. See Pierre Chevallier, *Les Ducs sous l'Acacia ou les premiers pas de la Franc-maçonnerie française, 1725–1743,* Paris: J. Vrin, 1964; and Jean Baylot, "James Hector McLeane ou l'Ecossais, second Grand Maitre" *Travaux de Villard de Honnecourt* 9 (1973): 58–63. See also Claude Nordmann, "Les Jacobites écossais en France au XVIIIe siècle," in Daniel Becquemont et. al., *Regards sur l'Ecosse au XVIIIe siècle,* vol. 3, Lille: Université de Lille 1977, pp. 81–108. These Jacobite links have been presumed for some time; see Daniel Mornet, *Les Origines intellectuelles de la Révolution française (1715–1787),* Paris: Armand Colin, 1933, p. 358.

78. Among the earliest records of French freemasonry are those for a lodge that met in Paris in 1736 and had in it John Coustos, who was a member of a London lodge; see B.N., FM MS 184, "Avis et Mémoires sur les affaires publiques, 1757–69," but in fact containing records from the 1730s, in particular, ff. 132–33. The lodge described here began in 1736, and Coustos appears on the list of members. See also B.N., FM 4.122, dated 1742.

79. Pierre Chevallier, *La première profanation du temple maçonnique ou Louis XV et la Fraternité, 1737–1755,* Paris: J. Vrin 1968, pp. 11–17.

80. Kloss MSS 190.E.47; letter cited earlier of 1774: "Avez vous plus de droit à ce titre parceque vous l'arrangez en 1770, que les G.L. créés par nous en Basse Saxe de 1729, en Russie de 1731 en Haute Saxony de 1737, en Danemark de 1747, à Hanovre en 1754."

81. See G.L. MSS Vignoles, history, f.2; others present were John Stanhope, Jacques Holtzendorff, Jeremy Strickland, Benjamin Hadley, and "un frère hollandois." This account has been accepted by contemporary Dutch historians of freemasonry.

82. Van Reijn, "John Theophilus Desaguliers," pp. 190–96.

83. See Margaret C. Jacob, *The Cultural Meaning of the Scientific Revolution,* New York: McGraw-Hill, 1988, pp. 143–44.

84. Gilbert W. Dayes, "The Duke of Lorraine and English Freemasonry in 1731," *Ars Quatuor Coronatorum* 37 (1924): 107–28.

85. *De Rotterdam Hermes,* [ed. J. C. Weyerman,] 9 September 1720 to 9 September 1721, no. 30, no. 54, no. 58; *De Amsterdam Hermes,* [ed. J. C. Weyerman,] 1721+, vol. 1, no. 25, no. 36; vol. 2, no. 26. On Weyerman see C. M. Geerars, "De vrijdenkerij in de journalistieke werken van Jakob Campo Weyerman," *Tijdschrift voor de studie van de verlichting* 2 (1975): 7–15.

86. For a photographic copy and transcription of this document, that also disputes its masonic character, see Christiane Berkvens-Stevelinck, "Les Chevaliers de la Jubilation: Maçonnerie ou libertinage? A propos de quelques publications de Margaret C. Jacob," *Quaerendo* 13 (1983): 50–57. For corrections of this transcription and an overview of the controversy surrounding my interpretation of this text, see my "The Knights of Jubilation—Masonic *and* Libertine," *Quaerendo* 14 (1984): 63–75. The emphasis is in the original.

87. On the use of the term "constitution" in French in this period to refer to the universe, and if in an institutional setting to be the antithesis of customary laws, see Marina Valensise, "The French Constitution in Prerevolutionary Debate," *Journal of Modern History* 60 (September 1988): S26–S27 (suppl.).

88. See [Anon.,] *La Reception mysterieuse. Des Membres de la celebre Société des Francs-Maçons . . . Par Samuel Prichard . . . ,* London: Par la Compagnie des Libraires, 1738. This is almost certainly a false imprint as to place; for a discussion of this tract see pp. 27–28.

89. For a complete copy of this text see John E. Cox, ed., *The Old Constitutions belonging to the Ancient and Honourable Society of England and Ireland . . . 1722, 1723, ms 1726, Dublin, 1730,* London: Richard Spencer, 1871, pp. 1–26. On the publisher J. Roberts's text, see P. Girard-Augry, "Les Constitutions de Roberts de 1722," *Travaux de la Loge nationale de recherches Villard de Honnecourt* 9 (1984): 21–46.

90. Samuel Prichard, *Masonry Dissected,* London, 1730, pp. 6–7; text most conveniently consulted in Harry Carr, ed., *Samuel Prichard's Masonry Dissected, 1730. An Analysis and Commentary,* vol. 8, Bloomington, Ill.: Masonic Book Club, 1977.

91. Kloss MSS, 190.E.47: "Le Chev. Chr: Wren fameux architecte, intendant des Bâtimens du Roi, membre du Parlement, ayant été êlu en 1710 pour la seconde fois G.M. de la Société tint la chaire jusqu'en 1716, tems ou les frères s'appercevant que l'âge de 88 ans ne lui permettait plus de veiller à leur conduite, résolurent à se réunir pour lui donner un successeur. Il ne se trouva que 4 [here double boxes given, the traditional sign for lodges] dans Londres, elles s'assemblèrent, firent répresenter le fr. Wren par le Mâitre de la plus ancienne Loge. Est ce là votre [cas?] non certainement." The letter is to Count Zinnendorf, the leader of the schism; hence the final question. In J. S. M. Ward, *Freemasonry and the Ancient Gods,* London, 1926, pp. 159–60, the author cites a manuscript note in the Bodleian by John Aubrey, "This day [18 May 1681] is a great convention at St. Paul's Church of the fraternity of the free ["free" then crossed out and "accepted" put in its place] Masons, where Sir Christopher Wren is to be adopted a brother & Sir Henry Goodrie of ye Tower." Wren is also claimed as a member in Edward Oakley, *A Speech Deliver'd to the Worshipful Society of Free and Accepted Masons at a Lodge, held at the Carpenters Arms, 30st of December, 1728,* [n.p., n.d.] pp. 28–29.

92. Letter given in full in E. A. Boerenbeker, "The Relations between Dutch and English Freemasonry from 1734 to 1771," *Ars Quatuor Coronatorum* 83 (9): 164.

93. Vermij, op. cit.

94. B.L., MSS ADD 40060, ff. 1–2. In York tradition has it that masters of the lodge were called "presidents."

95. Nicholas Rogers, *Whigs and Cities. Popular Politics in the Age of Walpole and Pitt,* Oxford: Clarendon Press, 1989, p. 365.

96. For Rousset's use of this address to other brothers, see B.A., Brievenarchief, Rousset to Schreuder, 1 January 1755: "Je salue par 3 + 3 le tres venerable, les respectables surveillants and les freres maitres & compagnons." This form of salutation was in use in the French lodges by the 1740s; see B.N., MS 15176, f. 380: "Je vous embrasse par 3 & 3." For the first use of "pantheist" see John Toland, *Socinianism Truly Stated. A Letter from a Pantheist to an Orthodox Friend,* London, 1705. Cf. Stephen H. Daniel, *John Toland. His Methods, Manners, and his Mind,* Kingston, Ont.: McGill-Queen's University Press, 1984, pp. 212–15.

97. University Library, Leiden, Marchand MSS, Rousset to Marchand, 18 October [year not given, but clearly toward the end of Marchand's life, i.e., 1756], University Library, Leiden, MS 2, f. 35.

98. [Anon.,] *Nouvelles libertés de Penser,* Amsterdam, 1743, containing five anonymous tracts, one entitled *Le Philosophe,* pp. 165, 188. It is from this tract that the term as applied to men of the Enlightenment originated.

99. See James E. Force, "The Origins of Modern Atheism," *Journal of the History of Ideas,* 1989, pp. 153–62; an excellent summary of recent work on the spread of materialism with attention to Toland, LaMettrie, and d'Holbach.

100. Venturi, op. cit., p. 8.

101. See, for example, "L'Age d'Or. Ode." in [Anon.,] *La Muse Maçonne,* The Hague: Van Laak, 1773, pp. 8–10.

Chapter 4

1. See Margaret C. Jacob, *The Radical Enlightenment. Pantheists, Freemasons, and Republicans,* London: George Allen and Unwin, 1981, especially chapters 5 and 6 for the career of Rousset de Missy. By revolution I mean to exclude palace revolts and dynastic upheavals.

2. Ibid., p. 236, citing a letter from Rousset to Bentinck dated 26 June 1748, and now located at British Library, Egerton MS 1745, f. 486.

3. In 1755 Schreuder also brought out a French edition of Locke's epistemology, *Essai philosophique concernant . . . ;* on Schreuder see I. van Eeghen, *De Amsterdamse Boekhandel, 1680–1725,* Amsterdam: Scheltema and Holkema, 1965, vol. 3, p. 265, vol. 5 (part 1), p. 220.

4. On the power of the regents, see Pieter Geyl, "Historical Appreciations of the Holland Regent Regime," in A. O. Sarkissian, ed., *Studies in Diplomatic History and Historiography in Honour of G. P. Gooch,* London: Longman, 1961, p. 287.

5. See the essay by Jan de Jongste in Margaret C. Jacob and W. W. Mijnhardt, eds., *Decline, Enlightenment and Revolution. The Dutch Enlightenment in the Eighteenth Century,* Ithaca, N.Y.: Cornell University Press, 1991.

6. On this whole movement, see I. Leonard Leeb, *The Ideological Origins of the Batavian Revolution. History and Politics in the Dutch Republic, 1747–1800,* The Hague: Nijhoff, 1973, pp. 60–67.

7. H. Rodermond, *De Vrijmetslaarsloge "La Bien Aimée", Amsterdam, 1735–1985,* The Hague: Maçonnieke Stichting, 1985, ISBN: 90–9000–9973, chapter 2, esp. p. 20. I am following here the convention of calling this lodge by its second name bestowed at its reconstitution, and not by its original title, "de la Paix."

8. [Anon.,] *Redevoering, Uytgesprooken door een Broeder Orateur, In eene Wettige Loge . . . 27 December 1755,* p. 6: Although this is a printed text, we cannot assume that it was intended for circulation beyond the confines of the fraternity. I am treating it as a particularly frank statement, as language not primarily intended for the larger public.

9. Ibid., p. 7: "Hoe wy, alschoon zwak in 't getal, egter sterk van moed, ons vereenigden en na ontfanging van behoorlyke en wettige volmagt, ons weerzyds begroetende als wettige leeden, van eene wettige Loge; van eene Loge die in ons heroopend wierd; van eene Loge die de oudste in onze stad is, en uyt de welke de meeste der overige leeden zyn voortgesprooten?" This sense of being beleaguered continued; see [J. van der Lijn,] *Vertoog, dienende tot aantooning van de ongegrondheid der lasteringen, de Order der Vry-Metselaars, ten onrechte aangewreeven,* 1764; a discourse given before the lodge and printed only for its use.

10. Ibid., p. 8.

11. G.L. MS 41:48 (1), 20 June 1762.

12. B.A. MS 41:6, ff. 1–5: "Dat, hier . . . , eenige der Broederen, meerendeels Leeden van de voorgenoemde Loge de La Paix, in een vereyst getal en van behoorlijke Qualiteiten, om een compleete Loge uyt te maaken, te zaamen zynde, met een zuyver voorneemen en opregten Vry Metzelaars yver elkandere hebben aangespoord en opgewekt tot het opregten eener Loge, en daar toe, allen, wat hier booven, gemeld is, geconsidereerd hebben en daar over rypelyk, ieder byzigzelfs gedagt, vervolgens met elkanderen geraad pleegd en overlegt, [?] tweede Byeen komst, eyndelyk beslooten hebben . . . uit hoofden van het voorgemelde om by den Tres Venerable Meester, den Broeder Rousset de Missy te verzoeken en aan te houden, ten eynde Hy, uyt zyne magt en authoriteit, door een Authentique Acte, wilde Vergunnen magtigen om, onder hen, eene reguliere Loge te formeren, en daar toe, te willen benoemen en van zynent Wege, aanstellen een Broeder, wiens bekwaamheid, hen bekendzynde, zy aan Hem zouden recommenderen, om op bekwaamen tyd en plaats, in Zynen naame en van Zynent wege, de, tot nu toe geslootene Loge de La Paix weder te oopenen, de Broederen tot eene Wettige Loge te formeeren en, in de zelve, als Hunnen Venerable en Meester te ageeren."

13. B.A. MS 41:6, letter dated 10 December 1754: "Nous aprenous avec la plus grande satisfaction et une veritable joye par une lettre de notre frère Schreuder du 9 du courant, que le Veritable Zèle pour notre tres respectable ordre n'est pas encore éteint parmi quelques freres de notre très chere et venerable Loge de La Paix constituée par. . . . Nous aprouvons donc la proposition qu'il nous fait de votre part et nous consentons très volontiers à la demande de nos Honorables freres . . . nous aprouvons volontiers lui recommandant de n'admettre aucune des nouveautés pernicieuses que des faux freres tachent d'introduire, et de se tenir attaché aux—Constitutions angloises, nous vous recommandons à ses soins paternels. . . . Votre tres affectionne frere & Maitre, Rousset de Missy." The signature includes his sign as a master and the seal of the old lodge.

14. B.A., Brievenarchief no. 54, in the rules which must be observed by the holder of the office of "trés venerable": "Als mede geenen, die weegens Religie of Staatkunde spreeken, of over de Galanterie &." The prohibition also turns up in the general rules for all officers of the lodge, 1757; B.A. MS 41, Notulen, f. 116 where the prohibition against cursing and taking God's name in vain also appears: "nog die Vloeken of De Heeren Naam misbruijken."

15. [Anon.,] *Therese philosophe, ou Mémoires pour servir à l'Histoire de D. Dirrage, & de Mademoiselle Éradice,* The Hague, n.d., but almost certainly 1748, p. 4: "où tout inspire la joie & le plaisir: la galanterie semble y former seule tout l'interêt de la société." Cf. [J. Duplain, Libraire,] *Dictionnaire de l'Académie françoise,* Nouvelle édition, Lyon, 1777, entry under "galanterie."

16. B.A. MS 41, Notulen, f. 141: "Niemand vermag in de Loge van verschillende

Streidstukken en den Godsdienst te spreeken; nog van eenige byzondere Staatkundige en Regeeringswyze gevoelens; en eyndelyk niet van het geene de Galanterie raakt of de eerbaare Leevenswyze zoude kunnen kwetzen."

17. G.L. MS 23.1 (kast 158.B), f. 113. "Recever donc de mes mains par le consentiment unanime de tous nos Freres Membres, les signes de votre nouvelle dignite! Et vous, mes trés chers Freres! recever votre trés Venerable Maitre! porter lui tout amour et attachement, qu'il merite!" These are the minutes of the lodge La Philantrope, meeting in Middelburg in the province of Zeeland, a town of some 30,000 souls in this period. I am grateful to W. Mijnhardt for having brought these records to my attention.

18. Ibid., f. 16, 1758: "Puis le Frère la Sage a fait la proposition de proceder à l'Election du Venerable Maitre de notre Loge future, en vertu de la faculté qui nous été accordée par la dite Constitution, ou qui etant agreé, le Frere Macaré a été elu Maitre de la Loge par voix unanimes de tous les Frères, et avec toutes les solennites requises."

19. Ibid., f. 115. The past master speaks to the new master and his brothers: "Accepter le suffrage publicq que vous avez [?] . . . avec le soin d'un Père tendre, l'application d'un vrai et veritable maçon, un zèle, capable à donner l'exemple à tous les Frères, et un amour vrai Fraternel pour nôtre auguste Ordre, et sa propagation dans nôtre Province." The orator continues: "Recever le temoignage publicq, que vous avez parfaitement achevé tous le devoirs de cette charge importanté: que vous avez sauvé nôtre loge, jusqu'ici des situations critiques, où elle s'est trouvée tant par rapport aux circonstances publicques, qu'au peu de zéle, qui nous a animé jusqu'ici."

20. B.A. MS 41:6, ff. 106–7, 29 April 1757: "maar dat echter nopens het 21 artikel, de Loge voor als nog zig liever voorbehoud om de oude Constitutien en reglementen van Engeland, als mede de Nadere Resolutien die tot opheldering van deselve Strekken niet in te Voeren, als een Vaste en onveranderlyke Basis van hun Werk en gedrag, maar deselve aan te zien als Goede hulpmiddelen om in opkomende gevallen tot een eerste point van Deliberatie te neemen en deselve als dan so verre te gebruijken als den aart der Zaake en de Constitutie der Order in deese Landen als meede die van de respective Loges . . . bijzonder zullen overeenbrengen."

21. G.L. MS 41:42b, ff. 162/174/168, 9 December 1761, and f. 176, 22 December 1761 on deliberation.

22. G.L. MS 23.1 (Kast 158.B), f. 2: "Qu'à leur grande Satisfaction ils viennent d'être informés de l'heureuse Revolution arrivée à la fin de l'Annee 1756, ou toutes les Loges de la Hollande assemblée, ont retabli un très Respectable Grande Loge." It is to be noted that the same text in Dutch translates "happy revolution" as "gelukkig tydstip," that is, as "happy moment," rather than the stronger word used commonly in the late 1780s, "omwenteling."

23. Ibid., f. 2. The Dutch text uses the term *Souvereiniteit,* f. 4. On this lodge see the fine essay by W. W. Mijnhardt, "Sociability in Walcheren 1750–1815," *Tijdschrift voor de studie van de verlichting en van het vrije denken* 12 (1984): 289–310.

24. G.L. MS 23.1 (Kast 158.B), minutes of the lodge La Philantrope, Middelburg, f. 4: "Que par là la Province de la Zeelande à été separée des autres, et que cette Province faisant une Souverainété à part, les Freres, qui y resident, pour participer à l'heureuse Union de leurs Freres Voisins, ont besoin de reconnaitre et de l'unir specialement à la Tres Respectable Grande Loge, qui vient d'être constituée en Hollande, pour que de leur part ils rendent complette son etendue sur toute la Republique." The same resolution is repeated in the minutes in Dutch, and there the term again is *Souvereiniteit.* This language is exactly repeated in the formal request to the Grand Lodge; MS 23.3, ff. 3–7.

25. G.L. MS 38:1, f. 67, meeting of 22 7bre 1756.

26. G.L. MS 23.3, ff. 16, 17 April 1758.

27. G.L. MS 123.B.4: "Hoe grote Verpligting heeft men niet aan die Verhevene Geesten,

die sonder vriy gewin sonder selfs gehoor te geven aan de natuurlyke lust die de mensch heeft om te heerschen, een instelling hebben versonnen, waar van 't enigste oogmerk is, de geesten en harten te verenigen, om se te verbeteren, en om in vervolgten tyden eene gantsch geestelyke Natie te formeren." Translated from French by brother Cornelis De Brauw.

28. See the essay by Jan de Jongste, op. cit.

29. G.L. MS 123.B.4., f. 31: "Le trés Venerable a proposé, qu'un des principaux devoirs de la Maçonnerie consistent dans l'obeissance à ses Souverains, et dans l'exacte observation des loix, qui tendrent aux biens de la Societé commune. . . . Sur quoi etant deliberé, tous les Freres d'un consentiment unanime ont rémercié le Tres Venerable en temoignant leur zelé pour le bien publicq et leur soumission entiere à leurs Souverains legitimes."

30. B.A., Brievenarchief, no. 70, "Remarques van P. B. Bunel."

31. B.A. MS 41:6, f. 16: "De Venerable (pro tempore) vermaand de Broederen tegen het houden van Clandestine Loges . . . byzonder teegen eene zeekere Joodse Loge, die zeedert eenige tyd hier ter Steede gehouden is."

32. Ibid., ff. 26–27. They conversed in French.

33. B.A., Brievenarchief, 3/35, no. 17, Amsterdam, 10 April 1756; the French terms are "profanisme" and "assemblées des clairvoyans."

34. G.L. MS 41:42b, 9 January 1762, answer to the lodge Philadelphia in Halle.

35. B.A., Brievenarchief, no. 12, to the lodge in Amsterdam La Charité, from La Bien Aimée, the opening saluation is "Ma chere soeur" and the closing, "Votre affectionnée Soeur." Ibid., no. 15, to the lodge in Nijmegen, "aan haare Zuster." Note that the lodge La Charité was made regular by the British Grand Master in 1755; see ibid., no. 19; the text speaks of "la legalité d'une Loge." Ibid., no. 18, where Minerva zum Zirkel addresses the officers of La Bien Aimée: "Comme nous prenons toujours à coeur la renommée & la splendeur de toutes nos Soeurs, légitimement établies."

36. G.L. MS 38:1, ff. 32, 38–39.

37. Ibid., f. 74: "puisque les Statuts de la maçonnerie ne permettent point qu'un pareil document sorte de loge. Ce qu'il a promis de faire observer, a la Vénérable Loge dont il est caracterisé: secondement, le dit frère Dagran en sa qualitâ de deputé a promis de ne donner aucune Constitution qu'apres l'Election du Grand Maitre National a supposer que le pouvoir lui en reste." And ff. 80–81 for the exhortation to scrutinize "chaque deputation."

38. B.A., Brievenarchief, no. 116, J. Buys to J. Schreuder, 27 July 1757: "te werken om zoo ampel en volmaakt eene Constitutie voor ons te bekoomen als mooglyk is . . . Wy hebben ons liever aan de Nationaale Loge willen adresseeren dan aan eenige andere, hoe veel gelegenheid wij ook hadden om eygenhandig van den Mylord Carnarvon of Comte de Clermont zulks te verkrygen."

39. B.A., Brievenarchief, no. 116, Curaçao, 27 July 1757.

40. B.A. MS 41, Notulen, f. 143: if ten or fewer brothers were present, one negative vote could be cast; twenty or fewer, two, etc.

41. G.L. MS 23.1 (Kast 158.B), f. 9: "Nous convenons, et tout Veritable Frère dont convenir, que tout honnete homme, dont le caractere, et les moeurs et la discretion ne portent rien de reprochable, peut etre aspirer à l'avantage d'etre initié dans nos Mysteres." This is the thirty-second meeting of the lodge, 17 December 1760.

42. G.L. MS 38:1, ff. 34–35; the rejection, for the second time, of one Teissier by 7 to 6 vote in the lodge Concordia vincit Animos.

43. G.L. MS 23.1 (Kast 158.B), f. 111: "Surtout, mes Frères, j'ai taché de Vous animer toujours dans le but principal de notre Institution, dans l'observance de cette Philantropie, de cette charité, de cette douce Egalité primitive des Hommes, qui fait le fonement de notre Art, et qu'il Nous convient de retablir du moins dans nos coeurs et dans nos Assemblees." This is from a verbatim oration, copied by hand, probably as it was spoken, or shortly thereafter, dated approximately 1763.

44. Ibid., f. 118: "La bonne compagnie mes Frères, sera donc toujours une suite necessaire de la moralité, et nous dictera en detail les devoirs de la société."

45. "Discours . . . à Amsterdam chez Jean Schreuder," pp. 42–51, in *Almanach des Francs-Massons. Pour l'Année Bissextile 1768,* [The Hague,] 1768.

46. G.L. MS 23.1, f. 119: "Sur ces conditions, mes Frères, conditions, que j'ose appeller des principles Nobles, qui n'ont en vue, qu'un but egalement glorieux et solide, sur ces conditions, dis je, je m'offre comme vôtre Maitre, Ami, Concitoyen, et comme votre Frère."

47. Ibid., f. 145, late 1760s: "Je finis, mes frères, en vous exhortant de nous unir de plus en plus par les liens les plus sacrés, pour donner un exemple à tout le monde, que par cette voye nous sommes en état de faire parvenir nôtre supérbe Edifice au plus haut point de la perfection!"

48. G.L. MS 41:48 (2), 23 December 1764: the minutes of the Grand Lodge where it is thanking Van der Lyn for an oration given in La Bien Aimée, "tegens de ongegrond lasteringen van het blind gemeen." Mention of a decree against the order proclaimed in Danzig.

49. Ibid., ff. 46–47: "zo is heeden de Verkiezing by boone. . . ." On the fees, ff. 62–63. Cf. Brievenarchief, no. 103: "Project om de harmonie in de minsaame verkiezing der Broederen deser Loge vaster te Maken, en meer en meerder aante queeken."

50. Ibid., f. 66: "en goedgevonden aan de Loge te proponeeren, omme het bovengenoemde 20th artic: van onse huishoudelyke wett in deser Voege te altereeren, van namentlyk by de Ballotteringe der Voorgestelde hierboven in plaatse van Witte Boonen te gebruyken, koopere penningen, en in plaatse van de swarte Boonen, een stuk geld bedragende de Waarde van dertig stuyvers voor het overige blykt het articel van de wett in zyngeheel dus wel te volstaan . . . 14 Maart 1760."

51. The list is at the G.L. MS 41.43, "La Bien Aimée lyst der gebannen & geexcludeerde BB . . . 1756–1835."

52. B.A., Brievenarchief, no. 50, letter of Baron de Boetzelaer, 7 January 1757.

53. B.A., Brievenarchief, no. 51, "preparatie voor St. Jansdag, 1757," actually 27 December 1756.

54. *The Constitutions of the Ancient and Honourable Fraternity of Free and Accepted Masons . . . Worcester,* [Mass.], 1792, pp. 137–39.

55. B.A., Brievenarchief, no. 102. For more information on Smith and a portion of a treatise he wrote on freemasonry, see Harry Carr, ed., *The Collected Prestonian Lectures, 1925–1960,* London: Quatuor Coronati, 1965, pp. 80–82. G.L. MS 926, "Various Tracts concerning Freemasonry or the Royal Art by George Smith, A.B. & Lector Math. of a Constituted Lodge at Amsterdam, Grand Master," 1757.

56. B.A. MS 41.7, Notulen, f. 16, 10 February 1758.

57. This whole process is carefully analyzed in W. Kat, *Een Grootmeestersverkiezing in 1756 uit het archief van de A. L. La Bien Aimée,* Amsterdam, published by the lodge, 1974, pp. 18–19.

58. G.L. MSS of Concordia vincit Animos, MS 38:1, "Diplome de Constitution et d'Etablissement en faveur de la Loge des Franc-Maçons, qui a eté decoré de ce titre, Concordia vincit animos . . ."; the original text is in Latin and was translated into French by the abbé Claude Yvon. This appears to have nothing to do with the lodge that George Smith is proposing.

59. For the significance of this usage for the political history of the period, see Marina Valensise, "The French Constitution in Prerevolutionary Debate," *Journal of Modern History* (1988): S22–S29 (suppl.). To the question "Was there a constitution in France before the Revolution?," the answer might now be given: Yes. There were many, in various masonic lodges.

60. See Johan A. van Reijn, "Een Rotterdamse Loge omstreeks 1721," *Thoth* 33, no. 5 (1982): 237–44.

61. W. Kat, *Een Grootmeestersverkiezing,* p. 17; the Dutch translation of the original letter reads: "in 1749 tenslotte, zag onze Loge door een gevolg van deze onlusten, haar Très Vénérable et Très Eclairé Maître heengaan, die haar gedurende meer dan twaalf jaren had geleid met een ijver, een waardigheid en didactische gaven, waarvan men weinig voorbeelden zal vinden."

62. Letter dated 7 November 1756 from Dagran to Schreuder; printed in Kat, op. cit., p. 112; pp. 43 ff. provides a photocopy of the initiation record for 24 February 1735 where it is evident that Rousset's name has been added in the margin. See also W. Kat, *Machtsstrijd in de Vrijmetselarij, 1757–1759,* Amsterdam: privately printed for La Bien Aimée, 1982.

63. Kat, *Een Grootmeestersverkiezing,* p. 25.

64. B.A., Brievenarchief, no. 37, 2 December 1756: "Je ne sçais si vous savez qu'il y a eu icy dans les Pays une grande Loge Nationale qui a commencé ses fonctions le 19 Novembre 1734 et qui a été constituée par la Grande Loge d'Angleterre au Mois de Mars 1735. Toutes les autres Loges de ces Provinces ont du lui etre soumises et recevoir d'Elle ou de son Grand-Maître leurs Constitutions. . . . Dans cette flatteuse supposition de votre zèle et de Votre bonne volonté Franc-Maçonne, je vous prie Chers et Vénérables Frères, dans ma susditte qualité exposée et prouvée, de me marquer si vous avez quelque Constitution en vertu de laquelle vous pouvez légitimer votre travail et votre formation en Loge." French was a second language for Dagran.

65. This recognition seems to have been made "legal" only in 1770; G.L. MS 41:48(2), 19 August 1770; minutes of the Grand Lodge.

66. Quoted from the *Constitutions* reprinted in Jacob, *The Radical Enlightenment;* see the appendix, p. 280.

67. B.A., Brievenarchief, no. 141e, Groote Loge gehouden den 18e December 1757.

68. Ibid., no. 141d: "Werdende aan alle Wettige Broederen stricktelijk geinterdiceerd; die van La Bien Aimée in hunne versaameling immer te visiteeren, ofte met de Leeden van deselve eenige correspondentie of ommegang te hebben over het geene de Broederschap eenigsints aangaat, op poene van te sullen werden gehandeld a's hunne meedepligtigen; en dewijl de Groote Loge het seer kwaade Gedrag bij die van La Bien Aimée gehouden . . . word gedeclareert dat de Heer J. Schreuder meester van gemelde versaemeling nooit admissibel zal zijn in eenige wettige Loge deezer landen, veel min als meester eenige wettige Loge zal kunnen regeeren; en word aan de verdere leeden van dat gesellschap de tydt van drie maanden gegeeven om sig daarvan af te zonderen, en aan den Grootmeester den blijken geevende van derselver onschuld omtrent het gepasseerde, often wel van hun berouw over 't selve te mogen worden gereadmitteerd in de geregelde Loges deeser Landen."

69. G.L. MS 412:7, f. 109 (1763).

70. B.A., Brievenarchief, no. 3/35, P. Bunel (master of the lodge) to his brothers, 9 March 1756: "Wij verklaaren ons bij deese, niet alleen geen Party te zyn aan de nog in duysternis omswervende."

71. B.A. MS 41:48(1), notes taken at the Grande Lodge, 20 June, 1762: "Wyders heeft den zeer Verligten Gedeputeerden Groot Meester aan deese aanzienelyke Vergaadering voorgedragen, zyne bevinding nopens de Utrechtse zaak in questie, en dezelve verzogt hunne consideratien in deese te willen opgeeven, ten einde die neeteligh e en moeielyke Verschillen, zoo mogelyk, te beslissen ofte andersints tot eene finale decisie te komen; en de weder zydse Partyen te ordonneeren zig naar het Besluit van dien te gedragen. . . . Het [?] gedrag der Leeden thans uitmakende de Loge L'Astrea, en hunne ongehoorzaamheid, in't niet willen companeeren met de Partyen van hunnen Meester; in't overtreeden van de suspensie; in't clandestin vergaaderen." Earlier, in defending the lodge, brothers described officers as knowledgeable about true masonic practices because of someone who had been in place in "du tems de Mr. Rousset." See B.A. Brievenarchief, no. 151e, 15 October 1760.

72. G.L. MS 41:42, 24 August 1759.

73. Ibid., 131c/120, 14 December 1759, where it is once again threatened.

74. Ibid., 132a, 19 August 1759.

75. Ibid., 135/125, 12 October 1759, P. Bunel to the lodge: "verklaaren het presidium van gemelde broeder voor onregtmatig & usurpatent."

76. B.A. MS 41:9, f. 126.

77. G.L. MS 41:48 (2), passim.

78. G.L. MS 41:42, f. 128, and ff. 129–30. Notes or draft of letters, undated but from 1759.

79. For an excellent analysis of this both absolute and relative decline see Jonathan Israel, *Dutch Primacy in World Trade, 1585–1740,* Oxford: Clarendon Press, 1989, final chapter.

80. As do the minutes of the G.L. MS 41:48 (2).

81. Ibid., 19 May 1782.

82. Ibid., 20 June 1762, on the rebellion of the lodge Frederik Royale.

83. Ibid., 6 June 1779, minutes of the Grand Lodge: "En wyders door voorleezen een Tractaat van Alliantie, dat, ingevolge het geresolveerde in de Groote Loge van 17 May 1778, met het Groot Oosten van 't Duytsche Ryk, onder bewind van den doorlugtigen Groot Meester. . . . Welke Alliantie van groot nut zoude zyn, zo ten oprigte van het algemeen belang der beide Natien."

84. F. Bourdet, *Le Patriotisme universel. . . ,* Berlin, 1777, p. xv. Bourdet was the official engineer and inspector of hydraulics for Frederick the Great, and orator of his lodge, Frédéric aux trois Séraphins, in Berlin.

85. *La Très-respectable Grand-Loge de France, a toutes les l.r. du Royaume . . . ,* 1773, p. 5. Property is directly mentioned.

86. *A La Gloire du G.A. de L'Universe . . . le G.O. de France, a toutes L . . . 1774,* pp. x–xi. G.L. sign 199.B.12.

87. In July 1749 Rousset's journal, *Mecure historique et politique,* had been condemned by the States of Holland; see W. P. C. Knuttel, *Verboden Boeken de republiek der Vereenigde Nederlanden,* The Hague: Nijhoff, 1914, p. 78. Few works made this category. Aside from anonymous texts, it includes works by Aretino, B. Bekker, Voltaire, La Mettrie, Hume (1766), and Priestley (1784), to name the most famous authors. The description of The Hague comes from a letter in Dr. Williams's Library, London, MS 24.157, dated 6 August 1760, and describing a trip to The Hague and Amsterdam.

88. *Du Gouvernement Civil, par Mr Locke. Traduit de l'Anglois. Sixième Edition, Exactement revue & Corrigée sur la dernière édition de Londres & augmentée de quelques Notes. Par L.C.R.D.M.A.D.P.,* The Hague: J. Schreuder and P. Mortier, 1755. The 1780 edition of this text is a page-by-page reprint published by Barthelemi Vlam. The 1755 edition was also reprinted in Paris in 1795.

89. B.A., Brievenarchief, 5.d, 1 January 1755, Rousset to Schreuder. I have written extensively on this correspondence and the identification of Rousset in "In the Aftermath of Revolution: Rousset de Missy, Freemasonry, and Locke's *Two Treatises of Government,*" an essay in the festschrift in honor of Franco Venturi, *L'Età dei lumi. Studi storici sul settecento Europeo in onore di Franco Venturi,* vol. 2, Naples: Jovene Editore, 1985, pp. 487–522. For mention of "le frère Silo," see B.A. Brievenarchief, 3/35, letter from Rousset to Schreuder, dated 21/1 [1756]. And in B.A., no. 5d, the text reads: "Monsieur Silo m'a envoyé une revision du la 1re. du portefeuille où vous avez fait quelque changemen[t]. . . ." In B.A. no. 5f, "le frère Silo." There is also a letter from Rousset to Marchand, University Library, Leiden, Marchand MSS 2, 23/6 [?], but from context, 1755, mentioning Silo, who is delivering books, in this case "de edition de Gibert." It should be noted that Locke is never mentioned by name, but the evidence seems overwhelming that this is the book being proofed.

90. Ibid., 21 January 1755, mentioning "la grande lettre que vous m'editez depuis si

longtemps sur le de Witt." This must refer to *Lettres et négociations entre Mr. Jean de Witt . . . I–IV,* Janssens-Waesberge, 1725. Schreuder worked for P. Mortier in this period and he had dealings with Waesberge. It is not possible to associate Schreuder with any other known edition of De Wit. This translation from the Dutch would prove Rousset's fluency at this early date. See *Biographie Universelle,* vol. 39, Paris, 1825, p. 165n.

91. Rodermond, op. cit., chapter 2, esp. p. 20. I am following here the convention of calling this lodge by its second name bestowed at its reconstitution, and not by its original title, Loge de la Paix.

92. In the discussion that follows I am indebted to Salvo Mastellone, "Sur l'origine du langage constitutionnel: Une traduction anonyme de l'anglais (J. Locke et D. Mazel)," *Bulletin de Société de l'histoire de Protestantisme français* 125 (1979): 364, and passim.

93. [Anon.,] *Redevoering, Uytgesprooken door een Broeder Orateur, In eene Wettige Loge . . . 27 December 1755,* p. 6: "Als de bitse nyd, het onkundig en lasterziek Gemeen, kwaadmeenende huychelaars, vooringenomene Schryvers, verjaagende Vorsten, vervloekte Inquisitie, donderende Vatikaanen en daverende Preedikstoelen, over al de [?] vervolging aankondigen, en alarm zonder ophouden blaazen!" Although this is a printed text, we cannot assume that it was intended for circulation beyond the confines of the fraternity. I am treating it as a particularly frank statement, as language not primarily intended for the larger public.

94. Cf. J. Hampton, "Les traductions françaises de Locke au XVIIIe siècle," *Revue de littérature comparee* 29 (1955): 240–51. The Dutch translation of Locke's *Two Treatises* gives both the first and second; *De Vryheid van Godsdienst in de Burgerlyke Maatschappy . . . door . . . Locke, Noodt, Barbeyrac, Hoadly en Drieberge, door den Heer R.D.B.G.D.I.H.M.V.,* Amsterdam: Jan Doll, 1774.

95. For an excellent list of all these editions and translations of Locke, see Peter Laslett, ed., *John Locke. Two Treatises of Government,* Cambridge: Cambridge University Press, 1960, p. 126. The original French text appeared as [Anon.,] *Du Gouvernement Civil. Traduit de l'Anglois,* Amsterdam: Wolfgang, 1691. See also John Attig, ed., *The Works of John Locke,* Westport, Conn.: Greenwood Press, 1985, pp. 31–33, which repeats the commonly made error that this edition was a Jansenist work; the 1780 and 1795 editions reprint the 1755 edition. It is interesting to note that in 1755 there also appeared a reprint of the 1702 translation of Algernon Sidney, *Discours sur le gouvernement,* vols. 1–4, The Hague: Louis and Henri van Dole, 1755, with a new preface by van Dole. The original translation was by the Huguenot refugee P. A. Samson, who had connections with Marchand and Rousset's youthful coterie.

96. *Du Gouvernement Civil . . . augmentée de quelques Notes. Par L.C.R.C.M.A.D.P.,* pp. xv–xvii, for all passages quoted. The passage on natural laws reads "j'en ai changé quelques expressions louches. . . . J'aurois pu étouffer, pour ainsi, dire, le Texte sous un amas de notes ou remarques tirées de Cumberland, des Lois Naturelles, de Burlamaqui, Principes du Droit Naturel, et de Mr Strube de Piermont du Droit Primitif." It should be mentioned that the 1749 Brussels edition of the French text had identified Locke as its author, but his authorship was widely known in the republic of letters from at least the early eighteenth century.

97. Ibid.: "chez nous les Nobles sont citoiens comme le reste des Habitans, et n'ont pas plus à dire que les Magistrats établis par la Constitution."

98. See Herbert H. Rowen, *The Princes of Orange. The Stadtholders in the Dutch Republic,* Cambridge: Cambridge University Press, 1988, pp. 191–93.

99. As quoted in Alice Clare Carter, *The Dutch Republic in Europe in the Seven Years War,* London: Macmillan, 1971, pp. 31–32.

100. E. J. B. Rathery, ed., *Journal et mémoires du marquis d'Argenson,* Paris, 1902, vol. 8, p. 466; the passage goes on to report that his Majesty has 80,000 men amassed on the frontiers of Holland.

101. Archives du Royaume de Belgique, Brussels, MS 34, Rousset to "Votre Excellence," 7 February 1755: "Mais votre politique de ceux qui l'employent; mais c'est aussi que la Republique est gouvernée, l'intérêt particulier y règle tout." For just how precarious Austrian loyalty to the alliance was by 1755, see J. C. D. Clark, ed., *The Memoirs and Speeches of James, 2nd Earl Waldegrave, 1742–1763,* Cambridge: Cambridge University Press, 1988, pp. 64–72.

102. Archives du Royaume de Belgique, Brussels, MS 34, 3 February 1755: "dans la plus grande securité, elle n'étoit pas plus grande en 1672 et peut être que si la [?] nous chercherit querelle il se trouveroit dans nos villes des Regens antistathouderois. . . . Amsterdam surtout est oposée [sic] au Consul du Stathoudre au de là de ce qu'on peut imaginer. Cette puissante ville a conservé le droit de nommer ses magistrats."

103. Haus-Hof-und Staatsarchiv, Vienna, GC.277,328,395, letters from the 1740s. After his death, Rousset's daughter requested a pension for her mother from the Austrians.

104. Cf. Richard Ashcraft, *Revolutionary Politics and Locke's Two Treatises of Government,* Princeton, N.J.: Princeton University Press, 1986, pp. 212–14, 393–94, with salutary comments on drawing these distinctions too clearly.

105. For Rousseau's encounter with Locke, whom as late as 1754 he knew only through the writings of Barbeyrac, see Ira O. Wade, *The Structure and Form of the French Enlightenment,* vol. 2, Princeton, N.J.: Princeton University Press, 1977, pp. 145–46; Réné Hubert, *Rousseau et l'Encyclopédie. Essai sur la formation des idées politiques de Rousseau (1742–56),* Paris: Gamber, 1928, pp. 61, 66, and 99n on Barbeyrac; cf. Robert Derathé, *Jean Jacques Rousseau et la science politique de son temps,* Paris: Vrin, 1970, pp. 47–49, 84–89. It is interesting to note that Derathé relies on this 1755 edition of Locke as reprinted in 1780. On the debt of Rousseau to Locke, see Richard Ashcraft, ed., *Locke's Two Treatises of Government,* London: Allen and Unwin, 1987, pp. 279–80.

106. B.A. MS 41.6, Notulen, ff. 147–49. There are nearly fifty rules put in place on 11 December 1754. From that date on, new members put their signatures to those rules.

107. B.A. Notulen 7, "Huyshoudelijke Wet van La Bien Aimée," 11 December 1754. The phrase is "dat alles in de loge in goede orde toega."

108. B.A. MS 5, 10 December 1754: "J'espère qu'on vous établira Maître de cette nouvelle Loge de la Paix, fondée sur l'ancienne & que vous la gouvernerez de la manière à ne s'y laisser glisser aucun abus françois & surtout que vous en bannirez l'yvrognerie en fixant la dépense du vin dans chaque repas a une bouteille par tête jusqu'à ce que la loge soit fermée."

109. Ibid., 1 January 1755: "je ne puis qu'aprouver souverainement tout ce que vous me marquez d'être passé; puisque j'y trouve toutes les marques d'une véritable et légitime Loge angloise, exempte de toutes les impertinents additions françoises."

110. Janet Mackay Burke, *"Sociability, Friendship and the Enlightenment among Women Freemasons in Eighteenth-Century France,"* Ph.D. diss., Arizona State University, 1986, p. 118, citing a text of 1779.

111. Ibid.: "je l'exhorte à ne pas porter la Loge au de là de 24 ou 25, autrement c'est une confusion, comme nous l'avons vû dans La Loge de la Paix ou il avoit 93 membres."

112. *Du Gouvernement Civil . . . augmentée de quelques Notes,* Amsterdam, 1755, p. 14.

113. Cf. Fred L. Pick and G. Norman Knight, *The Freemason's Pocket Reference Book,* London: Muller, 1955, rpt. 1983, p. 237. For a contemporary discussion of the importance of Noah, see [Anon.,] *Noblesse des Francs-Maçons, ou Institution de leur Société . . . Par un Prophane,* Frankfurt am Main: chez Jean-Auguste Raspe, 1756. The concern with drunkenness may also be related to the Noah theme; see Genesis 9:20, where one of his sons finds Noah drunk.

114. B.A. MS 46a, 25/26 December 1756: "Circa half negen was het eeten gereed en de tafel in order. Schielijk werd de Loge geopent. De eerste conditie was de Staten Generaal,

daarna d'Erf Stadhouder. Vervolgens de Grootmeester Nationaal." Notes taken on the meeting describe "daar komende was te propositie van een of twee politieke surveillants te hebben [?] balotteerde en wel per Loge, also de surveillants; Eensgesind met Haar: meester waren en dus bij meerderheyd een politiek—de 2de ter verkiezing van de Venerable de gedeputeerdens rapporteerde, dat het geaccordeerd wierd." Note the active presence of the abbé Claude Yvon at this assembly. A copy of the rules and statutes adopted by the Grand Lodge of The Netherlands can be found in *Les Devoirs, Statuts, ou Reglemens Généraux des Francs-Maçons; mis dans un nouvel ordre, et approuvés par la Grande Loge des sept provinces unies des Pais-Bas,* Frankfurt and Leipzig, 1764.

115. B.A., Brievenarchief, no. 35, La Charité to La Bien Aimée: "aiant pris pour objet de ses occupations, l'arrangement de diverses affaires purement domestiques, au Vendredi dernier le 26 de ce mois." And in the records of Concordia vincit Animos, also G.L. MS 38:1, f. 56: on refusing someone for membership, "qu'il a eté refusé chez nous uniquement pour raisons domestiques." He was judged to be too young, although he was not as young as some other members who were admitted. In Dutch the term used that implies the domestic is generally "onse *huishoudelyke* zaaken."

116. On the last word see B.A., Brievenarchief, no. 150a, from the lodge in Curaçao, 25 March 1760. For similar language see [Anon.,] *Rede, gehalten am 5.September 1777, in der Loge la Royale Yorck . . . ,* [Berlin, 1778]; spoken by a Swedish brother and translated from the French.

117. G.L. MS 23.1 (Kast 158.B), minutes of the lodge La Philantrope, Middleburg, Zeeland.

118. G.L. MS 41:42b, 150a/123, 25 March 1760; and the response (sent to Curaçao), 30 September 1760, f. 150b.

119. B.A. MS 41:9, f. 128. The orator is Jan Valkenburg.

120. Kloss MS 240.A.59, f. 66.

121. Ibid.

122. Franco Venturi, *Utopia and Reform in the Enlightenment,* Cambridge: Cambridge University Press, 1971.

123. B.A., Brievenarchief, no. 6b, where she is carefully described. She is also intended as a reference to the wife of King Pompilius. Oral tradition within the lodge also claims that she was meant as a virtuous spoof on the mistress of the French king.

Chapter 5

1. G.L. MS 38:1, minutes of the lodge Concordia vincit Animos, here excerpted. The minutes cited begin "A l'abrÿ de la vue des profanes & dans la maison du frère Chevalier le 23 Juillet l'an de Grace 1755. . . . La Loge ayant eté ouverte le frère Rodde . . . ont demandé leur demission de Membres, & comme aucun frère n'est gené dans la Maçonnerie à cet Egard, il leur a eté accordé, cependant au regret unanime de tous les frères."

2. Ibid., f. 58: "A l'abry de la vue des Profanes & dans la maison de Croze le 18 Juillet l'an 1756. La Vénérable Loge decorée du titre Concordia vincit animos s'y est assemblée comptant y trouver un appartement pour ouvrir Loge en presence des frères . . . Mais ayant trouvé que nous ne pouvoins y être nulle part a couvert, on a conclu de ne point l'ouvrir; quoi que pour satisfaire aux conventions qui subsistent entre la loge de la Paix." In the 1780s La Bien Aimée had to meet in private homes in order to save money; MS 41:9, f. 148.

3. G.L. MS 38:1 passim; Chevalier was thirty-six years old in 1756, a native of Rouen, and also a schoolmaster. Some are described as *marchands,* others as *négoçiants.* They all

paid the 2 ducat initiation fee. On at least one occasion Dutch was used for an initiation ceremony because the candidate did not know French.

4. See Franco Venturi, *Le Origini dell' enciclopedia,* Rome: Edizione U, 1946; and D. W. Smith, *Helvétius. A Study in Persecution,* Oxford: Clarendon Press, 1965, pp. 144–52.

5. See Margaret C. Jacob, *The Radical Enlightenment,* London: George Allen and Unwin, 1981, pp. 256–57. On the various interpretations put forward about the intellectual roots of the *Encyclopédie,* see Frank A. Kafker, "Some Observations on Five Interpretations of the Encyclopédie," *Diderot Studies* 23 (1988): 85–100. Yvon's name also appears on the complete membership list of this lodge housed in the masonic manuscripts at the Bibliothèque Nationale, Paris, MS FM 2.563, Portefeuille met Oude Naamlijsten, no. 5, f. 23; Yvon is among the founders who formed together on 5 July 1755. On de Prades, see Jean F. Combes-Malaville, "Vues nouvelles sur l'abbé de Prades," *Dix-Huitieme siècle,* no. 20 (1988).

6. G.L. MS 38:1. The oration was given at "L'Hotel du Comte d'Hallande."

7. [Anon.,] *L'Ordre des Franc-maçons trahi, et Le Secret des Mopses revelé,* Amsterdam, 1745, pp. 4–5. This tract is widely attributed to the abbé Perau.

8. B.N.U. MS 5437, ff. 20–30, Registre des Procès Verbaux de la Loge de la Candeur . . . constituée mere des Loges du Grand Orient de Strasbourg, 1763. The text of this important discourse is published in Jean Bossu, "La Baronne de Flachslande, Protectrice de la Loge La Candeur, O.de Strasbourg," *Travaux de la Loge nationale de recherches Villard de Honnecourt,* 1980, 2nd ser., no. 2, pp. 147–49. There is an early and obscene literature, with reference to sodomy, aimed against British masons; see [Anon.,] *The Free Masons,* 1723, B.L., sign 164.1.25.

9. B.A., Brievenarchief, no. 111, 10 May 1758.

10. [Anon.,] *La Très-Respectable Grand-Loge de France, à toutes les L[oges] . . . du royaume . . . , 1773,* p. 5.

11. B.A. MS 38:1; records of Concordia vincit Animos for 1755.

12. Kloss MS 192.A.33, *Premier discours prononce dans la cent vingt-unieme assemblee . . . de L. des Amis-reunis, 22 Fevrier, 1778,* p. 7. This discourse, although printed, is very rare and is bound with manuscripts concerning the establishment of this lodge.

13. Kloss MS 240.A.59, f. 16.

14. Bibliothèque Municipale de Bordeaux, MS 828/XXXVI, 4ff, undated but the hand is from the second half of the century.

15. *Almanach des Francs-Massons. Pour l'Année commune 1773,* n.p., 1773 [Library of The Grand Lodge of The Netherlands, shelf mark 4.F.10], p. 46.

16. *Gedenkteeken by eene plegtige Gelegenheid opgerecht,* a printed oration intended only for the brothers, dated 1773, p. 10; in speaking of "oproeren. . . . Speelt niet het laage gemeen daarin altoos de hoofdrol?"

17. Heather Swanson, "The Illusion of Economic Structure: Craft Guilds in Late Medieval English Towns," *Past and Present,* no. 121 (November 1988): 29–48. See also Bridget Hill, *Women, Work, and Sexual Politics in Eighteenth-Century England,* New York: Basil Blackwell, 1989.

18. Peter King, *The History of the Apostles Creed: With Critical Observations On its several Articles,* London, 1702, pp. 18–20. A portrait of King was in the Grand Lodge of London.

19. I owe the point to Mary Ann Clawson, *Constructing Brotherhood. Class, Gender, and Fraternalism,* Princeton, N.J.: Princeton University Press, 1989, pp. 46–47.

20. *Almanach des francs-maçons pour l'annee 1762,* p. 42. This song entitled "Aux Profanes" appeared in many places; "Moins curieux que plein de zèle / Viens: avec nous tu peux entrer."

21. [Anon.,] *Cinq Chansons maçonniques . . . ,* Berlin, 1777, p. 8: "O Frères! Méprisez

la race / Des esprits foibles, mal instruits: / Fuyez la vile populace / Qui trouve un venin dans nos fruits."

22. *La G[rand] L[oge] de France à toutes les loges regulières,* 1774, p. 1.

23. [Anon.,] *Discours prononcé à l'occasion de la fête de Saint Jean 24 Juin 1766. Dans la loge françoise établie à Brunswig sous les glorieux auspices de Monseigneur Le Duc Régnant* . . . , p. 4.

24. University Library, Leiden, Marchand MSS 2, f. 36, no date, but from the 1750s.

25. For the repetition of these prohibitions see M. Paillard, ed., *The English and French Masonic Constitutions,* London, 1940, pp. 38, 56. (Privately printed.) For the attitude of present-day British Freemasons, who even condemn the American women's auxiliary, The Order of the Eastern Star, see A. S. Frere, *Grand Lodge, 1717–1967,* Oxford: printed for the Grand Lodge, 1967, p. 164. For the standard eighteenth-century defense of this exclusion, see [Anon.,] *A Defense of Freemasonry, As practiced in the Regular Lodges both foreign and domestic, Under the Constitution of the English Grand Master* . . . , London, 1765, p. 36, against the egalitarian reformers of the 1760s.

26. B.A. MS 122.C.10, "Various Tracts concerning Freemasonry, or the Royal Art . . . 1575," f. 3.

27. [Anon.,] *Lettre de M.L'abbé D.F.*** à Madame La Marquise de ***. Contenant le véritable Secret des Franc-Maçons,* Anvers, 1744, p. 26: "Est-il deshonorant pour le beau Sexe de n'être point assis sur les Fleurs-de-Lys?"

28. Joan B. Landes, *Women and the Public Sphere in the Age of the French Revolution,* Ithaca, N.Y.: Cornell University Press, 1988, p. 40.

29. On Swedish government and society in this period, see Michael Roberts, *The Age of Liberty. Sweden, 1719–1772,* Cambridge: Cambridge University Press, 1986, pp. 135–50. The king is Adolf Frederick. It would be interesting to compare the list of officers with men known to be Hats and Caps, the two main political parties of the time. For one of the earliest records of Swedish freemasonry, see B.N. MS FM 1.95, ff. 19–11; rules for the lodge in Stockholm dated 1737.

30. B.A. MS 41:42b, f. 181, 29 December 1761: "en waar in de Ryks Raad Schaeffer, in 's konings plaats, als des Lands Grootmeester presideert." Finnish masons were also present.

31. B.A., Brievenarchief, no. 80, a contemporary hand gives the date of this letter as 24 June 1757; the masonic date given is 2785. Parts of the text are especially important to this discussion and are therefore given in the original: "tous les membres des 3 loges se trouvèrent à l'Eglise de Ladugårdsland, pour entendre le Sermon qu'a prononcé le frère Halman, Docteur en Théologie, & Curé de la Ditte eglise. . . . Et là nous allames avec une Suite de 70 Carosses au Palais Royal de Carlberg, que le Roy nous ceda pour ce jour la, avec promesse d'assister Lui même à nôtre Assembleé, si l'etât de sa Santé le lui auroit permit. . . . Durant ce tems la, une multitude de monde nous entourra, entrainées par la Curiosité; Entre augres L'Ambassadrice d'Espagne, nous ont invité à nous couvrir, à mêttre le chapeau; & pas même regarder la Dame, pour marquer du Dedain pour tant ce qui est profane. Et elle est entré et Sortie, sans que personne L'aye regardé ou parût faire quelque Attention à Elle. Il y a de remarquables, qu'autant qu'auparavant les maçons ont été jaloux de leurs habillements, sans les montrer aux profanes, tant ils ont été prodiguales ce jour la de les montrer. Et durant le repas même, plusieurs sont sorti de tables, pour se promener dans le jardin, tout habillés qu'ils étoient. . . . Jugez, s'il vous plait, qu'elle Attention le Vulgaire y a fait, & c'étoit un vray plaisir d'entendre leurs raisonnements; Quelques uns nous croyaient les Causes de plusieurs bouleversements dans le ministère. D'autres, que nous etoins intentionnés à rebattir la tour de Babilone, suplierent le Grand Dieu de ne pas nous punir, comme cy devant il les avoit puni; D'autres s'imaginèrent que nôtre unique bût êtoient d'aimer le Sexe, & produire des Enfants illegitimes."

32. See B.N. MS FM 1.95, f. 11; general rules for the lodge in Stockholm founded in 1737.

33. For The Hague as a town and its development, see *Enige Grondslagen voor de Stedebouwkundige ontwikkeling van 's Gravenhage,* The Hague: Gemeetebestuur van 's Gravenhage, 1948. For evidence of early contact between freemasons in The Hague and the Comédie, see H. Gerlach, "De Grondvesting van de nederlandse vrijmetselarij te 's Gravenhage," *Thoth* 2 (1981): 53.

34. Dr. Williams's Library, London, MS 24.157(41), dated 6 August 1760, written from Utrecht by Samuel Kenrick to James Wodrow.

35. B.N. FM 1.136, f. 431: "Soeur Dupont ayant été adoptée à la loge des parfaits Elus depuis l'année 1757. . . . Le jour de son adoption, on lui présente un coeur qui fut le seul garant de leur amitie." Signed by Soeur Dupont, this letter seeking charity is in a collection from the 1780s and sent to the Grand Lodge in Paris. On adoption practices, see James F. Traer, *Marriage and the Family in Eighteenth-Century France,* Ithaca, N.Y.: Cornell University Press, 1980, pp. 152–54, 178.

36. For a catalogue of that vast literature from later in the century, see the collection housed at the library of the Grand Lodge of The Netherlands, George Kloss, *Beschrijving der Versamelingen van het Groot-Oosten der Nederlanden,* The Hague, 1888; and for mysticism and masonic symbolism see Ronald D. Gray, *Goethe. The Alchemist,* Cambridge: Cambridge University Press, 1952. On this lodge, see also B. C. van Uchelen, "De Vrijmetselarij en de Vrouw," *Thoth* 26 (1975): 145–58.

37. On those ties, see David Stevenson, *The Origins of Freemasonry. Scotland's Century, 1590–1710,* Cambridge, Cambridge University Press, 1988, chapter 5. This discussion is largely based on the work of Frances Yates, *Giordano Bruno and the Hermetic Tradition,* London: Routledge & Kegan Paul, 1964.

38. Ruth Perry, *The Celebrated Mary Astell. An Early English Feminist,* Chicago: University of Chicago Press, 1986, pp. 50–52, 89–90, passim.

39. The episode is surveyed in Arend H. Huussen, "Sodomy in the Dutch Republic during the 18th Century," *Eighteenth Century Life* 9, no. 3 (the entire issue devoted to sexual behavior): 169–78. A fuller treatment occurs in Theo van der Meer, *De wesentlijke sonde van sodomie en andere vuyligheeden. Sodomietenvervolgingen in Amsterdam, 1730–1811,* Amsterdam: Tabula, 1984. On sodomy in France see Michel Rey, "Parisian Homosexuals Create a Lifestyle, 1700–1750," in Robert Maccubbin, ed., *'Tis Nature's Fault: Unauthorized Sexuality during the Enlightenment,* Cambridge: Cambridge University Press, 1988, pp. 179–91.

40. See *Daily Advertiser,* London, December 1735. See also *Europische Mercurius,* 1730, vol. 1, pp. 283–304; vol. 2, pp. 289–304.

41. C. Gerretson and P. Geyl, eds., *Briefwisseling en Aantekeningen van Willem Bentinck, Heer van Rhoon,* vol. 1, The Hague: Nijhoff, 1976, p. 114 (1744).

42. Ibid., vol. 2, F. Hemsterhuis to Bentinck, curator of Leiden University.

43. For the Bentincks, see Jacob, op. cit., pp. 198–201, 235–38, 261; and Herbert H. Rowen, *The Princes of Orange,* Cambridge: Cambridge University Press, 1988, pp. 160–203. On Rousseau, see M. Paquot, "Voltaire, Rousseau, et les Bentincks," *Revue de la littérature comparée* 6 (1926): 293–320; and H. L. Brugman, "Diderot, le Voyage de Hollande," in M. Boucher et. al., eds., *Connaissance de l'Etranger. Mélanges offerts à la mémoire de Jean-Marie Carré,* Paris: Didier, 1964. Cf. Walter Gobbers, *Jean-Jacques Rousseau in Holland. Een onderzoek naar de invloed van de mens en het werk (c. 1760–1810),* Ghent: Vlaamse Academie, 1963, pp. 358–59. On Rousseau, see also R. A. Leigh, ed., *Correspondance complète de Jean-Jacques Rousseau,* Banbury, Oxfordshire: The Voltaire Foundation, 1973, vols. 17, 18, and 19, passim.

44. Harry C. Payne, *The Philosophes and the People,* New Haven, Conn.: Yale University Press, 1976, p. 160.

45. Joanne Boeijen et. al., "Notre Misère est Générale. Gedachten van Charlotte-Sophie

Bentinck over de positie van de vrouw," *Documentatieblad Werkgroep 18e Eeuw,* no. 44 (1979). There is also a good novel based on primary sources about this relationship, Hella S. Haasse, *De Groten der Aarde. Of Bentinck tegen Bentinck,* Amsterdam: Querido, 1981. The book claims that they examined scientific subjects together and shared certain common intellectual interests.

46. Gemeente Archief, The Hague, records of births and marriages, no. 1773, 1774.

47. The Gemeente Archief has no baptism records for any of these women. On the troupe, see J. Fransen, *Les comédiens français en Hollande au XVIIe et au XVIIIe siècles,* Paris: Campion, 1925. rpt. This book is invaluable in identifying these women.

48. Pierre Clément, *Les Fri-maçons, hyperdrame,* London: J. Tonson, 1740; cf. Clarence D. Brenner, *A Bibliographical List of Plays in the French Language, 1700–1789,* New York: AMS Press, 1979.

49. See the text of *Les Fra-Maçonnes. Parodie de l'Acte des Amazonnes; Dans l'Opéra des fétes de l'Amour & de l'Himen.* Paris, 1754. Bibliothèque de Grand Orient de France lists one Poinsinet as the author.

50. Fransen, op. cit., pp. 210–11, 232–36, 251.

51. On Scottish freemasonry as simply a more elaborate form of masonic philosophizing, see J. M. Roberts, *The Mythology of the Secret Societies,* London, Secker & Warburg, 1972, pp. 94–100, and C. H. Chevalier, "Maçons écossais au XVIIIe siècle" *Annales historiques de la Révolution française* 41 (1969): 393–408. Cf. Paul Naudon, *Histoire et rituels des hauts grades maçonniques. Le Rite écossais ancien et accepté,* Paris, 1966, pp. 61–62. By 1761 there were at least twenty-five grades within French freemasonry, of which the nineteenth grade was that of grand architect.

52. Letter dated 1757 to the Grand Lodge of the Netherlands, from T. Manningham of the Grand Lodge of London, having consulted with the Scottish Grand Master; printed in P. J. van Loo, *Geschiedenis van de Orde van Vrijmetselaren onder het Grootoosten der Nederlanden,* The Hague: Maçonnieke Strichting, 1967, pp. 254–57.

53. I owe this point to Lynn Hunt.

54. Mr. L'abbé Coyer, *Découverte de l'isle frivole,* La Haye, 1751, pp. 8, 11, 15, 19. There are various editions of this French tract dated 1751 and 1752; there is also an English translation, which bears the date 1750 (*A Discovery of the Island Frivola,* London, 1750), but there is no antecedent in French for that text and the date may therefore be purposefully wrong.

55. Coyer, *Découverte,* p. 38: "A l'arrivée de l'Admiral on formoit un establissement où le sexe subalterne pourroit perdre sa vertu avec décence." And see p. 41: "Ils adorent le Soleil. . . . Ils ont proscrit la Poligamie, parce qu'il n'y a qu'n soleil et qu'une lune."

56. On Coyer, see L. Adams, "Coyer and the Enlightenment," *Studies on Voltaire and the Eighteenth Century* 123 (1974): 24.

57. *Amusements de la Toilette ou Recueil des Faits . . . les plus singuliers tragiques et comiques de l'amour passés en Hollande en Angleterre et en France . . . ,* vol. 1, The Hague, 1756, pp. 121–28, in particular, p. 127. Note that these pages are dated 1755 and bound in the volume published in 1756. The publisher also did many works by Rousset.

58. Ibid., p. 127: ". . . se peut-il qu'il y ait des Hommes qui ayant l'orgueil de croire que la Nature les ait mis au dessus d'un Maçon ou d'un Boulanger."

59. *L'Anti-Calomniateur, ou défense du theatre françois de la Haye,* Liège, 1755, p. 25.

60. Arthur M. Wilson, *Diderot,* Oxford: Oxford University Press, 1972, pp. 262–64, 330–31.

61. Frances A. Yates, *Shakespeare's Last Plays,* London: Routledge & Kegan Paul, 1975, pp. 123–31. I owe this point to Phyllis Mack.

62. *Livre de Constitution,* The Grand Lodge of The Netherlands, ff. 10r, v.

63. J. A. Dijkshoorn, *L'Influence française dans les moeurs et les salons des provinces-unies,* Paris, Ph.D. diss., 1925, University of Groningen, pp. 213–19.

64. This is in a different hand from the one that wrote the Livre; the manuscript is entitled "Amelie grande Maitresse du pretieux Orde de l'Union de la joye." It appears to contain a copy of a 1653 letter by one of the leaders of the salon. Cf. Haijo Zwager, *Waarover Spraken Zij? Salons en Conversatie in de achttiende eeuw,* Assen, 1968, pp. 175–78.

65. Abbé Perau, *L'Ordre des franc-maçons trahi, et le Secret des Mopses révelé,* Amsterdam 1745, pp. 120–22; and J. L. Carr, "Gorgons, Gormogons, Medduists and Masons," *Modern Language Review* 58 (1963): pp. 73–74. Cf. Harry Carr, ed., *The Early French Exposures,* London, 1971, pp. 113 et seq. (Privately printed.) In the G.L. manuscripts two folios entitled "Tableau des Mopses" in an eighteenth-century hand are all that remains of what may have been an interest in this organization.

66. G.L., Maçonnerie d'Adoption Ecossoise, 1751, MS in folder with Livre de Constitution, f. 11, ceremony entitled "Ouverture de la Loge." It begins with the instruction: "Les frères et soeurs entrent dans la chambre du travail et prennent chacun leur place."

67. G.L. MS Livre de Constitution, ff. 15–16, ceremony labeled "Reception au grade d'architecte"; and ff. 25–26, "Catéchisme des architects de l'adoption écossoise."

68. "Discours, prononcé par le Fr. Comte de Medini, dans la L. D'Adoption, érigée par les FF. de la L. régulière l'Indissoluble, à la Haye, le 29 Mars 1778," in *Almanach des Franc-Maçons. Pour l'Année Bissextile 1780,* The Hague: van Laak, 1780, p. 60.

69. *Almanach des Francs-maçons pour l'Année 1751,* The Hague: Pour le Compte des la Fraternité, 1751, no pagination. A pocket-size book of no more than forty pages, the annual masonic almanacs are invaluable sources of information on various lodges, in various countries. For other songs used in lodges of adoption, see *Nouveau Recueil de Chansons de la Tres-Vénérable Confrérie des Franc-Maçons . . . ,* Berlin, n.d., pp. 65, 83–84; songs for women masons possibly from the 1750s.

70. I owe this information to Bruce Alan Brown, University of Southern California, who is studying this troupe.

71. For an excellent analysis of this symbolism, see Dorothy Koenigsberger, "A New Metaphor for Mozart's Magic Flute," *European Studies Review* 5 (July 1975): 229–75.

72. For an intelligent discussion of the meaning of masonry in the life of Mozart, see H. C. Robbins Landon, *1791. Mozart's Last Year,* New York: Macmillan, 1988. I am grateful to Peter Upton for bringing this book to my attention and for discussions about it.

73. Bibliothèque Sainte-Geneviève, Paris, MS 1973, 1776, f. 4: "Un Sexe vain, indiscret et volage, qui n'a de loi qu'un instinct dangereux, en s'unissant avec un peuple sage, peut-il former de bien solides? Vivons pour nous, oui, connaissons la femme, son fol espirt, son coeur inconsequent, c'est l'interêt, ou l'orgueil qui l'enflamme, c'est le plaisir, jamais le sentiment, la femme n'a que moitie de notre ame et l'inconstance est son seule element."

74. [Anon.,] *Apologie Pour l'Ordre des Francs-Maçons. Par Mr. N . . . Membre de l'Ordre. Avec deux Chansons composées par Le Frère Américain,* The Hague: chez Pierre Gosse, 1742, pp. 70–71.

75. Mr. Uriot, *Lettres sur la Franche-Maçonnerie, A Stougard,* [n.p.] chez Diederich, 1769, p. 40.

76. *Chansons de l'Ordre de l'Adoption ou la Maçonnerie des Femmes, Au temple de l'Union, Le premier May 1751, à la Haye,* pp. 1–5. The only known copy is in the Bibliothèque Nationale, Paris, YE 17876. I am grateful to Gordon Silber, who discovered this text.

77. *Livre de Constitution,* f. 9: "Que tous frères et soeurs auront pour vêtement de maçons et de maçonnes, un tablier et des gants de peau blanches. Le tablier doublé de taffetas blanc et garni de ruban même couleur: qu'ils porteront pour simbolle de leur travail."

78. Fransen, op. cit., p. 304. See also Franz Pick and René Sedillot, *All the Monies of the World. A Chronicle of Currency Values,* New York, Pick Publishing Co., 1971, for some sense of comparable sums in other eighteenth-century countries.

79. Fransen, op. cit., p. 218.

80. B.A. MS entitled "Mémoire Général de la Recette et de la Dépense des finances de la loge d'adoption depuis l'origine de la loge, jusque, et compris l'assemblée du onze d'avril." Only three months are included and the lodge met once almost every week in that period. On wages in this period, see Jan de Vries, "An Inquiry into the Behaviour of Wages in the Dutch Republic and the Southern Netherlands, 1580–1800," *Acta historiae neerlandicae* 10 (1978): 96, where we learn that in Haarlem and Leiden in 1759 a stableman earned 312 guilders annually, whereas in Ghent in 1760 a servant earned 120 guilders. On the Amsterdam guild, see Richard W. Unger, *Dutch Shipbuilding before 1800,* Assen: Van Gorcum, 1978, p. 91. The fee was 63 guilders.

81. Anthony Vidler, *The Writing of the Walls. Architectural Theory in the Late Enlightenment,* Princeton, N.J.: Princeton Architectural Press, 1988, pp. 83–102, on the architectural designs of the lodges with attention paid to the lodges of adoption.

82. Fransen, op. cit., p. 327n. The records of this lodge are in the library of the Grand Lodge.

83. *Nederlandsche Vry-metzelaars Almanach, voor het Jaar 1793,* Rotterdam, prints a discourse given at the establishment of the lodge for actors.

84. *Almanach des Francs-Maçons, Pour l'Année 1763,* Amsterdam: chez la Veuve de Jean François Jolly, 1763, p. 44.

85. B.A. 41.9, 11 March 1778: "Theodorus Adrianus Craayenschot wyders deed de vener. Mr eene cierlyke redenvoering over het werktuig den Troffel, waarnade Br. Melissen mede eene redenvoering deed wegens het weeren van de Sexe uit onze vergaderingen."

86. For a defense of these Dutch lodges of adoption, see *Tweede Memoire van Defensie van de A . . . L'Union Royale . . . werdende onder het G.O. van Holland,* n.d.

87. B.N. MS FM 1.3, f. 651, 2 September 1779.

88. From the *Journal für Freymaurer,* 1785, quoted in Janet Mackay Burke, "Sociability, Friendship and the Enlightenment among Women Freemasons in Eighteenth-Century France," Ph.D. diss., Arizona State University, 1986, p. 115.

89. Ibid. This thesis should soon see publication. Cf. Janet M. Burke, "Freemasonry, Friendship and Noblewomen: The Role of the Secret Society in Bringing Enlightenment Thought to Pre-Revolutionary Women Elites," *History of European Ideas* 10 no. 3 (1989): 283–94.

90. *Recueil de cantiques maçonniques,* p. 101, bound with *La vraie maçonnerie d'adoption . . . ,* Philadelphie [probably Paris], 1783.

91. *Seconde Esquisse des travaux d'adoption . . . de la Candeur . . . de Paris,* 1779, p. 37: "au milieur d'un Temple consacré à cette Déesse."

92. Cited in Burke, *Sociability,* p. 276.

93. Ibid., pp. 288–89.

94. Charles Alan Kors, *D'Holbach's Coterie. An Enlightenment in Paris,* Princeton, N.J.: Princeton University Press, 1976, pp. 94–98, esp. pp. 106, 213.

95. There is a vast phamphlet literature from the lodges of adoption. A good place to begin is *La Vraie maçonnerie d'adoption; précédée de quelques Réflexions sur les Loges irrégulières & sur la Société civile . . . dediée aux dames. Par un Chevalier de tous les Ordres Maçonniques,* Philadelphie: chez Philarethe, 1783; cf. G. H. Luquet, *La franc-maçonnerie et l'état au XVIIIme siècle,* Paris: Vitiano, 1964, pp. 58–65, 205–7, 227. The lodges of adoption were also attacked as "a disastrous abuse"; see [Anon.,] *Les Francs-Maçons, plaideurs,* Geneva, 1786, p. viii.

96. *Seconde Esquisse des travaux d'adoption, . . . par les officiers de la loge de la Candeur . . . de Paris,* n.p., 1779, p. 5.

97. Copy of the letter from the French adoptive lodge La Candeur to the queen, in *Almanach des Francs-Maçons. Pour l'Année commune 1779,* The Hague: van Laak, p. 22.

98. See *Les Franc-maçons, plaideurs.*

99. Bibliothèque Municipale, Dijon, MS 1415, "Discours prononcé par Madame de D . . . 25 January 1782": "applaudissons nous d'avoire trouvé des hommes justes qui au lieu de nous offir cette condescendance, cette soumission apparente, gages trop certain de l'orgeuil et de la superiorité nous presentent une association, un partage, signe precieux de l'estime et de l'égalité." There are four different copies of this discourse, each in a different hand.

100. Ibid., ff. 331–32.

101. Ibid., f. 344.

102. André Dore, "La Maçonnerie des Dames. Essai sur les grades et les rituels des loges d'adoption 1745–1945," *Bulletins de la Grande Loge de France,* 1981, pp. 1–26. Reprints the text of "L'Amazonie Anglaise."

Chapter 6

1. Van Laak was also Clerk to the Grand Lodge; see B.A. MS 41:48 (1), 23 December 1761; and MS 41:48 (1), 18 March 1762, where he is described as the bookseller of the Grand Lodge. At this meeting he is asking permission to publish a songbook in Dutch and French; and see meeting of 28 September where there is a discussion of the widow Jolly reprinting an "incomplete" songbook and Constitution: "these books would be very damaging to the Grand Lodge of this country." Van Laak's sole rights were reaffirmed. She continued to publish and did an almanac in 1763.

2. B.A. MS 41:42, f. 244b, 8 November 1765, from Van Laak to La Bien Aimée: "Zynde deeze Collectie thans, zo door vermeerderingen welke my nog van Engeland en Frankryk in handen zyn gekomen, als van de Nationale Broederschap [toegezegd?]."

3. William J. Hughan, *Constitutions of the Freemasons of the Premier Grand Lodge of England, 1723–1784,* London, 1899, p. xxi. Preston was paid 20 pounds in 1776 for his services as secretary to the Grand Lodge.

4. Thomas Dunckerley, *A Charge, delivered to the Members of the Lodge . . . at the Castle-inn, Marlborough . . . 1769,* p. 27; bound with Rev. William Martin Leake, *A Sermon . . . Colchester . . . 1777 . . . ,* Colchester, 1778. And in the same volume, Rev. Mr. Panting, *Address . . . 1767,* p. 34: "the unenlightened are ever ready to impeach the harmony and improvement we profess."

5. [Anon.,] *Les Francs-maçons, plaideurs,* Geneva, 1786, p. ix. Note this was in the context of attacking mixed lodges, or lodges of adoption.

6. Kloss MS 240.C.33, f. 21. An undated French manuscript in a hand common at midcentury, entitled "Cahiers concernant les Receptions et Céremonies des Grades d'Apprentis et Compagnons." The library dates the text c. 1760.

7. *Almanach des Francs-Maçons. Pour l'Année commune 1787,* The Hague: Van Laak, 1787, p. 35.

8. [Anon.,] *Lettres de T*** au venerable Grand Maitre et à l'orateur de la loge de V . . . 27 Juillet 1749,* p. 3: "Si l'amour de Dieu nous engage à l'adorer, l'estime & l'amitié qui unissent deux tendres amis doivent les porter à se secourir réciproquement dans leurs besoins. L'homme Philosophe, c'est à dire vraiment sage, ne trouve jamais qu'il a fait assez de bien; on peut avoir assez de beauté, mais on a jamais assez de vertus."

9. William Smith, *A Sermon preached in Christ-Church, Philadelphia, [For the Benefit of the Poor]*, Philadelphia, 1779, passim. Dedicated to George Washington, with an appendix on Cincinnatus among other ancient republicans.

10. Quoted in Wayne A. Huss, "Pennsylvania Freemasonry: An Intellectual and Social Analysis, 1727–1826," Ph.D. diss., Temple University, 1984, p. 61.

11. Kloss MS 240.E.25, f. 53.

12. [Anon.,] *Faustin ou Le Siècle philosophique*, Amsterdam, 1784, pp. 72–78, 211–13. Found in B.N., shelf mark Baylot Imp. 354.

13. Archives Municipales, Strasbourg, Legs Gerschel, box 34/33, no date but clearly from the latter part of the century. The speaker is the orator of the lodge St. Geneviève (see pp. 188–89).

14. B.N. FM 1.63, a dossier of discourses from Paris, many of them from the early nineteenth century.

15. Kloss MS 192.A.33, dated 1778, "Règlement pour les Grades." For the symbolism used with this grade, which was largely cosmological (i.e., sun, moon, stars, arrayed around a globe), see Kloss MS 192.A.51, f. 39.

16. [Anon.,] *Origine et objet de la Franche Maçonnerie, Augmentés de Discours relatifs à cet Ordre; par le F.B***, aux depens des orientaux genevois*, 1774, G.L., shelf mark 202.C.24, p. 11.

17. [Anon.,] *Règlemens de la R.L. des A.R. à L'O[rient] de Paris 6 Mars 1788* . . . bound with *Discours prononcé en loge par un Franc-Maçon . . . 1755*, p. 14: "Le vrai Maçon n'est pas seulement vertueux; il est tout à la fois Philosophe, raisonnable, sociable, vertueux . . . il est parfait."

18. Kloss MSS 240.E.25, ff. 108–9: "Je vous l'ai dit autrefois, M.F. et vous en étés à présent bien persuadés ils sont disparus ces tems de barbarie, de superstition, l'ignorance, si contraires au bonheur de la terre, à tout état de civilisation, à la société en général et à notre ordre en particulier. Les lumières de la Vérité pénétrant dans tous les esprits, l'insinuant dans tous les coeurs, éternisent pour jamais le règne maçonique, parce qu'un art qui parle à la raison, doit être accueilli nécessairement dans le siècle de la Philosophie." Undated but from a collection of discourses from the 1780s.

19. G.L. MS 23:1, the lodge in Middelburg, Zeeland, f. 119 (early 1760s): "Et Vous, mon illustre, mon digne, mon cher Predecesseur, dont je reçois avec un double plaisir le Maillet . . . et surtout de m'éclairer de vos lumieres profondes, que nous avons vues briller à notre Orient."

20. Ibid., MS 41:42b, f. 152b, 13 December 1760, La Bien Aimée to l'Astree, lodge in Utrecht. Note the custom of communicating in French: "que nous sommes charmés de voir luir la lumiere dans une Ville, où jusques à present l'epaisseur des tenebres n'avoit pas permis jusques à la plus petite etincelle de percer les nuages de l'ignorance & de la prevention."

21. Ibid., f. 145 (1769).

22. *Nederlandsche Vry-Metzelaars Almanach, Voor het Jaar 1793*, Rotterdam: C. R. Hake, 1793, pp. 51–52, printing a discourse of 1766: "in het burgerlyke zyn wy medeleden van het lichaam, waar toe wy behoren, en wel verre dat deze gelykheid in ons Genoodschap, waarin wy staat nog rang kennen."

23. [Fr.***] *Discours prononcé le jour de S. Joseph devant une assemblée de Maçons civils et militaires*, Liège, 1785, pp. 6–7.

24. Archives Départementales, Côte d'Or, "Livre des Constitutions et Reglemens Generaux des Francs et Reçus Maçons en particulier pour La Loge de Lausanne, Aprouvés par tous les Frères le 30 Decembre 1741."

25. Kloss MS 240.E.25, f. 41; from a French military lodge of the 1770s in Bastia, Corsica.

26. Ibid.; addressed to French troops leaving Bastia in the 1770s.

27. [Anon.,] *Discours prononcé par le Grand-maître des Francs-Maçons de France . . . 1740,* p. 113; bound with *La muse Maçonne . . .* , The Hague, 1773. One of the most frequently cited masonic orations; copies in The Hague, Reims (Bibliothèque Municipale, MS 2068, piece 48).

28. *Almanach des Francs-Maçons, Pour l'Année 1763. Dressé & calculé sur la Longitude and la Latitude d'Amsterdam,* Amsterdam: chez la Veuve de Jean François Jolly, 1763, p. 43: "Ami sincere, Pere tendre, Époux affable, le Franc-Maçon est à la fois le plaisir de ses amis: la gloire de ses enfans & le triomphe de son épouse; il porte les vertus de la Loge dans le sein de sa famille."

29. *Almanach des Francs-Maçons. Pour l'Année commune 1774, Imprimé pour l'usage des frères, 5774* [1774], pp. 24–25; *Discours de Mr. Le Comte de T***, Lors de la reception de son Fils, faite le 29 Nov. 1763.*

30. *Almanach . . . 5774,* pp. 25–26: "Songez, que cet ordre illustre, devient pour vous une second patrie, rappellez vous que le premier Brutus & Manlius ont sacrifié leurs propres enfants, à l'amour de la patrie, & que mes devoirs pour l'ordre, sont aussi sacrés, aussi redoutables pour moi, que ceux qui leur firent repandre leur propre sang. Mais mon fils, vous qui dans ce moment, me devez le jour pour la seconde fois, quels charmes n'allez vous pas repandre sur ma vie, si vous repondez, à tout ce que l'Ordre attend d'un véritable Franc-Maçon. . . . En devenant frère, je suis devenu veritablement homme, & je ne dois rien faire, qui puisse me degrader du plus eau titre qui honore meme les plus grands Rois."

31. Archives Municipales, Strasbourg, Legs Gerschel, box 34, f. 212, 5 June 1776, from Pierre Antoine Griffon.

32. [Anon.,] *Discours d'Installation de la [loge] Ferdinand aux Neuf Étoiles, prononcé le 22 Févr. 1782,* bound in *Discours prononcés à la [Loge] Ferdinand aux IX Étoiles à l'O. de Strasbourg,* 1782, p. 3. G.L. sign 208.A.4.

33. B.N. MS FM 1.111, f. 423: "dont le devoir de son côte est d'eviter le Faste et la Tyrannie pour ecraser ses Enfans."

34. *De Nederlandsche Vry-Metzelaars Almanach, Voor het Jaar 1791,* The Hague: Isaac van Cleef, 1791, p. 38: "waar sneeuw en ys, zedert de schepping, de kruinen der bergen dekt, tot het afgelegenste voorgebergte in Afrika, leven en arbeiden broeders van my. In welk ryk, in welke vermaarde stad ik kom, daar zyn nu de stille wooningen der Vrymetselaary voor my een vaderland, en de schoot der vriendschap waarin ik veilig rust kan genieten."

35. Kloss MS 240.E.25, ff. 116–21: "qu'à l'esprit maçonique seul d'opérer cette étonnante révolution. Mais si nos lois ne peuvent rien encore sur le bonheur de l'homme dans lÉtat politique, combien elles ajoutent à son bonheur, à ses vertus dans l'État social. . . . Je vous dirai le Grand Orient vous compte au nombre de ses enfans chéris, il rend justice à la régularité à la distinction de vos travaux; continuez, comme vous avez commencé, soyes surtout très difficile sur le choix des profanes qui demandent l'entrée du Temple; le peu d'attention que l'on aporte à cet égard est le principe de tous les désordres qui troublent les L[oges] et qui vont au discrédit de la maçonnerie; Je vous dirai, ne vous trompes jamais sur le précieux mot d'égalité qui a été la source de tant d'abus—songes qu'elle consiste moins dans la différence des conditions que dans une égalité de principes d'éducation, de sentiment, de convenances sociales."

36. For a copy of this discourse and a discussion of Ramsay, see G. M. van Veen, "Andrew Michael Ramsay," *Thoth* 28, no. 11 (1977): 27–58.

37. *Almanach des Franc-Maçons. Pour l'Année commune 1782,* The Hague: Van Laak, 1782, p. 43, and passim.

38. Henry Plard, "La place de Lessing dans la Franc-Maçonnerie allemande de son temps," *Revue de l'Université de Bruxelles,* no. 3–4 (1977): 345–71.

39. [Gotthold E. Lessing,] *Ernst und Falk. Gespräche für freymäuery,* Wolfenbuttel, 1778, pp. 20, 32.

40. Ibid., p. 42: "ist Bemantelung der Tyrannen. Anders nichts." And see also pp. 68–70 for the masonic solution.

41. For example, *Fête Maçonne, célébrée dans la R. Loge La Charité à L'O. d'Amsterdam pour les 25 ans de présidence du T.V.M.R. . . . Le 7 du 4e mois de l'an 5781 [1781],* p. 65; [Anon.,] *Discours prononcé a l'Occasion de la fête de Saint Jean 24 Juin 1766. Dans la loge françoise établie a Brunswig sous les glorieux auspices de Monseigneur Le Duc Régnant de Brunswig et de Lunebourg . . . ,* p. 9; Mons MS, the lodge at Mons, Belgium, "Discours . . . Licurge, et tous les autres Legislateurs politiques n'ont pas rendre leurs etablissements durables, quelques sages qu'aient été leurs loix; elles n'ont pas s'etendre dans tous les pays, comme elles n'avoient en vue que les victoires, les conquettes, et l'elevation d'un peuple audessus de l'autre, elles n'ont pas devenir universelles, ni convenir au gout, au genie, et aux interets de toutes les Nations. La maconnerie au contraire si illustrée de nos jours, rassemble une société d'hommes de tout age, de toute condition et de tout pays." This manuscript ends with a paean of praise for Joseph II.

42. He already appears in the famous oration by Ramsay; cf. *La Muse Maçonne,* The Hague, 1773.

43. Helmut Reinalter, "Freimaurerei und Demokratie im 18. Jahrhundert," in H. Reinalter, *Aufklärung und Geheimgesellschaften. Zur politischen Funktion und Sozialstruktur der Freimaurerlogen im 18. Jahrhundert,* Munich: Oldenbourg, 1989, p. 43.

44. [Anon.,] *Rede so ben der aufnahme Zweener Candidaten in den Freymauerorden gehalten worden,* 1784, p. 4; while proclaiming the peace and quiet of the state, p. 14.

45. Reinalter, op. cit., p. 46.

46. [Anon.,] *Considérations filosofiques sur la Franc-maçonnerie. Dédié A tous les Oriens en France, par un Député de Jerusalem,* Hamburg, 1776, pp. 78–86.

47. *Mémoire pour la Loge des Neuf-Soeurs,* n.p., n.d., but date mentioned in the text, p. 17; G.L., sign 199.B.159.

48. *Discours Prononcé par le F . . . Comte de M . . . I, Dans la Grand Loge Nationale . . . de la Haye, le Juin 1783,* in *Almanach des Francs-Maçons. Pour l'Année Bissextile 1784,* The Hague, 1784, pp. 23–30: "En effet, decoré de nouveaux titres; eclairé de nouvelles lumieres, ayant continué mes voyages, j'ai parcouru une grand partie de l'Allemagne. . . . La distance que la noblesse ou les dignités civiles apportent entre les individus disparoissant dans les Loges, elle y laisse des germes feconds d'un bien general." And later, "C'est de cette façon, que la Maçonnerie interesse l'humanité. . . . Où est elle cetter fameuse Republique Romaine." Also contains discourses from the Nine Sisters.

49. Ibid., p. 28: "Quant a moi, je regarde, d'un oeil philosophique toutes les revolutions des États; & je les trouve dans l'ordre naturel des choses: à la lumiere d'une bonne critique, cherchant la cause qui élève ou abaisse une nation, je la découvre dans sa propre legislation, dans son gouvernement, dans son genie, dans ses moeurs & dans ses passions."

50. [Anon.,] *Rede der Ferer des St. Johannisfestes Gewidmer und in der Loge Ferdinand zum Felsen in Hamburg,* 1793, p. 6. Copy in Olin Library, Cornell University.

51. Kloss MSS 240.E.25, "Discours prononcé par le F . . . Orateur de la L. de la Parfaite Union à l'O. de Bastia dans une assemblée publique tenue à l'occasion de la fête de St. Jean où les Dames avoient été invitées," ff. 26–27.

52. *Almanach des Francs-maçons. Pour l'Année Bissextile 1776,* n.p., 1776, p. 20: "Que le pouvoir de ces G.M. Nationaux égale celui des G.M. d'Angleterre, & qu'ils ont, comme eux, la faculté de créer à leur tour des G.M Provinciaux, pour former des Loges Provinciales; le tout néanmoins, suivant les Conventions ultérierues, dans les Limites du Gouvernement Politique de leurs États respectifs." This last phrase is frequently repeated in the text.

53. Ibid., pp. 21–22: "La Liberté est une autre prérogative de la Franche Maçonnerie, où elle régne généralement dans toutes ses parties . . . cette préciceuse Liberté, qui rend la Constitution de l'Ordre si admirable, & qu'aucun Monarque ne peut lui ôter sans le détruire, parce qu'elle en est comme *l'essence.*"

54. *Almanach oder Taschen-Buch für die Brüder Freymäuer der vereinigten Deutschen Logen . . . 1776,* "Jetzt aber, da die Nationen releuchteter, und gleichsam durch eine menschlichere und geselligere Politick vereinigt sind."

55. [Anon.,] *Discours prononcés à la [Loge] Ferdinand aux IX Étoiles à l'O. de Strasbourg,* 1782, p. 7.

56. Kloss MSS 240.A.59, ff. 81–83; cf. Jacques Lemaire, "L'image de Voltaire dans l'historiographie maçonnique de langue française," *Revue de l'Université de Bruxelles,* no. 3–4 (1977): 320–30 (whole issue devoted to freemasonry).

57. *A La Gloire du Grand Architecte de l'Universe. Réquisitoire du V.F.G.***, grand Orateur de la très R.G.L. de France . . .* ,Donné à l'Orient de Paris, le dix-neuf du dixieme mois de l'an maçonnique 5774 [1774], p. 4: "Si cet abus subsistoit, la Maçonnerie ne seroit plus une république dans laquelle chaque individu partage également le pouvoir; on n'y trouveroit qu'un despotisme affreux, sous lequel on seroit obligé de baisser la tête, & la liberté, ce bien si cher, cet apanage le plus précieux de notre Ordre, seroit absolument anéantie." Printed copy to be found in Archives de la Ville, Strasbourg.

58. Text of the French Grand Lodge's regulations printed in *Almanach des Francs-Maçons. Pour l'Année commune 1777,* Amsterdam: Schreuder, 1777, p. 22; in the commentary the establishment of the French Grand Lodge is described as "this happy revolution."

59. B.N. FM 1.13, correspondence to the Grand Orient from lodge in Le Havre, f. 263, 21 December 1789.

60. Ibid., f. 393, from the lodge L'Ecole des Moeurs in Morlaix, no date but in correspondence from the late 1780s and early 1790s: "Dans l'ordre civil, les deputes d'une Province la representant aux assemblées générales de la Nation; il en est de même des LL . . . celles ci voient dans nos déliberations par le ministère de leurs fondes de pouvoirs, et ce qui ces Députés arrêtent a force de loi pour les LL."

61. [Anon.,] *Le Voile Levé pour les curieux, ou le secret de la Révolution révélé a l'aide de la franc-maçonnerie,* 2d ed., Paris, 1792, pp. 7, 25–27. This tract is sometimes attributed to abbé Lefranc.

62. The quotation is from *Almanach des Francs-Maçons pour l'annee 1762,* n.p., p. 17. Probably published in The Hague.

63. G.L. MS 41:42b, 22 December 1761, letter from La Bien Aimée to Frederik Royale.

64. Kloss MSS 240.E.25, "Discours . . . Mai 1779 . . . Bastia," ff. 66–67.

65. B.N.U. MS 5437, ff. 43–49.

66. [Anon.,] *Essai sur les mysteres et le véritable objet de la confrérie des francs-maçons,* 2d ed., Amsterdam, 1776, p. 31, article 6 of the statutes of the Grand Orient of France.

67. [Anon.,] *Dass Die Gesellschafft derer Freymäurer vollkommen und gerecht sen wurde an dem Johannis-Feste des 5747 Jahres . . . in Halle in einer Rede . . . Halle im Magdeburgischen,* 1748, p. 9. Copy in Olin Library, Cornell University.

68. Bibliothèque Municipale, Dijon, MS 1279, f. 63.

69. Ibid, Fonds Baudot, "Recueil de pièces concernant la Franc-Maçonnerie," f. 52, "discours de 10 9bre 1765."

70. [Anon.,] *Rede so ben der Aufnahme zweener Candidaten in den Freymaurerorden gehalten worden,* 1784, p. 11.

71. Ibid., p. 17. This same language is used in 1740 by the Grand Master of France, Chevalier Ramsay; see *La Muse Maçonne,* The Hague, 1773, pp. 116–17.

72. John Bartier, "Les Constitutions d'Anderson et la Franc-Maçonnerie continentale," *Revue de l'Université de Bruxelles,* no. 3–4 (1977): 286.

73. On the ancient origins of the order, see *Almanach des Franc-Massons. Pour l'Année Bissextile 1772,* p. 18; and *Almanach des Francs-Massons. Pour l'Année Bissextile,* 1768; printing an oration by Schreuder and possibly intended for the French-speaking and often Catholic brothers in the Low Countries.

74. *Almanach des Francs-Maçons. Pour l'Année commune 1781,* The Hague: Van Laak, 1781, p. 26.

75. Kloss MSS 240.E.25, f. 8, *Discours pronouncé a la L . . . de la parfaite union à l'Orient de Bastia . . . par le F. D'Orly . . . 29 June, 1778,* ff. 7–8.

76. [Anon.,] *Essai sur les Mysteres et le veritable objet des Franc-Maçons,* 2d ed., Amsterdam, 1776, p. 8. The first edition is Paris, 1771.

77. *Almanach des Francs-Maçons. Pour l'Année commune 1787,* The Hague: Van Laak, 1787, p. 36; G.L. sign 4 F 24. And see [Anon.,] *Recueil de Discours prononcés en différentes époques solemnelles, Dans la Vble & Très ancienne Loge Française La Royale Yorck de l'Amitie . . . 1767,* [Berlin,] 1781, p. 104. See this last also for the cult of Frederick.

78. *Almanach oder Taschen-Buch für die Brüder Freymäurer der vereinigten Deutschen Logen auf das Jahr Christi 1776;* unpaginated (3).

79. [Anon.,] *Zwei Maurerreden in der Magdeburgischen Loge, Ferdinand sur Glückseligkeit gehalten vom Bruder J.G.,* Magdeburg, 1785, p. 31.

80. [Anon.,] *Les Franc-maçons, plaideurs,* Geneva, 1786, p. vii.

81. Ibid.

82. *Almanach des Francs-Maçons. Pour l'Année Bissextile 1780,* The Hague: Van Laak, 1780; containing "Discours, prononcé le Fr. Comte de Medini, dans la L. d'Adoption, érigée par les FF. de la L. régulière l'Indissoluble, à la Haye, le 29 Mars 1778," p. 59.

83. G.L., Notulenboek no. 2, f. 264, from Bordeaux, 6 July 1769: "pendant 28 ans de travaux de tout alliage étranger ou suspect. Elle forme un saim de vrais amis et de citoyens que [?] l'intégrité, la Candeur et la Sociabilité."

84. Bartier, op. cit., pp. 285–87; cf. Jacob Katz, *Jews and Freemasons in Europe, 1723–1939,* Cambridge, Mass.: Harvard University Press, 1970.

85. [Anon.,] *Essai sur les Mysteres et le veritable objet des Franc-Maçons,* Amsterdam, 1776, p. 8: "Les institutions de la société maçonnique ne se proposoient point d'autre but que de ramener l'homme à sa bonté primitive, et de faire renaitre en son coeur les loix de la nature dans leur plus grande perfection.

86. Ibid., p. 9.

87. Ibid., p. 12: "Un infortuné qui est opprimé par la puissance, par la calomnie & la haine, est souvent perdu sans ressource, est-il Franc-Maçons! il lui sera facile de trouver chez toutes les nations une patrie, des freres, des protecteurs, & quelquefois même une fortune."

88. Ibid., p. 14.

89. Ibid., p. 18.

90. Ibid., p. 21: "Nous avons adopté en France le mot franchise, terme beaucoup plus encore pour exprimer la liberté du coeur, & c'est de lui que dérive l'épithete de Franche-maçonnerie & Franc-maçon."

91. Archives Municipale, Strasbourg, Legs Gerschel, box 34/7, a printed circular from the Grand Lodge dated 1773: "Depuis l'establissement de la Maçonnerie en France, on avoit toujours désiré de pouvoir former une Assemblée générale, où des Députés de toutes les parties du Royaume, apportant en commun les pouvoirs & les lumières de tous leurs Oriens[sic], concourussent à des opérations génerales, & généralement utiles à l'Ordre."

92. Kloss MSS 240.E.25, "Discours prononcé le 13 Janiver Jour désigné par la loge de la parfaite union l'Orient de Bastia . . . 1780," f. 136: "Respectables frères dont la présence ajoute en ce moment à l'illustration de cet atelier. . . . Elevés sous le plus modéré des Gouvernements; vous et vos concitoyens, conservez cette franchise nationale, heureux fruit de la liberté: elle vous distingue entre tous les peuples."

93. Ibid., f. 21.

94. R. A. Leigh, ed., *Correspondance complète de Jean Jacques Rousseau,* Banbury, Oxfordshire: The Voltaire Foundation, 1974: C. Bentinck to Charles Bonnet, vol. 18, 1763, p. 263; C. Bentinck to Charles Bonnet, vol. 19, 1764, p. 115.

95. B.A. MS 41:8, f. 26, 10 December 1766: "de Broeder orateur vertoonde ons op eene leersaame wyze, wat de grond oorzaak was geweest, waarom de Vrymetselary onder de verlichte menschen so veel opgang hadde gemaakte; betoogende [?] klaar, doordien de Natuurlyken Staat van het mensdom volkomen daarin wierd hersteld."

96. Bibliothèque Municipale d'Etude et d'Information, Grenoble, MS Q 50, f. 3: "Discours de M. Barral, fête de St. Jean, 24 Juin 1779: plus philosophes que ceux qui en affichent les livrées fastueuses, quand ceux ci etalent sterilement leurs sublimes maximes, les maçons cherchent modestement à les mettre en pratique."

97. Ibid.: "Dans les beaux jours de Lacedemone, dans les siècles brillants de Rome vertueuse, être citoyen etait une affaire assez importante & assez noble pour remplir tous les instans de la vie, & satisfaire les desirs de l'ambition . . . dans nos institutions modernes, ou la forme des Gouvernemens n'offre plus une carriere aussi à [?], où le plus grand nombre des sujets restent à la place qu'ils ont choisie ou qui leur est assignee par le Nature, où l'on contribue plus encore à la puissance commune."

98. Ibid.: "On a vanté beaucoup les epoques brillantes de l'histoire des peuples, où le sentiment de la liberté & des grandes choses germaient dans des ames fieres & republicaines—on a raison sous de certains raports; c'etaient des momens d'orgueil & de gloire pour le genre humain. Etait-ce ceux de son bonheur? Helas! je ne voir que les lauriers ensanglantés, l'humanité—pleurant sur des trophées, & comptes ses malheurs par le nombre des pompes triomphales. Je vois de grandes vertus effacés par de plus grand crimes; des briguées, des factions, des troubles, des assassinats politiques, des guerres civiles, & ces proscriptions plus affreuses encore où l'amour de la Patrie etait puni comme une revolte & l'amitie, la nature, la reconnaissance suffisaient pour armer la vengeance d'un tyran jaloux & inquiet: où le couroux du vainqueur servait de pretexte aux ressentimens particuliers, aux haines héréditaires, aux jalousies, à l'avarice. & à la cupidité; au milieu de ces crises horribles, de ces convulsions meutrieres & trop frequentes, le citoyen pouvait—il etre heureux? . . . il semble que la fraternité & les vertus maçonnique ne soient qu'une vaine decoration que nous quittons en sortant la société; ne nous retrouvez plus zelé que nous affectons de nous montrez ici; & toutes les belles maximes de notre morale disparaissent souvent au premier choc de l'interet ou de la rivalité."

99. [Anon.,] *Discours pour le Jour anniversaire de la naissance de sa majesté le Roi de Prusse . . . 1778,* Berlin, p. 4.

100. [Anon.,] *L'Ulissipeade. Poeme ou Les Calamités de Lisbonne, par le Tremblement de Terre . . . par un Spectateur de ce desastre suivi de l'Arche-Heros, Admiré de Tout l'Univers dans la Personne Sacrée de Frederic Le Grand, Roi de Prusse,* no date or place, but probably the late 1750s.

101. See [Anon.,] *Recueil de Discours prononcés en différentes époques solemnelles, Dans la Vble & Très ancienne Loge Française La Royale Yorck . . . , 1767,* Berlin, 1781; and bound with it, *Discours pour le jour anniversaire de la naissance de sa majesté Le Roi de Prusse prononcé le 24 Janvier 1777,* pp. 107 et seq.

102. *Almanach des Francs-Maçons, Pour L'année commune 1779,* The Hague: Van Laak, 1779, pp. 37–39.

103. Ibid., pp. 37–41. These almanacs were commissioned by the Grand Lodge of The Netherlands.

104. Raoul Berteaux, *Le Rite Ecossais ancien et accepté,* Paris; E.D.I.M.A.F. [1985], pp. 219–25, using the Kloss MS 240.E.92, an undated manuscript but clearly from the second half of the eighteenth century.

105. [Anon.,] *Sammlung neuer freymäurer-reden, oden und leider,* Berlin, 1777, p. 7. And Frederick praised in [J. C. A. Theden,] *Rede bei der fererlichen Aufnahme einer Gesellschaft in den Freymäuerorden . . . ,* Berlin, 1775.

106. [Anon.,] *Recueil de Discours et autres pièces tant en prose qu'en vers sur l'Art Royal par le F.L.*** Or.de la R.L.Angloise de St.J.du Secret & de l'Harmonie de Montpellier . . . ,* Amsterdam, 5751 [1751], pp. 11–12.

107. [Anon.,] *Esquisse des travaux d'adoption . . . ,* Paris, 1778, p. 19.

108. Bibliothèque Municipale, Dijon, MS 1263, "Discours prononcé a la loge de la Concorde à l'Orient de Dijon, en loge d'adoption, 2 Jan. 1783."

109. G.L. MS 23:1, the records of the lodge in Middelburg, Zeeland, f. 31, meeting of 22 August 1758.

110. G.L. MS 41:48 (2), 25 December 1765.

111. *Nederlandsche Vry-metselaars Almanach, Voor het Jaar 1793,* Rotterdam: C. R. Hake, 1793, p. 53, printing an oration from 1766.

112. *Almanach des Franc-Maçons. Pour l'Année commune 1779.* The Hague: Van Laak, 1779, p. 37–39.

113. Helmut Reinalter ed., *Joseph II und die Freimaurer,* Vienna: Böh/Au, 1987, pp. 12–13.

114. *Discours prononcé le jour de S. Joseph devant une assemblée de Maçons civils et militaires . . . ,* Liège, 1785, "La gloire de Joseph II est la sienne, la gloire de Louis XIV ne fut que le résultat des circonstances & des gens superieurs qui fleurirent sous son regne." (Copy in the B.N.)

115. Text printed in *Almanach des Franc-Maçons. Pour l'Anné commune 1787,* The Hague: Van Laak, 1787, pp. 24–26: "Ces assemblées, abandonnées entierement à elles mêmes, & n'étant soumises à aucune direction, peuvent fort bien donner lieu à des excès, également nuisibles à la Religion, au bon ordre & aux moeurs, & peuvent induire, surtout les supérieurs, & par une laison fanatique."

116. *Almanach des Francs-Maçons. Pour l'Année Bissextile 1788,* The Hague: Van Laak, 1788, p. 32: "On voulut les imiter; & les Rois, les Souverains & les Magistrats furent établis: mais hélas! le pouvoir fut sans bornes, l'autorité sans limites, l'esclavage absolu; & le Maçon ne trouva plus généralement que dans ses Loges l'heureuse alliance de la Souveraineté & de la Liberté."

117. Ibid., p. 37.

118. [Anon.,] *Rede auf den Geburtstag des Königs,* 1777, bound in *Sammlung neuer freymäurer-reden, Oden und Lieder,* Berlin, 1777. Despite its title, the oration is more interesting for its nationalism.

119. Kloss MSS 240.A.59, f. 81; ff. 82–83 for Franklin.

120. Kloss MSS 240.E.25, "Discours prononcé le 3 Juillet 1780 pour la réception des nouveaux dignitaires par le F. Dorly qui avoit été continué Orateur," f. 167. Spoken before the lodge in Bastia, Corsica. Later in the oration, which must have taken at least an hour, mention is made of the Calas affair (f. 221).

121. Ibid., ff. 170–73; and ff. 191–93.

122. *Almanach des Francs-Maçons. Pour l'Année 1785,* The Hague: van Laak, 1785, pp. 23–32.

123. *Almanach des Francs-Maçons. Pour l'Année 1785,* The Hague: Van Laak, 1785, p. 31.

124. A copy of the thesis is in B.N., MSS Joly de Fleury, 292, f. 354. For a summary of it, see Francisque Bouillier, *Histoire de la philosophie cartésienne,* vol. 2, Paris: Delagrave et Cie., 1868, pp. 632–37. See also D. W. Smith, *Helvétius. A Study in Persecution,* Oxford: Clarendon Press, 1965, pp. 144–52. Cf. Jean F. Combes-Malaville, "Vues nouvelles sur l'abbé de Prades," *Dix-Huitieme siècle,* no. 20 (1988): 376–98.

125. G.L. MS 38.1, "Notulen der Vergaderingen van . . . Concordia Vincit Animos, van den 13 Juli 1755 tot en met 30 Augustus 1761"; written entirely in French but Dutch was also spoken in the lodge.

126. Ibid., f. 20: "L'ordre dans lequel vous venez d'etre Initiés, a été longtemps l'objet des Calomnies publiques. Le monde, a qui il est plus commode de penser mal, que de penser bien des choses qu'on soustrait a sa connoissance, ne pouvoit s'imaginer que l'ordre rigoureux, qui lient nos assemblées secretes, & en ferme l'entrée a tous les profanes, put etre innocent de ces soupçons injurieux contre l'ordre tout ensemble. Ainsi autrefois la Corruption payenne rejetta sur le Christianisme naissant les Crimes qu'il vouloit guerir en elle, & extirper entirement de son sein."

127. Ibid., f. 21: "Oui, mes frères, c'est un temple que nous batissons a la Vertu. Ses fondemens sont posés dans notre Coeur. Les Vertus morales et Civiles en sont les ornemens. La Concorde, en Unissant les Esprits & les Coeurs, est le Ciment. . . . Nous sommes nous memes, mes fréres, les pierres Vivantes de ce temple."

128. Ibid.: "Enfin le très Venerable, / tous les freres presens y ayant donné leur approbation: / a établi les peines suivantes. Sçavoir que tout membre de notre loge, qui seroit convaincu d'avoir joué aux Cartes le matin avant midi, payera pour la premiere fois 30 sols d'amende, au profit de notre boite des pauvres, pour la second fois trois florins, & a la troisieme il sera procedé a une peine plus rigoureuse; & que ceux qui tomberont dans cette faute apres minuit, ou qui passeront la nuit au jeu, Comme aussi ceux qui decour veront de chez eux, soit aux Musicos ou autres endroits malhonnetes, payeront a la premiere fois 3 florins."

129. Cf. [Anon.,] *Julie Philosphe ou le Bon Patriote,* vols. 1 and 2 [n.p., but Paris], pp. 65–66: "je l'appris par la suite, etait un musico; tout le monde fait ce que c'est que ces musico' les hommes y viennent chercher le plaisir & la joie." She is visiting a house of prostitution in Amsterdam.

130. G.L. MS 41:6, ff. 117–53. There were over forty written rules in those kept for La Bien Aimée.

131. Ibid., ff. 23–24; Yvon's oration of 6 September 1755.

132. Ibid.: "Vous serez sans doute surprise du silence religieux que nous gardons sur nos Mystères, & vous croirez que des Lecons, si utiles au bonheur du monde, ne sauroient etre trop repandues; que bien loin de les dérober aux regards des profanes, nous devrions les prêcher publiquement."

133. Ibid.: "Pour jouter nos leçons, mon Cher frère, il faut avoir l'Esprit préparé par de longues instructions, il faut s'élever au dessus des préjugés populaires, il faut même étre philosophe jusqu'a un certain point."

134. Ibid.: "Né dans le sein du despotisme, & ne connoissant la liberté que de nom, vous la trouverez dans nos assemblées."

135. Ibid., f. 24: "Principe de ces sentimens nobles & généreux, qui élevent l'Homme au dessus de lui même, nous ne pouvons trop la Chérir. Nous la regardons comme le plus bel appanage de l'Humanité."

136. Van Veen, op. cit.

137. *Féte Maçonne, célébrée dans la R. Loge La Charité a Amsterdam . . .* 1781, p. vi.

138. *Almanach des Francs-Massons. Pour l'Année Bissextile 1772,* p. 17. Found in the G.L., shelf mark F no. 9.

139. *Premier Discours prononcé dans le cent vingt-uniéme assemblée, Le jour de la Fête de l'Installation de la R.L. des Amis-Reunis . . . Le 22 Février, 1778,* [Paris,] p. 7: "L'établissement des Médailles que vous avez adopté dans votre soixantième Bureau de Fondateurs, doit vous prouver aussi qu'en formant, parmi nous, des Classes successives pour l'instruction, en les distinguant par des couleurs & des ornemens consacrés par la plus haute antiquité, ils n'ont pas perdu de vue la base inaltérable de notre Société, cette précieuse

égalité, qui pour jamais préserve nos Temples." This is a printed discourse located at G.L., 192.A.33; although printed, it is not clear that it was ever published.

140. *Discours prononcé dans l'assemblée générale de toutes les classes réunies . . . Mars 1779* [Paris]; same location as previous discourse. The passage on p. 14 reads: "Mais comme le but civil, quelque distinct qu'il soit du but Maçonique, ne peut pourtant en être absolument séparé, chaque classe resserre les liens de ceux qui s'y font admettre, sans augmenter leurs droits dans la Société;* le Maître à tous Grades n'y en a pas plus que le simple Maître bleu, * tous nos faisceaux symbole du lien social, sont tous égaux."

141. *Discours prononcé dans l'assemblée générale . . . Paris . . . 1780;* same location at G.L., 192.A.33, p. 32: "Renonçant donc absolument à toute prétension à l'antiqueté, notre époque est fixée à l'établissement dans cette Loge des Commissaires aux Grades & Archives en 1775."

142. Kloss MSS 240.A.59, f. 18.

143. On the importance of these donations, Vivian P. Cameron, "Approaches to Narrative and History: The Case of the Donation of September 7, 1789 and Its Images," in Leslie E. Brown and Patricia Craddock, eds., *Studies in Eighteenth-Century Culture,* vol. 19, East Lansing, Mich.: Colleagues Press, 1989, pp. 413–32.

144. See "L'Alchimie du Bonheur. La Fin de l'âge des lumières et la société morave de 1770 à 1810," *Alchymie Stesti. Folklorist Library of Moravia* 51, pp. 263–81. Journal published by the Museum of Kromeriz.

145. G.L. MS 191.E.2, Discours du f[rère] Docteur Chaumeton, prononcé l'an de la v.I. 1800, f. 55: "Nous devons à cette admirable fonction de l'esprit la perfectibilité indéfinie dont nous sommes susceptibles. C'est par son moyen que l'immortel Newton à pour ainsi dire rivalisé la puissance creàtrice."

146. Ibid., f. 60: "Infortuné Rousseau! si tu avais connu nos augustes assemblées, si tu avais pu jouir des douceurs de l'union qui règne parmi nous, avec quelle énergie tu aurais donné l'essor à cette tendre philanthropie dont ton coeur était embrasé."

147. Ibid., bound with "G.F. Feret, Discours d'inauguration à la place de professeur d'historie naturelle & l'hopital militaire d'instruction de Milan (S.Ambroise)."

Chapter 7

1. Dr. Williams's Library, London, Wodrow–Kendrick correspondence, MS 24.157, f. 41, Utrecht, 6 August 1760. Our writer got it slightly wrong; Holland paid about 58 percent of the revenue. In general this is a fascinating correspondence with mention of Hume and matters Scottish, descriptions of travel in the Low Countries, and in the 1790s (f. 173) a favorable reference to Mary Wollstonecraft's "Rights of Woman which will delight you and still more perhaps your daughters. She possesses the same original genius, undaunted intrepedity." For a good general essay on Dutch history focused on the institution of stadtholder, see Herbert Rowen and Andrew Lossky, *Political Ideas and Institutions in the Dutch Republic,* University of California, Los Angeles, William Andrews Clark Memorial Library, 1985.

2. Joel Coutura, "L'Activité d'une Loge de Bordeaux entre 1780 et 1782," *Dix-Huitième siècle,* no. 21 (1989): 265–76.

3. G.L. MS 41:42, f. 128, "Concept en copy van het antwoord van L.B.A. op de aankondiging van La Charité . . . Juli, copie van 18 Aug. [1759]." Here the lodge is boldly stating its position in relation to the quarrel with the Grand Lodge.

4. The membership of this lodge must be pieced together from its minutes; ibid., MS 41:6, 1757, f. 103: "laastelyk zyn tot adspiranten voorgesteld de Herren Cornelis Vygh, woonagtig in de Warmoesstraat alhier Coopman in Engelse Manufactuuren." And f. 108: "de Heer Willem Vrucht wonende te Alkmaar, commandeur in dienst van d' Oostind. Compagnie." And in f. 28 et seq.: "Jac. de Tombe oud scheepen der stad Rotterdam als Frere." In f. 38: "Baron van Heeckeren Heere van Walien beschreeven in de Ridderschap van Gelderland gecommitteerd ter Oostind. Comp. wonende te Zutphen." Few occupations are given directly. See MS 41:7, f. 74 (1762), for the admission to two Italians, one from Genoa and the other from Milan; f. 76 for the professor of anatomy and surgery and for a surgeon. See same, f. 108, for a lieutenant in the garrison near Campen; (1775) where "brother musicians" are given a small remuneration. Cf. H. Rodermond, *De Vrijmetselaarsloge "La Bien Aimée" Amsterdam, 1735–1985,* The Hague: Maçonnieke Stichting, 1985, p. 37. For a general but brief discussion of the lodge in relation to the Revolution see H. Reitsma, "Genootschappen in Amsterdam en de revolutie van 1787," in Th.S.M. van der Zee, J.G.M.M. Rosendaal, and P.G.B. Thissen, eds., *1787. De Nederlandse Revolutie?* Amsterdam: De Bataafsche Leeuw, 1988, p. 158. On the question of decline and revolution in the Republic, see Margaret C. Jacob and W. W. Mijnhardt, eds., *Decline, Enlightenment, and Revolution: The Dutch Republic in the Eighteenth Century,* Ithaca, N.Y.: Cornell University Press, 1991.

5. For example, G.L. MS 41:6, ff. 109–13: from 1755 to 1757 visitors came from another lodge in Amsterdam, Antwerp, Surinam, Geneva, Stockholm, Bordeaux, Berne, Nijmegen, Hambourg, Leipzig, Leiden, Nantes, The Hague, London.

6. Ibid., MS 41:7, f. 161: "Giacomo Casanova de la loge de S. Andrée grand inspecteur de toutes les loges de France a Paris."

7. Robert Darnton, *Mesmerism and the End of the Enlightenment,* Cambridge, Mass.: Harvard University Press, 1968, pp. 92–93.

8. For a very useful list of names, see G. J. Schutte, *De Nederlandse Patriotten en de Koloniën. Een onderzoek naar hun denkbeelden en optreden, 1770–1800,* Groningen: Willink, 1974, p. 194. And for Valckenaer, see I. Schöffer, "Een kortstondig hoogleraarschap. Johan Valckenaer in Leiden 1795–1796," in S. Groenveld et. al., eds., *Bestuurders en Geleerden. Opstellen over onderwerpen uit de Nederlandse geschiedenis van de zestiende, zeventiende en achttiende eeuw, aangeboden aan Prof. Dr. J. J. Woltjer . . . ,* Amsterdam: De Bataafsche Leeuw, 1985, pp. 193–208; and Simon Schama, *Patriots and Liberators. Revolution in the Netherlands 1780–1813,* Knopf, New York: 1977, pp. 144–52, and passim.

9. G.L. MS 41:6, minutes for 1754–57, f. 1: "verstrooyde Schaapen zonder herder."

10. Ibid., f. 3: "Om by den Tres Venerable Master, den Broeder Rouset de Missy te verzoeken en aan te houden, ten eynde Hy, uyt zyne magt en Authoriteit, door een Anthentique Acte, wilde vergunnen en magtigen om, onder hen, eene reguliere Loge te formeeren . . . de Broederen tot eene Wettige Loge te formeeren."

11. Ibid., f. 30: "Hier op stond de Broeder afgezand overeind en deed eene korte reede in het frans, behelsende zyne vergenoegdheyd dat hy by eene zo Eerwaerdige Loge was afgezonden geweest, betuygde zyne dankbaarheid over het goede onthael & bejeegening hem aangedaan zo van weegens deeze Eerwaerdige Loge, als van veele der Broederen; verzeekerende dat hy vertrok met gevoeligheid & leetweese, & dat hij deeze Loge en de Leeden van dezelve, nooyt zoude vergeeten maar altoos aan dezelve met veel dankbaarheid, vriendschap & respect [sic] zoude gedenken."

12. See also ibid., MS 41:7, f. 89, from the lodge La Candeur in Strasbourg seeking a constitution from the Grand Lodge in The Hague.

13. Ibid., MS B.A., f. 200 (1763).

14. Ibid., MS 41:6, f. 46: "In aanmerking van de noodwendigheid dat de meubelen der

Loge zorgvuldig en zuyver bewaart worden is beslooten twee Broederen, *meubelmeesters* aan te stellen, en daartoe opte maaken eene Instructie, volgens dewelke zy deeze bezorging zullen." And f. 59: "Dat Echter omtrent den Venerable Mr. eene uytsondering is en aan den selven wanneer, een opvolger in den Stoel geplaatst is, hy zyne zitting zal hebben alle naast den dirigeerende Meester en aan Zyne Linkerhand, dat men hem de Benaming zal geeven van *Venerable passé maitre* en zynen rang en teekening na de surveillants." And in f. 79: "Nieuwe Christalle kroonen met waskaarsen verlichten de Zaal." And in f. 86: 294 florins spent on three silver candlesticks, a silver square and one pair of compasses; f. 88: cost of installation 5 ducats plus 10 for the reception.

15. Ibid., the last thirty folios contain their rules and guidelines; MS 41:7, f. 13: "en de Vervolgens wierd de processie begonnen in order als volgt de broeder 2de surveillant trok vooruyt draagende het eerste licht, en wierd gevolgt door de Broederen van het noorden . . . en de secretaris dragende het Wetboeck wierd geadsisteert door twee gewaapende broederen." The Law Book, or *Constitutions,* was carried in the ceremony and some brothers wore ceremonial swords.

16. Ibid., MS 41:6, f. 62: "Project om de Harmonie en de Minsaame Verkeering des Broederen deser Loge vaster to maken, en meer en meerder aan te queecken; als meede om Weg te neemen de meenigvuldige moeijtens die den Tresorier overkomen uit de veelvuldige boetens van absentie." And in f. 80, where we learn that the grade of master required a 6 ducat donation; f. 119: each brother paid 24 guilders a year.

17. Ibid., MS 41:7, f. 2: "Laastelyk Erinnerde de Tres. Vener: het interest [sic] van de Loge Cas, en de Br. Thresorier Leeverde aan yder der present zynde Leeden Eene Nota van haar agterstallen." And in f. 14 the poor box is said to contain 55 guilders (1758); in 1759 it contained 81 guilders. See f. 16, for the treasury which contained 3,133 guilders. The poor box grew steadily, reaching 105 guilders in 1760.

18. Ibid., f. 73.

19. Ibid., MS 44:6, f. 66 (1760): "20st Artic: van onse huishoudelyke wett in deser voege te altereeren, van namentlyk by de Ballotteringe der Voorgestelde hierboven in plaatse van Witte Boonen te gebruyken Koopere penningen, en in plaatse van de Swarte Boonen, een stuk geld bedragende de Waarde van dertig stuyvers."

20. Ibid., f. 101: "Broeder orateur ofte hy aen de Loge Eenige aenspraek te doen had. . . . Een Stightelyke redenvoering aen de Broederen vooroogen te stellen de Waerdy van 't mededoogen, daerby voorstellende hoe men door de Wisselvalligheyt der teyden tot den alderjammerlykste Staet kan gebraght worden." And again the theme in 1765; MS 41:8, f. 1.

21. Ibid., f. 105 (1763): "Waerna de broeder assistent orateur [C.] *van der Lyn* een aenspraek deed betreckelyk op de troebelen & vervolging aen ons broederschap sedert haere opkomst overgekomen."

22. Ibid., f. 38: "orateur ons allen stigtende met eene welgepaste en cierlyke reedenvoeringe, namentlyk ons voor oogen houdende, de Waare en Zeedelyke pligten van een opregt maçon."

23. Ibid., f. 43 (1759): "De Tres. Venerb. deed dien volgens Eene welgepaste Reedenvoeringe over de omstandigheid van desen dag . . . is men overgegaan tot de Electie der Nieuwe officieren."

24. Ibid., MS 41:8, f. 29 (1767): "Venb. Mr. betoogde uyt de oude Romynse Historien de Plegtigheedens de welke men gewoon was te doen by de verkiesing en aansteelinge der Romynse Burgermeesteren." And f. 121 (1775): "Hier op deed den Vener: Mr. eene Cierlyke Redevoering over de inhuldiging der Burgermeesteren by de Romynen, dezelve toepasselyk makende op de Inhuldiging onzer nieuw verkorene officieren . . . wierden de nieuwe Br. Officieren in hunne posten geinstalleerd."

25. Ibid., MS 41:7, f. 67 (1761): "Vervolgens ook bedankende de Officieren dewelke dit jaar in de Loge het bewindt hebben gehad & eyndelyk voor sigh selfs van den Throon afklimmende, syn ampt nederleide, de vercierselen & het Maillet op het Constitutie Boek nederleggende, & de broederen verzogt om toe te treeden tot de verkiezing van eenen nieuwen Grootmeester."

26. Ibid., f. 76: "soo declareerde de Broeder 1ste. Surveillant dat hoe gevoelig het ons was tot de verkiesing overtegaen, Eghter Syne presentie daer in niets soude hinderen, waer op de venerable Meester repliceerde dat hy niet tegenstaende sigh Liever wilde retireeren om [?] verkiesing in alles vry te laten."

27. Ibid., MS 41:8, f. 117 (1774).

28. Ibid., MS 41:7, f. 68: "Welke aenspraek door den tres venerable seer herderlyk beantwoord wierd, met betuyging ten volle aengedaen te wesen over de Liefde & het Vertrouwe van de Loge." In Dutch *vertrouwen* conjures up intimacy; see also MS 41:8, 13 November 1765; f. 14, for brotherly love.

29. Ibid., MS 41:7, f. 124: "De broeder orateur door de venerable aengesoght zynde, deed eene seergeleerde & welgepaste redenvoering over de besondere plegtigheden die oude Romynen gewoon waren te verrighten wanneer hunne soonen den jongelinghs tabbers met het mannelyk gewaet verwisselde, brengende het selve op eene seer gepaste wyze over tot de besondere omstandigheden der bovegemelde receptie."

30. Ibid., MS 41:8, f. 9: "orateur onser loge onderhieldt hiernae de vergadering met een reedenvoering waarinne die waardige broeder aantoonde, hoe dat het de pligt van een Vrye Metzelaar is, niet alleen onsen vergaderingen met vlyt, en yver by te woonen, maar selfs die boven allen anderen byeenkomsten te waarderen." I owe the point about humanism to W. W. Mijnhardt.

31. Ibid., MS 41:7, f. 83: "Vervolgens door den broeder orateur een seer geleerde aenspraek aan de loge gedaen, uitleggende de Bouwkunst van alle volkeren & orders; beginnende van den Tempel Salomons tot die van de Roomse, Griekse, & andere Geleerde kysers, vorsten, & bekende soo oude & nieuwe Bouwkundige als mathemathise & andere beroemde konstenaeren." The orator is Cornelius Jacob van der Lyn (see p. 168).

32. Ibid., MS 41:8, f. 19 (1766).

33. Ibid., f. 41: "reedenvoeringe aantoonde de gezellinne der Eendragt te zyn de vryheid; die aan de Deugt en goede en gegronde wetten is verbonden."

34. Ibid., f. 26 (1766): "de broeder orateur vertoonde ons op eene leersaame wyze wat de grond oorzaak was geweest, waarom de Vrymetselary onder de verlichte menschen zoveel opgang hadde gemaakte; betoogende . . . klaar, doordien de Natuurlyken Staat van het mensdom volkomen daarin wierd hersteld; sonder eenige Vermomming hoegenaamt in hun Tesamenkomst te dulden."

35. Ibid., f. 123 (1775).

36. Ibid.

37. Ibid., f. 45 (1768), on the need for "Orthodoxie": "Naauwkeurig gade te slaan omme ter verbeetering meede te werken, tendien eynde vooral eerst 't onderzoeken ende te beproeven, of in de voorgestelde nieuwigheedens ook iets ten besten van den order in 't algemeen verborgen was." The reference to "onse Koninklyke Wetenschap wel onderregt te zyn" occurs earlier in this oration.

38. Ibid., f. 37 (1767): "hem geevende eenen Meesterlyken raad om zig in alles te gedraagen als een opregt V.M. ten dien eynde zyn [?] geevende het voorbeeld van zynen door de Natuur verknogten broeder onse glansryke starr in het Westen."

39. Ibid., f. 50 (1768): "Een Goed V.M. door zijne Daaden toont eene goede smaak te hebben."

40. Ibid., f. 53: "dat niemand meer regt had zig te beroemen gesprooten te zyn uyt een [oud?] aadelyk of roemrugtig geslacht dan die geene, dewelke tot hunnen Stamvader of [aucteur] hadden een deugdsaam man."

41. Ibid., f. 56, 8 November 1769.

42. Ibid., f. 60 (1769).

43. Ibid., ff. 66–67 (1770): "Elk sig door eene yverige oplettendheidt in kunsten en Weetenschappen kan bequaam maaken."

44. Ibid., f. 121 (1775).

45. Ibid., Notulenboek no. 2 (letters to La Bien Aimée), f. 263 (1769): "dat ik . . . herhaalde bombardeeringen van Breslau, Myne huizen, meubelen, have en goed den vlammen het moeten zien opofferen . . . weederom na Warschauw te gaan, om myne aldaar te rug gelatene Vrouw en kinderen, uit te grote levensgevaar."

46. Ibid., f. 81: statement by the Grand Master to that effect (1771).

47. Ibid., f. 87 (1772): "de Liefde tot den Evenmensch en desselfde aantoonende, dat het niet genoeg is in sommige geleegendheidt noodlijdende bijgestaan en geholpen te hebben, maar dat het te Wenschen was, dat de Broederen Vrije metselaaren hier te landen de prijsenswaerdigen voorbeelden sommige onser buitenlandsche broederen naevolgden, met te gedenken en ten uitvoer te brengen een Vast bestaan voor verminkte, Oude, en afgesloofde [Zuijluiden], voor wie . . . nadat sij hun leeven tot nut en voordeel onser stad gewaagd hebben, in hunne oude day geen heenkoomen is." And again later in the year, f. 92, we find similar sentiments.

48. W. Mijnhardt, *Tot Heil van 't Menschdom. Culturele genootschappen in Nederland, 1750–1815 [For the Good of Mankind. Dutch Cultural Sociability, 1750–1815. With a summary in English], Proefschrift, University of Utrecht,* Amsterdam: Rodopi, 1987, pp. 106–23.

49. B.A. MS 41:8, f. 100 (1773): "den broeder orateur deed een welgepaste & breedvoerige reedevoering, zo weegens de overtreffelytheid onser order in alle haare puncten booven alle de andere Ridder orde."

50. Ibid., f. 108: "den broeder orateur een welgepaste reedevoering over de viering der feesten . . . aantonende haaren oorspong & nuttigheid."

51. Ibid., f. 101.

52. Ibid., MS 41:8, f. 104 (1773): "onsen venerable meester eene welgepaste reedevoering ter zyner verdeediging & ter handhaving zyner hooge waardigneid teegens den laster schryver van zeekere brief aan den Heer . . . te G.Waarover dien waardige meester voor het aflossen onser geschut werd bedankt."

53. Ibid., f. 105: "den venerable meester dewelke vervolgens ook een cierlyke reedevoering deed over de wisselvalligheid des Levens."

54. Ibid., f. 111 (1774): "den broeder Levenmeusilen [?] meede eene welgepaste reedevoering over de kenisse van onszelven & onsen afhangelykheid van anderen . . . uitleggende aan de Nieuwaangenomen broederen." And f. 113 for constancy.

55. Ibid., f. 127 (1775); f. 132.

56. *Gedenkteeken by eene plegtige Gelegenheid opgerecht,* pp. 10–12; dated March 1773 and found in the Library of the Grand Lodge, sign 2.C.74.

57. G.L. MS 41:9, f. 6.

58. Ibid., ff. 9, and 13.

59. Ibid., ff. 17–19.

60. Ibid., f. 39: "de Br. orateur eene Redenvoering over de dingen die buiten ons zyn en onze opmerkzaamheid verdienen."

61. Ibid., f. 41: "over de nuttigheid der Wetenschappen."

62. Margaret C. Jacob, *The Cultural Meaning of the Scientific Revolution,* New York: McGraw Hill, 1988, pp. 194–98.

63. G.L. MS 41:9, f. 46: "by geleegenheid van het ingevallen nieuwe Jaar, eene plechtige Zeegenwensch aan de Loge, waarin dezelfs zucht voor onze Koninglyke order, byzonder met betrekking tot het tegenwoordig hachlyks tydsgewricht, van ons dierbaar Vaderland, en de hooge Regeering."

64. Ibid., f. 52: "met die edele gevoelens, welken den Nederlandschen vryheid minnenden broeder de hoogste eere aandoen. . . ."

65. Ibid., f. 62: "de liefde voor het dierbaar Vaderland, in een tydstip daer Trotsche en zinnelooze heerschzucht, benevens verfoeyelyken eigenbaat, haar ondergang bedoelen; die liefde ons met de melk der kindscheid, als ingegeeven, vertoonde zich aldaar in haar volste kracht . . . dat de echte Vrymetselaaren, Goede Vrienden, en getrouwe Patriotten zyn, en met die gevoelens wierd den arbeid beslooten."

66. Ibid., f. 63.

67. Ibid., f. 64 (1781): "De Venerable Meester las aande loge voor, een Contract, of Conditien van een Collegie, onder de Zinspreuk la bien aimée, strekkende om het finantie weezen der loge, en derselver jaarlyksche contributien, voortaan op een vasten en duurzaamen voet te brengen."

68. Ibid., f. 70 (1781): "De zeer verlichte gedeputeerd Meester deed eene uitmundende redenvoering ten betoog, dat het volstandig in acht neemen der goede orde; de handhaaving der grondwetten, en eene redelyke vryheid, de zuilen zyn waarop een Genootschap [a private society] rust; dat denselver betrachting, natuurlyk geschikt is, om haeren groei en bloei te bevorderen; terwyl denzelver verwaarloozing, onvermydelyk haaren ondergang ten gevolge heeft." And f. 97 (1783): "tot een point van deliberatie hebben opgegeeven of het niet volstrekt nodig voor het domestique en economische belang den loge zyn zonde, dat het getal den broederen visiteurs uit de werkende loges deezen stad tot een bepaald getal wierd gebracht, in Conformiteit of op den voet den oude archiven en costume berustende ter secretarie der loge."

69. Ibid., ff. 78–79 (1781): "den oorsprong en voortgang onzer order, uit de kerkgeleerden der bygeloovige eeuwen opgedolven, in onze beter verlichte tyden overgebracht. . . . De Jaarlykschen ommegang, wierd met de vereischte staatigheid gehouden . . . in gulle gastvryheid, als mede van de vaderlandsche belanggelooze, en vryheidlievende gevoelens, welken den achtbaeren meester, in deze tyden van ongehoorde aanvalling, heerschzuchtige onderdrukking, en schending der heiligste verbonden, van onze nabuuren, in zynen boesem koesterde."

70. Ibid., f. 82–83 (March 1782): "door den Broeder Redenaar een Vertoog voorgeleezen, ten onderwerp hebbende *Het Heil des Volks, is de opperste wet,* 't welk door hem in het Schetsen der drie bekende Regeringsvormen wierd uitgebreid." (Emphasis in original.) "Logedag als meede die van de Groote Loge geleezen, uit welke laatste dan ook bleek dat de propositie van onze zeer verligte en voor ons ontschatbare Groot Mr. op de Groote Vergadering in 's Hage gedaan, ten einde met de Loges van het Groot Oosten, van het Vryheid minnenden en thans onafhankelyk verklaard Noord America een alliantie te sluiten en vriendelyk correspondentie te onderhouden."

71. Schama, op. cit., pp. 58–63.

72. G.L. MS 41:9, f. 90: "Den hoogverligten . . . mr Vaillant, die zo veel luister geduurende zyn bestier aan de bien aimee heeft bygezet, dezelve tegen verdrukking beveiligd en de maitrice loge tot billykheid heeft gebragt . . . die de in zyn hart gegrondvesten vryheid heeft doen uitblinken in zyne pogingen om met de ons zo gelyk zynde broederen Noord Americanen eenen kring van vriendschappen getanden rand ter onzer wederzeidse bescherm-

ing en beveiliging te sluiten." R. R. Palmer noted the many channels of communication through which knowledge of the American Revolution made its impact in the Dutch Republic in *The Age of the Democratic Revolution,* vol. 1, Princeton, N.J.: Princeton University Press, 1959, p. 242.

73. Wayne A. Huss, *The Master Builders. A History of the Grand Lodge of Free and Accepted Masons of Pennsylvania, vol. 1: 1731–1873,* Philadelphia, Grand Lodge, 1986, p. 49.

74. See W. Fritschy, "De patriottenbeweging in Nederland. Een verzetsbeweging tegen een financiële oligarchie?," in Th. S. M. van der Zee, J.G.M.M. Rosendaal, and P.G.B. Thissen, eds., *1787. De Nederlandse revolutie?,* Amsterdam: De Bataafsche Leeuw, 1988, pp. 52–69; with much appreciation for the work of J. G. A. Pocock.

75. G.L. MS 41:9, f. 100 (1783): "in het vertrek tot de loge geformeerd gebragt zynde, vertoonde zig aan het onverzaatbaar oog zodanige pragt, Schoonheid en Kiesse order dat een ieder, als buiten zig zelve vervoert, zig aan de stilzwygendheid verpligt was voor een geruime tyd toe te wijden, zynde het niet mogelyk het heerlyke zo van deeze nieuwe Loge als van de veelvuldige Ciradien alhier te beschrijven, waarom aan de Posteriteit [vagelyk] word overgelaten. . . ."

76. Ibid., f. 104 (1783): "Hier op nam de processie een anvang welke op de statelykste wyze en zonder eenige de minste verwarring alschoonde de menige der Bren. onder het gewoone Musiecq wierd verrigt, waarna deeze Loge, nadat de verligte Mr.van La Charite, zyn uiterste genoegen over ons werk betuigd had, wierd geslooten."

77. Ibid., f. 120 (1784); and ff. 135–36, a report of quarreling; f. 140 on hypocrisy; f. 140 (1785): "de gevolgen der Veinzery daar in ten duidelykste bewyzende dat den Veinzaart door zig zelve altoos eindelyk werd ontdekt en in zyn snood caracter beschouwd" (Underlined in the original); and f. 140: "redenvoering deed over het Schadelyke en afschuwelyke der Gramschap."

78. Ibid., f. 162 (October 1786): "Redenaar Michell eene zeer cierlyke redenvoering deed over de waare vereischtens der vrye Metzelary aantoonende dat de zelve eene Grondwettige herstelling vorderde enteens dat dezelve facieler te beryken was dan een staatkundige."

79. Ibid., f. 164 (February 1787): "Meester verzeld van twee broederen meesters zich in een an der vertrek begaf ten einde aan de Loge eene onbepaalde Vrijheid tot het verkiezen van een Meester overtelaaten."

80. Birminghtam City Library, Boulton and Watt MSS Box 36, 12 February 1788, van Liender to Watt, writing from Rotterdam.

81. G.L. MS 41:10, f. 6 (March 1788): "om na eene buitengewone rust niet veroorzaakt door dat een hamerslag van tweedragt in ons tempelgebouw gehoort was, maar door de ongelukkige omstandigheden des tijds daar buiten, ons werk met nieuwen iever weder te beginnen."

82. Ibid., ff. 10–11 (1788): "over de Deugt van zigzelve te verzaken, stellende tot een 1e grond om tot die hoge trap te geraken als eene noodzakelykheid voor 't bedwingen van zijn humeur . . . 't doelwit onser ordre, bestaande in een Vrij-metselaar menschlievend redelijk en deugdzaam te maaken."

83. Ibid., f. 13 (January 1789): "Den Broeder Redenaar deed eene aandoenlyke redenvoering over de behoeftigheden der tegenswoordige aanhoudende barre winter, met aanprysing van mededeelzaam medelyden voor zynen mede broeder en evenmensch."

84. Ibid., f. 27 (1793): "met gewoone formalityte gulhartig, vrolyk, geschikt & vriendelyk gehouden . . . vervoegde de Broederen zig na huys zeer vergenoegd & weltevreeden om ook hunne metzelaarinnen in hunne vreugd & Weltevreedenhyd te doen deelen."

85. Ibid., f. 48 (Winter 1794): "Dat eeven gelyk een vader zyne kinderen geen beeter

erfgoed kan naalaaten, dan eine goede opvoeding, de Vry metzelaary ook alzoo, zyne beoefenaaren, als eene bestendige Erfenis, de Deugd & Goede Zeeden laat genieten."

86. Ibid., f. 31 (1793): "een geschikt Voorwerp." This is one Christiaan Pettenaar.

87. Ibid., f. 32 (1793): "Dat deeze Loge aan Neegen Heeren van de Joodsche Natie & Godsdienst welke van een onbesprooken Leeven & Wandel zyn, zoude kunnen accordeeren het Lidmaatschap onser Loge onder deese voorwaarde: Dat deeze Neegen hetzy gerecipieerde het zy geassocieerde leeden onser loge, behoorende tot de Joodsche Natie & Godsdienst alle prerogatieven & Vryheeden, tot welke alle andere effectieve leeden onser loge geregtigd zyn, meede in alle opzigten & in alle gevallen genieten zullen & daartoe voor gerigtigd gehouden worden onder deese uytdrukkelyke conditie & bepaaling, dat geene deeser Heeren van de Joodsche Natie & Godsdienst welke nu of vervolgens tot effectieve Leeden onser loge zullen gerecipieerd of geassocieerd worden, immer of ooyt tot eenig Bestier der Loge, zal kunnen of moogen genomineerd, verkoozen & nog veel minder aangesteld worden." Cf. John Bartier, "Les Constitutions d'Anderson et la Franc-Maçonnerie continentale," *Revue de l'Université de Bruxelles,* no. 3–4, (1977): 285–86; p. 305 on responses to Jews in earlier Belgian and Swiss lodges.

88. A point made in Schama, op. cit., p. 141. On the French-language press, see Jeremy Popkin, *Revolutionary News. The Press in France, 1789–1799,* Durham, N.C.: Duke University Press, 1990, with some attention to the *Gazette de Leyde.*

89. G.L. MS 41:10, f. 32 (1793).

90. Ibid., f. 39: "eene korte beschryving van de Vieringen der Feester ter Eere van Saturnus by de Romynen als meede van dat ter Eere van St.Jan by laatere volken met overbrenging van de viering van dit laatste feest onder onse voor ouderen, ten tyde der kruys vaarten teegens de ongeloovige Saraceenen als by welke gelegenthyd de vrymetzelaaren onder de banniere der Ridders van Maltha anders Ridders van St.Jan genaamt, strydende ook deezen Heyligen tot hunne Patroon aannaamen." And see note 91.

91. Ibid., f. 42 (1794): "Na dit allen trat onsen Zagtaardigen Mentor op den Catheder en deed ons in eene weldoorwerkte Verhandeling onsen aandagt bepalen op het bedryf & de Gewoonte der Egyptische Priesteren, in het Schetzen van 's Lands Geschiedenissen of merkwaardige voorvallen in hieroglyphische teekenen op gedenkzuylen & naalden alsmeede op de Wanden hunner tempelen & in het byzonder op de Wyze op welke zy de wysgeeren Plato & Pythagoras tot leeden hunner order hebben aangenoomen toegepast op onse verheeven Werkzaamheeden."

92. Schama, op. cit., p. 61, in 1784.

93. Ibid., pp. 42 and 58.

94. Ibid., f. 46: "Een korte Schets van de voornaamste Vereyschtens, die den Bloey & bestendighyd der Genoodschappen over het algemeen en die der Vrymetzelary in het byzonder, bevorderen; toonende onsen waardigen mentor ons daar by treffelyk aan, hoe sterk de broederlyke Eensgezindhyd, Vryhyd & Gelykhyd daartoe medewerken."

95. Birmingham City Library, Boulton and Watt MSS, box 36/17, 26 July 1790, van Liender to Watt.

96. B.A. MS 41:10, f. 52 (1795): "Voor het openen der loge wenschte onsen geliefden Voorzitter de vergaderde broederschap geluk met de zoo lang gewenschte Omwending van zaaken in ons dierbaar Vaderland, waardoor nu Vryhyd, Gelykhyd & Broederschap de Zinspreuk van onse daagen was & gaf voorts der broederen kennis dat van nu voortaan alle eernaamen by ons voor afgeschaft gehouden wierden."

97. Ibid., f. 54: "waarby den voorzitter de Broederen Dienaaren verzogt binnen te koomen, als uyt kragt van gelykhyd by deezen Graad behoorende & hun als leeden der Order aanmerkende waarvoor den oudste broeder Dienaar J. Voogt Zeer nadrukkelyk & vryhydlievend bedankt wierd, zynde het te wenschen dat de door hem zoo yverig gewenschte knoop

van verbintenis tusschen de Fransche & Bataavsche Gemeenebesten, onoplooselyk stand houden moogen. . . . Eerstelyk! Wierd staande & plegtelyk een sterk Canon gelost, na eene Aanspraak hierop Relatie hebbende van het Hoofd deeser Loge, & na het speelen van de Marseillaanschen Marsch op het welzijn van de gezaamentlyke broederschap der vrye metzelaaren verspreyd over de oppervlakte der aarde & het zelve beslooten door onzen gewoonlyken Marsch & het Afzingen [?] van ons gezang, Accourez tous Maçons."

98. Ibid., ff. 56 et seq. (1795).

99. Ibid., f. 59: "dat onsen waardigen Papa op Woensdag verpligt was het groot Basoigne van de Municipalityt deeser stad, als van het welke hy mede lid is, bytewoonen."

100. Ibid., ff. 60–61 (November 1795), where there is a lengthy discussion of the delay in calling a national meeting in The Hague; and again, f. 73 (1796). On being too busy to attend the lodge in France see Archives Municipales, Strasbourg, Legs Gerschel, box 41/20–25, Paris, 17 October 1790: "Je suis si occupé depuis le commencement de la révolution."

101. G.L. MS 41:10, f. 67 (1795): "Hoe de Romijnen het feest der gulden eeuw, ter eere van Saturnus geviert hebben, by Gelegenthyd dat de dwingeland Tarquinius met zyn doemwaardig Wyf Tullia & verdere snooden aanhang uyt Roomen verdreeven waaren & dit toepasselyk maakende op cnse teegenswoordige Omstandigheeden in het algemeen, en voorts in het byzonder op den Oorsprong van ons S. Jans Feest."

102. Ibid., ff. 82–83 (1797).

103. Ibid., f. 85 (February 1797): "De Broeder orateur Hagedoorn het spreek gestoelte beklommen hebbende deed eene voortreffelyke verhandeling over de kragt der zinnebeeldige voorstellingen ter beoeffening der zedelyke plichten."

104. Ibid., ff. 88–89 (1797); and ff. 90–91.

105. Ibid., f. 101 (1798): "der schoone Sexe nit onse vergaderinge wordende sulks met blyke van algemeine goedkenning aangehoord en na het eindige daarvoor met toejuiching bedankt."

106. Ibid., f. 127 (1799).

107. Ibid., f. 133 (1799): "6. dat er in de wyze van verkiezing der officieren zodanige verandering zal worden gemaakt, als dienen kan, om eene vrye verkiezing niet inschyn maar in der daad, schoon eenigzints bepaald te verzeekeren."

108. On Middleburg culture, see J. J. Kloek and W. W. Mijnhardt, *Leescultuur in Middelburg aan het begin van de negentiende eeuw,* Middelburg: Zeeuwse Bibliotheek, 1988, pp. 35–43.

109. Schutte, op. cit., pp. 219–22. We have no study as yet, although Alison Blakeley is preparing one, that tells us about blacks in the Republic, or about Dutch representations of them. For the English language see Henry Lewis Gates, "The Voice in the Text: Messianism, Millenarianism, and the Discourse of the Black in the Eighteenth-Century," in Richard Popkin, ed., *Millenarianism and Messianism in English Literature and Thought, 1650–1800,* Leiden: Brill, 1988, pp. 193–210. Cf. Johannes M. Postma, *The Dutch in the Atlantic Slave Trade, 1600–1815,* Cambridge: Cambridge University Press, 1990.

110. On those events and for conditions in the colony where 3,000 whites ruled over 50,000 blacks, see John Gabriel Stedman, *Narrative of a Five Years Expedition against the Revolted Negroes of Surinam,* eds. Richard Price and Sally Price, Baltimore, Md.: Johns Hopkins University Press, 1988.

111. Sj. Groenman, *Met vallen en opstaan. De Vrijmetselaarsloge "Le Préjugé Vaincu" te Deventer, 1784–1984,* Deventer: Ankh-Hermes, 1983, pp. 46–64.

112. A. W. F. M. van de Sande, "Vrijmetselarij in Nijmegen in de achttiende en negentiende eeuw. Een socio-culturele schets," *Numaga. Tijdschrift gewijd aan heden en verleden van Nijmegen en omgeving* 32–33 (1985/86): 57–60.

Chapter 8

1. David D. Bien, "Offices, Corps, and a System of State Credit: The Uses of Privilege under the Ancien Régime," in Keith Michael Baker, ed., *The Political Culture of the Old Regime,* Oxford: Pergamon Press, 1987, pp. 110–12.

2. [Anon.,] *Discours prononcés à la [loge] Ferdinand aux IX étoiles à l'O. de Strasbourg, 1782,* G.L., shelf mark 208.A.4, passim.

3. [Anon.,] *Discours prononcé à la réception du Sér. F.M.P. d. D. en 1777,* pp. 18–19; bound with discourses cited in note 2.

4. Bertrand Diringer, *Franc-Maçonnerie et Société à Strasbourg au XVIIIeme siècle,* Memoire de Maitrise, 1980, p. 140. In Alsace many legal documents were in German.

5. Ibid., p. 120.

6. E. Pelzer, "La Noblesse alsacienne sous la monarchie française," *Revue d'Alsace* 113 (1987): 305–19. In Alsace 25 percent of the population was noble out of some 624,000 souls in the 1780s. Thirty-six *lettres de noblesse* were issued by the crown from 1648 to 1789.

7. B.N.U. MS 5437, registre des procès-verbaux de la Candeur, 1763–76, f. 25, 1763: "Le Venerable a ensuite proposé d'augmenter le Prix des réceptions d'aprentis et de compagnons qui étoient fixes à quatre louis ou quatre vingt seize livres, et de les porter à cent vingt livres ainsi et six livres pour les Servants."

8. Diringer, op. cit., p. 190. Cf. Th. Vetter, "Les relations scientifiques entre la Grande-Bretagne et l'Alsace dans la deuxième moitié du XVIIIe siècle," *Revue d'Alsace* 115 (1989): 37–68; and David A. Bell, "Nation-Building and Cultural Particularism in Eighteenth-Century France: The Case of Alsace," *Eighteenth-Century Studies* 21 (1988): 477.

9. Diringer, op. cit., p. 148.

10. We know so much about Strasbourg freemasonry because of the fine work of Diringer, op. cit., pp. 232, 15, 20, 24, 27, 37–41; p. 153 gives the known religious affiliations for all brothers from the 1760s to 1780s. Cf. Jules Keller, "Le théosophe alsacien, Frédéric-Rodolphe Saltzmann et les milieux spirituels de son temps," *Revue d'Alsace* 113 (1987): 326–27.

11. Daniel-Paul Lobreau, *Franc-Maçonnerie et Sociétés secrètes à Beaune aux xviiie et xixe siècles,* Université de Dijon, 1976, pp. 12–22.

12. Michel Taillefer, *La Franc-Maçonnerie Toulousaine sous l'ancien régime et la Révolution, 1741–1799,* Paris: E.N.S.B.-C.T.H.S., 1984, pp. 179–81.

13. The records of the dispute rest in the Bibliothèque Nationale, Paris, FM 1.111, ff. 401–45. For example, in ff. 401–2, they indicate that although Litzelman would be allowed to visit La Candeur, he could not be admitted as a member.

14. B.N.U., MS 5437, f. 293. On the establishment of the new Grand Lodge and the resulting schisms in French freemasonry, see Pierre Chevallier, *Histoire de la Franc-maçonnerie française,* vol. 1, Paris: Fayard, 1974, pp. 149–85.

15. Alexis de Tocqueville, *The Old Régime and the French Revolution,* trans. Stuart Gilbert, New York: Doubleday, 1955 (1st ed. 1856), p. 89. Cf. Bernadette Fort, "Voice of the Public: The Carnivalization of Salon Art in Prerevolutionary Pamphlets," *Eighteenth Century Studies* 22 (1989): 390.

16. Michael Laguionie, *Historie des Francs-Maçons à Limoges,* Paris: Lucian Souny, 1986, pp. 33–36.

17. Jean Quéniart, *Culture et Société Urbaines dans la France de l'Ouest au XVIIIe siècle,* Paris: Klincksieck, 1978, p. 446.

18. Alice Joly, *Un Mystique lyonnais et les secrets de la franc-maçonnerie, Jean-Baptiste Willermoz, 1730–1824,* Paris: Demeter, 1986 (originally 1938), pp. 84–85.

19. For members of La Candeur in the Society for the Revolution founded in 1790, see Diringer, op. cit., pp. 228–29; by then these brothers were bourgeois; B.N.U., MS 5437, registre des procès-verbaux de la Candeur (1763–76). And B.N., FM1, ff. 401–58; FM2 423.

20. Diringer, op cit., pp. 15–20, 66–67.

21. B.N. FM 1.111, f. 408, 7 January 1763.

22. Ibid.: "un objet d'amusement . . . qui les uns par leur état, les autres par leurs moeurs ne doivent point être membres de cette grande république."

23. B.N. FM 2.72, f. 7, 1779, from Fr. Dusausson: "M'objecterait-on mon état civil? Le V.ble qu'on m'a substitué est mon ami, j'estimé sa personne et sa probite; mais il n'est que marchand comme moi. Aurait-on porté atteinte à la moralité de mon caractere? J'ose repondre avec assurance que je suis honnèste homme et reconnu pour tel par tout mes commettans dans le commerce. Je suis regardé comme un bon père de famille & je suis estimé de mes amis."

24. B.N. FM 2.426, f. 28, where the Strasbourg lodge St. Geneviève is assuring the Grand Lodge of the probity of its merchant members of "meilleur reputation"; and f. 30, 1778, where the Grand Lodge is concerned because the orator of the same lodge is an actor.

25. On the military lodges, see Jean-Luc Quoy-Bodin, *L'Armée et la Franc-Maçonnerie au déclin de la monarchie sous la Révolution et l'Empire,* Paris: EDIC, 1987.

26. Archives Municipales, Strasbourg, Legs Gerschel, box 31, "Statuts et Reglemens particulier de la loge Saint Jean de la Candeur."

27. Diringer, op. cit., pp. 195–96; written in 1776.

28. B.N.U. MS 1432, f. 1, dated 1785 from Mad. Boecklin. Cf. Diringer, op cit., p. 199.

29. In this view I depart somewhat from the interpretation found in what remains an important, indeed classic, book on the subject: Robert Darnton, *Mesmerism and the End of the Enlightenment in France,* Cambridge, Mass.: Harvard University Press, 1968; for emphasis on the radical nature of mesmerism, see esp. pp. 3, 45, 79–80, 92–93.

30. André Schaer, *La Vie paroissiale dans un doyenné Alsacien d'ancien régime (1648–1789),* Ostheim: Edité par l'auteur, 1971, p. 152.

31. Diringer, op cit., p. 237; Strasbourg, Archives Municipales, Legs Gerschel, box 34/6, for printed *Tableau.* We can date it roughly because it lists Mr. Marchand as a former master and we know that he was master in the late 1770s.

32. Archives Municipales, Strasbourg, Legs Gerschel, box 34, "Esquisse de la cérémonie de réinstallation . . . de la loge d'Hérédon de Sainte Geneviève."

33. Ibid., f. 1: "Décoration ordinaire de la loge. La loge dans la forme d'un quarré long est décorée d'une tenture de serge bleue céleste ornée dans la partie supérieure d'un double galon d'or, de guirlandes et de fleurs du même métal artistement attachés à distances égales par des noeuds de rubans en or. A l'entrée du Sanctuaire que est élévé par les dégrés misterieux du premier grade sont placées les deux columnes simboliques de l'ordre, posées sur leurs bases et surmontées de leurs chapitaux en or d'ordre Corinthin. Le trone est couvert d'un baldaquin bleu de même etoffe enriché de galons et franches d'or, le dossier est d'une etoffe riche d'un trés grand Eclat. L'Autel est chargé de trois flambaux d'argens, du livre des statuts et reglemens de la [loge], et ce livre de l'evangile, d'un gloire, d'un compas, d'un maillet et du Bijou du Vénérable. Au dessus du Baldaquin est placée l'etoile flamboyante, et dans les ceintres du Sanctuaire sont representés le Soleil et la lune, ces trois astres sont supérieurement bien rendus. Les trois grandes Etoiles placées dans l'ordre usité autour du tableau de la loge sont sculptées et d'orées; une quantité d'autres moindres étoiles eclairant cette loge elles sont portées par des Bras d'orés attachées a des plaques de glaces fines & triangulaires. Les officiérs de la loge ont chacun devant eux une table couverte d'un tapis [?] à la tenture orné de galons et de franges d'or, sur ces tables de flambaux [sic] d'argent

semblables a eux qui sont sur l'autel du Venerable et les attributs analogues à leurs fonctions. L'orateur est placé dans une chaire revêtue des mêmes ornemens, aint aussi devant lui des flambaux comme y dessus. Enfin chaque dignitaire est décoré du Bijou qui lui est propre. A l'occident derriere les Surveillans sont des armes de France, celles du S. Grand Maitre et le chiffre de la loge dans des cartouches tout en or: au milieu de la Loge au midi, est le tableau des freres qui la composent, dans le sanctuaire à droite du Venerable les reconstitutions du Grand Orient de France, et à la gauche les Statuts et règlemens particuliers de cette loge composés de quarante articles, ces trois objets sont placés dans des cadres d'orés et sculptés."

34. Ibid., Esquisse de la Cérémonie à la Réinstallation de la [loge] de St. Jean . . . , f. 6 (by my count): "Tres Illustres et Tres Chers frères Visiteurs de toutes les Respectables loges de cet Orient, foible interprete des sentimens des maçons aggregés à la [loge] St. Geneviève, les expressions ne manquent pour vous peindre la Joye délicieuse et pure dont leurs coeurs sont pénétrés à l'occasion de la faveur que vous [?] bien leur faire de réhausser par votre presence l'eclat de l'auguste cérémonie qui doit consacrer . . . ; [f. 7:] Les officiers qui les dirigerent, n'aiant plus pas ce moyen de emouvoir ny caractere spécial sont rentrés dans la classe des simples ouvriers pour concourrir avec ces derniers par leur suffrages a l'etablissement de la nouvelle loge et a la création des trois lumieres qui doivent s'eclairer les etoiles qui sont éteintes . . . frère, vous annoncent allegoriquement cet heureux changement et cette régeneration prochaine de la Loge. . . . [Fr. Marchand is chosen as the master]. . . . Le F.M. des cérémonies conduit le Venerable à l'autel pour prendre possession de sa place et faire l'ouverture de la [loge] avec les formalités requises."

35. Ibid.: "du bonheur qu'on ne trouve point dans le tourbillon du monde. Quoi! tandis que l'orgueil écrase impitoyablement la portion de l'espèce humaine la plus considerable et la plus precieuse, tandis qu'il met entre les individus une distance immense, ce monstre fuit loin de cette enceinte sacrée ou un peuple de frères cultive un paix l'humanité que est d'autant plus durable que les noeuds ne sont tissus par l' égalité. Tandis que l'intérêt perfide désole les Sociétés, porte la ruin et la désolation dans les familles et dévore les fruits des succes du pauvre, la commode [?] regne dans cet attelier, une joye toujours pure anime les ouvriers et vivifie leurs travaux, l'or qui est pour les hommes la boite fatale de Pandora, ne peut alterer les douceurs que goutent les Maçons ils ne savent point sacrifier a l'idole de la fortune, s'ils travaillent a acquerer des richesses par des voyes honnetes, c'est pour payer leur contingent à la patrie, c'est pour s'acquitter des devoirs de Cytoyen, c'est enfin pour verser le surplus dans le sein de l'indigence."

36. Ibid.: "Tandis que le feu de la guerre embrase les deux hemispheres, les braves militaires prets a verser leur sang pour la patrie, profitent des momens. . . . Société heureuse! qui est la Société qui la formé . . . telle une mere prudente . . . ce sont les leçons touchantes de la Vertue les mortels élévés dans tons sein semblent des etres privilegés, ils sont exempts de tous les vues qui dégradent les autres hommes. Les Solons, les Licurges et tous les legislateurs vantés dans les fastes de l'histoire ont fait des recherches inutiles pour trouver le grand art de rendre les peuples heureux et vertueux, leurs Institutions politiques n'etant pas appuyées sur cette base inébranlable ont subi les révolutions des tems, et sont tombées; ce grand art, le code Maçonnique seul le renferme, c'est par son secours que les maçons se sont multiplés même au fort des persécutions."

37. B.N. FM 2.426, ff. 22–48.

38. B.N. FM 2.426, ff. 28–30, dated 1778, and f. 143, where the orator is identified.

39. Archives Municipales, Strasbourg, box 34/29a, Discours prononcé par le frère Mainglet . . . 1780 . . . et combien d'exemples n'avons nous pas de Monarques qui ont favorisé du titre glorieux de frères les plus pauvres Artisans, pourvu que leurs moeurs soyent honnètes et sans reproches.

40. Ibid., box 34, Discours prononcé dans la Loge de St. Geneviève le jeudi 20 Avril

1780: "Il ne se laisse pas eblouir par le faste des grandeurs, ni par la pompe des Cours; il remarque souvent sous ces dehors imposants et sous ces brillant couleurs les efforts impuissants de l'orgueil pour cacher les faiblesses et meme quelque fois les crimes de ces hommes élevés qui ne doivent les rangs qu'ils occupent, qu'au hazard de la naissance, ou à l'intrique ou à la flatterie, ou peut-être à d'autres moyens encore plus infames."

41. Ibid., box 34/29a, Discours prononcé par le frère Mainglet en l'occasion de la fête de St. Geneviève, 1780. For text see note 42.

42. Ibid., box 43/33, no date but located with material from the late 1770s and the 1780s, Oraison funèbre du frère Travitz par le frère Crax orateur de la Loge de Sainte Geneviève: "Aussi, quoique n'ayant pas été supérieur en grades, sa mémoire ne doit pas moins nous intéresser, il ne doit pas moins revivre dans nos coeurs. Nous n'accordons point nôtre estime aux marques exérieurement honorables, celles cy ne portent que trop souvent le faux mérite! mais aux vertus, à l'intrinsèque d'un homme vraiement fait pour en être decoré quoique la main de ses semblables ne lui ait pas donné cette satisfaction. Quelques ayant été ses merites civils et maçonniques, il n'est plus le frère Travitz . . . notre ordre est fondé sur ses sages principes et, en rejettant tout matérialisme, nous ne pouvons qu' envisager avec chagrin la mort prompte. . . . Nos prétendus esprits forts ont beau s'appuier sur l'innéffable bonte d'un dieu."

43. Diringer, op. cit., pp. 114–15. The majority of the lodge was in their twenties and thirties.

44. Archives Municipales, Strasbourg, "Planche à tracer de l'Installation de la R.L. St. Jean sous le Titre distinctif des Beaux Arts à l'Orient & Strasbourg. Faite le 29 Juillet 1782 par les FF. Députés de R.L. St. Jean sous le Titre distinctif d'Hérédon de St. Geneviève . . . 10 June 1782," ff. 7–8 (by my count).

45. Ibid.: "Vous les sentirez ces Avantages, t.c.f. [very dear brothers] dans le bonheur inappréciable d'être membres d'une Societé d'hommes vertueux, dans les douceurs d'une liaison intime que vous rapprochera d'une multitude de personnes de tous ages et tous rangs doués des plus grandes qualités, dans la protection des illustres chefs qui président l'ordre, dans la Satisfaction de trouver partout un peuple de ff. empressé à vous servir et à vous prodiguer tous les temoignages de la plus tendre affection."

46. Ibid.: "c'est à un grand Prince que les maçons françois sont redevables de la félicité qu'ils goutent; c'est ce Prince qui par rendre à la Maçonnerie francaise son premier lustre."

47. Ibid.: "d'être protegés par un prince . . . des Bourbons, l'amour de la nation entiere, le bienfaiteur de l'univers et la terreur de ses ennemis, Prince qui . . . mon discours, pour donner libre essort à l'expression de votre éternel attachement pour la personne de ce prince qui tient la premiere place parmi vous."

48. Ibid.: "abandonnons à ces egoistes inhumains que dévore l'ambition de couvrir leur naissance par le brillant des titres et les dons de la fortune . . . et engraisser leurs viscères du sang du deffenseurs de la patrie; le coeur du maçon n'est pas fait pour se repaiître et se nourrir de sentimens aussi dures et aussi detestables."

49. Ibid.: "journellement dans la Carriere des Sciences pour en approfondir les Misteres et se rendre utils à l'humanité! des Bourgeois reputables de tous les rangs, qui s'efforcent."

50. On this see Robert A. Schneider, *Public Life in Toulouse, 1463–1789,* Ithaca, N.Y.: Cornell University Press, 1989, pp. 307–17.

51. Archives Municipales, Strasbourg, box 35/1, letter of 1780.

52. Ibid., box 34/52; the first quote is from a letter dated 20 August 1765: "si les f. de la Candeur avoient traité avec moins de hauteur tous ceux quils ne croient pas leurs egaux dans l'Etat Civil, il y auroit certainnement moins de Loges irregulieres et nous n'aurions pas eû la douleur de vous porter." And then from a letter of 22 February 1765: "La Candeur n'omettra

pas de dire qu'elle n'est composés que de commerçants vous verrez qu'exepté cinq ce sont tous des bourgeois qui la composent."

53. Ibid.: "Grand Architecte de l'Univers, à Toi! qui conduis nos crayons, tu connois les plans que nous avons tracés pour la construction de ton auguste temple, & daignes aussi présider à nos travaux et diriger les ouvriers qui sont ici rassemblés. . . . Nous ses députés chargés de pouvoirs installons à perpetuité a l'Orient de Strasbourg la Loge St.Jean, sous le titre distinctif du Beaux Arts. La [loge] des beaux arts est installée. Cette derniere phrase fut repetée par les deux Surveillans et suivie d'un applaudissement général: le V. fit sur la lecture des lettres de patentes de Constitution, qu'il plaça dans le sanctuaire à la droite du trône dans un cadre."

54. Diringer, op. cit., p. 222: "Autre signe de cette médiocrité, les querelles intestines qui jalonnent toute l'histoire de la maçonnerie strasbourgeoise. Scissions, dénonciations, trafics de grades, évictions, loges clandestines: Nous ne commenterons pas toutes les 'affaires' qui inspirèrent factums, libelles et mémoires, lesquels constituent une part non négligeable des archives maçonniques. Le phénomène n'est d'ailleurs pas spécifique à Strasbourg."

55. Archives Municipales, Strasbourg, box 34/10, Legs Gerschel: "de commettre des actes de despotisme tout à fait oposér aux loix maçonniques . . . nous cherchions à sortir de la léthargie ou l'inaction et une cabale sourde nous avaient plongér . . . nous vous suplions de croire que ce qu'ils avancent est une imposture qui ne merite pas la moindre confiance . . . les trois frères qui en etaient coupables à une exclusion perpetuelle."

56. Ibid.: "Nous voici arrivés T.C.F. à l'Epoque de complot le plus monstrueux qui ait paru dans cet orient, complot aussi repréhensible au Civil que digne de Votre animadversion maçonnique . . . où les faux frères justement proscrit des charges du temple résolurent par le plus indigue complot d'employer la force et la trahison pour y regner en maitre."

57. Ibid., box 34/43: "Arretons nous un moment TT.Ch. FF. et contemplons de sang froid cette scène préparée par la pusillanimité, l'Egoisme, l'ambition et la Vengeance. Regardés de braves gens se présenter sur la foi des traités, sans autre d'armes que leurs droits et leur innocence." Dated 27 day of 9th month, 1784.

58. B.N. FM 2.563; ff. 4–32; from 1786. The Grand Lodge in The Hague is trying to mediate.

59. Ibid., f. 32: "cet esprit de Liberté et de franchise qu'emporte le nom de Francs et Libres Maçons, que nous avons le bonheur de porter. Oui, la voix de ce sentiment de Liberté gravé dans le Coeur de tous les hommes, mais qu'un Franc-Maçons sont plus vivement encore."

60. B.N.U. MS 5437, ff. 163–64.

61. Archives Municipales, Strasbourg, Legs Gerschel, box 36: "philosophes téméraires et ambitieux qui préfèrent leur réputation au bon ordre de leur patrie et à Dieu même raison qui échoue tous les jours contre un atome."

62. Ibid., f. 305 (1776): "que l'egoisme devenue presque géneral dans ce siècle les aggrave encore, en repandant son poison jusque sur les liaisons les plus sacrées du sang qu'il dissout, en ne rendant que trop souvent les parents les plus proches, des ennemis irréconciliables."

63. Ibid., box 31/4; Discours mac. du mois de Juin 1781.

64. Ibid.: "il a reparé sa faute par des actes sublimes de soumission & de repentir. Comment ne seroit-il pas rigoureux vis-à-vis lui-même, lui, qui connoit les secours efficaces qui lui sont offerts pour combattre le mal; qui ne peut se dissimuler la voix intérieure, qui l'appelle l'exhorte & l'anime à faire la volonté de son Dieu."

65. Guy Chaussinand-Nogaret, *The French Nobility in the Eighteenth Century*, Cambridge: Cambridge University Press, 1985, pp. 5–6.

66. Archives Municipales, Strasbourg box 31/4; Discours . . . 1781: "certes cet homme, porteroit-il tous les Cordons & Bijoux qui ont jamais été mis en usage pour distinguer les connoissances, possederoit-il tous les grades, produiroit-il les plus belles patentes—il ne seroit point franemaçon; il n'en auroit que l'apparence; la *Vertu* lui manqueroit. . . . Rein de plus beau dans la Nature qu'une ame pleine de Candeur, qui sent sa droiture."

67. Ibid.: "C'est cette elévation, cette grandeur d'ame, qui rend le vrai maçon préférable aux autres hommes. Il connoit la valeur des choses, il sait apprécier les actions, il rapporte tout à l'unique but digne de ses soins. De son pieds il touche la terre, mais sa tête est dans le Ciel. Intimément persuadé de sa haute destination, il a toujours devant les yeux le plus grand des exemples, & travaille sans relache à sa perfection, en avançant le bonheur de ses semblables."

68. Cf. David Bien, "The Army in the French Enlightenment: Reform, Reaction and Revolution," *Past and Present,* no. 85 (1979): 68–98. Similar arguments were put forward for the reform of the officer corps, for virtues that would work solely among nobles.

69. B.N.U. MS 5437, f. 215: "Elles travaillent sans relache conférant tous les grades à prix d'Argent, tandis que nous avons supprimé cette coutume mercenaire. Que deviendront les ornements de notre temple?"

70. Ibid., f. 29 (1763): "Dans les connoissances humaines le sage ne croit que ce qui luy est demontré, il repugne et [?] ce qui l'étonne ou le surprend aussy n'est ce pas sans raison que nous gemissons de la critique amere de la pluspart des prophanes; exités par la curiosité & nos mysteres ils paroissent revoltés de notre fidelité a observer nos engagemens.

71. Ibid., f. 31: "peut être serai je trop temeraire que d'oser entreprendre de tracer son portrait si les charmes dont la nature la douce sont embelis par ceux d'un esprit cultivé, si la nobless de ses sentiments, la bonte de son ame, la droiture de son coeur, l'Egalité de son caractere, les attraits de sa societé, la douceur de ses moeurs, et tout ce quelle inspire, encore, que l'on sent bien mieux que l'on ne peut l'exprimer, ne vous parloit plus eloquement que [?] ne puis le faire a toutes ces belles qualites, qui est ce qui pourroit meconnoître Madame la Baronne de Flachslande." On f. 30 we find the names of the women patrons of the 1740s.

72. Ibid., f. 32: "Le Titre distinctif de Protectrice de la loge de la Candeur est trop flatteur, messieurs, pour ne pas l'accepter avec reconnoissance, malgré le Voile impénétrable qui vous cache aux yeux de mon sexe, les vertus que vous pratiquez sont venu jusqu'a moy. . . . Signé Truchser de Flachslande." This was a distinguished noble family: Jean François Henry de Flachslanden took part in the counterrevolutionary army of Condé.

73. Diringer, op. cit., pp. 146–47.

74. Schaer, op. cit., p. 264.

75. B.N.U. MS 5437, ff. 43–56. The dispute dragged on for months.

76. Ibid., f. 38 (1763): "Elle luy à été accordée, il a dit que lors qu'il avoit été au scrutin pour M.de Le Klingen; il avoit trouvé une Boitte bouchée avec de la cire, qu'il avoit mis son jeton dans l'autre, mais que s'étant aperçù qu'il s'etoit trompé il avoit ouvert la dit Boitte pour reprendre son jetton et quil ne sçavoit pas s'il en avoit pris d'autres avec le sien, le Vénérable la prie de sortir de la loge pour qu'on pesat ses raisons—avec l'atrocité de l'action, il a refusé d'obeir, le Vénérable luy a dit que s'il insistoit dans son réfus, il alloit fermer la loge et qu'on le laisseroit seul, il a repondu qu'il sortiroit pour ne plus revenir, et comme il continuoit a parler le Vénérable a chargé le maitre de cérémonies de conduire ce rebele."

77. Tocqueville, op. cit., p. 80.

78. In this respect see Nina Rattner Gelbart, *Feminine and Opposition Journalism in Old Regime France. Le Journal des Dames,* Berkeley: University of California Press, 1987, chapter 3.

79. Ibid., ff. 105–5; and B.N., FM 1.111, f. 403 (1763): "qu'un maçon soit d'un etat

libre et son propre maitre." And in f. 405 the master of La Candeur notes that the lodge is "composée de la plus haute noblesse."

80. On this affiliation with La Candeur, see Diringer, op. cit., passim.

81. B.N.U. MS 1432, MS Société harmonique des amis réunis, 1786–89, f. 70, and ff. 31–33.

82. Darnton, op. cit., p. 73; and for the radicals, p. 80.

83. B.N.U. MS 1432, f. 1, from Mme. de Brochtlin (née de Roeder), 1785: "Rassurée! que la foiblesse de mon sexe, ne met point d'obstacle à la participation de la sublime Découverte de M. Mesmer; en vertue de la quelle, la société bienfaissante, qui m'a reçu avec tant de bonté à son traitement, propage et reprend avec un succés egal au zèle qui l'anime, le premier honneur de l'humanité. J'ose, aprés la grande foi, qui m'impriment et m'affirment les progrès particuliers que je fais sur ma santé . . . depuis deux ans, supplier en qualité de Mere de famille, l'illustre société pour l'advantage dêtre initiée en Disciple."

84. Ibid., f. 70 (1786): "m'a intimement convaincu de l'existence d'un Agent puissant, nommé par vous *fluide magnetique,* le quel mis en action, par des procédés, qui ne sont véritablement bien connus que des initiés, peut produire une grand révolution, dans un objet aussi intérressant, pour des ames honnêtes & sensibles."

85. Ibid., f. 5: "et à l'entretien des forces de l'homme, en supplément d'actions momentanément ajoutées à celles dont il est en possession, retablira dans son être l'équilibre qui n'est jamais troublé que par la diminution du movement qu'occasionnent des abberations diverses."

86. Ibid., MS 3678, f. 2; cf. Darnton, op. cit., pp. 68–69, 115–16.

87. B.N.U. MS 3678, f. 6: "L'action de l'homme sain sur le malade sera donc puissante en raison de la foiblesse de ce dernier, mais cet empire de la force n'étant employé que pour vaincre la maladie, au lieu d'opprimer l'individu, cette auguste fonction de l'humanité sera un lieu de plus pour les sociétés, et probablement les hommes deviendroit d'autant meilleurs qu'ils auront plus de moyens de se rendre heureux."

88. Ibid.: "L'homme vu dans son état purement physique comme toutes les autres parties de la matière, & le mouvement propre à son organisation subordonné aux mouvemens généraux, auxquels il obéit dans cet instant. . . ."

89. For example, see Keller, op. cit., pp. 326–27.

90. [Anon.,] *Essai sur la secte des illuminés,* Paris, 1789, pp. 41–47.

91. Ibid., p. 91.

92. Gary Kates, *The Cercle Social, the Girondins, and the French Revolution,* Princeton, N.J.: Princeton University Press, 1985, pp. 91–92.

Chapter 9

1. Bibliothèque de Institut de France, Paris, MS 2048, ff. 159–65 (1793): "dans un temps où assurément personne ne prévoyoit notre révolution, je m'étois attaché à la franche [sic] maçonnerie qui offroit une sorte d'image de l'égalité, comme je m'étois attaché aux parlements qui offroient une sorte d'image de la liberté. J'ai depuis quitté le phantome pour la réalité."

2. A similar point is made about German freemasonry in Horst Möller, "Enlightened Societies in the Metropolis: The Case of Berlin," in Eckhart Hellmuth, ed., *The Transformation of Political Culture. England and Germany in the late Eighteenth Century,* London: Oxford University Press, 1990, pp. 221–25.

3. Michael Sonenscher, *Work and Wages. Natural Law, Politics and the Eighteenth-century French Trades,* Cambridge: Cambridge University Press, 1989, p. 332.

4. [Anon.,] *Discours prononcés à L[oge] Ferdinand aux IX Étoiles à l'O. de Strasbourg 1782,* p. 10.

5. Archives Municipales, Strasbourg, Legs Gerschel, box 35/9. Cf. René Brassel, ed., *Inventaire des archives de la Ville de Strasbourg,* Strasbourg: Archives de la Ville de Strasbourg, 1975, pp. 40–43. For the national figures the following is very helpful: Ran Halévi, *Les Loges maçonniques dans la France d'Ancien Régime aux origines de la sociabilité démocratique,* Paris: Armand Colin, 1984, p. 43.

6. Daniel Roche, *Le Siècle des lumières en province. Académies et académiciens provinciaux, 1680–1789,* vol. 1, Paris: Mouton, 1978, p. 260.

7. See Sonenscher, op. cit., pp. 299, 302, 327, where the supposed relationship between *compagnonnages* and freemasonry is definitively laid to rest.

8. B.N., FM 1.118, ff. 125 etseq., "Observations Préliminaires sur le Plan"; entire box is devoted to minutes from the meetings of the assembly in the 1700s and 1780s.

9. This less than satisfactory approach is adopted in Halévi, op. cit., p. 97. Cf. Jacques Feneant, *Francs-Maçons et Sociétés secrètes en Val de Loire,* Cambray: C.L.D., 1985, pp. 11–16.

10. Durand Echeverria, *The Maupeou Revolution. A Study in the History of Libertarianism. France, 1770–74,* Baton Rouge: Louisiana State University Press, 1985, pp. 48–49.

11. On Jacobitism as perceived in London see Nicholas Rogers, *Whigs and Cities. Popular Politics in the Age of Walpole and Pitt,* Oxford: Clarendon Press, 1989, pp. 77–78.

12. As cited in Alain Le Bihan, *Franc-Maçons et ateliers parisiens de la grand loge de France au xviiie siècle (1760–1795),* Paris: Bibliothèque Nationale, 1973, p. 111.

13. Michel Taillefer, *La Franc-Maçonnerie toulousaine sous l'ancien régime et la Révolution 1741–1799,* Paris: E.N.S.B.-C.T.H.S., 1984, pp. 217–27.

14. Alexis de Tocqueville, *The Old Régime and the French Revolution,* trans. Stuart Gilbert, New York: Doubleday, 1955, p. 92.

15. Box 36/24, Archives Municipales, Strasbourg, Lecture du Royal Ordre H.R.D. Kilwining . . . 1st Grade, 1789 (no month given): "Je ne viendrai pas de m'opposer / Aux Ennemis de mon Souverain, / De ma Patrie, & de ma Religion."

16. Diringer, op. cit., p. 233; on Jacobins, see pp. 227–31. Cf. Vivian R. Gruder, "The Society of Orders at Its Demise: The Vision of the Elite at the End of the Ancien Régime," *French History,* 1, (1987): 210–36.

17. Bibliothèque Municipale, Reims, MS 1940, ff. 48–50; Prieur MSS.

18. E. F. Bazot, *Manuel du Franc-Maçon* 3d ed., Paris, 1817, p. 95.

19. Kloss MSS 192.A.33, dated 1778, Paris; the lodge of les Amis Réunis.

20. *Statuts de l'Ordre Royal de la Franc-Maçonnerie en France,* (1773), p. 2.

21. Ibid., "Cette Assemblée ainsi composée Députés, tant des Provinces, que de Paris, représentant véritablement le Corps Maçonique de France, sous la dénomination de Grande-Loge National, s'est fait un objet capital d'arrêter les Status, & de dommer au régime de l'Ordre un forme qui pût déraciner les abus dont on croyoit trouver le principe dans l'ancienne administration." And on p. 18: "Les Secrétaires donneront aux Orateurs de leurs Chambres communications des affaires contentieoses qui leur seront respectivement adressées, afin de les mettre en état d'y donner leurs conclusions."

22. The story of the suppression and the copy made in this century by Cochin is found in Pierre Chevallier, ed., *Mémoire justificatif du F . . . de la Chaussée 1773,* Paris: Lauzeray, 1977, p. 25: "Dans les premiers temps de la Maçonnerie en France, le Corps des Maçons était lui-même parfaitement bien composé; on était délicat sur le choix des Prosélytes quoi-

que les principes d'égalité ne permissent pas de s'arrêter au hasard de la naissance ou du rang."

23. Ibid., p. 26.

24. Ibid., p. 32.

25. Quoted as the opening line in a dispute which made its way into print: [Anon.,] *Mémoire contre le projet d'établissement d'une nouvelle Loge à l'O . . . de Rochefort,* dated 19th day of 8th month, 1776, and signed by Brothers Gillet and Chevallier.

26. On the concern about servants see circular dated 10 February 1779. These circulars have no title and always begin with the words "A La Gloire du G.A. de L'Univers. . . ." I shall cite them by date, with the vast majority I have found coming from the Municipal Archives in Strasbourg. For orations, see those printed in *Planche à Tracer Générale de l'Installation Du . . . Louis-Philippe-Joseph d'Orléans, Duc de Chartres, Prince du Sang, en qualité de Grand Maître . . .*, 1773, p. 14: "c'est sur nous qu'elle se repose pour la débarrasser de tout ce qu'elle avoit d'impur; nous repoussons de son sein les sociétés indécentes; nous y replaçons les Maçons honnêtes."

27. Archives de la Ville de Strasbourg, "Nouveau mode d'existence pour le G.O. et pour les LL. de son régime"; printed circular for 1791.

28. Circular dated 9 April 1780. In Archives Municipales, Strasbourg, box 13/3a.

29. *Projet Maçonique de Bienfaisance et plan d'Association,* dated 30 November 1780, pp. 1–14.

30. B.N. FM 1.136, ff. 393–486, for an entire collection of these letters. I quote from them at random.

31. Ibid., f. 420, from one Joseph Schwartzmann, originally Danish.

32. Circular for 16 December 1781: "Dans l'ordre physique & dans l'ordre politique, le lieu que ce centre commun de la Maçonnerie Françoise doit occuper, étoit déja fixé, lorsque le concours de vos suffrages, dirigés vers le bien commun, en avait légitimer la position. . . . S'il faut un centre de lumières, dans l'Ordre Maçonnique, il n'est pas moins nécessaire dans l'ordre politique. . . . Les Maçons, soumis au Souverain, quel qu'il soit, ou comme Citoyens ou comme Sujets, se font un devoir plus strict que le reste des hommes de respecter les loix. . . . Il faut donc que le Gouvernement ait sans cesse sous les yeux une partie considérables des Maçons de l'Etat qu'il gouverne, afin d'être à porté d'observer leurs actions. . . . La nécessité d'un centre Maçonnique dans la Capitale est donc démontrée."

33. Ibid., p. 3: "Quel est ce régime? Vous le savez, [tres cheres frères] celui qui convient le mieux à une association libre; celui dans lequel nul ne reçoit la loi d'un seul, & dans lequel chacun la reçoit de tous & par conséquent de lui-même. Tout arrêté général est l'ouvrage de l'association entière: & comme tout Maçon a concouru à l'élection du Député qui vote au G.O. pour L. dont il est membre, tout Maçon vote en quelque sorte dans la confection des règlemens, par la bouche du Député commis par la L. & par conséquent tout maçon vote dans la confection des obligations qu'il s'impose."

34. Circular for 14 April 1781; Archives Municipales, Strasbourg, box 13/31.

35. Circular of 17 April 1782; Ibid.

36. Circular for the 7th day of 3rd month, 1781; Ibid., p. 6: "Empressons-nous . . . de seconder les vues paternelles du Gouvernement, qui sans doute accueillera notre offrande aussi favorablement." For a large selection of letters requesting charity see B.N., FM 1.136, ff. 393–486.

37. Circular of 24 June 1787, "Statuts et Réglemens Généraux et Particuliers de la T.R. Grand-Loge, ancien et unique Grand Orient de France, Jerusalem, 5787 [1787]," p. 8. Copy to be found in The Library of the Grand Lodge, The Hague, shelf no. 211.F.154.

38. Ibid., p. 5: "elle a repoussé fermement les innovations dangereuses qu'on a cherché à propager sous les couleurs les plus séduisantes. . . ."

39. Circular for the 7th day of November 1787; Archives Municipales, Strasbourg, box 13/31.

40. The phrase is from a letter written by *frère* Salivet to *Fr.* Marchand, a master of a lodge in Strasbourg, from Paris, 10 June 1786: "Differens membres de LL. de l'O. de Paris ont formé un chap. de hauts grades. L'eclat avec le quel on les y a donnés, l'empressement de [?] de MM de venir les y prendre, le choix qu'on y a fait de qu'il y a de meilleur dans le fatras énorme de hauts grades, nous a bientot suscité des envieux, et par consequent des ennemis ou s'est couvert du manteau du bien general: ou nous a denoncés au G.O. comme tendant a les renverser."

41. Halévi, op. cit.

Conclusion

1. For the kind of scholarship I am thinking of, see George H. Williams, *The Radical Reformation,* Philadelphia: Westminister Press, 1962; or any of the work of Gerald Strauss, for example, *Luther's House of Learning: Indoctrination of the Young in the German Reformation,* Baltimore, Md.: Johns Hopkins University Press, 1978.

2. Franco Venturi, *Utopia and Reform in the Enlightenment,* Cambridge: Cambridge University Press, 1971, introduction.

3. Note the essays by D. Bien and R. Chartier in Keith M. Baker, ed., *The French Revolution and the Creation of Modern Political Culture,* vol. 1: *The Political Culture of the Old Regime,* Oxford: Pergamon Press, 1987; for the Dutch Enlightenment, see the essay by W. W. Mijnhardt, "The Dutch Enlightenment: Humanism, Nationalism, and Decline," in Margaret C. Jacob and W. W. Mijnhardt, eds., *Decline, Enlightenment and Revolution: The Dutch Republic in the Eighteenth Century,* Ithaca, N.Y.: Cornell University Press, 1991. For Scotland I am thinking of Richard Sher, *Church and University in the Scottish Enlightenment: The Moderate Literati of Edinburgh,* Princeton, N.J.: Princeton University Press, 1985. See N. T. Phillipson and Rosalind Mitchison, eds., *Scotland in the Age of Improvement. Essays in Scottish History in the Eighteenth Century,* Edinburgh: Edinburgh University Press, 1970; and for Franco Venturi, see his magisterial *Settecento Riformatore,* 5 vols., Torino: Einaldi, 1969+; vol. 3 in English translation, *The End of the Old Regime in Europe, 1768–1776: The First Crisis,* trans. R. Burr Litchfield, Princeton, N.J.: Princeton University Press, 1989.

4. See in particular the essays in Eckhart Hellmuth, ed., *The Transformation of Political Culture. England and Germany in the Late Eighteenth Century,* London: Oxford University Press, 1990.

5. Foremost among them, Keith M. Baker, *Inventing the French Revolution. Essays on French Political Culture in the Eighteenth Century,* Cambridge: Cambridge University Press, 1990.

6. See, for example, Peter Burke and Roy Porter eds., *The Social History of Language,* Cambridge: Cambridge University Press, 1987.

7. Joyce Appleby, "One Good Turn Deserves Another: Moving beyond the Linguistic; A Response to David Harlan," *American Historical Review* 94 (December 1989): 1326–32; for an example of the social construction of a text, see Joan DeJean, *Fictions of Sappho 1546–1937,* Chicago: University of Chicago Press, 1989.

8. Dena Goodman, *Criticism in Action. Enlightenment Experiments in Political Writing,* Ithaca, N.Y.: Cornell University Press, 1989, p. 2.

9. Ibid., p. 3.

10. Ernst Cassirer, *The Philosophy of the Enlightenment,* trans. Fritz C. A. Koelln and James P. Pettegrove, Boston: Beacon Press, 1951, p. 13.

11. Pierre Bourdieu, *Outline of a Theory of Practice,* trans. Richard Nice, Cambridge: Cambridge University Press, 1977, p. 25.

12. Peter Gay, *The Enlightenment: An Interpretation,* New York: Random House, 1967; his differences with the platonizing schools of the 1930s are most clearly articulated in a symposium on the writing of Carl Becker held in 1956; Raymond O. Rockwood, ed., *Carl Becker's Heavenly City Revised,* New York: Archon Books, 1968. For a latter-day attempt to write in the Gay tradition see Henry Vyverberg, *Human Nature, Cultural Diversity, and the French Enlightenment,* Oxford: Oxford University Press, 1989.

13. See, for example, Daniel Roche, "Académies et politique au siècle des lumières: les enjeux pratiques de l'immortalité," in Keith M. Baker, ed., op. cit., pp. 331–46.

14. For the Commonwealth tradition in France see Michael Sonenscher, *Work & Wages. Natural Law, Politics & the Eighteenth-Century French Trades,* Cambridge: Cambridge University Press, 1989, chapter 10; the phrase belongs to Dale van Kley, "The Jansenist Constitutional Legacy in the French Prerevolution," in Keith M. Baker, ed., op. cit., p. 180.

15. For what they would be reading, see Jeremy Popkin, "The Prerevolutionary Origins of Political Journalism," in Keith M. Baker, ed., op. cit., pp. 203–24.

16. Margaret C. Jacob, *The Cultural Meaning of the Scientific Revolution,* New York: McGraw-Hill, 1988, pp. 148–50.

17. For example, see van Kley, op. cit., pp. 169–202.

18. L. W. B. Brockliss, *French Higher Education in the Seventeenth and Eighteenth Centuries,* Oxford: Clarendon Press, 1987, pp. 366, 455.

19. See Alan C. Kors, *Atheism in France, 1650–1729, vol. 1: The Orthodox Sources of Disbelief,* Princeton, N.J.: Princeton University Press, 1990.

20. See Dena Goodman, "Enlightenment Salons: The Convergence of Female and Philosophic Ambitions," *Eighteenth Century Studies* 22 (1989): 329–50.

21. *Traité des trois imposteurs, des religions dominantes et du culte, D'après l'analyse conforme à l'histoire: contenant Nombre d'observations morales, analogues à celles mises à l'ordre du jour pour l'affermissement de la République . . . ,* Paris, 1796; copy in Newberry Library, no. C.525.2187. I owe this reference to members of Richard Popkin's seminar on the three impostors, Leiden University, summer 1990. From the work of Sylvia Berti we now know that part of the text came from a translation of Spinoza and that one Mr. Vroese, from Brabant, as identified in the Marchand MSS, University of Leiden, authored much of the manuscript that Rousset sent into the world.

22. The point is made in Aram Vartanian, "The *Annales* School and the Enlightenment," in O. M. Brack, Jr., ed., *Studies in Eighteenth-Century Culture,* vol. 13, Madison: University of Wisconsin Press, 1984, p. 233. See Robert Darnton, *The Business of Enlightenment: A Publishing History of the Encyclopédie,* Cambridge, Mass.: Belknap Press, 1979; Daniel Roche, *Le Siècle des Lumières en province: Académies et académiciens provinciaux,* Paris: Mouton, 1978.

23. See the treatment given it in Ernst Wangermann, *The Austrian Achievement, 1700–1800,* New York: Harcourt Brace, 1973; and of course the works cited in my introduction.

24. Vartanian, op cit., p. 237.

25. Cf. Marie-Cécile Révauger, "De la Révolution Américaine à la Révolution Française: Le Franc-Maçon dans la Cité," in Élise Marienstras, ed., *L'Amérique et la France: Deux Révolutions, Publications de la Sorbonne,* Paris: Publications de la Sorbonne, 1990, p. 17.

26. For that interpretation see Robert Wuthnow, *Communities of Discourse: Ideology and Social Structure in the Reformation, the Enlightenment, and European Socialism,* Cam-

bridge: Cambridge University Press, 1989. For a similar point about the democratic implications of sociability, see Daniel Gordon, "'Public Opinion' and the Civilizing Process in France: The Example of Morellet," *Eighteenth Century Studies* 22 (1989): 327–28.

27. R. R. Palmer, *The Age of the Democratic Revolution. A Political History of Europe and America, 1760–1800,* vols. 1 and 2, Princeton, N.J.: Princeton University Press, 1959.

28. For a discussion of this historiography, see Jack R. Censer, "Commensing the Third Century of Debate," *American Historical Review* 94 (1989): 1315.

29. See Lynn Hunt, *Politics, Culture, and Class in the French Revolution,* Berkeley: University of California Press, 1984.

30. Lucien Goldmann, *The Philosophy of the Enlightenment. The Christian Burgess and the Enlightenment,* trans. Henry Maas, Cambridge: MIT Press, 1973; originally published in German in 1968.

Index

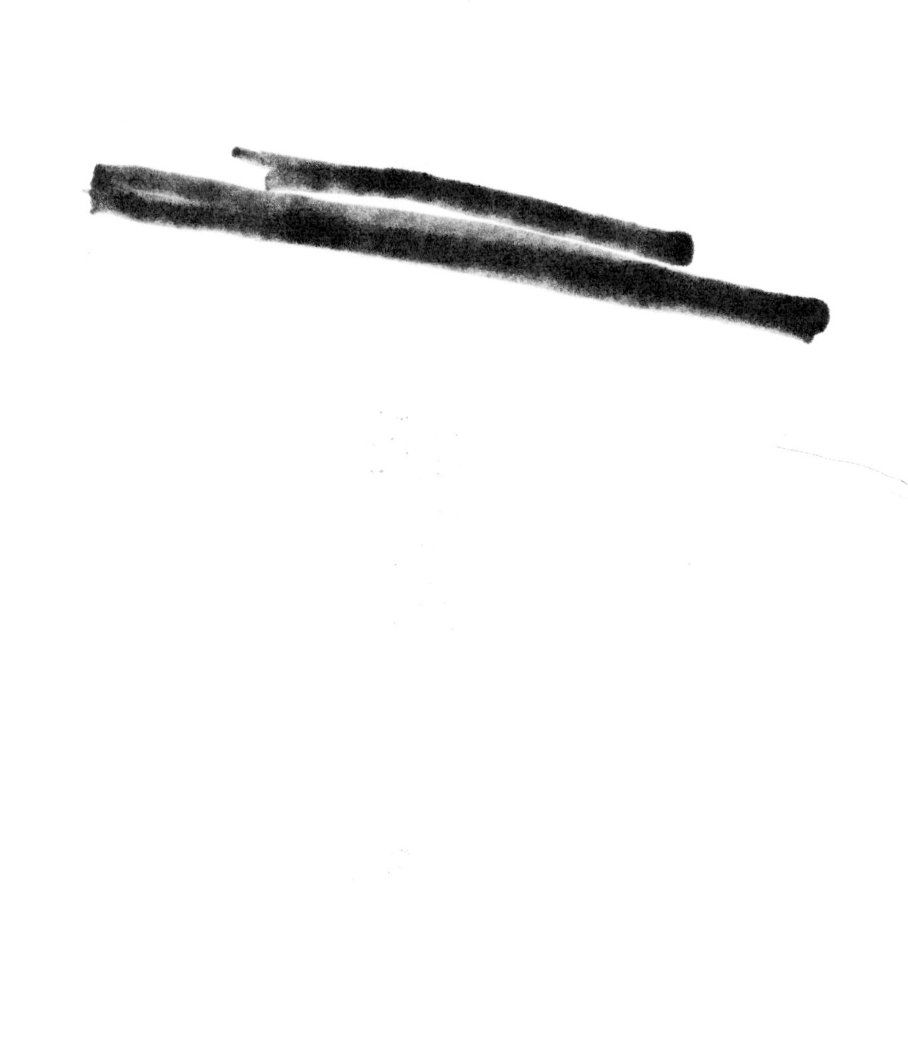